Pastoral Counsel

THOMAS C. ODEN

Classical Pastoral Care

VOLUME THREE
PASTORAL COUNSEL

Baker Books

A Division of Baker Book House Co
Grand Rapids, Michigan 49516

For A. Johan Noordsij and in memory of Frank Lake—
admirable psychiatrists and friends

Contents

Preface to the Baker Edition

EVANGELICALS STAND POISED to rediscover the classical pastoral tradition. This series seeks the revitalization of a discipline once familiar to evangelical Protestant scholarship, but now regrettably crippled and enervated.

It has been commonly observed that there is a deep hunger and profound readiness among evangelicals for neglected classical Christian roots as a resource for counsel, teaching, exegesis, and the work of ministry (see the writings of Robert Webber, Mark Noll, Ward Gasque, Donald Bloesch, James I. Packer, Michael Horton, Clark Pinnock, and Os Guinness).

It is well known that classic Protestant and evangelical teachers made frequent and informed references to the ancient Christian pastoral writers. Calvin was exceptionally well grounded in Augustine, but was also thoroughly familiar with the texts of Cyprian, Tertullian, John Chrysostom, Ambrose, Jerome, Leo, and Gregory the Great, and ecumenical council definitions such as those of Nicea, Constantinople I, and Chalcedon. Philipp Melancthon and Martin Chemnitz were especially gifted scholars of classical pastoral care. This tradition was carried forth and deepened by Reformed pastoral theologians (Gerhard, Quenstedt, Bucanus, Ursinus, Wollebius, and Cocceius), and survived healthily well into the eighteenth-century evangelical revival among leading teachers like J.A. Bengel, Philip Doddridge, Jonathan Edwards, John Wesley, and Johann Neander, all of whom read classic Christian writers handily in their original languages. Not until the late nineteenth century did the study of the ancient pastoral writers atrophy among Protestant pastors.

What is notably missing in today's picture is the classic pastoral texts themselves in accessible form, and a vital community of pastors and care-givers in living dialogue with these foundational prototypes.

1

A major long-range objective of this edition is the mentoring of young evangelical pastors and counselors toward greater competence in the classical pastoral tradition. Deliberately included in this collection are the voices of women from the classic Eastern and Western traditions of spiritual formation, exegesis, martyrology, catechesis, and piety. While the documentation of their poignant utterances is regrettably infrequent, they still are exceedingly powerful commentators on care-giving—I am thinking of such voices as Amma Theodora, Julian of Norwich, Hildegaard of Bingen, and Teresa of Avila.

Will benefits accrue to persons in teaching and helping professions who have no evangelical commitments or interests? The study of classical pastoral care is fitting not only for pastors and professionals, but for lay readers interested in their own inward spiritual formation. The arguments contained in this series tend to elicit ripple effects on diverse readers in such widely varied fields as psychology, Western cultural history, liturgies, homiletics, and education. Classical pastoral care is long overdue in contributing something distinctive of its own to the larger dialogue on care-giving, empathy, behavioral change, and therapeutic effectiveness.

By the early eighties it began to be evident that someone needed to pull together a substantial collection of essential sources of classic Christian writers on major themes of pastoral care. The series was first published by Crossroad/Continuum Publishing Company, a general academic publisher of religious books with strong ties to the erudite Herder tradition of Catholic scholarship. In the intervening years, no serious rival or alternative to this collection has appeared. There exists no other anthology of texts of classical pastoral care that presents the variety of textual material offered in this series. I am now deeply pleased to see it come out in an edition more accessible to Protestants. This is the first time the series has been made available in paperback.

The four books can be read either as a single, unified sequence or separately as stand-alone volumes. To this day some readers know of only one or two volumes, but are not aware that each volume is part of a cohesive series. Baker has made this unity clearer by offering the four volumes as a series.

I am deeply grateful for the interest that many working pastors, counselors, and lay persons have shown in this Classical Pastoral Care series. Even though these volumes were chosen as a Religious Book Club selection over several years, the circulation has been disseminated largely through academic audiences. I am pleased that it is now being offered by Baker for the first time to evangelical pastors and evangelically oriented pastoral and lay counselors and lay readers.

These texts are sometimes hard to locate if one is approaching them topically in crumbling, antiquated editions with poor indexes. This edition provides for the first time a well-devised index for the whole series that makes the anthology much more accessible to readers who wish to dip into it thematically.

These four volumes are designed to display the broad range of classical Christian reflections on all major questions of pastoral care. Many practical subjects are included, such as care of the dying, care of the poor, marriage and family counseling, pastoral visitation and care of the sick, counsel on addictive behaviors, vocational counsel, the timing of good counsel, the necessary and sufficient conditions of a helping relationship, body language in pastoral counsel, pastoral care through preaching, pastoral care through prayer, the pastor as educator of the soul, preparing for the Lord's table, clergy homosexuality and sexual ethics, equality of souls beyond sexual difference, the path to ordination, charismatic, healing ministries, and preparation for the care of souls.

The four volumes are:

I. *On Becoming a Minister* (first published 1987)
II. *Ministry through Word and Sacrament* (1989)
III. *Pastoral Counsel* (1989)
IV. *Crisis Ministries* (1986)

This edition for the first time identifies the order of volumes more clearly. Since in the first edition the fourth volume (*Crisis Ministries*, with its bio-bibliographical addendum) appeared first, the sequential order of the series has been confusing to some readers. Many have never seen the four volumes in a collection together, and do not yet realize that the whole sequence is constructed in a well-designed order to cover all major topics of pastoral theology.

There is reason to believe that this series is already being regarded as a standard necessary accession of theological seminary libraries, as well as of the libraries of most colleges and universities in which religious studies are taught, and in many general public libraries.

Meanwhile, out of rootless hunger the prefix "pastoral" has come to mean almost anything. There is no constraint on ascribing any subject matter to the category of pastoral care. In this game pastoral can mean my ultimate concern, transcendental meditation, or worse, my immediate feeling process or group hugging or my racial identity or crystal-gazing—you name it, anything. Then what is called pastoral is no longer related to the work of Christian ministry at all.

The preaching and counseling pastor needs to know that current pastoral care stands in a tradition of two millennia of reflection on the tasks of soul care. If deprived of these sources, the practice of pastoral care may become artificially constricted to modern psychotherapeutic procedures or pragmatic agendas. During the sixties and seventies, these reductionistic models prevailed among many old-line Protestant pastors, and to some degree as the eighties proceeded they also took root among evangelicals. This anthology shows the classic historic roots of contemporary approaches to psychological change, and provides to some degree a critique of those contemporary models.

Pastors today are rediscovering the distinctiveness of pastoral method as distinguished from other methods of inquiry (historical, philosophical, literary, psychological, etc.). Pastoral care is a unique enterprise that has its own distinctive subject-matter (care of souls); its own methodological premise (revelation); its own way of inquiring into its subject-matter (attentiveness to the revealed Word through Scripture and its consensual tradition of exegesis); its own criteria of scholarly authenticity (accountability to canonical text and tradition); its own way of knowing (listening to sacred Scripture with the historic church); its own mode of cultural analysis (with worldly powers bracketed and divine providence appreciated); and its own logic (internal consistency premised upon revealed truth).

The richness of the classic Christian pastoral tradition remains pertinent to ministry today. The laity have a right to competent, historically grounded pastoral care. The pastor has a right to the texts that teach how pastors have understood their work over the centuries. Modern chauvinism has falsely taught us a theory of moral inferiority: that new ideas are intrinsically superior, and old patterns inferior. This attitude has robbed the laity of the pastoral care they deserve, and the ministry of the texts that can best inform the recovery of pastoral identity.

Thomas C. Oden
June, 1994

Introduction

LONG BEFORE PSYCHOLOGY was a distinct profession, pastors engaged in activities that required psychological wisdom. Pastors have struggled for the health of persons and the life of souls in ways that anticipate and resemble contemporary psychotherapies. We will show that many essential elements of psychotherapeutic care are were well understood before the modern period.

Nine key questions await unpacking:

- How do sources of the classic pastoral tradition describe the necessary and sufficient conditions of *helping relationship,* the essential elements of the therapeutic relationship and how do these descriptions correspond with recent accounts?
- What constitutes *counsel,* what should one expect from it, and how is an apt counselor found?
- How does God's own *empathic caring* and providential guidance shape the process of human care-giving?
- Why is the *timing* of seasonable wisdom such a crucial prudential element of pastoral counsel?
- How did the classic Christian psychologists understand *the language of the body,* and its relation to the struggle for language in self-disclosure, as well as the significance of silence?
- Why are *admonition and discipline* such distinctive features of constructive behavioral change?
- Can responsible freedom be rightly nurtured without *moral guidance?*
- How do classic therapeutic understandings and procedures *anticipate contemporary psychotherapeutic assumptions* and procedures?
- Finally, what patterns recur in classic analyses of the psychological dynamics of the *will* that have been rediscovered by modern behavioral science?

5

1 Necessary and Sufficient Conditions of a Helping Relationship

WHAT RELATIONAL qualities are required in the care-giver? What elicits increased self-understanding and constructive behavioral redirection? What sort of person must one become to serve as an effective *therapon* (therapeutic agent)? Numerous writers of the ancient pastoral tradition have deliberately pursued these questions we are about to pursue. They connect with questions being actively investigated by psychologists about relational qualities requisite to effective therapeutic relationships, and conditions of constructive psychological change.

Five pivotal points recur in classical pastoral care that describe the effective therapeutic relationship: (1) accurate empathic listening; (2) congruent, open awareness of one's own experiencing process, trusting one's own soul, one's own most inward experiencing, enabling full self-disclosure; (3) unconditional accepting love; (4) rigorous self-examination; and (5) narrative comic insight. These are the texts awaiting our examination.

An embryonic theory of psychotherapeutic effectiveness has been implicitly operative in the classical pastoral tradition from its early times. These premodern views are ordered and set forth in such a way that they may be easily compared with various contemporary psychotherapeutic views of how constructive behavioral change occurs.

Therapeia in the Greek means a helping, serving, healing relationship. A *therapon* (from which our term "therapist" comes) is one who helps, serves, and heals. The Latin translation for *therapon* is *ministerium*, from which our word "minister" (helper, servant) comes. Thus the roots of therapy and ministry are closely intertwined in our language. The pastoral office has from its beginnings been thought of literally as a therapeutic relationship.

Three factors have been consensually identified in much recent psychotherapy as essential to a helping relationship. I refer to the familiar "therapeutic triad" that governs relational effectiveness—accurate empathy, self-congruence and unconditional acceptance. These are viewed by many as "necessary and sufficient conditions of therapeutic personality change" (Carl R. Rogers, *Journal of Consulting Psychology*, 21, 1957, pp. 95–103). Freud and the psychoanalytic tradition focused upon the

7

transference relationship, accurate analysis of Oedipal relationships, and the nurturing of ego-strength. The behavior therapists developed procedures for relearning dysfunctional behaviors through carefully sequenced reinforcement exercises. We will show how each of these approaches (Rogerian, Freudian, and Skinnerian) is found proleptically in ancient Christian pastoral care.

There is considerable evidence that the early Christian pastoral writers thought deeply about issues we today call "therapeutic effectiveness." The pastoral writers reflected especially upon the nature of an effective personal relation between givers and receivers of counsel. The texts that follow set forth key elements of classic Christian reflection on conditions necessary for constructive psychological change.

I. 🦚 ACCURATE EMPATHIC LISTENING

Repeatedly the Christian pastoral tradition has grasped and articulated this pivotal insight: The primary condition of a caring relationship is the capacity for accurate, empathic listening, where one enters into the emotive sphere of reference of another, willing to participate attentively to what is here and now occurring inwardly. This human empathy has characteristically been understood in correspondence with divine empathy. A profound analogy emerged in the Christian tradition between the human capacity to enter into the experience of another and God's empathic engagement in human experience in the incarnation.

The capacity for "as if" experiencing was viewed as a crucial element of pastoral counsel. We begin with Ambrose's concise description of the heart of empathic caring:

> Show compassion for those who are bound by chains, as if you yourself were bound with them. . . . Suffer with those who are in trouble, as if being in trouble with them. (Ambrose, *Letters*, 59, To the Church at Vercelli, FC 26, p. 361)

As if bound, one enters imaginatively the chained inner world of another, seeing the troubled soul from within the frame of the other's experience.

The extent to which the empathic imagination can indeed reach in to penetrate the consciousness of another is remarkably described by Catherine of Siena:

> They made themselves infirm with those who were infirm, so that they might not be overcome with despair, and to give them more courage in exposing their infirmity, they would ofttimes lend countenance to their infirmity and say, "I, too, am infirm with thee"! They wept with those who wept, and rejoiced with those who rejoiced; and thus sweetly they knew to give every one

his nourishment, preserving the good and rejoicing in their virtues, not being gnawed by envy, but expanded with the broadness of love for their neighbours, and those under them. They drew the imperfect ones out of imperfection, themselves becoming imperfect and infirm with them, as I told thee, with true and holy compassion, and correcting them and giving them penance for the sins they committed—they through love endured their penance together with them. For through love, they who gave the penance, bore more pain than they who received it. (Catherine of Siena, *A Treatise of Prayer*, p. 253)

Empathy is an imaginative act, an engagement of the compassionate imagination, an event of the understanding. When it becomes more than that—an act of actual suffering with and for another—it does not cease being empathy but becomes more than empathy, namely, taking another's suffering upon oneself. That is not what modern writers usually mean by empathy. That goes a decisive step beyond empathy. It is fundamental to life in Christ. If we are to speak descriptively of empathic understanding in the pastoral tradition, we must examine what it means to understand another, or to share understanding between persons. Thomas Aquinas provided a clear conceptual window into this important process:

Understanding implies intimate knowledge. For *intelligere* (to understand) is the same as *intus legere* (to read inwardly). . . . [which] penetrates into the very essence of a thing. . . . Since, however, human knowledge begins with the outside of things as it were, it is evident that the stronger the light of the understanding, the further can it penetrate into the heart of things. Now the natural light of our understanding is of finite power; wherefore it can reach to a certain fixed point. Consequently man needs a supernatural light, in order to penetrate further still so as to know what it cannot know by its natural light: and this supernatural light which is bestowed on man is called the gift of understanding. . . . Understanding denotes a certain excellence of a knowledge that penetrates into the heart of things. (Thomas Aquinas, *Summa Theologica*, Part II–II, Q. 8, Art. 1, Vol. II, p. 1204)

Empathy is a type of understanding. Its key feature is the capacity to penetrate the understanding of another from within, to read something inwardly, or view one as one views oneself, to see from the inside. We may even speak of empathy toward a plant or animal. But if we are speaking of empathy toward a free, self-determining person, we are seeking to grasp that person's developing experience in its here and now complexity and subtlety from within that person's unique frame of reference. Empathy is often described by the ancient pastoral writers as the primary precondition of soul care. They emphasized the importance of the care-giver's willingness to listen, to be quiet, and not constantly to need to talk. The impulse to talk must be deliberately constrained by the soul guide on behalf of a greater end than wordy self-disclosure:

A brother asked Abba Poemen, "How should I behave in the place where I live?" The old man said, "Have the mentality of an exile in the place where you live, do not desire to be listened to, and you will have peace." (Poemen, *Sayings of the Desert Fathers*, p. 163)

The Desert Fathers often use hyperbole to state their counsel sharply and at times even humorously. The desire not to be listened to requires a bit of savoring to grasp. In our ordinary human condition we are prone to want to speak loud and often, and listen seldom or half-heartedly. The way to prune that bad habit, says Poemen, is by reinforcing its opposite, the desire to be unheard. Later Ignatius Loyola and Viktor Frankl made use of this same dialectic of paradoxical intentionality, where one wills oppositely from the flow of impulse in order to constrain the libidinal energies and gain freedom and self-control.

Right hearing is the essence of the process:

The speaker indeed expresses his thoughts but is understood only by himself. . . . Often we do not rightly hear what is said, and enter into lengthy arguments over things we wrongly thought we heard. . . . If I had heard you aright I should not have thought it absurd. . . . It is said that definition is the remedy for this mistake. (Augustine, "The Teacher," XIII.43, LCC VI, p. 99)

While there is a time to listen, there is also a time not to listen. Whether to listen, or how deeply to listen, is itself a moral and prudential judgment:

Listen not to those who disparage their neighbors, lest while you listen to other you be stirred up to dishonor your neighbors. (Ambrose, *Letters*, 59, To the Church at Vercelli, FC 26, p. 336)

Richard Baxter delineated the blessings that pour forth when the pastor is open and accessible to parishioners. One who preaches must first listen:

When we are familiar with them, they will be encouraged to open their doubts to us and deal freely with us. But when a minister knows not his people, or is as strange to them as if he did not know them, it must be a great hindrance to his doing any good among them. . . . By means of it, we shall come to be better acquainted with each person's spiritual state, and so the better know how to watch over them. We shall know better how to preach to them, and carry ourselves to them, when we know their temper, and their chief objections, and so what they have most need to hear. . . . We shall know better how to lament for them, and to rejoice with them, and to pray for them. For as he that will pray rightly for himself must know his own wants, and the diseases of his own heart, so he that will pray rightly for others, should know theirs as far as possible. (Baxter, *RP*, pp. 177–178)

Aelred of Reivaulx provided a model for the pastor to pray for grace to engage empathically in ministry to persons:

Teach me your servant, therefore, Lord, teach me, I pray you, by your Holy Spirit, how to devote myself to them and how to spend myself on their behalf. Give me, by your unutterable grace, the power to bear with their shortcomings patiently, to share their griefs in loving sympathy, and to afford them help according to their needs. Taught by your Spirit may I learn to comfort the sorrowful, confirm the weak and raise the fallen; to be myself one with them in their weakness, one with them when they burn at causes of offence, one in all things with them, all things to all of them, that I may gain them all. Give me the power to speak the truth straightforwardly, and yet acceptably; so that they all may be built up in faith and hope and love, in chastity and lowliness, in patience and obedience, in spiritual fervor and submissiveness of mind. And, since you have appointed this blind guide to lead them, this untaught man to teach, this ignorant one to rule them, for their sakes, Lord, if not for mine, teach him whom you have made to be their teacher, lead him whom you have bidden to lead them, rule him who is their ruler. Teach me, therefore, sweet Lord, how to restrain the restless, comfort the discouraged, and support the weak. Teach me to suit myself to everyone according to his nature, character and disposition, according to his power of understanding or his lack of it, as time and place require, in each case, as you would have me do. (Aelred of Rievaulx, *Treatises, The Pastoral Prayer*, CF 2, pp. 114–115)

This prayer epitomizes spiritual direction in the medieval period. Its intense humility must not be taken with jaded skepticism by modern readers as if a phony pretense. Its key feature is the prayer for empathy: that I might feel my way into the neighbor's disposition, to be "one with him" in his weaknesses and offenses, that I might respond uniquely and personally as time and place require.

II. 🍎 GOD'S OWN EMPATHIC UNDERSTANDING

It has been early and consistently recognized in the pastoral tradition that there is a similarity between God's engagement in human suffering and our efforts at empathy with the suffering neighbor. Much of the energy of empathic engagement in the classical pastoral tradition has come from the special dynamic of the comparison of God's care and human care.

The incarnation was viewed as the overarching pattern of the willingness of God to enter fully into our human situation of alienation and suffering. God's self-giving incarnate love calls for energetic human response, for entering the situation of suffering of the neighbor to redeem, show mercy, heal and transform, so as to manifest Christ's love amid the world. Athanasius set forth the empathy of God with these moving words:

What was God to do in the face of this dehumanizing of mankind, this universal hiding of the knowledge of Himself by the wiles of evil spirits? Was He to keep silence before so great a wrong and let men go on being thus deceived and kept in ignorance of Himself? . . . What, then, was God to do? What could He possibly do, being God, but renew His Image in mankind, so that through it men might once more come to know Him? (Athanasius, *On the Incarnation*, sec. 13, p. 22)

God overcomes the deceptions of humanity by doing what only God would think of doing, and what only One who was incomparably good and powerful could have done. God entered fully and bodily into the alienated human situation, participating in its limits and struggles, sharing its condition, redeeming it by participation—all without ceasing to be God. This engaging image reverberates through much Christian reflection on compassion and empathy for others. The powerful theme of Christ descending into hell became a replete model of engaged, empathic ministry:

It was for this reason, too, that the Lord descended into the regions beneath the earth, preaching His advent there also, and [declaring] the remission of sins received by those who believe in Him. . . . These things, therefore, He recapitulated in Himself; by uniting man to the Spirit, and causing the Spirit to dwell in man, He is Himself made the head of the Spirit, and gives the Spirit to be the head of man: for through Him (the Spirit) we see, and hear, and speak. He has therefore, in His work of recapitulation, summed up all things, both waging war against our enemy, and cursing him who had at the beginning led us away captives in Adam. . . .

But the case was that for three days He dwelt in the place where the dead were, as the prophet says concerning Him: "And the Lord remembered His dead saints who slept formerly in the land of sepulcher; and he descended to them, to rescue and save them" [see ANF I, 451n]. And the Lord Himself says, "As Jonas remained three days and three nights in the whale's belly, so shall the Son of man be in the heart of the earth" [Matt. 11:40]. Then also the apostle says, "But when He ascended, what is it but that He also descended into the lower parts of the earth?" [Eph. 4:9]. This, too, David says when prophesying of Him, "And thou hast delivered my soul from the nethermost hell" [Ps. 86:23]. (Irenaeus, *Against Heresies*, Bk. IV, Ch. XXVII, sec. 2, ANF I, p. 499, Bk. V, Ch. XXI.1, p. 548 XXXI.1, p. 560; the "sepulcher" quote Irenaeus thought to be from Isaiah)

In the descent into hell, Christ struggled with the demonic powers and broke their fury and deceit. The strong man who held the human spirit captive was defeated. The tradition of commentary on these scriptural passages has suggested penetrating analogies with our human attempts to bind up the demonic powers to enable new life to emerge from a previously imprisoned life. Irenaeus argued that Jesus' ministry recapitulated the entire human situation. The descent into hell was a critical and dramatic moment of that recapitulation that echoes through ordinary one-on-one conversations.

Is it possible that one may become so attuned to another's feelings that one senses in advance the response of the other?

Indeed, from my own feelings I can in turn judge yours, believing I am never far from you nor you from me, so closely are we united in our souls. (Ambrose, *Letters*, 64, to Antonius, FC 26, p. 400)

Ambrose thought that the aim of counseling was to elicit an inner witness already buried deeply within the partner in dialogue. He wrote in reference to the judgment of Solomon on which claimant was mother of the surviving child (see 1 Kings 3:16–27):

What can be more hidden than the witness that lies deep within; into which the mind of the wise king entered as though to judge a mother's feelings, and elicited as it were the voice of a mother's heart. For a mother's feelings were laid bare when she chose that her son should live with another rather than that he should be killed in his mother's sight.

It was therefore a sign of wisdom to distinguish between secret heart-thoughts, to draw the truth from hidden springs, and to pierce as it were with the sword of the Spirit not only the inward parts of the body but even of the mind and soul. (Ambrose, *Duties of the Clergy*, Bk. II, Ch. VIII, sec. 46, NPNF 2, X, p. 51)

The central model for empathic care was Jesus' own ministry. Note the maternal and medical metaphors by which Catherine of Siena spoke of God's radically empathic way of caring:

The coming of the great Physician, that is to say, of My only-begotten Son, cured this invalid, He drinking this bitter medicine, which man could not drink on account of his great weakness, like a foster-mother who takes medicine instead of her suckling, because she is grown up and strong, and the child is not fit to endure its bitterness. He was man's foster-mother, enduring, with the greatness and strength of the Deity united with your nature, the bitter medicine of the painful death of the Cross, to give life to you little ones debilitated by guilt. (Catherine of Siena, *A Treatise of Discretion*, p. 69)

This is a striking feminine metaphor for the atoning work of the Savior: like a foster-mother who takes bitter medicine for her suckling who could not tolerate it, passing the healing medication through her milk. This is how far the empathy of God is willing to go for us—taking our medicine for us on the cross. This refracts the Pauline metaphor that "God made him who had no sin to be sin for us, so that in him we might become the righteousness of God" (2 Cor. 5:21, NIV). Catherine celebrated God's empathic care as analogous to a surrogate mother who becomes wholly attentive to the desperate needs of the sick child, using whatever means available to bring health.

III. ❦ RADICAL OPENNESS TO ONE'S EXPERIENCING PROCESS

That care-giver is termed *congruent* who is thoroughly open to his or her own experience, aware of what is occuring emotively within. Congruence with one's own feeling process is widely regarded as one of the necessary conditions of a relationship of constructive behavioral change. The counselor who does not have access to his own feeling process is not likely to be trusted by others.

This same idea is found frequently in the tradition of Christian pastoral care. Openness to one's experience was, in a sense, more radically conceived in the Christian tradition, because it included a vastly more profound and extensive assumption about the self viewed as *psuche* (soul): that one's life transcends this temporal sphere, that one's struggle is rightly understandable only in a world-historical and finally eschatological context. Hence the process of becoming aware of oneself was placed in an wider cosmic-historical arena in which one's openness to one's current experiencing had to be seen in the light of God's openness to all historical experience. Instead of viewing internal congruence merely as an intrasubjective matter, as is the case in contemporary psychotherapies, the Christian pastoral tradition viewed personal congruence as finitely reflective of and analogous to radical divine self-awareness, the congruence of God's life with God's self-knowing, the incomparable range of the triune God's self-knowing.

We begin this part of our exploration by asking: On what grounds may one actively welcome new experience and celebrate its constant unfolding? Among the earliest writings of the apostolic period was a letter ascribed to Barnabas, whose author grasped the essential point concisely:

Whatever experience comes your way, accept it as a blessing, in the certainty that nothing can happen without God. Never equivocate, either in thought or speech. . . . Do not be one of those who stretch out their hands to take, but draw back when the time comes for giving. (*The Epistle of Barnabas*, sec. 19, ECW, p. 218)

The injunction to accept emergent experiencing was a familiar theme of the early oral tradition in Christian pastoral care. For similarly the *Didache* had said, "Accept as good whatever experience comes your way" (ECW, p. 229). The fluxuating experiencing process occurs always in the companionship of God. All events minus none are to be received in the context of divine self-knowing and self-giving. This provides a universal-historical context in which to place all attempts to be "openness to experience."

Assuming soul as that which enlivens body, Tertullian urged: "Trust your soul."

In order to trust nature as well as God, trust the soul. It will bring it about that you trust yourself. It certainly is the soul which you value in proportion to the greatness it gives to you; to which you belong totally; which is all to you; without which you cannot live or die. (Tertullian, "Testimony of the Soul," Ch. 6, FC 10, pp. 141–142)

To trust one's soul is to trust the deep resonances of meaning within oneself that correspond to the concrete unfolding of one's very life. The idea of trusting our own organismic responsiveness, which was later taken to be a primary indicator of psychological full-functioning and a precondition of effective therapeutic agency, was clearly anticipated by ancient Christian writers.

If, as Tertullian argued, the soul is to be trusted, listened to carefully, and valued in proportion to its greatness, then how does that process of listening to the *psyche* differ from listening to oneself, one's feeling process, becoming attuned to the flow of one's own affective life—a theme that so predominates in late 20th century psychology? Classical pastoral writers differ from modern psychologists in that they place the emotive process within a world-historical (and ultimately an eschatological) context. Tertullian effectively grasped the notion of the ambivalence of the soul, and the need for listening precisely and accurately to the soul's ambivalences:

> Every soul justly proclaims those things which we are not allowed even to hint at. Deservedly, then, every soul is a defendant as well as a witness of the truth. . . . O soul, thou didst always proclaim God, yet not seek Him; didst detest the demons, yet adore them; didst invoke the judgment of God, yet not believe in its existence; didst foresee the infernal punishments, yet not guard against them. (Tertullian, *Testimony of the Soul*, Ch. 6, FC 10, p. 143)

The soul can be torn by contrary passions. We can know the good and not do it. But however we may fail to follow the soul's better vision of the truly good, it nonetheless remains available to us. We cannot ever fully stamp out that part of ourselves which glimpses the reality and goodness of God, even when we do not follow. The congruent person is relatively more aware of those ambivalences, attentive to what the soul is saying at any given moment.

Athanasius painted a remarkable word-picture of the face of his own soul guide, Anthony, an early model of the care-giver. For what appeared on Anthony's face, he said, corresponded perfectly with the ebb and flow of his inward life. Anthony was congruent with his own feelings. The inward depths were beheld openly in his face:

> [Anthony was not] embarrassed to put himself in a position to learn. For indeed, often he would raise questions and ask to hear from those with him. And he acknowledged that he was helped if someone said anything useful. His face had a great and marvelous grace, and this spiritual favor he had from the Savior—for if he was present with a great number of monks, and someone who had not formerly met him wished to see him, immediately on arriving, he would pass by the others and run to him, as though drawn by his eyes. It was not his physical dimensions that distinguished him from the rest, but the stability of character and the

purity of the soul. His soul being free from confusion, he held his outer senses also undisturbed, so that from the soul's joy his face was cheerful as well, and from the movements of the body it was possible to sense and perceive the stable condition of the soul, as it is written, "When the heart rejoices, the countenance is cheerful; but when it is in sorrow, the countenance is sad" [Prov. 15:13]. (Athanasius, *Life of St. Anthony*, ACW 10, p. 81)

This leads one to believe that congruence of inner spirit with outer behavior was viewed early in the tradition as a mark of spiritual maturity, of saintliness, of a holy life fully responsive to the love of God. John Climacus would later write that even a single word of a reliable spiritual guide would reveal the flavor of the entire life behind it:

Often one cup of wine is sufficient to reveal its flavour, and one word of the hesychast [one who follows the way of quietness] makes known to those who can taste it his whole inner state and activity. (Climacus, *Ladder of Divine Ascent*, Step 27, Sec. 79, p. 210)

If every soul guide must be true to his own inner self, and each one is different, that suggests an hypothesis concerning why the types of persons who model care of souls are extremely varied in the Christian tradition·

What a dissimilarity there is between the spirit of St. Augustine and that of St. Jerome! it may be remarked in their writings. Nothing can be more gentle that St. Augustine; his writings are sweetness itself. St. Jerome, on the contrary is very austere; to be convinced of this, look at him in his epistles, he is almost always angry. Yet both were extremely virtuous, only one had more gentleness, the other a greater austerity of life, and both (although not equally gentle or equally stern) were great saints. (Francis de Sales, Conference IV, *SC*, p. 60)

The underlying principle is this: If the soul guide must be true to his own temperament, and if different persons have different temperaments, then the better the soul guide the more individuated, the more unique. These soul guides were remembered as being extraordinarily congruent, however varied. A rigorous ethic of honesty prevailed in relation to temperament. John Climacus sharply distinguished between guile and honesty:

Simplicity is a constant habit of soul that has become immune to crafty thinking. Guile is a science, or rather a diabolical deformity, bereft of truth and thinking it can escape the notice of the many. Hypocrisy is a contrary state of body and soul interwoven with every kind of subterfuge. Guilelessness is a joyous state of soul far removed from all ulterior motive. Honesty is unmeddling thought, sincere character, frank and unpremeditated speech. (Climacus, *The Ladder of Divine Ascent*, Step 24, Sec. 14–18, pp. 146, 147)

The care-giver speaks with *simplicity*, which is that habit of soul that yearns for the plain truth, and which therefore is seldom trapped in guile or hypocrisy. Since speech wells up directly from the depths of the soul, it is unpremeditated. It does not play games.

IV. 🦌 LEARNING TO TRUST ONESELF

Learning to feel one's feelings accurately, to trust one's own organismic process, to gain confidence that one's feelings are not fundamentally distorted—these are long-recognized habits of healthy psychological functioning. The model of healthy affective expression, accordingly, is the neonate who expresses feelings accurately and readily, without intro-jections of what one should or should not feel to distort that expression. A definitive recent expression of these view is found in Carl R. Rogers, but these views are much older, as will be shown.

The need for recovery of child-like trust and organismic responsive-ness was beautifully stated in this passage from Francis de Sales:

Cordial love is attached to another virtue, which is as it were a consequence of that love, namely a childlike confidence. When children have, say a fine feather, or something else which they think pretty, they cannot rest until they have found their little companions to show them the said feather and make them share in their joy; and just in the same way they want them to share their grief, for if they have but a finger-ache they go telling ev-eryone they meet about it, to get pity and have the poor finger breathed upon. Now I do not say that you must be exactly like these children, but I do say that this confidence ought to make you willingly communicate to your sisters all your little satisfac-tions and consolations, with no fear lest they should remark your imperfection. . . . So too as regards your faults, I should wish you not to take so much pains to hide them, for they are none the better for not being outwardly visible. The sisters will not think you have none because they are concealed, and your imperfec-tions will perhaps be more dangerous than if they were detected, and caused you the confusion which they do to those who are more ready to let them appear on the surface. You must not, then, be astonished or discouraged when you commit some fault or imperfection before your sisters, but, on the contrary, you must be very glad to be seen as you really are. (Francis de Sales, Conference IV, *SC*, pp. 66, 67)

From this passage we get an impression of life in a community that is seeking a rich quality of self-disclosure, with a common desire for mutually corrective love, each one willing to be seen as they are, and happy to share great or small discomforts and joys with each other. To the degree that such a community existed, it surely must have been a healthy environment for interpersonal growth.

Ironically, however, in the building of self-esteem and self-trust, some are most helped by not helping them. They are most benefited when quietly left to their own resources without overprotectiveness. The notion of benign neglect, or harmlessly letting another person be according to his or her own self-direction (later developed by Edmund Burke), had its roots in a rich pastoral tradition that valued giving space to letting self-esteem grow in its own due time. Such growth and self-initiative could be smothered by excessive paternalism or over-parenting:

Sometimes a rapid cure is not for the advantage of those who are healed. . . . Wherefore, in the case of such persons, the everlasting God, the Knower of secrets, who knows all things before they exist, in conformity with His goodness, delays sending them more rapid assistance, and, so to speak, in helping them does not help, the latter course being to their advantage. . . . They may afterwards be called to a more stable repentance; so as not to be quickly entangled again in those evils in which they had formerly been involved when they treated with insolence the requirements of virtue, and devoted themselves to worse things. (Origen, *De Principiis*, Bk. II, Ch. I, ANF IV, pp. 318–319)

God's way of helping those who want a quick remedy for the tough tasks of actualizing human freedom is to not rush in and fix things easily. Rather it is to allow persons to struggle with the consequences of their own choices so as to be given another, and again another opportunity for the growth of virtue through responsible freedom.

Ambrose anticipated in its essential form the modern notion of congruent self-esteem as a quality needed in the counselor, i.e., feeling one's feelings accurately rather than hearing one's feelings through the heavy filter of scripted, internalized voices:

Blessed, plainly, is that life which is not valued at the estimation of outsiders, but is known, as judge of itself, by its own inner feelings. (Ambrose, *Duties of the Clergy*, Bk. II, Ch. I, Sec. 2, NPNF 2, X, p. 43)

The care-giver does well to reveal his own feelings in a timely, modest, and appropriate way:

We have also said that courtesy of speech has great effect in winning favour. But we want it to be sincere and sensible, without flattery, lest flattery should disgrace the simplicity and purity of our address. We ought to be a pattern to others not only in act but also in word, in purity, and in faith. What we wish to be thought, such let us be; and let us show openly such feelings as we have within us. Let us not say an unjust word in our heart that we think can be hid in silence, for He hears things said in secret Who made things secret, and knows the secrets of the heart, and has implanted feelings within. (Ambrose, *Duties of the Clergy*, Bk II, Ch. XIX, Sec. 96, NPNF 2, X, p. 58)

The soul guide helps others to find *their own* way, as distinguished from *the guide's* own way. He serves as a modest usher to the truth about themselves (not an usher that leads others to himself):

His office is not to teach his own way, nor indeed any determinate way of prayer, etc., but to instruct his disciples how they may themselves find out the way proper for them, by observing themselves what does good and what causes harm to their spirits; in a word, that he is only God's usher, and must lead souls in God's way and not his own. (Dom Augustine Baker, "Holy Wisdom," p. 341; WSD, p. 27)

Methodius in the third century acknowledged the greatness of human powers of discovery. But these power are limited when it comes to digging spiritual wisdom out of the hard rock of human experience.

God has given great things to persons, sowing, as it were, in their nature the power of discovery, together with wisdom, and the faculty of art. The person, having received this power, digs metals out of the earth, and cultivates the earth. But the case stands differently with that wisdom which is conjoined with piety. For it is not possible in any place to discover easily. Man cannot obtain it speedily from his own resources, nor can he give it unto others. (Methodius, *Three Fragments on the Passion of Christ*, Sec. I, ANF VI, p. 401)*

Much is within the range of discovery by human initiative, as the arts of farming and mining show. But human wisdom needs transcendent help when it comes to discovering that wisdom that flows from divine revelation, that can feed the soul.

Luther warned, however, that amid stress we do not always do well simplistically to "trust our own feelings," insofar as that may imply that we do not allow scripture to speak to our feelings:

In times of trial we should learn to judge, not by our feeling but by the Word of God. This Word promises us that every trial is only the eventide upon which the morning of comfort follows. But our flesh does the opposite and, disregarding the Word, directs its attention only to the present feeling of affliction and judges by that feeling. Therefore it cannot conceive of the end of the trial in his heart. (Luther, WA 25, p. 151, in WLS 3, #4440, p. 1380)

The greater wisdom may lie in simply listening to scripture illuminate one's experience.

V. 🐾 THE CURATIVE POWER OF SELF-DISCLOSURE

There is great spiritual power in revealing one's temptations to a confessor or soul friend. For thereby, the Deceiver, a false lover, is disarmed. On the disclosure of temptation to a counselor, Ignatius Loyola wrote:

The enemy also behaves like a false lover who wishes to remain hidden and does not want to be revealed. For when this deceitful man pays court, with evil intent, to the daughter of some good father or the wife of a good husband, he wants his words and suggestions to be kept secret. He is greatly displeased if the girl reveals to her father, or the wife to her husband, his deceitful words and depraved intentions, for he then clearly sees that his plans cannot succeed. In like manner, when the enemy of our human nature tempts a just soul with his wiles and deceits, he wishes and desires that they be received and kept in secret. When they are revealed to a confessor or some other spiritual person who understands his deceits and evil designs, the enemy is greatly displeased for he knows that he cannot succeed in his evil design once his obvious deceits have been discovered. (Ignatius Loyola, *Spiritual Exercises*, p. 132)

Basil placed exceptionally high value upon full self-disclosure in the process of spiritual growth:

Every person who intends to make any worthwhile progress and to be in union in a way of life that corresponds with the commands of our Lord Jesus Christ should not hide deep within himself any movement of his soul. He should also not speak any thoughtless word, but he should reveal the secrets of his heart to those in the brotherhood whose office it is to show a compassionate and sympathetic care for the weak. (Basil, The Long Rules, WSD, p. 63; cf. Q. 46, FC 9, p. 324)

The search for means by which to avert and displace spontaneous "evil thoughts" remained a great preoccupation of the early ascetic tradition. John Cassian thought that the best antidote was full and untrammelled disclosure in confession:

An evil thought is made weak at the very second it is manifested to another person. . . . Evil thoughts can dominate us only as long as they are hidden in our hearts. (John Cassian, WSD, p. 64; cf. Second Conference of Abbot Moses, XI, NPNF 2, XI, p. 312)

But is it wise that one should become fully self-revealed? Should not some privileged information be held back?

I would urge them to give a discreet and total account of their conscience to their spiritual guide. Openness destroys curiosity and makes the soul simple. (Marie of the Incarnation, *Autobiography*, p. 78; WSD, p. 65)*

Complete and unreserved disclosure is also emphasized by the seventeenth century Cistercian abbot, John Cardinal Bona:

The absolute importance of manifesting our entire conscience and interior state of soul to our spiritual director is clearly established from all we have already written. . . . Our spiritual guides, if they have an intimate knowledge of our inner life, will fashion their advice and counsels appropriately for our state and personal need. He who does not open his heart to his spiritual guide closes it to God also. Since spiritual fathers watch over us in God's place, it is proper they should be able to see all the hidden chambers of our heart, as God penetrates the innermost secrets of the heart. (John Cardinal Bona, *A Treatise of Spiritual Life*, WSD, p. 66)

"The manner in which we should open our heart" was brilliantly described by the seventeenth century French Sulpician, Louis Tronson, using the metaphor of complete pouring out of conscience:

The manner in which we should open our heart, and declare all the secrets of our conscience to our spiritual director, is well explained by these words of the Prophet Jeremiah: "Pour out your heart like water in the presence of the Lord" [Lam. 2:19]. Other liquids do not pour out so entirely, that they do not leave something in the receptacles where they were before. You pour out, for example, a pitcher of oil; there always remains a little of it in the bottom of the vessel. If you pour out a jug of wine, the wine drops down, but the scent remains; it is the same with other fluids. But with water, it is poured out entirely and nothing remains in the container where it was, neither liquid, nor scent, nor taste, nor any other indication that could reveal that it was there. It is thus that you should pour out your heart before the person who directs you and who for you represents Our Lord Himself: "Pour out your heart like water in the presence of the Lord," that is to say, retain nothing, of however little importance it may be. Tell everything to your director. (Louis Tronson, "Obedience to One's Director," WSD, pp. 73–74, NIV)*

The same direction would later be given by Freud to his psychoanalytic patients.

Baxter thought that there was a direct correlation between quality of self-disclosure and truthfulness of preaching:

Preach to yourselves the sermons which you study. . . . I confess I must speak it by lamentable experience, that I publish to my flock the distempers of my own soul. When I let my heart grow cold, my preaching is cold; and when it is confused, my preaching is confused. . . . (Baxter, *RP*, p. 61)

The counselor who must dissemble will be disadvantaged in close encounter.

Such, then, ought the man of counsel to be. He must have nothing dark, or deceptive, or false about him, to cast a shadow on his life and character, nothing wicked or evil to keep back those who want advice. (Ambrose, *Duties of the Clergy*, Bk. II, Sec. 88, NPNF 2, X, p. 57)

The congruence of the counselor remains a crucial component of the effectiveness of counsel. To give good counsel, one must learn to hear good counsel within oneself.

The prophet David taught us that we should go about in our heart as though in a large house; that we should hold converse with it as with some trusty companion . . . Solomon his son also said: "Drink water out of thine own vessels, and out of the springs of thy wells" [Prov. 5:15]; that is: use thine own counsel. For: "Counsel in the heart of a man is as deep waters" [Prov. 20:5]. . . . Scipio, therefore, was not the first to know that he was not alone when he was alone, or that he was least at leisure when he was at leisure. . . . Also David says: "I will hear what the Lord

God will say within me" [Ps. 85:8]. (Ambrose, *Duties of the Clergy*, Bk. III, Ch. I, Sec. 1–2, NPNF 2, X, p. 67)

Precisely when alone, we remain in dialogue!—(with ourselves, our remembered experience, conscience and reason—all in the presence of the divine auditor). One does not learn to lead others to living waters until one learns to drink from deep inward well-springs. But how does one learn to listen deeply to what is said within oneself?

You have one cell [room] outwardly, another within you. The outward cell is the house in which your soul dwells together with your body; the inner cell is your conscience and in that it is God who should dwell with your spirit, he who is more interior to you than all else that is within you. The door of the outward enclosure is a sign of the guarded door within you, so that as the bodily senses are prevented from wandering abroad by the outward enclosure so the inner senses are kept always within their own domain. Love your inner cell then, love your outward cell too, and give to each of them the care which belongs to it. (William of St. Thierry, *The Golden Epistle*, Sec. 105, p. 47)

Do not dread being alone with yourself. For that is when the door opens for this inward conversation.

VI. 🐞 THE LIMITS OF OPENNESS: CONSTRAINTS UPON COMPULSIVE SELF-DISCLOSURE

The temptation to compulsive self-disclosure was strongly resisted, both on the part of the care-giver and care-receiver. Simple honesty was highly valued. One need not say everything in order to say what is pertinent. There was no absolute requirement that one ought to tell everything one knows about oneself. It would be a dull exercise to require another to listen to one endlessly spill out one's immediate feelings in perpetuity. Gregory's metaphor of the broken dam, where the excess of words is like the destructive and useless excess of water in a flood, made this point well:

Those who are addicted to much talking, are to be admonished to observe vigilantly from how great a degree of rectitude they lapse, when they fall to using a multitude of words. For the human mind behaves after the manner of water: when enclosed, it collects itself to the higher levels, because it seeks again the height from which it came down. But, when released, it loses itself, in that it scatters itself to no purpose through the lowest levels; indeed, all the superfluous words wasted when it relaxes its censorship of silence, are so many streams carrying the mind away from itself. Consequently, it does not have the power to return inwardly to self-knowledge, because, dissipated as it is by much talking, it is diverted from the secret places of inward considerations. It lays itself completely exposed to the wounds from the enemy lying in wait for it, in that it does not encompass itself with a barrier of watchfulness. Wherefore it is written: "As a city that lieth open and is not compassed with walls, so is a man that cannot refrain his own spirit from speaking" [Prov. 25:28]. (Gregory the Great, *Pastoral Care*, Part II, Ch. 14, ACW 11, p. 132)

Once the floodgates are opened, one cannot recover the water, or use it in a controlled manner for constructive purposes. If spare selection of words is commended, so is the quality of the relationship in which spare words are spoken. Great hope is invested by some recent psychologists in the immediacy and fullness of self-disclosure, as if health consisted essentially in unmitigated self-expression. We find instead that the pastoral writers were quite wary of excessive words. Much talk was not thought to be intrinsically healthy. And it is hardly psychologically healthy to say endlessly whatever comes to our mouths to whomever we please:

Some brothers were coming from Scetis to see Abba Anthony. When they were getting into a boat to go there, they found an old man who also wanted to go there. The brothers did not know him. They sat in the boat, occupied by turns with the words of the Fathers, Scripture, and their manual work. As for the old man, he remained silent. When they arrived on shore they found that the old man was going to the cell of Abba Anthony too. When they reached the place, Anthony said to them, "You found this old man a good companion for the journey?" Then he said to the old man, "You have brought many good brethren with you, father." The old man said, "No doubt they are good, but they do not have a door to their house and anyone who wishes can enter the stable and loose the ass." He meant that the brethren said whatever came into their mouths. (Anthony the Great, in *Sayings of the Desert Fathers*, p. 4)

Gregory the Great pitied one driven impulsively by ceaseless words:

Solomon [said]: A fool uttereth all his mind, a wise man deferreth and keepeth it till afterward (Prov. 28:11). Under the im-

pulse of impatience the whole spirit exposes itself, and its turbu-
lence drives it out the more speedily, in that there is no
interior discipline of wisdom to keep it in. The wise man, on
the other hand, keeps back and lets the future take care of matters. (Gregory the Great, *Pastoral Care*, Part III, Ch. 9, ACW 11,
p. 109)

Self-controlled speech was valued more than immediate self-
disclosure. If everything requires comment, we babble endlessly. The
tongue requires discipline to speak well.

If you say what you like, you will hear what you don't like. . . .
The first begetter of this adage appears to have been Homer, who
has this line in the *Iliad*, book 20: "The word you speak is the
word you will hear." . . . Plutarch quotes a much finer passage of
Sophocles:

> The man who rashly pours out many words
> Often must hear against his will the wrong
> He willed to say. (Erasmus, "Adages," I i 27/ LB II
> 37A, in *Collected Works*, Vol. 31, pp. 74–75.)

If one is going to lay open one's private thoughts and struggles of
conscience to another, in whose presence should this be done?

[Abba Poemen] said, "Do not lay open your conscience to anyone whom you do not trust in your heart." (Poemen, in *Sayings of
the Desert Fathers*, p. 163)

Shall one trust the secrets of one's heart to a stranger who appears to
be friendly?

Let not a stranger hear your secrets amid your striving, lest he
turns against you and hates you and uses your words against you;
for oftentimes he will talk deceitfully with you, or evilly use the
truth to hurt you. ("Testaments of the Twelve Patriarchs," sec. ix,
ANF VIII, p. 30)*

When a counselor has been deeply trusted, and in due course the
individual comes at some point to see the hidden vulnerabilities of the
counselor, a crisis may arise in the trust relationship:

Often the Lord has shut the eyes of those in obedience to certain failings of their superior, but when the superior himself
revealed these to them, he engendered distrust . . . We should beware lest we scatter in the open sea what we have gathered in
port; this will be understood by those who have entered upon

outer turmoils, being as yet unprepared for them. (Climacus, *To the Shepherd*, sec. 39, 42, in *The Ladder of Divine Ascent*, p. 237)

The pastor who values legitimate self-disclosure may overvalue his own disclosures. If failings of the pastor are abruptly or prematurely revealed, the eyes of the hearer may be opened too quickly and the relationship undermined. Hence avoid compulsive disclosure and time well the discrete disclosure.

Suppose a pastor says something profound but somewhat premature which the parishioner is not prepared to hear, which, being misunderstood, causes the person to stumble. Is the guide liable when one under his guidance stumbles and falls? This, according to Gregory, comes under the law of negligence:

If anyone dug a pit and neglected to cover it over, then if an ox or an ass fell into it, he should pay the price of the animal. So, when a man who has arrived at the deep streams of knowledge, does not cover them up before the unlearned hearts of his hearers, he is judged liable to punishment if by his words a soul, whether clean or unclean, takes scandal. (Gregory the Great, *Pastoral Care*, Part III, Ch. 39, ACW 11, pp. 231–232)

Accordingly, the pastor is responsible not only for his words, but to a high degree for how they are interpreted and received—a caution against loose language.

Should the counselor vent anger? The pastoral writers were keenly attentive to the dynamics of anger. They searched for a way of distinguishing between the proper expression of anger and its destructive forms. Ambrose stated this distinction wisely:

He that is double-minded is not consistent, nor is he consistent who knows not how to check himself in anger, of whom David aptly says: "Be angry, and sin not" (Ps. 4:5). He does not control anger but gives way to nature, which man cannot prevent but can moderate. Therefore, although we are angry, let our passion give vent to natural emotion, not to unnatural sin. For who would permit one who cannot govern himself to receive others to govern? (Ambrose, *Letters*, 59, To the Church at Vercelli, FC 26, p. 343)

Ambrose was not urging that we always repress anger but rather that one rightly may within appropriate limits feel one's anger when frustration builds, because it is a natural emotion which finally is impossible to prevent; but in being angry do not let it take charge of the soul. Moderate it in a fitting way so that it does not become an unnatural or sinful expression of unexamined aggression. One who harbors unexamined aggression is hardly fit to guide another.

VII. ❦ UNCONDITIONAL ACCEPTING LOVE

If one had to choose between analytical skills and unconditional love in choosing a soul guide, surely one had best choose love. Ambrose reflected upon the special efficacy of love in human relationships:

There is nothing so useful as to be loved, nothing so useless as not to be loved; for to be hated in my opinion is simply fatal and altogether deadly. . . . Goodness is agreeable and pleasing to all, and there is nothing that so easily reaches human feelings. And if that is assisted by gentleness of character and willingness, as well as by moderation in giving orders and courtesy of speech, by honour in word, by a ready interchange of conversation and by the grace of modesty, it is incredible how much all this tends to an increase of love. (Ambrose, *Duties of the Clergy*, Bk. II, Ch. VII, sec. 28, NPNF 2, X, p. 48)

One leg of Rogers' triad of therapeutic qualities was what he called "unconditional positive regard," viewed as a necessary precondition to effective therapeutic change. Nothing heals the bruises of life like unconditional love. The pastor who is called to mediate God's own healing love to others must first be grounded deeply in a highly personal awareness of being loved. Only then can the neighbor be beheld with prizing, affectionate personal regard.

One does not reach the depths of the neighbor by focusing merely upon human limitations:

There is no person on earth so bad that he does not have something about him that is praiseworthy. Why is it, then, that we leave the good things out of sight and feast our eyes on the unclean things? It is as though we enjoyed only looking at—if you will pardon the expression—a man's behind. . . . [The devil] gets his name from doing this. He is called *diabolus*, that is, a slanderer and reviler, who takes pleasure in shaming us most miserably and embittering us among ourselves, causing nothing but murder and misery and tolerating no peace or concord between brothers, between neighbors, or between husband and wife. (Luther, "The Sermon on the Mount," LW 21, p. 42)

The desire to see the best in another, and build upon what is good, is grounded in God's own unconditional love.

Love binds us fast to God. Love casts a veil over sins innumerable. There are no limits to love's endurance, no end to its patience. Love is without servility, as it is without arrogance. Love knows of no divisions, promotes no discord; all the works of love are done in perfect fellowship. It was in love that all God's chosen saints were made perfect; for without love nothing is pleasing to Him. It was in love that the Lord drew us to Himself. (Clement of Rome, *To the Corinthians*, sec. 49, ECW, p. 49)

Unfeigned love is the precondition of every act of pastoral care. It engenders tolerance and patience, and makes way for constructive correction:

When the people see that you unfeignedly love them, they will hear any thing and bear any thing from you; as Augustine said, "Love God, and do what you please." We ourselves will take all things well from one that we know entirely loves us. We will put up with a blow that is given us in love sooner than with a foul word that is spoken to us in malice or in anger. . . . If you be their best friends, help them against their worst enemies. And think not all sharpness inconsistent with love: parents correct their children, and God himself "chastens every son whom he receives" [Heb. 12:6]. Augustine said, "Better it is to love even with the accompaniment of severity, than to mislead by excess of leniency." (Thomas Aquinas, *Commentary on Sentences*, I, Distinction 27, Q. 1, a. 1–4, AR, pp. 261–262)*

Ambrose pointed to David as prototype of one who, as God's loving minister, elicited love easily from others:

He was brave in battle, gentle in ruling, patient under abuse, and more ready to bear than to return wrongs. . . . It is no small thing, especially in the case of a king, so to perform humble duties as to make oneself like the very lowest. It is noble not to seek for food at another's risk and to refuse a drink of water, to confess a sin, and to offer oneself to death for one's people. . . . He opened not his mouth to those planning deceit, and, as though hearing not, he thought no word should be returned, nor did he answer their reproaches. . . . It gives a very great impetus to mutual love if one shows love in return to those who love us and proves that one does not love them less than oneself is loved, especially if one shows it by the proofs that a faithful friendship gives. (Ambrose, *Duties of the Clergy*, Bk. II, secs. 32, 34–35, 37, NPNF 2, X, p. 49)

Hugh of St. Victor recognized the paradox that love could be at the same time so potentially hurtful and so wonderful. Why is this so?

Love, then, appears to be, and is, the attachment of any heart to anything, for any reason, whether it be desire or joy in its fruition, hastening towards it by desire, tranquil in its enjoyment.

Here lies your good, O heart of man, here also is your evil. . . .
For everything that exists is good; but, when that which is good is
wrongly loved, the thing in itself is good, but the love of it is bad.
So it is not the lover, nor what he loves; nor the love wherewith he
loves it that is evil; but it is the fact that he loves it wrongly that is
altogether evil. . . . If love be desire, let it make real haste; if it be
joy, then let it rest indeed. Love is, as we have said, the attachment of any heart to any thing for any reason, desire in the longing for it and joy in its fruition, hastening towards its object in
desire, at rest in its enjoyment, running to it and resting in it. . . .
There are three things that can be loved either rightly or
wrongly, namely, God, one's neighbour, and the world. God is
above us, our neighbour is our equal, the world is below us. . . .
When our desire sets out, only let God be in it in three ways, our
neighbour in two, and the world in one. . . . Set charity in order,
then, that desire may run from God, and with God, and unto
God, from our neighbour and with him, but not to him, from the
world, but neither with nor unto us. (Hugh of St. Victor, *SSW*,
pp. 188–190)

Note the three ways of love: One loves that which is from the world,
but one does not love the world as such or what the world loves. One
loves the neighbor, but not what the neighbor loves, and not the neighbor apart from his grounding in God. Hence ordered love flows from
God, flows with God's love, and all loves are directed in relation to God's
love, so that all loves return to God.

Why is it, asked Thomas, that when the lover acts against the inclination to love, he feels pain?

Just as fire cannot be restrained from the motion that befits it
according to the exigency of its form except through violence, so
neither can the lover do anything apart from love; and on account of this, Gregory says (*Homily* 30, Gospels) that love cannot
be idle, nay, rather that if it exists at all, it achieves great things.
And because everything violent is painful as though repugnant to
the will, as is said in *Metaphysics* V, 6, likewise it is also painful to
act against the inclination of love or even beyond it; to act, however, according to it, is to do whatever is befitting the beloved. For
since the lover will accept the beloved as one with himself, it follows that the lover wears the mask (*persona*), as it were, of the
beloved in all matters relating to the beloved. (Thomas Aquinas,
Commentary on Sentences, I, Distinction 27, Q. 1, a. 1–4, AR, pp.
261–262)

There is a profound interpersonal psychology embedded in this spare
passage. How is fire restrained? Only by repressing it, or hedging it

with limits. So with love. From this comes its distinctive pain. The reason love is masked is that the lover so identifies with the beloved that
they appear as one. Hence when one looks at one lover, one sees the
other. Such a love, like fire, is always active, never resting. Love cannot
passively stand aside, but is intrinsically active.

Thomas provided a concise way of clarifying the relation of knowing
and loving.

In respect to those things that are above the soul, love is nobler
and higher than knowledge, whereas in respect to those things
that are beneath the soul, knowledge is more important. Whence
also it is good to know many things that it would be evil to love.
(Thomas Aquinas, *Commentary on Sentences*, I, Distinction 27, Q.
1, a. 1–4, AR, pp. 265–266)

Love exceeds knowledge in that which transcends human selfhood,
for only love, not knowledge, can embrace the infinite. Where knowledge excels is in those natural things that underlie the body-soul interface—for knowledge can measure only that which is finite.

Like all good qualities, love can be distorted. Jeremy Taylor warned of
love that so degenerated into pleasing others that it came to lack judgment:

Strive to get the love of the congregation; but let it not degen-
erate into popularity. Cause them to love you and revere you; to
love with religion, not for your compliance; for the good you do
them, not for that you please them. Get their love by doing your
duty, but not by omitting or spoiling any part of it: ever remembering the severe words of our blessed Saviour, "Wo be to you,
when all men speak well of you" [Luke 6:26]. (Jeremy Taylor,
RAC, III, sec. 33, *CS*, p. 12)

Since the heart can attach itself wrongly to any perceived good, love
may take contorted forms. Love loves rightly when rightly ordered in
relation to God, neighbor, and world. Is it native to the heart, therefore,
to love?

"Tell us, Fool! Which existed first, your heart or love?" He answered and said, "Both my heart and love came into existence
together, for, if that were not so, the heart would not have been
made for love, or love made for reflection." (Raymond Lull, *The
Book of the Lover and Beloved*, sec. 74, p. 31)

VIII. 🦌 BEFRIENDING

Empathy, congruence and love become profoundly united in the best
exemplars of spiritual guidance, as seen in Pachomius, one of the
founders of monastic spiritual direction:

If he saw old people or people who were sick in body or children, he would take pity on them and care for their souls in all respects. And he took joy in those who made progress in virtue and increased in faith, for they pursued what was good with great zeal. . . . And he spent (time) for their needs and the needs of the strangers who came around, until a priest was appointed there. And as he himself read to them, he had such knowledge and piety, and his gaze was so proper and his elocution so consonant with the meaning of the words, that when these worldlings saw this man of God among them, they were all the more inclined to espouse the faith and become Christians. For he was very merciful and fond of their souls. And many times, when he saw people who did not know their God and maker, he wept for long periods all alone, because he desired, if at all possible to save everyone. (*The Life of Pachomius*, CSS 45, pp. 35, 37, 39)

His empathy was recognizable in his pity and tears, and his joy in the soul's progress. His congruence was seen in his gaze and in the correspondence of his speech and his life. His love welled up abundantly in spontaneous acts of mercy. Put simply, he was "fond of their souls."

Ambrose urged the complete and untrammeled opening of one's heart to a friend:

Preserve, then, my sons, that friendship you have begun with your brothers, for nothing in the world is more beautiful than that. It is indeed a comfort in this life to have one to whom you can open your heart, with whom you can share confidences, and to whom you can entrust the secrets of your heart. . . . [Christ] gave us a pattern of friendship to follow. We are to fulfil the wish of a friend, to unfold to him our secrets which we hold in our own hearts, and are not to disregard his confidences. Let us show him our heart and he will open his to us. Therefore He says: "I have called you friends, for everything that I have learned from my father, I have made known to you" [John 15:15]. A friend, then, if he is a true one, hides nothing; he pours forth his soul as the Lord Jesus poured forth the mysteries of His Father. (Ambrose, *Duties of the Clergy*, Bk. III, sec. 131, 135, NPNF 2, X, p. 89, NIV)*

The deeper the friendship, the less is hidden. It is as comforting as it is beautiful to have one friend from whom nothing is hidden. Such friendship transcends social class differences:

Friendship is the guardian of pity and the teacher of equality, so as to make the superior equal to the inferior, and the inferior to the superior. . . . Let no authority be wanting to the inferior if the matter demands it, nor humility to the superior. Let him listen to the other as though he were of like position—an equal, and let the other warn and reprove like a friend, not from a desire to show off, but with a deep feeling of love. (Ambrose, *Duties of the Clergy*, Bk. III, sec. 132, NPNF 2, X, p. 89)

Friendship may be subjected to four different tests, according to Aelred:

There are four qualities which must be tested in a friend: loyalty, right intention, discretion, and patience, that you may entrust yourself to him securely. The right intention, that he may expect nothing from your friendship except God and its natural good. Discretion, that he may understand what is to be done in behalf of a friend, what is to be sought from a friend, what sufferings are to be endured for his sake, upon what good deeds he is to be congratulated; and, since we think that a friend should sometimes be corrected, he must know for what faults this should be done, as well as the manner, the time, and the place. Finally, patience, that he may not grieve when rebuked, or despise or hate the one inflicting the rebuke, and that he may not be unwilling to bear every adversity for the sake of his friend. (Aelred of Rievaulx, *The Pastoral Prayer*, Sec. 61, CF 2, p. 105)

One who enters into an enduring friendship takes the faults and misfortunes of the friend as his own:

He does not yet have detachment who is not able, in case of temptation, to overlook the fault of a friend, whether it be real or apparent. . . . "Nothing can be compared to a faithful friend" (Ecclus. 6:15). Indeed he takes his friend's misfortunes as his own and endures with him in hardships until death.

The number of friends is great, but only in good times; in time of trial you will scarce find one. (Maximus the Confessor, *The Four Centuries of Charity*, Ch. 4, secs. 92–94, ACW 21, p. 207)

Friendship is like having a second self:

Friendship is equality. A friend is another self. These are also ascribed to Pythagoras as their author, containing as they do the same opinion, that friendship is equality and having one soul, and that a friend is a second self. For there is nothing not shared where there is equality of fortune nor is there any dissension where the mind is one and the same, nor any separation where two are joined in one. Aristotle in the *Magna Moralia*, Book 2:

"Wherever we wish to say emphatically 'friend' we say 'My soul and his are one.' " Again, in the same book: "for a friend, as we say, is a second self." (Erasmus, "Adages," I i 2/ LB II 14F, *Collected Works*," Vol. 31, p. 31)

Ambrose argued that the betrayal of friendship is particularly odious. Once trust is broken, friendship may be exceedingly difficult to recover.

There is unity of mind in friends, and no one is more hateful than the man that injures friendship. Hence in the traitor the Lord found this the worst point on which to condemn his treachery, namely, that he gave no sign of gratitude and had mingled the poison of malice at the table of friendship. So He says: "It was thou, man of like mind, My guide and Mine acquaintance, who ever didst take pleasant meals with Me" [Ps. 55:13] . . . An enemy can be avoided; a friend cannot, if he desires to lay a plot. Let us guard against him to whom we do not entrust our plans; we cannot guard against him to whom we have already entrusted them. (Ambrose, *Duties of the Clergy*, Bk. III, sec. 136, NPNF 2, X, p. 89)

Anyone who entrusts oneself to a friend makes oneself vulnerable. So precious is the friendship relation that it must be protected against any betrayal of trust.

IX. 🐝 The Call to Self-Examination

The pastoral writers frequently asked: By what method do we come to know ourselves more clearly? How does the soul guide achieve self-knowing in a way that facilitates self-knowledge in the neighbor? Essential to the constructive change process is self-examination, presupposed in the care-giver and sought in all.

Although others may help in self-examination, what is essentially needed is a lively, inquiring relation to oneself. One need not first look for tools or external goods as if they were prior to looking attentively toward oneself. Chrysostom's marvelous metaphor sets forth the point:

As jugglers need a lot of implements—wheels, ropes, and daggers—but the philosopher has his entire art stored in his soul and needs nothing from outside; so in our case, the [inquirer] needs a good bodily constitution, and a place suitable to his method of life, in order that he may not be too far from human society and yet may enjoy the quiet of solitude, and may not miss the most suitable climate. (Chrysostom, *On the Priesthood*, Ch. 15, VI.5, p. 143)

What one needs for self-examination is not an elaborate toolbag or a rearrangement of external conditions, but—more costly—a willingness to put oneself to rigorous test, to inquire honestly into one's actual motivations, to monitor accurately one's ongoing emotive processes, to distinguish real from apparent truth.

The soul who knows herself will notice whether she cares nothing for the things that she receives, or whether she rejoices over them as over something good. Such a soul will take stock also of her mental processes, so as to find out whether she is easily moved by the hearing of some apparent truth. (Origen, *The Song of Songs*, Bk. 2, ACW 26, p. 132)

Origen recognized the subtle complexity of layers of self-knowledge:

I do not think it is possible to explain easily or briefly how a soul may know herself; but as far as we are able, we will try to elucidate a few points out of many. It seems to me, then, that the soul ought to acquire self-knowledge of a twofold kind: she should know both what she is in herself, and how she is actuated; that is to say, she ought to know what she is like essentially, and what she is like according to her dispositions. She should know, for instance, whether she is of good disposition or not, and whether or not she is upright in intention; and, if she is in fact of an upright intention, whether, in thought as in action, she has the same zeal for all virtues, or only for necessary things and those that are easy; furthermore, whether she is making progress, and gaining in understanding of things, and growing in the virtues; or whether perhaps she is standing still and resting on what she has been able to achieve thus far; and whether what she does serves only for her own improvement; or whether she can benefit others, and give them anything of profit, either by the word of teaching or by the example of her actions. . . . And the soul needs to know herself in another way—whether she does these evil deeds of hers intentionally and because she likes them; or whether it is through some weakness that, as the Apostle says, she works what she would not and does the things she hates, while on the contrary she seems to do good deeds with willingness and with direct intention. Does she, for example, control her anger with some people and let fly with others, or does she always control it, and never give way to it with anyone at all? So too with gloominess: does she conquer it in some cases, but give way to it in others, or does she never admit it at all? (Origen, *The Song of Songs*, Bk. 2, ACW 26, pp. 130–131)

Ever-deepening layers of self-awareness require careful probing: Can I distinguish my characterological disposition from my very self? My disposition from my intention? Do I seek a balanced orbit of virtues, or only those that are momentarily desired? Do I enjoy misdeeds or resist them intentionally? Am I in charge of my anger or being controlled by it? If I am to deepen self-knowledge, it will require careful attentiveness to my discrete motivations, intentions, propensities, habits, affective states, and moods. It will require studied observation of where changes are taking place, and whether for good or ill.

Every behavioral failure has a history of being unattended:

He [Abba Poemen] also said, "Not understanding what has happened prevents us from going on to something better." (Poemen, in *Sayings of the Desert Fathers*, p. 163)

A key psychoanalytic principle of soul care was well understood early in the Christian tradition of counsel: Skewed interpretations of the history of one's own personal experience block future growth. To open up emergent potentialities for the *psyche*, one must examine where the blockages lie. The facilitator of self-knowledge will proceed as though he knew little or nothing, rather than everything, as we see in the case of Abba Anthony:

One day some old men came to see Abba Anthony. In the midst of them was Abba Joseph. Wanting to test them, the old man suggested a text from the Scriptures, and, beginning with the youngest, he asked them what it meant. Each gave his opinion as he was able. But to each one the old man said, "You have not understood it." Last of all he said to Abba Joseph, "How would you explain this saying?" and he replied, "I do not know." Then Abba Anthony said, "Indeed, Abba Joseph has found the way, for he has said: 'I do not know'." (Anthony the Great, *Sayings of the Desert Fathers*, Alpha, 17, p. 4)

Avoid the assumption that the guide knows everything, knows how one should respond situationally, or knows so as to circumvent the mystery of the person, or understands the concrete divine address to someone else. When the presumption of knowing everything is disavowed, counsel can proceed on the realistic basis of a humble effort at piecing together the intricate puzzles of self-awareness:

Wherever I can, I give counsel. When he is alert, and we sit down together, then, as if I wish to learn something, I ask a question about those matters which it is fitting for him to learn, and while we speak to one another, he will gain instruction. But it is even better to wait first to see if he himself will ask anything on his own initiative. If so, the occasion of the interaction will be all the more fitting. If he does not ask anything, however, let us put questions to one another spontaneously, wishing to learn something. (Clementina, *Recognitions of Clement*, Bk. X, Ch. III, ANF VIII, p. 193)*

The assumption of Socratic dialogue was that the learner already, at some unrefined level, knows the truth about him or herself, and that the task of dialogue is to put well-conceived, pertinent questions to the reasoning mind in order that it may discover clearly and articulate adequately what one had already "known" at some subliminal level intuitively. This occurs in good counsel.

X. 🦚 THE DEEPENING OF SELF-AWARENESS

It was a premise of Greek philosophy that all human beings have a rational requirement to know themselves. Early Christian writers argued that this premise was embedded in Jewish and Christian wisdom, and in fact had been anticipated by Solomon long before Socrates. Origen specifically argued this:

The admirable maxim "Understand thyself" or "Know thyself" is said to derive, among others, from one of the seven men whom popular opinion acclaims as having been of outstanding wisdom among the Greeks. But Solomon who, as we saw in our Introduction, anticipated all these sages in time and in wisdom and in the knowledge of things, says to the soul, as to a woman, and with the implication of a threat: "Unless you have known yourself, O fair one among women, and have recognized whence the ground of your beauty proceeds—namely, that you were created in God's image, so that there is in you an abundance of natural beauty; and unless you have thus realized how fair you were in the beginning—though even now you are so much more beautiful than other women that you are the only one to be called fair; and unless you have in this way known yourself for who you are—for I would not have your beauty to seem good by comparison with that of your inferiors, but rather that you form your judgement of yourself by looking squarely at yourself and your own comeliness—unless, I say, you have done this, I command you to go forth and put yourself at the very back of the flocks, and no longer to feed sheep or lambs, but to feed goats." (Origen, *Song of Songs*, Bk. 2, ACW 26, p. 128)*

The soul is not only knowable, but beautiful. The soul is not to judge herself in terms of others' criteria of beauty, but of her own distinctive beauty. The punitive judgment (go feed the goats!) is intended to call the soul back to her high task of radical self-awareness.

Does such a self-examining dialogue hope for a simple, absolute illumination? Or does it proceed gradually, step by step, through complex and hazy layers of recollection? Augustine described the uncovering of the soul as a gradual process that depended upon astute questioning:

It often happens that a man, when asked a question, gives a negative answer, but by further questioning can be brought to answer in the affirmative. The reason lies in his own weakness. He is unable to let the light illumine the whole problem. Though he cannot behold the whole all at once, yet when he is questioned about the parts which compose the whole, he is induced to bring them one by one into the light. He is so induced by the words of his questioner, words, mark you, which do not make statements, but merely ask such questions as put him who is questioned in a position to learn inwardly. For example, if I were to ask you the question I am at present discussing: "Can nothing be taught by means of words?" it might at first seem to you to be absurd because you cannot visualize the whole problem. So I must put my question in a way suited to your ability to hear the inward Teacher. (Augustine, *The Teacher*, XII.40, LCC VI, p. 97)

The wise teacher-counselor does not try directly to introject learnings into the mind of the other, but rather helps the individual move to an inward position in which one may oneself "hear the inward Teacher." How does such a process of self-discovery practically proceed? How may one person's inner world make contact with another's inner world of memory, desire, and hope?

He learns nothing unless he himself sees what he is asking about. . . . In the halls of memory we bear the images of things once perceived as memorials which we can contemplate mentally and can speak of with a good conscience and without lying. But these memorials belong to us privately. If anyone hears me speak of them, provided he has seen them himself, he does not learn from my words, but recognizes the truth of what I say by the images which he has in his own memory. (Augustine, "The Teacher," XII, LCC VI, p. 96)

Viewing memory as a lengthy hallway of pictures, the pictures of one soul are never the same as another's. If I am to help teach you about your private hallway, I must first listen carefully to your own descriptions of it. I may ask questions about your hallway, but the richness of the dialogue hinges upon how wisely I put those questions, and how much your responses correspond with the actual pictures in your hallway. Nothing that I say to you about my hallway will make much difference unless it corresponds with something in yours.

Why has a wise providence made self-knowledge so perplexing? Why is knowing oneself so much more difficult than knowing of things?

None can be good, unless they have in their power that perception by which they may become good. Only then may they become of their own intent what they choose to be. Otherwise they could not be truly good. If they were kept in goodness not by freely chosen purpose, but by necessity, they could not be good. God has given to every one the power of their own will, that each one may be what one wishes to be. . . . In order, therefore, that there might be a distinction between those who choose good and those who choose evil, God has concealed that which is profitable to them, i.e., the possession of the kingdom of heaven, and has laid it up and hidden it as a secret treasure, so that no one can easily attain it by one's own power or knowledge. Yet He has brought the report of it, under various names and opinions, through successive generations, to the hearing of all; so that whoever should be lovers of good, hearing it, might inquire and discover what is profitable and salutary to them. (Clementina, *Recognitions of Clement*, III, Ch. 53, ANF VIII, p. 128)*

The divine intention is to require us to make an effort to ask questions about ourselves, so that the healthy life will not simply be given us cheaply (lacking willing receptivity), but must be sought for by the exertion of moral energy to acquire and appreciate. Such hard won goodness of soul is more valuable than if easily won.

Cyril pondered about precisely what it is that we come to know in knowing ourselves. We find ourselves to be awesomely made, free, radically accountable creatures, capable of refracting the image of the Creator:

"Know thyself," who you are, that is to say that man has a two-fold constitution, combining soul and body, and that, as we said just now, the same God is creator of your soul and of your body. And, you must know your soul to be endowed with free-will, and to be God's fairest work in the image of himself, its maker. It is immortal in as far as God grants it immortality. It is a rational living creature not subject to decay, because these qualities have been bestowed by God upon it. And it has the power to do what it chooses. (Cyril of Jerusalem, *Catechetical Lectures*, IV, LCC IV, p. 109)

Can one know anything of oneself with certainty? Augustine argued that some forms of self-knowing can attain certainty: that I am, that I know that I am, and that I desire being more than not being. In this he saw an indirect analogy to the triune God, who is, who speaks his Word, and who affirms and delights in his own speech. Thus when we know ourselves properly, we gain some preliminary recognition of the triune God imaged already in our very selves. The argument is ingenious:

For we both are, and know that we are, and delight in our being and our knowledge of it. Moreover, in these three things no true-seeming illusion disturbs us; for we do not come into contact with these by some bodily sense, as we perceive the things outside of us . . . but, without any delusive representation of images or phantasms, I am most certain that I am, and that I know and delight in this. In respect of these truths, I am not at all afraid of the arguments of the Academicians, who say, What if you are deceived? For if I am deceived, I am. For he who is not, cannot be deceived; and if I am deceived, by this same token I am. And since I am if I am deceived, how am I deceived in believing that I am? For it is certain that I am if I am deceived. Since, therefore, I, the person deceived, should be, even if I were deceived, certainly I am not deceived in this knowledge that I am. And, consequently, neither am I deceived in knowing that I know. For, as I know that I am, so I know this also, that I know. And when I love these two things, I add to them a certain third thing, namely, my love, which is of equal moment. For neither am I deceived in this, that I love, since in those things which I love I am not deceived; though even if these were false, it would still be true that I *loved* false things. (Augustine, *The City of God*, Bk. XI.26, NPNF 1, II, p. 220)

This is a brilliant anticipation of the Cartesian argument on behalf of certain knowledge (*dubito, cogito, ergo sum*) over a thousand years before Descartes. Thus the charge that we can know nothing with complete certainty about ourselves is answered. For we can know that we exist, and that we know we exist, and that we love to be more than not to be. Thus without appeal to any empirical data whatever but purely by clear and distinct ideas alone, one must conclude that anyone who is deceived, must first *be* in order to be deceived.

But what does one know when one comes more fully to know one's own soul? If the soul mirrors God's goodness, does that not tempt one to self-congratulation so as perhaps to fail to see one's misdeeds? Catherine of Siena formulated this response with exceptional precision:

In the knowledge which the soul obtains of herself, she knows more of God, and knowing the goodness of God in herself, the sweet mirror of God, she knows her own dignity and indignity.

Her dignity is that of her creation, seeing that she is the image of God, and this has been given her by grace, and not as her due. In that same mirror of the goodness of God, the soul knows her own indignity, which is the consequence of her own fault. Wherefore, as a man more readily sees spots on his face when he looks in a mirror, so, the soul who, with truth knowledge of self, rises with desire, and gazes with the eye of the intellect at herself in the sweet mirror of God, knows better the stain of her own face, by the purity which she sees in Him. (Catherine of Siena, *A Treatise of Discretion*, pp. 62–63)

Thus when I know myself profoundly, and recognize that my soul mirrors the goodness of God, that paradoxically makes me simultaneously aware both of God's goodness reflected in me, and of my inadequate mirroring of God's goodness.

Richard Baxter strongly stressed the importance of the counselor studying himself in preparation for pastoral care:

Take heed therefore unto yourselves, and to all the flock, over the which the Holy Ghost hath made you overseers, to feed the Church of God, which He hath purchased with His own blood. Acts 20.28.

Let us consider, What it is to take heed to ourselves. See that the work of saving grace be thoroughly wrought in your own souls. Take heed to yourselves, lest you be void of that saving grace of God which you offer to others, and be strangers to the effectual working of that gospel which you preach; and lest, while you proclaim to the world the necessity of a Saviour, your own hearts should neglect him.... Take heed to yourselves, lest you perish, while you call upon others to take heed of perishing; and lest you famish yourselves while you prepare food for them.... many a preacher is now in hell, who hath a hundred times called upon his hearers to use the utmost care and diligence to escape it.... Many a tailor goes in rags, that maketh costly clothes for others; and many a cook scarcely licks his fingers, when he hath dressed for others the most costly dishes.... When you pen your sermons, little do you think that you are drawing up indictments against your own souls!... If you speak of hell, you speak of your own inheritance: if you describe the joys of heaven, you describe your own misery.... O miserable life! that a man should study and preach against himself, and spend his days in a course of self-condemning! A graceless, inexperienced preacher is one of the most unhappy creatures upon earth: and yet he is ordinarily very insensible of his unhappiness; for he hath so many counters that seem like the gold of saving grace, and so many splendid

stones that resemble Christian jewels, that he is seldom troubled
with the thoughts of his poverty; . . . Alas! it is the common danger and calamity of the Church, to have unregenerate and inexperienced pastors, and to have so many men become preachers
before they are Christians; who are sanctified by dedication to
the altars as the priests of God, before they are sanctified by
hearty dedication as the disciples of Christ; and so to worship an
unknown God, and to preach an unknown Christ, to pray
through an unknown Spirit. (Baxter, *RP*, pp. 51–56)

Those who pretend to escape the soul's ills by changing their external
environment or circumstances forget that one forever brings one's soul
into those new circumstances:

To try to escape ill-health of the soul by moving from place to
place is like flying from one's own shadow. Such a man as flies
from himself carries himself with him. He changes his place, but
not his soul. He finds himself the same everywhere he is, except
that the constant movement itself makes him worse, just as a sick
man is harmed by jolting when he is carried about. (William of
St. Thierry, *The Golden Epistle*, Sec. 95, p. 44)

XI. ❦ The Process of Self-Examination

John Donne commended a periodical review of one's entire life from
beginning to end. His own act of self-examination began with this as-
tonishing prayer, linking the endless grace of God with the linear temporal line of providence in history:

O Eternal and most gracious God, who, considered in thyself,
art a circle, first and last, and altogether; but, considered in thy
working upon us, art a direct line, and leadest us from our beginning, through all our ways, to our end, enable me by thy
grace to look forward to mine end, and to look backward too, to
the considerations of thy mercies afforded me from the beginning. (John Donne, *Devotions*, p. 11)

Bonaventure was chief among scholastic writers who believed that by
entering one's soul deeply one journeys to meet God:

Enter into yourself, then, and see
that your souls loves itself most fervently;
that it could not love itself
unless it knew itself,

nor know itself
unless it remembered itself,
because our intellects grasp only what is present to our
   memory.
From this you can observe,
not with the bodily eye, but with the eye of reason,
that your soul has a threefold power.
Consider, therefore,
the operations and relationships of these three powers,
and you will be able to see God
through yourself as through an image,
which is to see *through a mirror in an obscure manner.*
(Bonaventure, *The Soul's Journey into God*, CWS, pp. 79–80)

Bonaventure described the process by which the soul moves toward God through self-examination, moving from desire, and through the love of happiness, freely toward the good, which the soul can behold:

Now desire tends principally toward what moves it most; but what moves it most is what is loved most, and what is loved most is happiness. But happiness is had only in terms of the best and ultimate end. Therefore human desire seeks nothing except the highest good or what leads to or has some likeness to it. So great is the power of the highest good that nothing can be loved by a creature except out of a desire for it. Creatures, when they take the image and copy for the Truth, are deceived and in error.

See, therefore, how close the soul is to God, and how, in their operations, the memory leads to eternity, the understanding to truth and the power of choice to the highest good.

These powers lead us to the most blessed Trinity itself in view of their order, origin, and interrelatedness. From memory, intelligence comes forth as its offspring, since we understand when a likeness which is in the memory leaps into the eye of the intellect in the form of a word. From memory and intelligence love is breathed forth as their mutual bond. These three—the generating mind, the word and love—are in the soul as memory, understanding and will, which are consubstantial, coequal and coeval, and interpenetrate each other. . . . When therefore, the soul considers itself, it rises through itself as through a mirror to behold the blessed Trinity of the Father, the Word and Love: three persons, coeternal, coequal and consubstantial.

. . . It seems amazing when it has been shown that God is so close to our souls that so few should be aware of the First Principle within themselves. Yet the reason is close at hand: for the human mind, distracted by cares, does not enter into itself through memory; clouded by sense images, it does not turn back to itself through intelligence; allured by concupiscence, it does not turn back to itself through desire for inner sweetness and spiritual joy. Thus lying totally in these things of sense, it cannot reenter into itself as into the image of God. (Bonaventure, *The Soul's Journey into God*, CWS, pp. 84, 87)

Memory, intelligence, and love combine to enable this journey. In beholding oneself intently, one suddenly stands beheld by the triune God. Yet our passions constantly becloud and prevent full recognition.

Whether the soul mirrors God or God mirrors the soul remained a mystery to Raymond Lull. What was clear to him was that self-knowledge was being awakened and increased through the divine-human meeting and beholding:

The Lover gazed upon himself so that he might be a mirror in which to behold his Beloved, and he gazed upon his Beloved as in a mirror in which he might have knowledge of himself. Which of these two mirrors do you think was nearer to his understanding? (Raymond Lull, *The Book of the Lover and Beloved*, sec. 350, p. 104)

The modern pastoral counseling movement founded by Anton Boisen began with the premise that every person is a book of experience to be read. This idea is found much earlier in the pastoral tradition, as in Alan of Lille, who posited three mirrors in this beholding, the mirror of scripture, of creation, and of nature:

You may read about yourself in the book of experience. You may discover yourself in the book of conscience. The book of knowledge—written in a volume—may reprehend you, as well as the book of experience written in the heart. You read in the book of knowledge: "Know yourself." In the book of experience you will read that the flesh battles against the spirit, in the book of conscience that "The day of judgment circles on remorseless wings." O man, look at yourself in this threefold mirror, and you will not be pleased by the sight of yourself. The glass in which you should behold yourself is triple: the mirror of Scripture, the mirror of nature, and the mirror of creation. In the mirror of Scripture you will read of your condition. In the mirror of creation you will behold your wretchedness. In the mirror of nature you will see that you stand accused. (Alan of Lille, *The Art of Preaching*, Ch. 3, CSS 23, p. 29)

Self-knowledge is deepened by beholding the human condition as mirrored in scripture. The fall of freedom is mirrored by beholding its created goodness. The judgment of freedom is mirrored in what self actually beholds in an ordinary mirror, the mirror nature provides.

XII. 🐝 HUMOR IN COUNSELING

The pastoral writers thought that comic perception was a uniquely swift and effective vehicle of good counsel and spiritual instruction. They are misrepresented if thought to be disinterested in the essential psychological dynamics of humor, affability, and wit. As early as second century, Clement and other Christian thinkers were reflecting on the subtle dynamics of humor in interpersonal relationships:

Old men who look on young men as children may, perhaps, although only infrequently, jest with them, teasing them in a way that will teach them good manners. With a shy and taciturn youth, for example, they may make this pleasantry: "My son,"— indicating the youth who is so quiet—"never stops talking." Such teasing encourages the young man in his modesty, for, by accusing him of a fault he does not have, it jestingly calls attention to his good qualities. This is, indeed, a sort of instruction, securing what one has by reference to what one does not have. He who says that a man who confines himself to water and is self-controlled is always attending parties and getting drunk accomplishes the same sort of thing. (Clement of Alexandria, *Christ the Educator*, Bk. II, Ch. 7.57, FC 23, p. 143)

The jest is a paradoxical communication: by pointing overtly in one way it wishes to point precisely in the opposite way. Thus one may encourage by seeming to demean, or show what is there by pointing to what is not there. It is a complex communication, but a sharp tool in the hands of a skilled partner in dialogue. Clement also recognized that the jest, in the wrong hands, could be turned to destructive purpose:

If there should be present any of those who take delight in ridiculing others, we must still hold our tongue and dismiss their flow of words as a cup filled to overflowing. Such sport is dangerous. "The mouth of the fool-hardy comes near to a fall" (Prov. 10:14). "Thou shalt not welcome a foolish report, nor consent with an unjust man to be an unjust witness," (cf. Exod. 23:1), whether to accuse someone or to speak ill of him or to show ill-will toward him. (Clement of Alexandria, *Christ the Educator*, Bk. II, Ch. 7.57, FC 23, p. 143)

Even among the most rigorous ascetic traditions, pastoral writers have made a point of emphasizing the value of recreation and good humor in sustaining the spirit of the community:

Cordial love ought to be accompanied by two virtues, one of which may be called affability, and the other cheerfulness. Affability is a virtue which spreads a certain agreeableness over all the business and serious communications which we hold with one another; cheerfulness is that which renders us gracious and agreeable in our recreations and less serious intercourse with one another. All the virtues have, as you know, two contrary vices, which are the extremes of the virtue. The virtue of affability, then, lies between two vices: that of too great gravity and seriousness on the one hand, and on the other of too many demonstrations of flattery. Now the virtue of affability holds the golden mean between these two extremes, making use of affectionate terms according to the necessity of those with whom it has to deal, preserving at the same time a gentle gravity according to the requirements of the persons and affairs of which it treats. I say that we must show signs of affection at certain times, for it would not be suitable to carry into a sick room as much gravity of demeanour as we should display elsewhere, not showing more kindness to an invalid than if she were in full health. But we must not make such demonstrations too frequently, or be ready on every occasion to speak honeyed words, throwing whole handfuls of them over the first person we meet. Just as if we put too much sugar on our food it would disgust us, becoming insipid by being too sweet, so, in the same way, too frequent signs of affection would become repulsive. (Francis de Sales, Conference IV, *SC*, p. 59)

Keep in mind that the context of these observations is a strict community of convented nuns whose lives were fundamentally dedicated to prayer. This makes the appeal for a shared mood of affability, laughter, and recreation all the more winsome.

The sisters must have proper recreation, and it is specially important that it should be made cheerful for the novices. Our minds must not be kept always on the stretch; there would be danger of our becoming melancholy. I should not like you to give way to scruples when you have spent the whole of recreation on some occasion in talking about unimportant things. . . . Neither is there any harm whatever in laughing a little at something that a sister may have said. To utter some light, merry word, which may perhaps mortify her a little, provided it does not make her sad, and provided also that I said it not to hurt, but simply for recreation, is not a matter for confession. (Francis de Sales, Conference IV, *SC*, p. 70)

Humor reduces the tension, and serves as an antidote to sadness. George Herbert warned against "perpetual severity":

He sometimes refresheth himself, as knowing that nature will not bear everlasting droopings, and that pleasantness of disposition is a great key to do good; not only because all men shun the company of perpetual severity, but also for that, when they are in company, instructions seasoned with pleasantness both enter sooner and root deeper. (Geo. Herbert, *CP*, Ch. XXVII, CWS, pp. 94, 95)

This Part of our discussion has sought to identify key elements of the effective therapeutic relationship. They are: accurate empathic listening grounded in God's own empathic understanding, radical openness to one's own experiencing process, fitting self-disclosure, unconditional accepting love, the willingness to enter into rigorous examination of motives, and a sense of the comic amid the contradictions that characterize ordinary human existence.

2 The Nature of Pastoral Counsel: Its Prevailing Metaphors

FIVE COMPLEMENTARY metaphors amplify implicit layers of meaning in the work of pastoral counsel. In the chapter that follows each will be explored. These images occur repeatedly in classical discussions of soul care:

(1) The prevailing metaphor is that the pastor works like a *counselor*, offering timely wisdom.

(2) The pastor works like a *physician*, providing therapeutic remedies for ailing members of the flock.

(3) The pastor works like the *guide* of a hazardous journey, providing direction and situational mentoring to enable the flock to avoid obstacles and find their way through difficult passages.

(4) The pastor works like a *liberator*, freeing the soul from self-created prisons of fear, guilt, and depression.

(5) The pastor works like an *educator*, providing resources by means of which the soul can better learn the truth about herself.

Several metaphors may function simultaneously in a single passage. This chapter brings together classic pastoral texts that reveal how these five metaphors interlace and complement each other.

I. ❦ GOOD COUNSEL

The notions of "good counsel" and "counsel" (Hebr: *etsah, yaats,* Gk: *eubolia*) were familiar to classic Jewish and Christian writers. A classic definition of counsel was summarized by Thomas Aquinas in a section of the *Summa Theologica* on "The Gift of Counsel," which dealt with both the giving and receiving of good counsel (*euboulia*):

> Now among the acts of man, it is proper to him to take counsel, since this denotes a research of the reason about the actions he has to perform and whereof human life consists, for the speculative life is above man, as stated in Ethics, x. But *euboulia* signifies goodness of counsel, for it is derived from *eu*, good, and *boule*, counsel, being *a good counsel* or rather *a disposition to*

take good counsel. Hence it is evident that *euboulia* is a human virtue.... All sin is contrary to taking good counsel. For good counsel requires not only the discovery or devising of fit means for the end, but also other circumstances. Such are suitable time, so that one be neither too slow nor too quick in taking counsel, and the mode of counsel. (Thomas Aquinas, *Summa Theologica*, Part II–II Q. 51, Art. 1, Vol. II, p. 1409)

Counsel may do harm as well as good. All counsel is not good counsel. If so, it then becomes important to discern what makes counsel good. Generally speaking, it is good if it finds good means to a good end, and pursues these means at a good time, on a fitting occasion. Bad counsel would unwisely discern good means to a bad end or bad means to a good end, or propose good means to a good end at a bad time. How does the disposition to take good counsel (*euboulia*) differ, then, from prudence or from good judgment? Let Thomas answer:

Consequently *euboulia* which makes man take good counsel must needs be a distinct virtue from prudence, which makes man command well.... It belongs to prudence to take good counsel by commanding it, to *euboulia* by eliciting it. [Reply Obj. 2]. Different acts are directed in different degrees to the one end which is a good life in general: for counsel comes first, judgment follows, and command comes last. The last named has an immediate relation to the last end: whereas the other two acts are related thereto remotely. Nevertheless these have certain proximate ends of their own, the end of counsel being the discovery of what has to be done, and the end of judgment, certainty.... Hence in Greek some in respect of *sunesis* [judgment] are said to be *sunetoi*, i.e., persons of sense, or *eusunetoi*, i.e., men of good sense, just as on the other hand, those who lack this virtue are called *asunetoi*, i.e., senseless. Now, different acts which cannot be ascribed to the same cause, must correspond to different virtues. And it is evident that goodness of counsel and goodness of judgment are not reducible to the same cause, for many can take good counsel, without having good sense so as to judge well. Even so, in speculative matters some are good at research, through their reason being quick at arguing from one thing to another (which seems to be due to a disposition of their power of imagination, which has a facility in forming phantasms), and yet such persons sometimes lack good judgment (and this is due to a defect in the intellect arising chiefly from a defective disposition of the common sense which fails to judge aright). Hence there is need, besides *euboulia*, for another virtue, which judges well, and this is called *sunesis*. (Thomas Aquinas, *Summa Theologica*, Part II-II, Q. 51, Art. 2, Vol. II, p. 1410)

Summarizing and applying this point: If one is to act rightly and do well, one must first be well-counseled, either by oneself or another. One must then use good judgment in applying that counsel to circumstances. Then one must be prudent in contextually executing (commanding) an act for a particular circumstance. Thus it is possible for someone to be bright, quick-witted, and well-adapted to imaginative argument, yet still remain hampered in either giving or receiving good counsel. For good counsel is tempered by the common sense ability to judge and apply maxims rightly and proportionally in a specific context.

Earlier, Clement of Alexandria made a similar, but tighter, distinction between counsel and good counsel:

Now counsel is seeking for the right way of acting in present circumstances, and good counsel is wisdom in our counsels. (Clement of Alexandria, *Stromata*, Bk. II, Ch. XVI, ANF II, p. 363)

Baxter had recourse to biblical models and precedents in defining the task of the pastor as counselor for the soul, analogous to the physician who cares for the body or the attorney who advises on one's property:

We must be ready to give advice to inquirers who come to us with cases of conscience. Especially must we be prepared for that great question which the Jews put to Peter, and the gaoler to Paul and Silas, "What must I do to be saved?" (Acts 16:30). A minister is not to be merely a public preacher, but to be known as a counsellor for their souls, as the physician is for their bodies, and the lawyer for their estates. In this way each one who is in doubts and straits may bring his case to him for resolution, as Nicodemus came to Christ, and as it was usual with the people of old to go to the priest. "For the lips of a priest ought to preserve knowledge, and from his mouth men should seek instruction—because he is the messenger of the Lord Almighty" (Mal. 2:7). (Baxter, *RP*, p. 96, NIV)*

Eckhart thought that the inner freedom of the counselor was a more crucial credential than academic training.

If I were seeking a master of studies, I should go to the colleges of Paris where higher studies are followed, but if I wanted to know about living a perfect life, they could not help me there.

To whom should I go? To a person with a nature that is pure and free and to no one else. (Meister Eckhart, "Fragments," 8, *Meister Eckhart*, p. 236, cf. WSD, p. 4.)*

The confidence that persons could by grace live a perfect life was greater in the late medieval period than today, where the tradition shaped by Freud begins with the base-line premise of human self-deception and unconscious distortions.

If one seeks counsel, one seeks to know how to act in a specific situation. The counsel is good if it is tempered by wisdom. Thomas sought to distinguish counseling from five commensurable actions closely associated with it: instructing, comforting, reproving, pardoning, and forbearing:

> Spiritual needs are relieved by spiritual acts in two ways, first by asking for help from God, and in this respect we have prayer, whereby one man prays for others; secondly, by giving human assistance, and this in three ways. First in order to relieve a deficiency on the part of the intellect, and if this deficiency be in the speculative intellect, the remedy is applied by *instructing*, and if the practical intellect, the remedy is applied by *counselling*. Secondly, there may be a deficiency on the part of the appetitive power especially by way of sorrow, which is remedied by *comforting*. Thirdly, the deficiency may be due to an inordinate act; and this may be the subject of a threefold consideration. First, in respect of the sinner, inasmuch as the sin proceeds from his inordinate will, and thus the remedy takes the form of *reproof*. Secondly, in respect of the person sinned against; and if the sin be committed against ourselves, we apply the remedy by *pardoning the injury*, while, if it be committed against God or our neighbor, it is not in our power to pardon, as Jerome observes (*Super* Matt. 18:15). Thirdly, in respect of the result of the inordinate act, on account of which the sinner is an annoyance to those who live with him, even beside his intention; in which case the remedy is applied by *bearing with him*, especially with regard to those who sin out of weakness, according to Rom. 15:1. (Thomas Aquinas, *Summa Theologica*, Part II–II, Q. 32, Art. 1, Vol. II, p. 1325)

Thomas' purpose was to define counsel and distinguish it from those terms that lie nearby. In this complex and ingenious passage, he distinguished different types of help, the most fundamental being the distinction between divine help and human help. Those who want God's help must pray. Those who want to give and receive human help in response to God's help may offer

> instruction to the mind,
> counsel for practical actions,
> comfort for sorrow,

reproof and admonition for correction of ills,
pardon for sins,
and forbearance for those who are weak.

These constitute a basic catalogue of types of help. All types are concerns of soul care. Counsel is that mode of help that assists practical reasoning in making good and prudent judgments with good means leading to good ends at an appropriate time.

II. ❦ THE PHYSICIAN OF SOULS

Soul care is both like and unlike bodily care. The pastoral writers often struggled with analogies between medicine and ministry. They asked how the soul's peculiar diseases were to be diagnosed, how malaises were to be recognized at early stages, how treated without eliciting further complications, and restored to soundness. In all these ways pastoral counsel is similar to medicine, surgery, and physical therapy, even though certain differences are obvious. The anatomy of this highly functional metaphor is worth understanding. It begins early in the Christian tradition:

You are to be like a compassionate physician: heal all that have sinned. Make use of all available saving methods of cure: not only cutting and searing, or using corrosives, but binding up, and putting the patient in a safe place, and using gentle healing medicines, and sprinkling comfortable words. If it be an hollow wound, or great gash, nourish it with a suitable salve, that it may be again knitted together and become smooth with the rest of the surrounding flesh. If it be foul, cleanse it with corrosive powder, that is, with words of correction. If the wound is due to the swelling up of proud flesh, cauterize it down with a sharp plaister—the threat of judgment. If it spreads further, sear it, and excise the decaying cells—with fasting end the plague. . . . You must not be overly ready or hasty to do radical surgery. Do not quickly have recourse to the saw, with its many teeth. First use a lancet to lay open the wound, that the inward cause from which the pain is derived may be drawn out. (*Constitutions of the Holy Apostles*, Bk. II, sec. V.41, ANF VII, p. 415)*

The guiding principle of both medicine and soul care is *variability of treatment*. Each remedy must change according to particular causes and observed symptoms. The compassionate physician of souls will come to the therapeutic task resourcefully armed with a variety of approaches. He will be ready to clean the wound, bind it up, prevent its tendency to injure the rest of the body, protect against further infection. He will not overtreat, and not employ drastic methods while gentle ones are available. Caution and prudence are key elements of this gentle metaphor. Yet the comparison of medicine and soul care is plausible only if the two spheres compared are recognized as different. The primary difference is that soul care deals with the insidious malady of sin, while medicine deals primarily with physical ailment:

As a skillful and compassionate physician, heal all such as have wandered in the paths of sin; for "they that are whole have no need of a physician, but they that are sick. For the Son of man came to save and to seek that which was lost"(Matt. 9:12). Since you are therefore a physician of the Lord's Church, provide remedies suitable to every patient's unique case. Cure them, heal them by all means possible; restore them sound to the Church. (*Constitutions of the Holy Apostles*, Bk. II, sec. iii.20, ANF VI, p. 405)*

The "suitable remedy" principle makes it necessary that the pastor be an accurate observer of many levels of functioning that may be occurring simultaneously. If sin is viewed exhaustively as sickness, does not the metaphor tend to lose its moral dimension? Are all forms of sin, by analogy, to be viewed in such a morally neutral way as a physician would view infection or lesion?

If you wish to understand the nature of the sickness of the soul, contemplate with me the lovers of money, and the lovers of ambition, and the lovers of boys, and those overly fond of women; for it was just such as these that Jesus beheld among the crowds, took compassion upon, and healed them. For not every sin is to be considered a sickness, but that which has settled down in the whole soul. For so you may see the lovers of money wholly intent on money and upon preserving and gathering it; the lovers of ambition wholly intent on a little glory, for they gape for praise from the masses and the vulgar; and similarly you will understand the other cases. . . . Not every sin is a sickness. . . . Some are weak, and others sickly more than weak, and others, in comparison with both, are more like a moral slumber. (Origen, *Commentary on Matthew*, Bk. X, sec. 24, ANF X, p. 430)*

It is when a distorted behavior pattern has compulsively "settled down in the whole soul" that it becomes the intensive concern of pastoral care. The care-giver is less concerned with occasional maladies than with those deeply incapacitating, chronic moral distortions and compulsive hungers and driving passions that come to take charge of the whole soul. The deeply compulsive inner sickness is different from a temporary moral weakness, or moral laziness or stupor. It is an habituated character pattern that distorts the whole range of perception, action, memory, imagination and covenant relationships. The basic goal of medicine is restored equilibrium, as with a healthy balance of good diet, rest, and exercise. Soul care shares an analogous goal:

Further, because of disordered mingling of qualities and of broken continuity in the body, we require physicians and their art. When change takes place in some quality, we need to restore the balance by introducing the opposite quality, so as to bring the constitution of the body back to normal. The physician's art is not, as some think, just to cool a fevered body, but to restore it to an equable temperament. For were one merely to cool a man in a fever, his condition would turn into the exactly opposite ailment. (Nemesius, *On the Nature of Man*, Ch. I.6, LCC IV, p. 242)

Similarly, the physician of souls does not apply a single remedy unilaterally or absolutely, without seeking to avoid the imbalances that might arise from any excessive application. Amid the complexities of our spiritual malaise, how are we to know what to do, and to whom shall we turn? Ignatius trusted that God's own Word made flesh would become the incomparably helpful physician amid the mystery of iniquity that yields untold human affliction:

There is one Physician: both flesh and spirit, begotten and unbegotten, in man, God, in death, true life, both from Mary and from God, first passible and then impassible, Jesus Christ our Lord. (Ignatius of Antioch, *To the Ephesians*, sec. 7, AF, 80)*

The theandric union of God and humanity in Christ serves to heal the breach between God and humanity caused by sin. Clement of Alexandria viewed the healing work of the divine physician within a world-historical frame of reference. The healing work occurs differently within different spheres of need and possibility, according to the large design of God's incomparably wise providence:

The soul He heals in a way suitable to the nature of the soul: by His commandments and by His gifts. We would perhaps expect Him to heal with His counsels, but, generous with His gifts, He also says to us sinners: "Your sins are forgiven" [Luke 7:48]. With these words we have become born anew in spirit, for by them we share in the magnificent and unvarying order established by His providence. That providence begins by ordering the world and the heavens, the course of the sun's orbit and the movements of the other heavenly bodies, all for the sake of humanity. Then, it concerns itself with the human condition itself, for whom it had undertaken all these other labors. And because it considers this as its most important work, it guides the human soul on the right path by the virtues of prudence and temperance, and equips the body with beauty and harmony. Finally, into the actions of humankind it infuses uprightness and some of its own good order. (Clement of Alexandria, *Christ the Educator*, Bk. I, Ch. 2, FC 23, p. 8)*

The healing of the fundamental sickness of the soul—sin—occurs not merely by burdening humanity with another new requirement, but by proclaiming the good news of divine forgiveness as radical gift. It is a forgiveness that elicits a responsiveness that searches for the excellent behaviors of prudence and temperance that give moral evidence that divine forgiveness has been taken seriously. It is through the address of the forgiving Word of the Son that the intent of the Father in creation and providence is now clarified, and all this by the power of the Spirit.

George Herbert portrayed the pastor as always prepared for these contingencies, caring for the whole person. In that time many folk-medical functions were actually taken care of by pastors within the bounds of their own parish:

If there be any of his flock sick, he is their physician, . . . it is easy for any scholar to attain to such a measure of physic, as may be of much use to him, both for himself and others. This is done by seeing one Anatomy, reading one Book of Physic, having one Herbal by him. And let Fernelius be the Physic Author, for he writes briefly, neatly and judiciously; especially let his Method of Physic be diligently perused, as being the practical part and of most use. Now both the reading of him and the knowing of herbs may be done at such times, as they may be a help and a recreation to more divine studies, . . . For home-bred medicines are both more easy for the Parson's purse, and more familiar for all men's bodies. So where the Apothecary useth, either for loosing, Rhubarb: or for binding, Bolearmena [an astringent]; the Parson useth damask or white Roses for the one, and plantain, shepherds-purse, knotgrass, for the other; and that with better success. . . . yet he looks not in this point of Curing beyond his own Parish; except the person be so poor, that he is not able to reward the Physician. (Geo. Herbert, *CP*, Ch. XXIII, CWS, pp. 88, 89)

"Physic" here refers to the primitive practice of folk medicine. Every pastor should have sufficient knowledge of diet, herbs, and simple, serviceable remedies that when other medical services are not available to the poor, certain remedies can be applied. This has very old precedent in the Christian tradition.

Some may question whether soul care has been enough concerned with practically delivering actual remedies for the human predicament. Clement thought that Christian caring always seeks a palpable, actual remedy, not a seeming remedy.

Those who labor under some sickness are dissatisfied if the physician prescribes no remedy to restore their health; how, then, can we withhold our sincerest gratitude from the divine Educator when He corrects the acts of disobedience that sweep us on to ruin, and uproots the desires that drag us into sin, refusing to be silent and connive at them, and even offers counsels on the right way to live? Certainly we owe Him the deepest gratitude. (Clement of Alexandria, *Christ the Educator*, Bk. I, Ch. 12, [100], FC 23, pp. 88–89)

The fundamental purpose of soul care is the delivery of actual, situational remedies for the malaise of sin and moral dysfunction. The competence of the pastor must be assessed by asking: To what extent has the disease (sin) been cured? Has the patient been reasonably restored to full functioning, given the situation and its limits?

Coercion is never in order. One must be understanding when sick persons spit out bad-tasting medicine. So it is with spiritual medicine.

When a physician persuades the sick to take some bitter remedies, he does so by coaxing requests. He does not use a compelling command. He knows that weakness, not choice, is the reason why the sick man spits out the healthful medicines, whenever he rejects those which will aid him. (Peter Chrysologus, *Sermons*, 108, FC 17, pp.166–167)

By the end of the seventh century, the Synod of Quinisext, A.D. 692, drew together much of the standard pastoral teaching on how spiritual medications would be variously applied. It became one of the most influential ecumenical documents on pastoral care:

It behooves those who have received from God the power to loose and bind, to consider the quality of the sin and the readiness of the sinner for conversion, and to apply medicine suitable for the disease, lest if he is injudicious in each of these respects he should fail in regard to the healing of the sick man. For the disease of sin is not simple, but various and multiform, and it germinates many mischievous offshoots, from which much evil is diffused, and it proceeds further until it is checked by the power of the physician. Wherefore he who professes the science of spiritual medicine ought first of all to consider the disposition of him who has sinned, and to see whether he tends to health or (on the contrary) provokes to himself disease by his own behaviour, and to look how he can care for his manner of life during the interval. And if he does not resist the physician, and if the ulcer of the soul is increased by the application of the imposed medicaments, then let him mete out mercy to him according as he is worthy of it. For the whole account is between God and him to whom the pastoral rule has been delivered, to lead back the wandering sheep and to cure that which is wounded by the serpent; and that he may neither cast them down into the precipices of despair, nor loosen the bridle towards dissolution or contempt of life; but in some way or other, either by means of sternness and astringency, or by greater softness and mild medicines, to resist this sickness and exert himself for the healing of the ulcer, now examining the fruits of his repentance and wisely managing the man who is called to higher illumination. (Synod of Quinisext, Canon CII, The Seven Ecumenical Councils, NPNF 2, XIV, p. 408)

The pastor is here authorized to administer spiritual medicine in due proportion and season. For pastoral guidance is his specified duty, that for which he is called and ordained. He must diagnose accurately the temperament of the parishioner, and the extent to which the sinner has colluded freely to cause his own failings. The causes may be complex and interlacing, as in the case of a hidden ulcer. The medication must not be too harsh or too mild. Accurately assessing the disposition of the sufferer is crucial. The council fathers recognized that the sick person may be responsible for bringing sickness nearer, "provoking oneself to disease," and that a supposed cure can harm as well as help. Several pastoral metaphors subtly mesh: searching for and describing causes, leading the flock to safety, avoiding steep cliffs of despair, binding up the wounded, bearing fruit, bringing light.

Augustine spoke of the progress of the soul as a developmental process extending through time, through which the healing of faith enables the perspective of hope which empowers the energy of love:

There are three stages in the soul's progress: healing, looking, seeing. Likewise there are three virtues: faith, hope, love. For healing and looking, faith and hope are always necessary. For seeing, all three are necessary in this life, but in the life to come love only. (Augustine, "The Soliloquies," VII.14, LCC 6, p. 32)

If faith heals the sickness of the soul, then hope looks forward to the completion of what began in faith. If faith and hope begin and anticipate the completion or goal of the journey, then love itself constitutes that journey's fulfillment. Love is that for which the journey began, that which one has gone so out of one's way to see.

III. 🐚 THE GUIDE OF THE SOUL'S ARDUOUS JOURNEY

The physician metaphor is not complete without the complementary metaphor of guidance. For even one who is well needs a guide through hazardous territory. The soul needs not only a physician for sickness, but a guide through dangerous terrain. In the background of this metaphor is the hazard of the high mountain, the danger of the dark forest, the confusion of the trackless desert, the clamor of the distant city where one does not know the language. To be there without a guide is folly. These are the situations to which the soul's journey is analogous.

We wander in thick darkness; we need an unerring guide in life who will keep us from stumbling. The best guide is not that blind one who, in the words of Scripture, "leads the blind into a ditch," (Matt. 15:14), but the Word, keen of sight, penetrating into the secret places of the heart. Just as there cannot be a light that does not give light, nor a cause unless it produces some effect, nor a lover unless he loves, just so He cannot be good unless He rendered us service and led us to salvation. (Clement of Alexandria, *Christ the Educator*, Bk. I, Ch. 3, FC 23, p. 11)

Available guides may be better or worse, more or less competent. Some may lead others into ditches or cause them to stumble. The incomparably good guide is none other than God the Son—Word become flesh—who knows our hearts, having bodily shared our human condition. It is not accidental that God is willing to guide us and offers to do so. For as light cannot be light without bouncing off of things and making them brighter, so God's goodness could not be good if it did not make everything around it better. Our lives are illumined by God's own Life, as beheld in Christ. Persuasion, admonition and consolation all interweave in the guidance of habits, actions, and passions:

For, be it noted, there are these three things in man: habits, deeds, and passions. Of these, habits come under the influence of the word of persuasion, the guide to godliness. This is the word that underlies and supports, like the keel of a ship, the whole structure of the faith. Under its spell, we surrender, even cheerfully, our old ideas, become young again to gain salvation, and sing in the inspired words of the Psalm: "How good is God to Israel, to those who are upright of heart." [Ps. 72:1]. As for deeds, they are affected by the word of counsel, and passions are healed by that of consolation. These three words, however, are but one: the self-same Word who forcibly draws men from their natural, worldly way of life and educates them to the only true salvation: faith in God. That is to say, the heavenly Guide, the Word, once He begins to call men to salvation, takes to Himself the name of persuasion (this sort of appeal, although only one type, is properly given the name of the whole, that is, word, since the whole service of God has a persuasive appeal, instilling in a receptive mind the desire for life now and for the life to come); but the Word also heals and counsels, all at the same time. In fact, He follows up His own activity by encouraging the one He has already persuaded, and particularly by offering a cure for his passions. (Clement of Alexandria, *Christ the Educator*, Bk. I, Ch. 1, FC 23, pp. 3–4)

Here a subtle triune analogy is applied to the three strata of guidance: God seeks to address us at the threefold levels of habit formation, decisive action, and nurture. The triune God guides the believer along these paths by means of persuasion, counsel and consolation, yet all three dimensions of soul care remain a single unitive process of guidance. The living Word seeks to educate and persuade the habits, to guide the sphere of activity through counsel and admonition, and to increase the moral affections by means of encouragement and consolation. Thus as early as the late second century, the pastoral tradition already had achieved an elementary level of reflection upon the need for integration of three spheres that have tended to become somewhat bifurcated in contemporary psychology. Note how different today are these three schools: behavior modification of the habitual life, responsibility counseling of the active life, and empathic caring for the emotive life. In classic Christianity they were inseparably treated.

Clement further distinguished between three stages of spiritual counsel, analogous to athletic training—the beginner who watches proficient performance of the master; the maturing one who is learning to practice as exhorted; and the proficient one who has learned spiritual discipline:

Now the modes of all help and communication from one to another are three. One is by attending to another, as the master of gymnastics, in training the boy. The second is, by assimilation, as in the case of one who exhorts another to benevolence by practicing it before. The one co-operates with the learner, and the other benefits him who receives. The third mode is that by command, when the gymnastic master, no longer training the learner, nor showing in his own person the exercise for the boy to imitate, prescribes the exercise by name to him, as already proficient in it. The spiritual guide, accordingly, having received from God the power to be of service, benefits some by disciplining them, by bestowing attention on them; others, by exhorting them, by assimilation; and others, by training and teaching them, by command. (Clement of Alexandria, *The Stromata*, Bk. VI, Ch. XVII, ANF II, p. 518)*

Here is a remarkable glimpse into a primitive theory of communication and a process of counsel that must have been familiar to the oral tradition of the Christian community of second century Alexandria. Some persons need to learn to be attentive to an improved behavior; others need exhortation to practice; while others are sufficiently advanced that they need minimal but specifically targeted directives. The novices in spiritual discipline need to attend carefully upon the embodied example of the teacher-trainer. Guided by example, those who are moderately advanced need to be encouraged to practice it repeatedly, so they are provided with a structure for practice, so they can assimilate in their behavior what they have seen modeled. Then all that remains for the most proficient, who have in fact achieved this capacity for assimilation, is to apply the proper spiritual directive to the circumstance at hand.

Only one who never starts the journey does not need a guide. The mere desire for a safe journey is hardly enough to insure a safe journey. The soul guide, as Augustine knew, must be prepared to show the individual how what one earnestly wishes or desires to do may lead one in an entirely wrong direction:

There can be no error when nothing is sought, or when that is sought which ought to be sought. In so far as all men seek the happy life they do not err. But in so far as anyone does not keep to the way that leads to the happy life, even though he professes to desire only to reach happiness, he is in error. Error arises when we follow something which does not lead to that which we wish to reach. The more a man errs in his way of life, the less is he wise, the further he is from the truth in which the chief good is beheld and possessed. (Augustine, *On Free Will*, Bk. IX, Ch. 26, LCC VI, pp. 150–151)

There is a distinction here between envisioning the good life rightly, and reaching for it practically while one envisions it. Spiritual direction seeks to correct the errors of both perception and judgment.

We do not fail in seeking happiness, but rather in following a way that only appears to lead to happiness but really does not. A soul guide who knows the precipices and desert terrain is urgently needed. The complex and hazardous journey of the soul was graphically described by Origen in this way:

Before the soul reaches maturity, it dwells in the wilderness, where, of course, it is trained in the commandments of the Lord and where its faith is tested by temptations. And when it conquers one temptation and its faith has been proved in it, it comes to another one. And it passes, as it were, from one stage to another. So, when it proceeds through the different temptations of life and faith one by one, it is said to have stages in which increases in virtues are sought one by one. . . . The stages are repeated twice in order to show two journeys for the soul. One is the means of training the soul in virtues through the Law of God when it is placed in historical existence, where by ascending through certain steps it makes progress, as we have said, from virtue to virtue, and uses these progressions as stages. And the other journey is the one by which the soul, in gradually ascending to the heavens after the resurrection, does not reach the highest point unseasonably, but is led through many stages. In them it is enlightened stage by stage. (Origen, Homily XXVII On Numbers, sec. 5, CWS, pp. 252–253)*

Origen was using the journey of Israel from Egypt to the promised land as a paradigm for the journey of the soul, in order to make clear that the process occurs by stages of development. The metaphor is that of a long and difficult journey, where the destination is promised, but each stage is new and somewhat unexpected, testing and challenging faith at each point to grow in a distinctly new way. This is not merely a journey that is taken as an end in itself, but a journey that is taken as a means of maturation, progressing from virtue to virtue, continuing not only in this life, but also after this life. This journey has many potential starting places:

"And Moses wrote down their starting places and their stages by the Word of the Lord" (Num. 33:2). He wrote them down, then, "by the Word of the Lord" so that when we read them and see how many starting places lie ahead of us on the journey that leads to the kingdom, we may prepare ourselves for this way of life and, considering the journey that lies ahead of us, may not allow the time of our life to be ruined by sloth and neglect. The danger is that while we linger in the vanities of the world and delight in each of the sensations that come to our sight or hearing or even to our touch, smell, and taste, days may slip by, time may pass on, and we shall not find any opportunity for completing the journey that lies ahead. Then we give up halfway there, and there will happen to us what is reported of those who could not complete the journey but whose limbs fell in the wilderness (cf. Heb. 3:17; I Cor. 10:5). Thus, we are on a journey; and we have come into this world that we may pass from virtue to virtue. (Origen, Homily XXVII On Numbers, sec. 7, CWS, p. 247)

The purpose of the journey is the education of the living soul toward the full range of habits of excellence. Every new situation calls for a mode of counsel that is right for that situation. When counsel is exceptionally adept, it can steer a vulnerable ship away from hazardous waters:

As a ship which has a good helmsman comes safely into harbour with God's help, so the soul which has a good shepherd, even though it has done much evil, easily ascends to Heaven. (Climacus, *The Ladder of Divine Ascent*, Step 26, sec. 52, p. 195)

As the helmsman is judged more harshly than the passenger in a storm, so the counselor is judged more rigorously than the one receiving counsel amid a period of personal turmoil. The metaphor varies, but the responsibility of the care-giver is not slackened:

Often the sin which a superior commits in his mind is judged to be greater than the sin committed in actual deed by one in obedience, if indeed it is true that a soldier's error is less grievous than a general's ill counsel. (Climacus, *To the Shepherd*, sec. 60, *The Ladder of Divine Ascent*, p. 240)

If I put myself in the hands of a mountain climbing guide, and that guide leads me into a winter storm on a precipitous cliff, who is responsible? The conceptual error or interpretive deficiency of the counselor which misleads or harms the one receiving counsel is egregious.

These excellent qualities of a spiritual guide were outlined by Basil:

With much care and forethought seek to find a person adept at guiding those who are making their way toward God, who will be an unerring director of your life. He should be blessed with virtues—

> bearing witness by his own deeds to his love for God,
> familiar with the Holy Scripture,
> recollected,
> free from avarice,
> a good, quiet man, tranquil,
> pleasing to God,
> a lover of the poor,
> mild, forgiving,
> laboring hard for the spiritual growth of disciples,
> without vainglory or arrogance,
> impervious to flattery,
> not given to vacillation,
> preferring God to every thing else. (Basil, "On
> Renunciation of the World," FC 9, p. 19; cf. WSD, p. 41)*

Trying to be one's own spiritual guide is the height of folly, for:

No one is gifted with such prudence and wisdom as to be adequate for himself in the guidance of his own spiritual life. Self-love is a blind guide and fools many. (John Cardinal Bona, *A Treatise on the Spiritual Life*, WSD, p. 5)

The maxim that "the attorney who defends himself has a fool for a client," holds also for spiritual counsel.

IV. 🐝 Instructions Upon Choosing a Soul Guide

Some guides are more competent than others. It behooves the reasonable person to choose a soul guide well. Do not place the destiny of the soul in the hands of a novice, or manipulator, or exploiter. If one already has a significant, trustful relationship with one's pastor, then no weighty choice may be required. But that cannot always be presupposed.

The pastoral writers considered carefully how one might best find or leave a soul guide. How is trustworthiness to be identified and judged. If misjudged, how are costly misjudgments corrected? Are different spiritual guides more adept at some than other spiritual disabilities?

Let us judge the nature of our passions and of our obedience, and choose our spiritual father accordingly. If you are prone to lust, then do not select as your trainer a wonderworker who is ready for everyone with a welcome and a meal, but rather an ascetic who will hear of no consolation in food. If you are haughty, then let him be stern and unyielding, and not meek and kindly. Let us not seek those who have the gift of foreknowledge and foresight, but rather those who are unquestionably humble. (Climacus, *The Ladder of Divine Ascent*, Step 4, sec. 20, p. 52)

This suggests that one owes a duty to oneself to search for a guide whose special competencies correspond with the specific problems with which one is struggling. The obverse is implied: Take care that you do not merely select a guide who will reinforce behavioral deficits or fail to challenge precisely at major points of resistance and vulnerability.

Is some implicit notion of transference (similar to psychoanalytic transference) already at work in early Christian ideas of counsel? Is spiritual parenting something like another experience of actual parenting, or reparenting? The importance of this analogy seems to have been intuited early. One's counselors may be explicitly viewed as "spiritual parents":

For if the divine oracle says, concerning our parents according to the flesh, "Honour thy father and thy mother, that it may be well with thee;" and, "He that curseth his father or his mother, let him die the death;" how much more should the word exhort you to honour your spiritual parents and to love them as your benefactors and ambassadors with God, who have regenerated you by water, and endued you with the fullness of the Holy Spirit, who have fed you with the word as with milk, who have confirmed you by their admonitions. (*Constitutions of the Holy Apostles*, Bk. II, Sec. V.33, ANF VII, p. 412)

The psychoanalytic transference relationship was thereby in an embryonic way anticipated. The soul guide may function in a way something like a surrogate parent. Counsel is reparenting, redoing what may have gone awry in one's actual parent-child relationship. This differs from psychoanalytic views of transference largely in the tendency of psychoanalysis to resist rather than honor one's actual parents. The reparenting task contains both the elements of nurture and admonition, hence both positive and negative reinforcement.

To the degree that one projects unrealistic or perfectionistic expectations upon the counselor, that itself must become a subject of self-examination. No soul guide guides perfectly, as Francis de Sales remarked:

If we wait to find a perfect Superior to set over a Community, we must ask God to send some saint or angel to fill the post, for neither men nor women will be found suitable for it. (Francis de Sales, *SC*, XVI, p. 305)

One may be prone to give up too quickly on a physician of souls if expected results are not immediately forthcoming. Of this danger John Climacus spoke, warning against "sick souls who try out a physician and receive help from him, and then abandon him out of preference for another before they are completely healed:"

Do not run from the hands of him who has brought you to the Lord, for you will never in your life esteem anyone like him. It is dangerous for an inexperienced soldier to leave his regiment and engage in single combat . . . Two are better than one, says Scripture. That is to say, "It is better for a son to be with his father, and to struggle with his proclivities with the help of the Divine power of the Holy Spirit." He who deprives a blind man of his leader, a flock of its shepherd, a lost man of his guide, a child of its father, a patient of his doctor, a ship of its pilot, imperils all. And he who attempts unaided to struggle with the spirits is slain by them. (Climacus, *The Ladder of Divine Ascent*, Step 4, sec. 72, 73, pp. 42–43)

This passage shows how seriously the bonding of the relationship of counsel was taken in early Christianity. To leave a spiritual counselor prematurely would be like a young child leaving a parent, a desperate patient leaving a good physician, a blind man dismissing his guide on a steep mountain trail. Going it alone is not advised. Bouncing from one guide to another is even more dangerous. If, however, a soul guide is causing serious harm to one's soul, one may have to take direct initiative on one's own to break the relationship:

A brother questioned Abba Poemen, saying, "I am losing my soul though living near my abba; should I go on living with him?" The old man knew that he was finding this harmful and he was surprised that he even asked if he should stay there. So he said to him, "Stay if you want to." The brother left him and stayed on there. He came back again and said, "I am losing my soul." But the old man did not tell him to leave. He came a third time and said, "I really cannot stay there any longer." Then Abba Poemen said, "Now you are saving yourself; go away and do not stay with him any longer," and he added, "when someone sees that he is in danger of losing his soul, he does not need to ask advice." (Poemen, *Sayings of the Desert Fathers*, pp. 162–163)

This penetrating exchange reveals the patience of the soul guide in honoring the self-determination of the individual. The interplay between radical self-determination and radical obedience to counsel is a striking and sometimes comic one in the early monastic tradition. The stark criterion for breaking the relation is nothing less than loss of soul.

Thomas Aquinas was intrigued by the question of whether one should obey a spiritual guide who requires that one act contrary to divine law:

A prelate is not to be obeyed contrary to a Divine precept, according to Acts 5:29: "We ought to obey God rather than men." Therefore when a prelate commands anyone to tell him anything that he knows to need correction, the command rightly understood supports the safeguarding of the order of fraternal correction, whether the command be addressed to all in general, or to some particular individual. If, on the other hand, a prelate were to issue a command in express opposition to this order instituted by Our Lord, both would sin, the one commanding, and the one obeying him, as disobeying Our Lord's command. Consequently he ought not to be obeyed, because a prelate is not the judge of secret things, but God alone is. (Thomas Aquinas, *Summa Theologica*, Part II–II, Q. 33, Art. 8, Reply Obj. 5, Vol. II, p. 1340)

Acts 5:29 is sufficient authorization for a lay person to not listen to the counsel of a minister who seeks to persuade him to flaunt God's commands. This raises the question of how one may learn to not collude with bad counsel. Ignatius of Antioch placed primary responsibility on the hearer:

I have learned to know certain people who had passed by on their way from there with bad teaching: you did not permit them to sow it among you but stopped your ears (Ignatius of Antioch, *To the Ephesians*, 9, AF, p. 80)

One need not listen to bad counsel. Discernment of bad counsel is a function of conscience. If one could select a counselor who was wise and prudent, or another who is just, which should be chosen for counsel? Ambrose answered:

We entrust our case to the most prudent man we can find, and ask advice from him more readily than we do from others. However, the faithful counsel of a just man stands first and often has more weight than the great abilities of the wisest of men: "For better are the wounds of a friend than the kisses of others" [Prov. 27:6] . . . If one connects the two, there will be great soundness in the advice given. (Ambrose, *Duties of the Clergy*, Bk. II, Ch. X, secs. 50–51, NPNF 2, X, p. 51)

Three leading qualities of the adept spiritual director were concisely stated by the seventeenth century English Benedictine, Augustine Baker:

Now to the end to enable the soul to make a good choice (I mean such a soul as hath freedom to make her own choice), I will set down the qualities necessary to be found in a good director, by which title I do not mean simply a *Confessarius*, that is only to hear faults confessed, to give absolution, and there an end; for the ordinary qualities of learning and prudence are sufficient thereto. But by a spiritual director I intend one that, besides this, is to instruct the disciple in all the peculiar duties of an internal life . . . but especially that can teach her how to dispose herself to hearken to and follow God's internal teaching, and to stand in no more need of consulting her external director, etc. Such are the proper offices of a guide, to enable him whereto there are generally by spiritual writers required three principal guides: 1. a good natural judgment; 2. learning; 3. experience. (Dom Augustine Baker, *Holy Wisdom*, pp. 74, 75)

An attitude of receptivity to guidance is premised, and virtually necessary if the counsel is to have effect:

Do not begin calculating how you shall live by your own judgment or desire to have your behavior appear to be good to yourself alone. Rather, submit your mind and personal counsel to those who, in life, and time, and labor, have already cultivated and dug in the divine vineyard before; from them you will easily learn this duty thoroughly. It is clearly ridiculous, that we obtain teachers of the mechanical and menial arts, and we still blunder here and there, while we commit the divine science to ourselves as though it were something base and worthless. (Isidore of Pelusium, *Letters*, 260, MPL 78, WSD, p. 52)

One may shift to a different spiritual director for due cause:

Brother, invoke God with persistence, in order that He might show you a person capable of guiding you well, one whom you must listen to as God Himself... But if the Holy Spirit sends you to another person, do not hesitate in the least. We hear that it is Paul who plants, Apollos who waters, and Christ who gives the growth (1 Cor. 3:6). (Symeon the New Theologian, *The Discourses*, XX.2, CWS, p. 232; WSD, p. 36)*

At times the director does well to advise another counselor for the soul dissatisfied with a proposed way.

Spiritual directors should give freedom to people and support them in their desire to seek growth. The director does not know the means by which God may wish to honor a soul, especially if that soul is no longer satisfied with the director's counsel. This dissatisfaction is indeed a clear sign that the director is not helping the soul, either because God is making it advance by a road different from the one along which the director is guiding it, or because the director himself has changed his method. These directors should themselves advise people to change. (John of the Cross, *Living Flame of Love*, WSD, pp. 56–57)

William of St. Thierry offered specific counsel on how an ascetic might seek out a spiritual counselor, and how a significant relationship might be formed:

In order that your solitude may not appall you and that you may dwell the more safely in your cell three guardians have been assigned to you: God, your conscience, and your spiritual father. To God you owe devotion and the entire gift of self; to your conscience the respect which will make you ashamed to sin in its presence; to your spiritual father the obedience of charity and recourse in everything... If you will take my advice, you will choose for yourself a man whose life is such that it will serve as a model to impress upon your heart, one whom you will so revere that whenever you think of him you will rise up because of the respect you feel for him and put yourself in order. Think of him as if he were present and let the charity you feel for one another act in you to correct all that needs to be corrected, while your solitude suffers no infringement of its secret. Let him be present to you whenever you wish and let him come sometimes when you would have preferred him to stay away. The thought of his holy severity will make it seem as if he were rebuking you; the thought of his kindness and goodness will bring you consolation; the purity and sanctity of his life will set you a good example. For you will be driven to correct even all your thoughts, as if they were open to his gaze and visited by his rebuke, when you consider that he is watching. (William of St. Thierry, *The Golden Epistle* sec. 101, 103, pp. 45–46)

The advice of the spiritual father could not proceed without being confirmed by conscience, duly held up before God. Yet, assuming a harmony between these three voices—God, conscience, and spiritual counselor—the result is a powerful impression leading to behavioral transformation and constancy of recollected purpose.

V. 🦋 FREEING THE SOUL FROM BONDAGE

Among the more dramatic images of the soul guide is that of liberator, a powerful metaphor that assumes a prevailing condition of bondage to the powers of sin and death, to guilt, anxiety and boredom. These prison doors, having become tightly locked, must be unlocked to enable a new life of freedom. The soul guide shows the way out of self-made prisons.

The theme of freeing is intrinsically related to the previous metaphors of guiding and healing. Luther sharply contrasted these two words—"must" and "free." He sought to show that Christian counsel aims at a new freedom. Do not reduce Christian liberty to a "must," he argued:

Take note of these two things, "must" and "free." The "must" is that which necessity requires, and which must ever be unyielding; as, for instance, the faith, which I shall never permit any one to take away from me, but which I must always keep in my heart and freely confess before every one. But "free" is that in which I have choice, and may use or not, yet in such wise that it profit my brother and not me. Now do not make a "must" out of what is "free," as you have done, so that you may not be called to account for those who were led astray by your exercise of liberty without love. (Luther, "Eight Wittenberg Sermons," First Sermon, WML II, p. 395)

The gospel calls the faithful to freedom, not to another round of bondage of law.

The premise of counsel is accountable freedom. Without freedom there can be no counsel. Coercive actions are sharply distinguished from good counsel. If one has power to force another to an action, that power must be disavowed in good counsel:

> This expression of our Lord, "How often would I have gathered thy children together, and thou wouldest not" [Matt. 23:37], set forth the ancient law of human liberty, because God made human persons as free agents from the beginning, possessing their own power, even as they do their own souls, to obey the behests of God voluntarily, and not by compulsion. For there is no coercion with God, but a good will towards us is present with Him continually. And therefore does He give good counsel to all. And in humanity, as well as in angels, He has placed the power of choice (for angels are rational beings), so that those who had yielded obedience might justly possess what is good, given indeed by God, but preserved by themselves. (Irenaeus, *Against Heresies*, Bk. IV, Ch. XXXVII, sec. 1, ANF I, p. 518)*

Only free intelligent beings require counsel, and only to them is counsel possible or pertinent. Coercion is entirely ruled out of good counsel. God calls persons to responsible freedom, but permits freedom to fall. The prophets gave good counsel on the assumption that their hearers had the freedom to follow it. Were it wholly out of one's power to do good, one would not need counsel:

> If some had been made by nature bad, and others good, these latter would not be deserving of praise for being good, for such were they created; nor would the former be reprehensible, for thus they were made originally. . . . And therefore the prophets used to exhort men to what was good, to act justly and to work righteousness, as I have so largely demonstrated, because it is in our power so to do, and because by excessive negligence we might become forgetful, and thus stand in need of that good counsel which the good God has given us to know by means of the prophets. For this reason the Lord also said, "Let our light so shine before men, that they may see your good deeds, and glorify your Father who is in heaven" [Matt. 5:16]. . . . All such passages demonstrate the independent will of man, and at the same time the counsel which God conveys to him, by which He exhorts us to submit ourselves to Him, and seeks to turn us away from the sin of unbelief against Him, without, however, in any way coercing us. . . . If then it were not in our power to do or not to do these

things, what reason had the apostle, and much more the Lord Himself, to give us counsel to do some things, and to abstain from others? But because man is possessed of free will from the beginning, and God is possessed of free will, in whose likeness man was created, advice is always given to him to keep fast the good. (Irenaeus, *Against Heresies*, Bk. IV, Ch. XXXVII, secs. 2–4, ANF I, p. 519)

On what basis could one be exhorted to do good if it were intrinsically beyond one's power? Kant later concluded that the very sense of obligation is an *a priori* argument for freedom of the will. All counsel, advice, and exhortation silently assume responsible freedom and personal accountability. This is why it would be amusing to attempt to counsel a statue or a tree, which has no capacity for responsiveness. Only freedom can be meaningfully counseled.

Origen viewed the counselor as guest of the soul, invited by the individual into these special inner precincts where freedom takes counsel:

Apostle Peter says, "that our adversary the devil goes about like a roaring lion, seeking whom he may devour" [1 Pet. 5:8]. On which account our heart must be kept with all carefulness both by day and night, and no place be given to the devil; but every effort must be employed in order that the ministers of God—those who were sent to minister to them who are called to be heirs of salvation—may find place within us, and be delighted to enter into the guest-chamber of our soul, and dwelling within us may guide us by their counsels. (Origen, *De Principiis*, Bk. III, Ch. iii, sec. 5, ANF IV, p. 337)*

Good counsel constantly seeks to guard against threats to the soul's well-being. For this reason ministers are needed, called, and sent by God, and are to be welcomed as valued guests into the hidden chambers of the soul. Only there can they work effectively.

VI. 🐾 EDUCATOR OF THE SOUL

The last of our series of key metaphors of counsel is that of mentor or teacher or educator. That is eductive or educative which leads the way (from *ducere*, to lead, draw, bring out). The way in this case is from reliable premises to right conclusions.

One of the earliest Christian treatises on pastoral care used the metaphor of pedagogy as the central image of Christ's activity in the soul— Clement of Alexandria on *Christ the Educator* of the soul. The pastoral counselor teaches the soul the truth about herself by providing a fit context in which the soul can discover herself and learn the truth that is embedded in herself:

> Let us call [Christ], then, by the one title: Educator of little ones, an Educator who does not simply follow behind, but who leads the way, for His aim is to improve the soul, not just to instruct it; to guide to a life of virtue, not merely to one of knowledge. Yet, that same Word does teach. It is simply that in this work we are not considering Him in that light. As Teacher, He explains and reveals through instruction, but as Educator He is practical. First He persuades men to form habits of life, then He encourages them to fulfill their duties by laying down clear-cut counsels and by holding up, for us who follow, examples of those who have erred in the past. Both are most useful: the advice, that it may be obeyed; the other, given in the form of example, has a twofold object—either that we may choose the good and imitate it or condemn and avoid the bad. Healing of the passions follows as a consequence. The Educator strengthens souls with the persuasion implied in these examples, and then He gives the nourishing, mild medicine, so to speak, of His loving counsels to the sick man that he may come to a full knowledge of the truth. (Clement of Alexandria, *Christ the Educator*, Bk. I, Ch. 1, FC 23, p. 4)

Christ himself is the soul's Educator. The care-giver's language and actions seek to cooperate with Christ's educative intent. To educate the soul is not merely to teach conceptually or abstractly, but rather practically to lead the soul on the narrow path toward wiser behavioral patterns and a truer grasp of one's calling. The leading or educing of which Clement spoke was less concerned with objective description and empirical investigation than with mending the moral habits under which life is lived poorly or well. This educative counsel works constantly at two levels: by advice and by example, by talk and by deed. The talk may be persuasive, upbuilding, or advisory. The life of the counselor shows whether he is serious about his own teaching. Only in this way may the passions be healed, and the soul nourished and strengthened.

One who is prepared to give counsel must be prepared to receive his own counsel:

> For counsel is not the worse, but the better, if it be profitable both to him that gives, and to him that takes it. Only do it in simplicity, and principally intend the good of their souls. (Jeremy Taylor, *RAC*, II, sec. 21, *CS*, p. 9f.)

There are repeated injunctions in modern pastoral care against advice giving and preemptive diagnosis. Diagnosis is sometimes viewed as an introjection imposed by another upon the unique experience of the individual, and some think it better to allow the individual to make his or her own diagnosis (cf. C. Rogers, *Client Centered Therapy*, pp. 219–225). Advice is often viewed in even worse light. It is said that advice-giving tends to insert a needless dimension of moral requirement into the interaction, which is thought by some to be preferably value-free, or at least obligation-free. Recognizing these dangers, the classical pastoral writers nonetheless thought that accurate diagnosis and reliable advice were major duties of an effective counselor:

Awaiting the favorable opportunity, he corrects evil, diagnoses the causes of inordinate passion, extracts the roots of unreasonable lusts, advises what we should avoid, and applies all the remedies of salvation to those who are sick. (Clement of Alexandria, *Christ the Educator*, Bk. I, Ch. 12, FC 23, p. 99)*

The education of our souls requires diagnosis to grasp the reasons why the passions are trapped, and reliable advice concerning both extrication and avoidance. Without diagnosis and advice, counsel lacks effective remedies.

Our divine Educator is trustworthy, for He is endowed with three excellent qualities: intelligence, good will and authority to speak. With intelligence, because He is the Wisdom of the Father: "All wisdom is from the Lord and hath been always with Him." [Ecclus. 1:1]. With authority to speak, because He is God and Creator: "All things were made through Him, and without Him was made nothing" [John 1:3]. With good will, because He is the only one who has given Himself as a sacrifice for us: "The Good Shepherd lays down His life for His sheep" [John 10:11], and in fact He did lay it down. Surely, good will is nothing else than willing what is good for the neighbor for his own sake. (Clement of Alexandria, *Christ the Educator*, Bk. I, Ch. 11.97, FC 23, p. 86)

According to Clement, Christ the educator of the soul is the pattern of good counsel. Counsel does not take proper shape without astute intelligence that seeks to grasp the reasons why things have come to be as they are. It also requires personal congruence that engenders trust, and good will through which the individual comes to feel that another cares for him, even so far as being willing to act sacrificially on his behalf. Without experiencing the counselor in this threefold way as wise, congruent, and caring, the individual who seeks and needs counsel is hardly ready to receive it. All three were embodied by the prototype Educator whose counsel the pastor seeks proportionally to refract. The intelligence, authenticity, and self-sacrificing good will of the counselor must all work together for constructive behavioral change.

Accordingly, it is Jesus' own guidance that provides the most balanced model for Christian counsel:

His character is not excessively fear-inspiring, yet neither is it overindulgent in its kindness. He imposes commands, but at the same time expresses them in such a way that we can fulfill them. . . . He seeks to train us to the condition of a wayfarer, that is, to make us well girded and unimpeded by provisions, that we might be self-sufficient of life and practice a moderate frugality in our journey toward the good life of eternity, telling us that each one of us is to be his own storehouse: "Do not be anxious about tomorrow" [Matt 6:34]. He means to say that he who has dedicated himself to Christ ought to be self-sufficient and his own servant and, besides, live his life from day to day. (Clement of Alexandria, *Christ the Educator*, Bk. I, Ch. 12.98, FC 23, p. 87)

The Educator seeks a balance of moral clarity and kindness, combining strength and encouragement. The aim of good counsel is ego-strength—being one's own storehouse, taking one day at a time without inordinate anxiety. This intent to engender self-responsibility is quite different from the heteronomy of judgmental legalism. Good counsel is not legalistic brow-beating:

In counsel there is advantage; in precept, fetters. Counsel attracts the willing; precept binds the unwilling. If anyone has followed counsel, and has not regretted it, she has reached an advantage. But if one has regretted it, she has no reason to blame the Apostle. She herself should have decided her own weakness, and she is responsible for her own will. (Ambrose, *Letters*, 59, To the Church of Vercelli, FC 26, p. 334)

Ambrose was speaking here of Paul's commendation of "the unmarried woman" (1 Cor. 7:32–34). An act of counsel assumes responsible freedom. That is different from a hardened, inflexible, legalistic approach that leaves no room for freedom (in this case the freedom to decide about how one is to live out one's covenant sexuality).

Ambrose set forth a list of prototypes of the pastor as counselor, using biblical models. In Solomon we see the readiness of wisdom to be responsive to any question. In Joseph and Daniel we see foresight, planning, and courage. In Moses we behold prudence and trustability.

Even the queen of Sheba came to him and tried him with questions. She came and spoke of all the things that were in her heart and heard all the wisdom of Solomon, nor did any word escape her. . . . There was nothing which the truth loving Solomon did not tell her. . . . Joseph also when in prison was not free from being consulted about matters of uncertainty. His counsel was of advantage to the whole of Egypt, so that it felt not the seven years' famine, and he was able even to relieve other peoples from their dreadful hunger. Daniel, though one of the captives, was made the head of the royal counsellors. By his counsels he improved the present and foretold the future. . . . What shall I say of Moses whose advice all Israel always waited for, whose life caused them to trust in his prudence and increased their esteem for him? Who would not trust to the counsel of Moses, to whom the elders reserved for decision whatever they thought beyond their understanding and powers? (Ambrose, *Duties of the Clergy*, Bk. II, Ch. X–XI, secs. 51–56, NPNF 2, X, pp. 51, 52)

VII. ❦ THE PASTOR'S SERVICE

Parishioners may need to be specifically encouraged to seek out the pastor's service as counselor:

The people have become unacquainted with this office of the ministry, and with their own duty and necessity in this respect. It belongs to us to acquaint them with it, and publicly to press them to come to us for advice about the great concerns of their souls. We must not only be willing to take the trouble, but should draw it upon ourselves, by inviting them to come. What abundance of good might we do, could we but bring them to this! And, doubtless much might be done in it, if we did our duty. How few have I ever heard of, who have heartily pressed their people to their duty in this way! Oh! It is a sad case that men's souls should be so injured and hazarded by the total neglect of so great a duty, and that ministers should scarcely ever tell them of it, and awaken them to it. Were your hearers but duly sensible of the need and importance of this, you would have them more frequently knocking at your doors, and making known to you their sad complaints, and begging your advice . . . One word of seasonable, prudent advice, given by a minister to persons in necessity, may be of more use than many sermons. (Richard Baxter, *RP*, pp. 96–97)*

Pastors have a distinct duty to press parishioners to utilize their services, not simply to lay back and wait for people to come to them. The essential work of the pastoral counselor consists in searching hearts for the truth buried in them. Few ministers are adequately prepared for the subtleties of this task:

In searching men's hearts, and setting home the truth to their consciences —the ablest minister is weak enough for this, and few of inferior parts would be found competent to it. For I fear noth-

ing more than that many ministers who preach well will be found
but imperfectly qualified for this work, especially to manage it
with old, ignorant, dead-hearted sinners. (Richard Baxter, *RP*,
p. 46)*

No effective pastor sits around waiting for troubled people to come to
him. The word of consolation and divine providence must be taken to
people where they are:

The Country Parson when any of his cure is sick or afflicted
with loss of friend or estate, or any ways distressed, fails not to
afford his best comforts; and rather goes to them than send for
the afflicted, though they can, and otherwise ought to come to
him. To this end he hath thoroughly digested all points of consolation, as having continual use of them; such as are from God's
general providence, extended even to lilies; from his particular, to
his church; from his promises; from the examples of all saints
that ever were; from Christ himself, perfecting our Redemption
no other way than by sorrow; from the Benefit of affliction, which
softens and works the stubborn heart of man. (Geo. Herbert, *CP*,
Ch. XV, CWS, p. 77)

In the interest of more thorough and intensive pastoral care, Baxter
urged pastors to limit their responsibilities primarily to their own
parish:

Every flock should have its own pastor, and every pastor his
own flock. . . . Though a minister is an officer in the Church universal, yet is he in a special manner the overseer of that particular church which is committed to his charge. . . . when we have
undertaken a particular charge, we have restrained the exercise
of our gifts so specially to that congregation, that we must allow
others no more than it can spare of our time and help except
where the public good requireth it. (Richard Baxter, *RP*, p. 88)

Baxter pointed to the scriptural grounding of the assumption that
every pastor should know each member personally, in Paul's speech to
the elders of Ephesus:

"Take heed to all the flock" (Acts 20:28). It is, you see, *all* the
flock, or every individual member of our charge. To this end it is
necessary that we should know every person that belongs to our
charge. For how can we take heed to them, if we do not know
them? We must labour to be acquainted, not only with the persons, but with the state of all our people, with their inclinations
and conversations; what are the sins of which they are most in

danger, and what duties they are most apt to neglect, and what temptations they are most liable to. For if we know not their temperament or disease, we are not likely to prove successful physicians. . . . Does not a careful shepherd look after every individual sheep? and a good schoolmaster after every individual scholar? and a good physician after every particular patient? . . . But I shall quote only from Ignatius: "Let assemblies," says he, "be often gathered; inquire after all by name: despise not servant-men or maids." . . . But, some one may object, "The congregation that I am set over is so great that it is impossible for me to know them all, much more to take heed to all individually." To this I answer: Is it necessity or is it not that has cast you upon such a charge? If it be not, you excuse one sin by another. How dare you undertake that which you knew yourself unable to perform, when you were not forced to it? (Richard Baxter, *RP*, pp. 90–91)*

The pastor should be sufficiently close to each parishioner that he knows that individual's probable temptations. Each one deserves to be called and known by name. If the pastoral charge is too large to do this, Baxter thought, it should be reduced in size.

When the human condition is ablaze with destructive passions, it is better to take some action than watch it burn:

We must first imagine that we are in a shipwreck or in a fire, where one must labor to snatch at least one brand from the burning if it is impossible to control or to extinguish the whole blaze. . . . If you are a preacher of the Gospel, then do not preach as if you could win all for Christ; for not all obey the Gospel (Rom. 10:16); but give thanks if you can lead to Christ and convert three or four souls as the ends of smoking brands. (Luther, WA 20, p. 144; in WLS 3, pp. 1120f.)

VIII. ❦ THE NURTURING RELATIONSHIP

Care of souls cannot occur without a relationship of trust. It is remarkable that as early as the writings of Ignatius of Antioch (ca. 35–115), the Christian pastoral tradition had firmly grasped this principle: The witness to God's love must come to persons in a way consonant with God's own personal caring and sacrificial self-presentation.

Address yourself to people personally, as is the way of God Himself, and carry the infirmities of them all on your own shoulders (Ignatius of Antioch, *Letter to Polycarp*, 1, ECW, p. 127)

Luther compared the shepherding relationship to the radical caring of a loving mother for her child, a care that is willing to take risks:

Unless your heart toward the sheep is like that of a mother toward her children—a mother, who walks through fire to save her children—you will not be fit to be a preacher. (Luther, WA 52, p. 810; in WLS 2, p. 932, #2925)

Relational trust grows slowly through manifold seasons of caring, not immediately or absolutely. Once again, Luther turned to a feminine metaphor of care-giving:

How does a mother nourish her child? First, she feeds it with milk, then gruel, then eggs and soft food. If she weaned it and at once gave it the ordinary, coarse food, the child would never thrive. So we should also deal with our brother, have patience with him for a time, suffer his weakness and help him bear it; we should give him milk-food, too, as was done with us, until he likewise grows strong. (Luther, "Eight Wittenberg Sermons," First Sermon, WML II, p. 393)

Ambrose employed a military metaphor for intensive soul care: fighting a furious battle against the demonic Enemy for human souls. However powerful, these powers may be gradually overcome by the "gentle warrior":

Put on the armor of God in your fight against spiritual diseases and the cunning of the Devil who tempts our senses with cunning and fraud. Yet, he is easily crushed by the gentle warrior who does not sow discord, but, as befits the servant of God, teaches faith with moderation and refutes those who are his adversaries. Of this man Scripture says: "Let the warrior who is gentle arise" [Joel 3:9], and the weak man says: "I can do all things in him who strengthens me" [Phil. 4:13]. (Ambrose, *Letters*, 79, To Irenaeus, FC 26, p. 447)

The "gentle warrior" metaphor suggests both well-defended strength and tender kindness, both ready power and willing servitude. Without this combined consciousness, the pastoral counselor cannot enable strength to emerge through weakness. If these are qualities of good counsel, what deficient personal qualities are to be pruned away?

The pastor must be without guile, without falsehood; not rigid, not insolent, not severe, not arrogant, not unmerciful, not puffed up, not inordinately willing to please, not timorous, not double-minded, not one who insults people in one's charge, not one that conceals the divine laws or hides the promises to repentance, not hasty in thrusting out and expelling, but steady, not one that delights in severity, not heady. (*Constitutions of the Holy Apostles*, Bk. II, sec. iii.21, ANF VII, p. 405)*

This catalogue of undesirable pastoral behaviors hinges mainly on the pride of office that tempts those to whom others turn for spiritual counsel. The pastoral office is easily abusable. If so, then one might think it fitting that the counselor should be constantly aware of wrenching ambivalences within oneself as one seeks to counsel and comfort. Not so, according to the Didache:

You shall not be forever indecisive as to whether something shall be or not be. Do not be an extender of hands to receive, only to draw them back and not give. If you have anything at all, it is through your hands that the ransom for sins must flow. Do not hesitate to give, and do not murmur while you are giving. ("The Teaching of the Twelve Apostles," Ch. IV, ANF VII, p. 378)*

Excessive softness or harshness are opposite extremes to be avoided by the counselor:

A faithful servant of God, however, is in duty bound not to exceed the authority of his office and not to abuse it for the sake of his own pride but to administer it only for the benefit of those who are entrusted to him. . . . Thus in those people who in foolish humility try to get along with everybody everywhere and to be popular with their charges, the influence of authority is necessarily lost, and familiarity breeds contempt. How gravely do they sin! They allow the things that belong to God and that have been entrusted to them to be trampled underfoot. They should have seen to it that these things were honored. On the other hand, if he does not pay attention to the latter qualification (faithfulness), he will become a tyrant who always frightens people with his power. He wants to be considered grim. Instead of striving to make their authority as fruitful as possible for others, such people try to make it as frightful as possible, even though according to the apostle that power was given not to destroy but to edify. But let us call these two faults by name: softness and harshness. (Luther, "Lectures on Romans, 1515," LW 25, pp. 138–139; WA 56, p. 160)

Approachability is a crucial character trait of pastoral temperament. Lacking approachability, other pastoral virtues will be quickly spent:

Who will come to a man however well fitted to give the best of advice, who is nevertheless hard to approach? It goes with him as

with a fountain whose waters are shut off. What is the advantage
of having wisdom, if one refuses to give advice? If one cuts off
the opportunities of giving advice, the source is closed. (Ambrose,
Duties of the Clergy, Bk. II, Ch. VII, sec. 61, NPNF 2, X, p. 53)

Ambrose understood how to gain the confidence of one who is braced
for self-defense:

Fear does not force confidence, but affection calls it forth. . . .
Then arises confidence, so that even strangers are not afraid to
trust themselves to another's kindness. . . . Two things, therefore,
love and confidence, are the most efficacious in commending us
to others. There is also a third quality, giving good advice. . . .
Who will put himself into the hands of another whom he does
not think to be more wise than himself. . . . For why should we
consult another when we do not think that he can make anything
more plain than we ourselves see it? . . . Seek out the one who is
better fitted by example and experience than others; who can put
an end to immediate dangers, foresee future ones, point out
those close at hand, explain a subject, bring relief in time, be
ready not only to give advice but also to give help,—in such a
man confidence is placed, so that he who seeks advice can say:
"Though evil should happen to me through him, I will bear it"
[Ecclus. 22:31]. To a person of this sort then we entrust our
safety and our reputation, for he is, as we said before, just and
prudent. Justice causes us to have no fear of deceit, and prudence frees us from having any suspicions of error. (Ambrose,
Duties of the Clergy, Bk. II, Ch. VII–VIII, sec. 38–43, NPNF 2, X,
p. 50)*

One who unites ability, sincerity, and love, will develop significant pastoral relationships:

The chief means of all is this—for a minister so to conduct
himself in the general course of his life and ministry as to con-
vince his people of his ability, sincerity, and unfeigned love to
them. For if they take him to be ignorant, they will despise his
teaching, and think themselves as wise as he. If they think him
self-seeking, or hypocritical, and one that does not mean as he
says, they will suspect all he says and does for them, and will pay
no attention to him. Whereas, if they are convinced that he understands what he does, and have high thoughts of his abilities,
they will reverence him, and the more easily yield to his advice;
and when they are persuaded of his uprightness, they will the
less suspect his movements; and when they perceive that he in-

tends no private ends of his own, but merely their good, they will the more readily be persuaded by him. (Richard Baxter, *RP*, p. 232)*

IX. 🐚 Prudent Counsel

Prudence is the habit of acting with deliberation and discretion. It is the ability to regulate and discipline oneself according to right reason, so as to direct the will practically toward the good by selecting good means to good ends. Prudence is a quality of good counsel. The prudent act circumspectly, discreetly, not rashly or insensibly.

Good counsel manifests an orderly sequence of prudent behavioral patterns. Thomas Aquinas organized this sequence under the heading of the eight aspects of prudence, wisely synthesized and condensed out of a long-standing classical debate concerning the nature of prudence. That prudence which is necessary for good counsel is sorted out into five crucial intellectual excellences, and three excellent behaviors of practical action. Put simply, the counselor must remember well, reason consistently, understand empathically, be willing to listen tirelessly and acceptingly (docility), and not be conned (shrewdness); and in addition to these habits of mind and heart, the counselor must think ahead about future contingencies and consequences (foresight), be keenly attentive to the specifics of what is happening now in the life situation with which one is dealing (circumspection), and not act precipitously but cautiously to prevent misjudgments:

Tully (*De Invent. Rhet.* ii.53) assigns three parts of prudence, namely, memory, understanding and foresight. Macrobius (*In Somn. Scip.* i) following the opinion of Plotinus ascribes to prudence six parts, namely, reasoning, understanding, circumspection, foresight, docility and caution. Aristotle says (*Ethics*, vi. 9, 10, 11) that good counsel, *sunesis* [judgment] and *gnome* [advice] belong to prudence. Again under the head of prudence he mentions conjecture, shrewdness, sense and understanding. And another Greek philosopher [Andronicus] says that ten things are connected with prudence, namely, good counsel, shrewdness, foresight, regnative [authority], military, political and domestic prudence, dialectics, rhetoric and physics. . . . Out of all the things mentioned above, eight may be taken as parts of prudence, namely, the six assigned by Macrobius; with the addition of a seventh, viz., memory mentioned by Tully; and *eustochia* or shrewdness mentioned by Aristotle. . . . Of these eight, five belong to prudence as a cognitive virtue, namely, memory, reasoning, understanding, docility and shrewdness; while the three others belong thereto, as commanding and applying knowledge to action, namely, foresight, circumspection and caution. (Thomas Aquinas, *Summa Theologica*, Part II–II, Q. 48, Art. 1, Vol. II, p. 1400)

Is such prudential counsel to be considered a special gift of grace?

That a man be of such good counsel as to counsel others, may be due to a gratuitous grace; but that a man be counselled by God as to what he ought to do in matters necessary for salvation is common to all holy persons. (Thomas Aquinas, *Summa Theologica*, Part II–II, Q. 52, Art. 1, Vol. II, p. 1412)

Every believer is guided and helped by God in prayer. This is not to be considered a gift found only in a few. But the ability to give good counsel to others indeed is a remarkable gift. This counsel proceeds in an orderly sequence which Thomas described as follows:

The steps that intervene by which one ought to descend in orderly fashion are memory of the past, intelligence of the present, shrewdness in considering the future outcome, reasoning which compares one thing with another, docility in accepting the opinions of others. He that takes counsel descends by these steps in due order, whereas if a man has rushed into action by the impulse of his will out of a passion, without taking these steps, it will be a case of precipitation. (Thomas Aquinas, *Summa Theologica*, Part II–II, Q. 53, Art. 3, Vol. II, p. 1417)

Precipitate acts are contrasted with prudential acts, which have taken these steps in due order.

All believers are called to give prudent, practical help to those in need. These mercies were called corporal alms, that is, acts of mercy done for persons who suffer bodily. There is a profound analogy between these corporal alms, and another type of alms-giving, namely, spiritual alms, or acts of mercy done for persons suffering emotively, spiritually, and intrapersonally. This distinction, again, was classically stated by Thomas:

It would seem that corporal alms are of more account than spiritual alms. For it is more praiseworthy to give alms to one who is in greater want. . . . On the contrary, Augustine says (*De Serm. Dom. in Mont*, i. 20) on the words, Give to him that asketh of thee (Matt. 5:42): "You should give so as to injure neither yourself nor another, and when you refuse what another asks, you must not lose sight of the claims of justice, and send him away empty; at times indeed you will give what is better than what is asked for, if you reprove him that asks unjustly." Now reproof is a spiritual alms. Therefore spiritual almsdeeds are preferable to corporal almsdeeds.

I answer that, There are two ways of comparing these almsdeeds. First, simply; and in this respect, spiritual almsdeeds hold the first place, for three reasons. First, because the offering is more excellent, since it is a spiritual gift, according to Prov. 4:1; "I will give you a good gift, forsake not My law." Secondly, on account of the object succored, because the spirit is more excellent than the body, wherefore, even as a man in looking after himself, ought to look to his soul more than to his body, so ought he in looking after his neighbor, whom he ought to love as himself. Thirdly, as regards the acts themselves by which our neighbor is succored, because spiritual acts are more excellent than corporal acts, which are, in a fashion, servile.

Secondly, we may compare them with regard to some particular case, when some corporal alms excels some spiritual alms: for instance, a man in hunger is to be fed rather than instructed, and as the Philosopher observes (Top. iii.2), for a needy man "money is better than philosophy," although the latter is better simply. (Thomas Aquinas, *Summa Theologica*, Part II–II, Q. 32, Art. 3, Vol. II, p. 1326)

Even though there are exceptional cases, such as the starving person, in which caring for the body is immediately and contextually more urgent than caring for the soul through instruction, counsel, corrective love and pardon, nonetheless, in a simple and straightforward sense, spiritual almsdeeds were thought by Thomas to be more crucial to the welfare of the neighbor than bodily almsdeeds alone. For if one helps another's soul to health and mind to knowledge and emotive life to new energy, then benefits will in due time accrue to the body. Both merciful acts to the body and the soul, however, are important, and rightly are to be held in appropriate balance. Thomas then plunged into this speculative question: In what sense is it proper to say that God, the angels, and the blessed give and receive counsel?

God causes in the blessed a knowledge of what is to be done, not as though they were ignorant, but by continuing that knowledge in them. . . . Accordingly the gift of counsel is in the blessed, in so far as God preserves in them the knowledge that they have, and enlightens them in their nescience of what has to be done. . . . Counsel is in God, not as receiving, but as giving it. (Thomas Aquinas, *Summa Theologica*, Part II–II, Q. 52, Art. 4, Vol. II, p. 1414)

The nescience of the blessed is their not knowing, their blessed unawareness of that knowledge which lies beyond their competence, but which they trust that God knows fully.

The pastoral writers sought constantly to avert disastrous mistakes in counseling. They knew that the pitfalls were many and hidden. The pastoral literature abounds in advice to counselors that would circumvent bad outcomes. One cannot give bad advice with impugnity:

> *Malum consilium consultori pessimum*, Bad advice is worst for the adviser. This is a proverbial line of verse about people who give wrong advice to others, which rebounds on their own head. Indeed, as the Greeks say, counsel is a sacred thing. Just as it should be freely accepted when the situation demands it, so it should be conscientiously and honestly given if it is needed. Otherwise there will not be lacking a Power which will exact amends from anyone who treacherously isolates a sacred and divine thing. (Erasmus, "Adages," I ii 14/LB II 73E, *Collected Works*, Vol. 31, p. 155)

X. ❦ DECIDING TO ASK FOR HELP

The classic pastoral writers showed keen interest in the question of how one decides to ask for and receive help. One is not ready for help until there is some consciousness of need, and of the possibility for change. Feeling hurt is the precondition of asking for help. If one hurts and cannot recognize it, then the first task is to assist that recognition. No one seeks help who does not hurt in some way. The pastoral function which assists the individual in coming to that level of awareness in which he or she can reach out for help (called "pre-counseling" by Seward Hiltner), or "need recognition," was recognized as a pastoral function in the ancient Christian pastoral tradition.

Accurately defining how deeply one is experiencing pain is a necessary early step to healing:

> One who is not aware that he has fallen, simply has no desire to be lifted up, and one who does not feel the pain of a wound, will not seek any healing remedy. (Gregory the Great, *Pastoral Care*, Part III, Ch. 34, ACW 11, p. 219)*

The task is to turn unawareness into awareness. The ironic first task of the helper is to help sufferers feel the suffering that they experience but may not yet fully recognize.

No individual is to be coerced into counsel. Recognition of need remains a matter of personal volition. When an individual resists being helped or denies existing difficulties, then the options of the pastoral

counselor remain limited, but freedom must be honored. Using the physician's analogy, John Climacus recognized these limits in the seventh
century:

A pilot cannot save a ship by himself without help from the
sailors, nor can a physician cure a sick man unless the patient
first entreat him and urge him on by baring his wound with complete confidence. Those who are ashamed to consult a physician
cause their wounds to fester, and often many have even died. (Climacus, *To the Shepherd*, sec. 36, p. 236)

The first step toward recovery is the recognition that one is hurting,
so as to lead one to openly "bare one's wound" in the presence of a
competent care-giver. This may be perceived as an extremely difficult or
humiliating step. The mere awareness that one needs to be helped is
often viewed as a sign of disgrace. Recognizing this, John Chrysostom
countered:

To ask for aid bears the semblance of disgrace, but it ceases to
be so when the pastor boldly acts to make clear what must be
done. Only then can others recognize that from making a special
effort now they are likely to derive exceptional benefit later. So
they must be taught to look beyond appearances. Therefore Paul
writes: "Let him who is taught the word share all good things
with him who teaches. Do not be deceived; God is not mocked,
for whatever a man sows, that he will also reap" (Gal. 6:6,7) . . .
Let the disciple, says he, keep nothing to himself, but have everything in common. For what he receives is better than what he
gives. (Chrysostom, "Commentary on Galatians," Ch. VI, NPNF
1, XIII, p. 44, RSV)*

Some may think of it as a uniquely modern individualistic form of
denial that would interpret asking for help as a sign of moral weakness.
Rather this has been a perennial stumbling block for pastoral care. It
can only be overcome by a caring relationship that patiently welcomes
full disclosure, and so practices good counsel that its benefits are in due
time recognizable. Chrysostom took the description of Acts 2:44—that
the disciples held "everything in common"—as a metaphor of disclosure
in spiritual counseling. Thus it may be said of those who are personally
open with each other, that their thoughts and feelings are held fully in
common just as the earliest disciples held all material things in common.
     As it is unreasonable to hide one's illness from the physician, so it is
unreasonable to hide one's sin and despair from one's spiritual mentor:

But he who seeks medicine for a wound, however foul it is,
however smelly, must show it to a doctor so that an effective cure
may be applied. The priest in fact occupies the place of a doctor

and he, as we have said, must establish the satisfaction. (Peter Abelard, *Ethics*, p. 101)

It may happen, however, that one desires help, looks earnestly for help and still does not find it. This may go on for a very long time. The recognition of the depths of one's pain is what Teresa of Avila called "the gift of tears." Despite looking for twenty years for a soul guide, Teresa could not find any one who adequately understood her. Keenly aware of how much she needed guidance, she found that books alone could not substitute for a listening care-giver:

[My uncle] gave me a book called *Third Alphabet*, which treats of the Prayer of Recollection. During this first year I had been reading good books (I no longer wanted to read any others, for I now realized what harm they had done me) but I did not know how to practice prayer, or how to recollect myself, and so I was delighted with the book and determined to follow that way of prayer with all my might. As by now the Lord had granted me the gift of tears, and I liked reading, I began to spend periods in solitude, to go frequently to confession and to start upon the way of prayer with this book for my guide. For I found no other guide (no confessor, I mean) who understood me, though I sought one for fully twenty years subsequently to the time I am speaking of. This did me great harm, as I had frequent relapses, and might have been completely lost; a guide would at least have helped me to escape when I found myself running the risk of offending God. (Teresa of Avila, *Life*, Ch. IV, p. 80)

When people lack clear understanding about what pastoral counseling is, the pastor has a duty to teach the people about the possibilities and limits of the pastoral office. Richard Baxter urged pastors to communicate more clearly to parishioners that real human needs may be met by available pastoral services:

If our people grasped their responsibilities, they would readily come to us at the points at which they wish to be instructed, and to give an account of their knowledge, faith, and life. They would come of their own accord without being sent for, knock more often at our doors, and call for advice and help for their souls, asking "What must I do to be saved?" (Acts 16:30). But now the matter has come to a sad pass. They think a minister has nothing to do with them. If he admonishes them or if he calls them to be catechized and instructed, or if he would take an account of their faith and profiting, they would ask him by what authority he does these things? They might be prone to think that he is a busy, pragmatical fellow who loves to be meddling where he has nothing to do; or a proud fellow who only likes to tyrannize their consciences. (Baxter, *RP*, p. 181, NIV)*

Some parishioners remain wholly uninformed about the nature of ministry and the basis of pastoral service. When some feel that their minister is too busy to talk with them, or when others fear that the pastor will be overbearing or try inordinately to control their behavior, a preliminary conversation is needed to clarify the nature of pastoral care. Add to this the inveterate tendency of people to rationalize—it all adds up to tremendous resistance to counsel which the counselor has to recognize and do what can be done to overcome.

Significant spiritual progress is seldom made alone. Determination to go it alone may indicate a lack of valuing oneself and one's possibilities, as John of the Cross observed:

The person that falls down by himself remains on the ground alone and does not value his soul, since he entrusts it only to himself. If you are not fearful of falling alone, how do you dare to try to rise alone? Notice how much more can be done by two together than by one alone. (John of the Cross, *Spiritual Maxims and Sentences*, WSD, p. 5.)

The main reasons why we so fiercely resist asking for help are pride, individualism, and the illusion of self-sufficiency:

There is scarcely any truth of which we have naturally more difficulty in allowing ourselves to be convinced than the necessity of a director. . . . The good opinion that we have of our own talents persuades us that we have no need of outside help. There is almost nobody who doesn't experience deeply within himself a great repugnance toward allowing himself to be led. Whenever a person has the spirit of enlightenment, he claims the right to make for himself some rules of conduct. He believes it would be a weakness to do otherwise. He cannot persuade himself that he has any needs great enough that they can't be remedied in other ways than by a director. Yet the saints have always been very far from these thoughts; for they have thought that there couldn't be in this world any greater wisdom than to allow oneself to be directed in all things. (Louis Tronson, "Obedience to One's Director," WSD, pp. 5–6)

The saints recognized the need for direction. The seeker of spiritual health was urged first to pray to be given a good spiritual guide, then having found one, confide completely and listen well. Such an individual will not be disappointed.

Since you are going in search of a good guide, you ought with great insistence ask the Lord that He guide you with His hand to

such a person. Thus shown the way, confide your heart to him
with every confidence, and do not hide anything from him, good
nor evil, the good so that he may direct you and advise you, the
evil so that he may correct it in you. Do not do anything of importance without his counsel, putting your confidence in God,
who is a friend of obedience. God will put in the heart and on
the tongue of your guide whatever is best for your spiritual
health. (John of Avila, "Hear, O Daughter," WSD, pp. 18–19)

One had best not offer counsel when not asked:

Come not to counsel, before you are called. This saying, now
familiar under the name of Cato, seems to have been proverbial,
as Plutarch bears witness: his words in the "Table-talk," book I,
are these: "Surely therefore it was out of place and proverbially
wrong for Menelaus to become an adviser without being asked."
(Erasmus, Adages, I ii 90/LB II 103c, *Collected Works*, Vol. 31,
pp. 230–231)

The desert fathers had the habit of refusing to give guidance unless
there was clear evidence of its need and genuine contrition on the part
of the recipient:

We had heard of his inflexible rule never to give instruction in
the spiritual life except to persons who sought it in faith and
heartfelt contrition. For he was afraid that if he poured out the
water of life indiscriminately to people who had no use for it or
were hardly even thirsty, he would cast his pearls before swine.
(John Cassian, Conferences, I, First Conference with Abba
Moses, LCC XII, p. 195)

It does little good to offer good counsel to one who is not ready to
listen. Erasmus mused on this ancient proverb:

You are sprinkling scent on manure. All scent vanishes and is
overcome by the smell of manure. (Erasmus, "Adages," I iv 61/LB
II 171C, *Collected Works*, Vol. 31, p. 361)

The counselor who does not embody his own counsel is evidently lu-
dicrous. The daily behavior of the counselor remains a model to those
being counselled:

If you accept my counsel, you will select for yourself a man
whose life is such that it will act as a personal model to touch
your heart, one whom you will respect so much that whenever
you think of him you will keep on going because of the esteem

you have for him and keep yourself in check. Think of him as if he were present to you. (William of St. Thierry, *The Golden Epistle*, WSD, p. 24)

The pastor has the duty to teach the people about the possibilities and limits of the pastoral office. One who counsels must embody his own counsel. The counselor, however, does not coerce others into counsel, or come to counsel before called. Accurately defining how deeply one is experiencing pain is a necessary early step to healing.

In this second Part of our discussion we have attempted to identify the prevailing metaphors of pastoral counsel: The pastor works like a *counselor* who offers timely wisdom; a *physician* who provides therapeutic remedies; a *guide* for a hazardous journey who provides direction and situational mentoring; a *liberator* who works to free the soul from self-created prisons of fear, guilt, and depression; and an *educator* who teaches the soul the truth.

3 God's Own Caring

CLASSIC PASTORAL writers thought it unwise to speak abstractly of human caring as if it could be detached from God's active eternal caring. This part of our collection brings together major classical texts that place human caring in the context of divine care. These passages view God the Spirit as archetypal Counselor whose wisdom human counsel may to some degree reflect. They view scripture as the most reliable source of understanding of God's own caring for humanity and the world.

Pastoral Care does not occur in a social or historical vacuum. The pastor-parishioner relationship exists in a society, which lives out of a larger cultural history, which exists amid universal human history, which has its beginning and ending in God. The classical pastoral tradition has often pointed beyond the microcosmic situation of interpersonal care to the macrocosmic situation of God's own caring for the world. Put in terms of systematic theology, the providing of human care occurs in the context of divine providence.

I. 🐝 HUMAN CARING GROUNDED IN GOD'S CARE

The pastoral tradition has not viewed human care autonomously, as if everything were dependent upon fleeting, changing human initiative. Rather human caring is viewed as energized and embraced by God's own steady caring for the world.

Key qualities assumed in effective therapeutic relationships are viewed by analogy with God's own therapeutic relationship with history. This section sets out the providential context in which that interpretation is placed.

God's way of caring for souls does not work according to a short term plan, as Origen pointed out:

For God governs souls not with reference, let me say, to the fifty years of the present temporal life, but with reference to an illimitable age. It is for this reason that God made human intelli-

89

gence akin to eternity, in order that the rational soul would not be blocked from an ultimate cure, as it so often is in this life. (Origin, *De Principiis*, Bk. II, Ch. I, sec. 13, ANF IV, p. 314)*

God's care, as eternal ubiquitous Knower, penetrates yet transcends all historical reality. This care wells up from eternity. The unending caring of the eternal God for the soul is not limited to this life. Christian care for the soul is not, therefore, to be seen as focused narrowly upon human initiative—so vulnerable and prone to frustration—but as a response to the divine initiative-taking in salvation history. For this reason, God's care of the world cannot be subjected to objective physical measurement, which applies only to measurable temporal objects:

For although, in the creation of the world, all things have been arranged by Him in the most beautiful and stable manner, He nevertheless needed to exercise some healing influence upon those who were struggling with the debilitating effects of their misdeeds, and upon the whole world that had become polluted by sin. Nothing has ever been neglected by God, or ever will be. God does at each particular juncture what it becomes Him to do in a perverted and changed world. As a farmer engages in varied actions of care in relation to the soil and its products according to the varying seasons of the year, so God administers entire ages of time, as if they were, so to speak, so many individual years, performing during each one of them what is requisite with a reasonable regard to the care of the world. (Origen, *Against Celsus*, Ch. lxix, ANF IV, p. 528)*

Origen placed God's care of souls within a world-historical, and finally eschatological, frame of reference. God, the cultivator, the nurturer, takes care of the garden of history. That care extends over many extended seasons of growth, and not merely our own times, through innumerable seasons that finite human consciousness is too limited to grasp. Minucius Felix argued that the general trend of the divine purpose is nevertheless knowable on the basis of evidences seen in ordinary history:

Now if, on entering any house, you should behold everything refined, well arranged, and adorned, assuredly you would believe that a master presided over it, and that he himself was much better than all those excellent things. So in this house of the world, when you look upon the heaven and the earth, its providence, its ordering, its law, believe that there is a Lord and Parent of the universe far more glorious than the stars themselves, and the parts of the whole world. . . . But our heart is too limited to understand Him, and therefore we are then worthily estimating

Him when we say that He is beyond estimation. I will speak out in what manner I feel. He who thinks that he knows the magnitude of God, is diminishing it. (Minucius Felix, *The Octavius*, Ch. XVIII, ANF IV, pp. 182–183)

God's providing is recognizable through the excellence of its order and design. Human reasoning can to some small degree become aware of this ordering. Any measurement we make of God's design is bound to be an inadvertent diminution. If so, then how can we say that divine harmonies ring precisely through the ordinary sphere of this limited, bodily, material nature, where everything is temporal and corruptible? A beautiful metaphor was supplied by Alexander:

Don't you know that a lyre sometimes sounds out of tune, yet by the addition of harmony, everything is brought into concord. It is in this way that the divine goodness becomes intermixed with unordered motion, that is, the world of matter, and thus a certain order emerges out of what seems to be an innate disorder. (Alexander of Alexandria, *Of the Manichaeans*, Ch. XVIII, ANF VI, p. 248)*

Viewed from a wider perspective, the discords of history are made harmonious. Both tempo and harmony are made beautiful through God's capacity to bring good out of evil, though in themselves the times are rough hewn, unattractive, ill-timed, discordant, and noisy.

In his counsel to Frederick of Saxony during an illness, Luther developed a striking series of analogies between God's care of us and our care for others. They especially point toward the constancy of God's care. Human care that seeks to reflect God's infinite care may be sporadic and occasional, so as to reveal the limits of finitude and egocentricity, but in doing so points beyond itself to God's incomparable care:

Who had the care of us so many a night, while we slept? Who cared for us when we were at work, or at play, or engaged in all those countless things wherein we had no care for ourselves? Indeed, how much of our time is there in which we have the care of ourselves? Even the miser, careful as he is to gain riches, must necessarily set aside his care in the midst of all his getting and gaining. And so we see that, whether we will it or not, all our care falls back on God alone, and we are scarcely ever left to care for ourselves. Still, God does now and again leave us to care for ourselves, in order to bring home to us His goodness, and to teach us how great the difference between His care and ours. Hence, He permits us now and then to be assailed by some slight malady or other ill, dissembling His care for us (for He never ceases to care), and yet at the same time preventing the many evils that threaten us on every side from bursting in upon us all together. In this way He challenges us as His beloved children, to see whether we will not trust His care, which extends through all our past life, and learn how vain and powerless a thing is any care of ours. How little, indeed, do we or can we do for ourselves, throughout our life, when we are not able to stop a small pain in one of our limbs, even for the shortest space of time? (Luther, *The Fourteen of Consolation*, WML I, pp. 124–25)*

We may fancy that we are caring greatly for ourselves, until we compare that care with the eternal care that God has for all things. If God's care is so great, then does God require nothing of us? Why should we work so hard to care for ourselves and others, if God takes all this care of us in every way? In answering, Luther distinguished between legitimate and illegitimate external means of support. Two seemingly inconsistent metaphors are used, but they join together in a complementary way: self-initiative in military activity and the trusting behavior of birds. God gives the faithful ample external means of support (armor), yet asks them not to depend inordinately on these external means (as the birds of the air):

Why, since God wants to battle for them, does He bid them possess armor? He is an amazing God: He does not want to do the work without our armor, yet not through it. He wants us to use swords and yet not depend on them. Thus He also wants me to work in order to support myself; and yet He says He wants to support me, as He does the birds, without my labor. Therefore we must become accustomed to this: God wants us to use external means and yet not depend upon them. (Luther, WLS 2, #2937, p. 935; WA 17 I, 143f.)

It is no self-contradiction to say that instruments of self-defense have utility, yet are not absolute, and cannot be the source of absolute trustworthiness. Paradoxically, as one actively uses means of self-protection, one may come to depend all the more upon God. This suggests that God's way of caring is to be understood from an entirely different vantage point than human ways of caring—from the vantage point of God's incomparable power to care:

We seem many to ourselves, but to God we are very few. We distinguish peoples and nations; to God this whole world is one family. Kings only know all the matters of their kingdom by the ministrations of their servants; God has no need of information. We not only live in His eyes, but also in His bosom. (Minucius Felix, *Octavius*, Ch. XXXIII, ANF IV, p. 193)

When we view our human situation, it seems complex; but God beholds the whole simply. The cosmos is analogous to a family that God already knows intimately, and about which further information is not required in order to gain understanding. Human history is not an object of external awareness to God, but known as it were from the inside by God, from within the experience of being human. This awareness of the intimate care of God prompted the leading patristic psychologist, Nemesius, to ask to what extent God's providential care can be examined and demonstrated through careful reasoning, so that God's caring would be to some degree knowable to all humanity even apart from revelation.

It is not only, however, to Jews and Christians, but to pagans, also, that we must make good our contention. Come, then, and let us prove that there is a providence, arguing only from such things as Greeks themselves believe. One might then demonstrate the existence of providence by the same arguments that we have employed to prove that there is a God. For the continued existence of all things, especially where they are subject to genesis and decay, the place and order of whatever has being, maintained always according to the same pattern, and utterly undeviating courses of the stars, the circle of the year and the returning seasons, the equality of day-time and night-time, when taken over the year, and the measured and utterly regular lengthening and shortening of either—how could anything continue to be managed like that, if there was no one thinking it out beforehand?. . . . Another thing that shows the existence of providence is the agreement among all men to acknowledge the need to pray and to perform divine service by means of sacred offerings and holy places. For how, or to whom, should anyone pray, if there were no mind guiding the world? . . . Take away providence, and forthwith wickedness is conceded to those who have the power to work it. Mercy and the fear of God are taken away, and at the same time virtue and godliness. For unless God foresees, he neither punishes, nor distributes encouragement to those that do well, nor does he ward off their hurts from those that are wronged. Who then would any longer worship God, if he is nowise of a least service to us? Take away providence, and prophecy, and all foreknowledge is taken away also. But any such supposition is out of accord with events that are taking place almost every day. For many are the manifestations of divine aid to men in need. (Nemesius, *Of the Nature of Man*, Ch. XLII.61, LCC IV, pp. 424–427)

Four rational arguments thus establish the hypothesis that God cares: the fact that creation continues; the orderliness of nature; the persistence of prayer among widely different forms of human culture, which would be absurd without the premise of God's care; and the fact that morality requires providence.

Critics of providence say: God can't care about sticky details! It would be corrupting of God if God were involved in worldly particulars! Nemesius answered:

Suppose that these objectors disclaim any imputation of negligence to God, but say that providence over particulars does not beseem him. Suppose that they say that it is incongruous that such blessedness should condescend to mean and trivial details, and be involved to some extent in profanation by the absurdities that spring from material circumstances and human caprice, and that, for that reason, God does not choose to exercise providence over particulars. In making such assertions, they do not see that they are investing God with two of the basest inclinations, an inclination to be scornful, and a propensity for being easily defiled! That is to say, either the Creator disdains ruling and managing particulars because he scorns them (a thing most monstrous to affirm), or else he must, as these folk suggest, be shunning defilement. Now the rays of the sun naturally draw up moisture of every kind, yet no one says that the sun (or even his rays) is sullied by shining on dunghills. (Nemesius, *On the Nature of Man*, Ch. XLIV.67, LCC IV, p. 443)

If God would turn out to be hesitant to become involved in life's details either because easily corruptible or scornful of finitude, God would be less caring than humanity. But such is not God's way, for God is neither uninvolved nor corrupted by involvement. God neither withdraws from nor despises our humanity but engages in it bodily. Other critics have tried to argue that God did not create the cosmos but merely arranged and adorned what was previously given. Lactantius countered, aware that pastoral care could not proceed without an answer:

Nor are the poets to be listened to, who say that in the beginning was a chaos, that is, a confusion of matter and the elements; but that God afterwards divided all that mass, and having separated each object from the confused heap, and arranged them in order, He constructed and adorned the world. Now it is easy to reply to these persons, who do not understand the power of God: for they believe that He can produce nothing except out of materials already existing and prepared; in which error philosophers also were involved. . . . There is something more in God, whom

you verily reduce to the weakness of man, to whom you allow
nothing else but the mere workmanship. In what respect, then,
will that divine power differ from man, if God also, as man does,
stands in need of the assistance of another? But He does stand in
need of it, if He can construct nothing unless He is furnished
with materials by another. But if this is the case, it is plain that
His power is imperfect, and he who prepared the material must
be judged more powerful. By what name therefore, shall he be
called who excels God in power?—since it is greater to make that
which is one's own, than to arrange those things which are another's. But if it is impossible that anything should be more powerful than God, who must necessarily be of perfect strength,
power, and intelligence, it follows that He who made the things
which are composed of matter, made matter also. (Lactantius, *The
Divine Institutes*, Bk. II, Ch. IX, ANF VII, p. 53)

It makes a great deal of difference to the Christian tradition of pastoral care whether God is uncreated Creator *or* merely artificer of a creation made by another. If the one who cares amid the fall of a sparrow is
none other than the Almighty One who called creation forth out of
nothing, then that divine care, despite our confusions about it, is incomparable in power and goodness. The radical dependence of creature
upon Creator is not an incidental or ancillary concept of pastoral care.

There is a healthy awareness in the pastoral tradition that the will of
God is not at all times discernible by finite minds that are bound in time
and prone to sin. Prosper of Aquitaine (c. 390–c. 463) offered this
three-stage sequence of reasoning:

We should base our reasoning on these three propositions
which are perfectly sound and true. One of these declares that
God's goodness from all eternity and of His own free choice wills
all men *to be saved and to come to the knowledge of the truth*. With this
goes another, stating that every man who is actually saved and
comes to the knowledge of the truth, owes it to God's help and
guidance just as he owes to Him his perseverance in faith *that
worketh by charity*. A third acknowledges with modesty and circumspection that we cannot comprehend the motive of every divine
decree and that the reasons of many of God's works remain hidden from our human understanding. We see that God acts in a
different or even in a singular way at different times, when dealing with different nations or families, with infants or the unborn,
or even with twins. We have no doubt that here we are facing
those things which God in His justice and mercy does not wish us
to know in this fleeting world. (Prosper of Aquitaine, *The Call of
All Nations*, Bk. II, Ch. 30, ACW 14, pp. 142–143)

Soul care does not despair over the mystery by which God knows even though we do not know, and works differently in each situation. Rather the mystery is celebrated as known by God.

II. ❦ Avoiding False Starts on Questions Concerning Providence

The biblical teaching of providence often awakens earnest questions concerning the justice of God's way of caring. Although the sufferings faced today often seem to be unprecedented, on closer inspection they are found similar to those faced in previous periods of pastoral care.

One of the earliest and most persistent challenges that faced the Christian teaching of God's care was that which came from the hedonically-oriented Epicureans, whose ideas are still very much alive. Lactantius offered an early Christian reply to the Epicurean critique, and clarification of why it remains so attractive to so many audiences— the idle, the covetous, the timid, the impious, the ascetic, the upwardly mobile, the vainglorious, the egocentric, and various kinds of counselors. Epicureanism, he thought, stands as a complete and ever-expansive form of rationalization:

The system of Epicurus was much more generally followed than those of the others; not because it brings forward any truth, but because the attractive name of pleasure invites many. For every one is naturally inclined to vices. Moreover, for the purpose of drawing the multitude to himself, he says what every hearer already wishes to hear said. He does not encourage the idle to apply himself to learning. He releases the covetous man from giving generously to the people. He gives permission to the inactive man to not undertake the business of the state. He releases the sluggish from bodily exercise, and the timid from military service. The irreligious is told that gods pay no attention to human conduct. The one who is unfeeling and selfish is ordered to give nothing to anyone, since the wise man presumably does everything on his own account. To a man who avoids the crowd, solitude is praised. One who is already too sparing learns that life can be sustained on water and meal. If a man hates his wife, the blessings of celibacy are enumerated to him. To one who has unruly children, the happiness of those who are without children is proclaimed. Foster parents are advised that there is no bond of nature. To the man who is delicate and incapable of endurance, it is said that pain is the greatest of all evils. To those who are already courageous, it is said that the wise man is happy even

under tortures. The man who devotes himself to the pursuit
of influence and distinction is enjoined to pay court to kings.
One who cannot endure annoyance is enjoined to shun the house
of royalty. Thus the crafty counselor collects a constituency from
various types of needy characters. While he lays himself out to
please all, he becomes all the more at variance with himself in
order to please all, and he is even more inconsistent with himself
than they all are with one another. But we must explain from
what source the whole of this system is derived, and what origin it
has. . . . When Epicurus reflected on these things, induced as it
were by the injustice of these matters (for thus it appeared to him
in his ignorance of the cause and subject), he thought that there
was no providence. And having persuaded himself of this, he un-
dertook also to defend it, and thus he entangled himself in inex-
tricable errors. For if there is no providence, how is it that the
world was made with such order and arrangement?. . . . Thus,
because he had taken up a false principle at the commencement,
the necessity of the subjects which followed led him to absurdities.
(Lactantius, *The Divine Institutes*, Bk. III, Ch. XVII, ANF VII,
p. 86)*

The comic aspect underlying "Epicurean counsel" is that it tried to
give everyone just what they seemed to want or in fact already had. The
advice given was merely an echo of tendencies that already existed. The
aim was happiness, and the miscalculation was that if one only continued doing what one was already doing, now clothed with a pretence of
self-determination, then one would become happy. According to Lactantius, the deeper distortion underlying this convenient counsel is rejection of divine providence. The pivotal error is the assumption that
God does not care. From this comes a diverse range of misjudgments
that confirm biases already seated temperamentally in the soul. How did
Christian teaching reason about providence over against the seeming
plausibility of this Epicurean advice?

God, says Epicurus, pays no attention to the world, and therefore He has no power. For he who has power must of necessity
care about it. For if He has power and disavows the use of it, why
should humanity and creation be regarded as so far beneath God,
and contemptible in His sight? On this account Epicurus thinks
that God can only be pure and happy if he remains completely
immobile and at rest. To whom, then, has the administration of
so great affairs been entrusted, if these things which we see to be
governed by the highest judgment are neglected by God? Or how
can he who lives and perceives be completely immobile? . . . In
what can the action of God consist but in the administration

of the world? But if God maintains constant care of the world, it follows that He cares for human life, and takes notice of the acts of individuals, and earnestly desires that they should be wise and good. (Lactantius, "A Treatise on the Anger of God," Ch. XVII, ANF VII, p. 273)*

Does God directly and specifically predetermine all that God foreknows?

While God knows all things beforehand, yet He does not predetermine all things. For He knows beforehand those things that are in our power, but He does not predetermine them. For it is not His will that there should be wickedness nor does He choose to compel virtue. (John of Damascus, *OF* II.30, NPNF 2, IX, p. 42)

According to this premise, providence does not exclude either free choice or chance:

But it would be contrary to the essential character of divine providence if all things occurred by necessity, as we showed. Therefore, it would be contrary to the character of divine providence if nothing were to be fortuitous and a matter of chance in things. (Thomas Aquinas, *Summa Theologica*, I, Q. 47, I, pp. 246–247)

If God exists, whence comes evil?

Thus, Boethius introduces a certain philosopher who asks: "If God exists, whence comes evil?" But it could be argued to the contrary: "If evil exists, God exists." For, there would be no evil if the order of good were taken away, since its privation is evil. But this order would not exist if there were no God. (Thomas Aquinas, *Summa Theologica*, I, Q. 71, I, pp. 240–241)

Suppose then that God does care for the world, in contrast to the unconvincing notion that God could have created a magnificent world only to care nothing for it, we may remain perplexed by a speculative question posed by Origen: If to be God is to be active, then for what reason did God remain inactive prior to the creation of the world? Shall we assume that God did nothing before beginning to create and care for the world?

This is the objection which they generally raise: they say, "If the world had its beginning in time, what was God doing before the world began? For it is at once impious and absurd to say that the nature of God is inactive and immoveable, or to suppose that goodness at one time did not do good, and omnipotence at one time did not exercise its power."... To these propositions I consider that none of the heretics can easily return an answer that will be in conformity with the nature of their opinions. But we can give a logical answer in accordance with the standard of religion, when we say that not then for the first time did God begin to work when He made this visible world, but as, after its destruction, there will be another world, so also we believe that others existed before the present came into being. And both of these positions will be confirmed by the authority of holy Scripture. For that there will be another world after this, is taught by Isaiah, who says, "There will be new heavens, and a new earth, which I shall make to abide in my sight, saith the Lord" (Is. 64:22), and that before this world others also existed is shown by Ecclesiastes, in the words: "What is that which hath been? Even that which shall be. And what is that which has been created? Even this which is to be created" (Eccl. 1:9–10, LXX). (Origen, *De Principiis*, Bk. III, Ch. V, ANF IV, p. 341)

Though Origen's view cannot be considered consensual, and was in fact rigorously challenged, it shows evidence of an early Christian effort to assert the radical engagement of God in the world. Contemporary speculation on a continuing succession of worlds was thus anticipated by Origen, who viewed God's care for creatures as eternally springing from the heart of God. Augustine responded comically:

How, then, shall I respond to him who asks, "What was God doing *before* he made heaven and earth?" I do not answer, as a certain one is reported to have done facetiously (shrugging off the force of the question), "He was preparing hell," he said, "for those who pry too deep." (Augustine, *Confessions*, XI.12, LCC VII, p. 253)

III. ❦ Spirit as Counselor

In Christian counsel, the active agent of change is not the human analyst or agent alone, but God's own active Spirit, to whom the human spirit may respond. The human spirit is being addressed, constrained, and freed by the power of God's own Spirit. In this way pastoral counsel seeks to point beyond itself to God's own counsel in scripture and to God's active presence through God's own indwelling Spirit. Indeed the pastoral writers thought that the Holy Spirit intends to use human intelligence, human empathy, and human speech for the betterment of the human life. In this way, the triune God is actively engaged in redemptive interpersonal encounter.

If the Holy Spirit is the archetypal Counselor whose counsel our speech hopes to mediate or refract, then we must ask how the Spirit comes to be present and recognized as such amid human interaction? The very root word of *paraclesis*, so critical to the scriptural understanding of comforting counsel, serves as a hinge point:

Now Paraclete, when spoken of the Saviour, seems to mean intercessor. For in Greek, Paraclete has both significations—that of intercessor and comforter. On account, then, of the phrase which follows, when he says, "And He is the propitiation for our sins" [1 John 2:2], the name Paraclete seems to be understood in the case of our Saviour as meaning intercessor; for He is said to intercede with the Father because of our sins. In the case of the Holy Spirit, the Paraclete must be understood in the sense of comforter, inasmuch as He bestows consolation upon the souls to whom He openly reveals the apprehension of spiritual knowledge. (Origen, *De Principiis*, Bk. II, Ch. VII, sec. 4, ANF IV, p. 286)

By analogy, insofar as our human counsel mediates divine counsel, we empathize with and intercede for the neighbor, who is lifted up in prayer before God even amid ordinary conversation. The Spirit's work is consolation:

The Paraclete, who is called the Holy Spirit, is so called from His work of consolation, *paraclesis* being termed in Latin *consolatio*. For if any one has been granted the privilege of participating in the Holy Spirit by the knowledge of His ineffable mysteries, he undoubtedly obtains comfort and joy of heart. For since he comes by the teaching of the Spirit to the knowledge of the reasons of all things which happen—how or why they occur—his soul can in no respect be troubled, or admit any feeling of sorrow; nor is he alarmed by anything. (Origen, *De Principiis*, Bk. II, Ch. VII, sec. 4, ANF IV, p. 286)*

The early Christian community viewed the soul as a battle ground between God's own Spirit of truth-telling, and deceitful influences that tempt persons to distort the truth about themselves. The grace of baptism enables the radical confidence experienced by believers that in dying-and-rising one has finally renounced the self-deceiving power of evil, and turned to a life of telling the truth and living out of the truth.

Everyone stands basically under the influence of either the Holy Spirit or some destructive spirit. It is not possible to avoid the one or the other, unless one imagines that one could be simultaneously controlled by opposite spirits. For the Comforter hates every lie, and the devil hates all truth. But every one that is baptized agreeably to the truth is separated from the destructive spirit, and is under the Holy Spirit. The Holy Spirit remains with him so long as he is doing good, and fills him with wisdom and understanding. (*Constitutions of the Holy Apostles*, Bk. VI, sec. XX-VII, p. 462)*

Just as psychoanalysis assumes that learning the reasons for one's discomfort is itself an important aspect of therapy, so did the Christian pastoral tradition as early as the third century teach a similar maxim. When the soul learns how to describe accurately why things have occurred to her, then the soul tends to be consoled. This is one of the most crucial means by which the Paraclete teaches. Clement of Alexandria commented on the sense in which it is said that God the Spirit "sees into" the soul.

"He surveys all things, and hears all things," seeing the soul naked within; and possesses from eternity the idea of each thing individually. What happens in theaters, where one is able to look all around, is something like God's way of viewing: each part is seen, and the whole is seen together. For in one glance He views all things together, and each thing by itself. (Clement of Alexandria, *The Stromata*, Bk. VI, Ch. XXVI, ANF II, p. 517)*

As one can see everything in a good theatre, so does God see, not only this moment but all moments in divine simultaneity. God does not see into things as we do with finite vision, looking at this and then that thing partially, but with infinite cognition and wisdom, seeing the whole and its parts at once. This is why our notions of personal insight can hardly be extrapolated to encompass God. Language cracks and breaks under the strain. God's seeing into our souls is compared here to nakedness. We experience ourselves amid our sinful self-assertiveness as naked in the presence of the Holy. We are unable to maintain any secrets before this gaze:

God, who has made all things, and looks upon all things, from whom there can be nothing secret, is present in the darkness, is present in our thoughts, as if in the deep darkness. Not only do we act in Him, but also, I had almost said, we live with Him. (Minucius Felix, *Octavius*, Ch. XXXII, ANF IV, p. 193)

If this Holy One is so beyond our full comprehension, then how do our souls come to know such awesome holiness even partially? Athanasius argued that anyone can begin to become so acquainted by becoming quietly attuned to one's own soul:

The way of truth will aim at reaching the real and true God. But for its knowledge and accurate comprehension, there is need

of none other save of ourselves, but it is in us, and it is possible to
find it from ourselves, in the first instance, as Moses also taught,
when he said: "The word" of faith "is within thy heart" [Deut.
30:14]. Which very thing the Saviour declared and confirmed,
when He said: "The kingdom of God is within you" [Luke
17:12]. For having in ourselves faith, and the kingdom of God,
we shall be able quickly to see and perceive the King of the Universe, the saving Word of the Father. . . . What road is this? I say
that it is the soul of each one of us, and the intelligence which
resides there. For by it alone can God be contemplated and perceived. (Athanasius, *Contra Gentes*, II.30.1, NPNF 2, IV, p. 20)

If the soul through which God is beheld is already that which makes
us alive, then none need search externally for a means of beholding.
But this does not obviate the need for hearing the word of scripture
instructing the soul through the Spirit, who assists this process of
listening.

Augustine argued that the Holy Spirit speaks all human languages.
Otherwise the church could not be universal:

The Holy Spirit deigned to reveal himself in the languages of
all nations, so that a man may realize that he has the Holy Spirit
when he is contained in the unity of the Church, which speaks
with all languages. (Augustine, *Sermons*, 268.2, LCF, p. 237)

The universality of the redemptive community, its cross-cultural character, its ability to embrace all human conditions and cultures, stands as
historical evidence of the capacity of the Holy Spirit to address all humanity in all times and places.

A fascinating musical metaphor was used by Ambrose, who himself is
credited with nurturing a new form of music (the Ambrosian Chant).
He compared the well attuned soul with a musical instrument (cithara,
zither, guitar) that can be played and brought into harmonious accord
by God's own Spirit:

"I will give praise to you upon the cithara, my God" (Ps. 43:4).
Our soul has its own cithara, for Paul would not have said, "I will
pray with the spirit, but I will pray with the understanding also; I
will sing with the spirit, but I will sing with the understanding
also" [1 Cor. 14:15], unless he had a cithara that resounded at the
touch of the pick of the Holy Spirit. The cithara is our flesh
when it dies to sin to live to God; it is a cithara when it receives
the sevenfold Spirit in the sacrament of baptism. For while the
tortoise is alive, it is sunk in the mire; but when it has died, its
covering is adapted to the uses of song and the gift of holy in-

struction, to sound forth the seven changing notes in rhythmic measures. (Ambrose, *The Prayer of Job and David*, Bk. Two, 10.36, FC 65, p. 419)

The metaphor is surprising: As the tortoise only becomes a means of song through death, and as the harp in itself is dead, but only becomes a means of beautiful music at the hands of a living artist, so does the soul become vibrant with beauty when, dying to sin, it is touched by God's own Spirit of mercy, truth and love. The seven notes of the scale resonate with the seven gifts of the Spirit.

Augustine hoped that his own counsel would diminish in importance as his hearers came to listen to God's own counsel in scripture:

Would that you, giving earnest heed to the word of God, did not require counsel of mine to support you under whatsoever offences may arise! Would that your comfort rather came from Him by whom we also are comforted. (Augustine, *Letters*, LXX-VIII, To the Church of Hippo, 1, NPNF 1, I, p. 345)

Augustine was hoping in this particular situation (in a letter to the people of the Church of Hippo in 404 A.D. concerning a scandal) that his hearers would be able to receive the counsel and comfort of God directly through Word and Spirit.

IV. 🦋 Scripture as Source of Good Counsel

There is no Christian pastoral care in any period of its history without scripture, without the law and gospel, without the prophetic and apostolic witness through which God's own care is made known. The practice of pastoral care, according to the classical tradition, does not proceed as if it were an independent psychological wisdom, or as if pastoral wisdom were to be achieved apart from the previous study of scripture and the immediate personal address of scripture. The role that scripture plays in the guiding, comforting, and caring process was stated powerfully in the Westminster Confession. It did not deny natural knowledge of emotive life, but viewed that natural knowledge as corrupted and incomplete without God's own self-disclosure:

Although the light of nature, and the works of creation and providence, do so far manifest the goodness, wisdom, and power of God, as to leave men inexcusable; yet are they not sufficient to give that knowledge of God, and of his will, which is necessary unto salvation; therefore it pleased the Lord, at sundry times, and in divers manners, to reveal himself, and to declare that his will unto his Church; and afterwards, for the better preserving and propagating of the truth, and for the more sure establishment and comfort of the Church against the corruption of the flesh, and the malice of Satan and of the world, to commit the same wholly unto writing; which maketh the holy Scripture to be most necessary; these former ways of God's revealing his will unto his people being now ceased. (Westminster Confession, Ch. 1, *CC*, p. 195)

The pastor is ordained and authorized to offer the comfort of scripture to the anxious, guilty, and despairing. One serving in this office must study it carefully and be ready to offer the whole counsel of God where needed. This is why we have the written word, and not merely a bare uninterpreted event:

The inspired Word exists because of both obedience and disobedience: that we may be saved by obeying it, and educated because we have disobeyed. (Clement of Alexandria, *Christ the Educator*, Bk. I, Ch. 2.5, FC 23, p. 7)

This question plunges deeper than at first it might appear. The issue hinges on why the Word spoken in Christ is needed, and why the scripture is needed to communicate that Word, and whether if we had already been obedient, we might have no need of the Word. Scripture is needed at both levels: when we have obeyed and when we have disobeyed, to restore us through hearing obedience, and to teach us when we have fallen away.

Must the context of a scriptural passage be taken into account when scripture is brought to bear in counsel? Tertullian answered with this example:

"Art thou loosed from a wife? Seek not a wife" [1. Cor. 7:27]. Here it is quite evident that persons are referred to who had been called only recently and were asking for advice regarding the circumstances in which they found themselves at the time of their conversion. This, then, is our interpretation of the passage. We must examine it to see whether it harmonizes with the time and occasion of writing, with illustrations and arguments used earlier, as well as with assertions and opinions which follow later on, and— most important of all—whether it agrees with the advice of the Apostle and his own personal practice. Obviously, there is nothing to be more sedulously avoided than inconsistency. (Tertullian, *On Monogamy*, ACW, 13, p. 98)

When scripture is heard and received as a source of counsel, it is not to be treated woodenly as if it were an object, but rather as divine address, spoken in a particular time and place, and therefore seeking to be understood as speaking to us from within that time and place, accurately understood, utilizing whatever historical and rational resources are available to us to allow it to speak its own word to us.

Cyril of Jerusalem urged the pastor to be ready to speak where scripture speaks, and be silent where scripture is silent:

Let us say about the Holy Spirit exactly what Scripture says and nothing else, and do not let us pry where Scripture does not answer. The Scriptures were spoken by the Holy Spirit himself, and what he said about himself is exactly what he pleased, or we could comprehend. So, let what he spake be said, which is to say, let us not dare to utter anything that he did not. (Cyril of Jerusalem, *Catechetical Lectures*, XVI, LCC VI, p. 168)

This passage does not imply that Christian counselors can only quote scripture and nothing else, for the entire history of pastoral counsel testifies that counselors do not treat scripture that inflexibly. On the whole the pastoral tradition has been well-aware of secular psychological understandings that were available to it in different historical periods. Rather the primary concern is to not stand in the way of allowing scripture to speak clearly and directly to the present situation. That word can only reach its intended depth through the concrete address of the Holy Spirit. The assumption is that the scriptures are sufficient if we only attend closely enough to them, and pray for the Spirit's own illumination. They provide sufficient instruction for each human challenge. This is coupled with a strong injunction that the counselor not distort the simple address of scripture with some gloss of his own, nor hide the depth of God's own mercy through some insensitivity of his own. It is fundamentally through scripture that the word is mirrored to the emotive life:

And it seems to me that these words become like a mirror to the person singing them, so that he might perceive himself and the emotions of his soul, and thus affected, he might recite them. ... Therefore, when someone sings the third psalm, recognizing his own tribulations, he considers the words in the psalm to be his own. ... And so, on the whole, each psalm is both spoken and composed by the Spirit so that in these same words, as was said earlier, the stirrings of our souls might be grasped, and all of them be said as concerning us. (Athanasius, *A Letter to Marcellinus*, CWS, p. 111)

In this way the address of the Spirit through scripture begins to impact human affections. One views oneself imaginatively as present by analogy in the events that the scriptures recount. This is why the Christian counselor makes diligent study of scripture.

The Spirit, which by the providence of God through the Word who was in the beginning with God, illuminated the ministers of truth, the prophets and apostles. . . . in order that he who is capable of instruction may by investigation, and by devoting himself to the study of the profundities of meaning contained in the words, become a participator of all the doctrines of his counsel. (Origen, *De Principiis*, Bk. IV, Ch. 1, sec. 14, ANF IV, p. 362)

Daily scripture study was thought by Theonas of Alexandria (c. 300) to be required in soul care:

My dearest Lucianus, since you are wise, bear with good-will the unwise. Then they too may perchance become wise. Do no one an injury at any time, and provoke no one to anger. . . . Let no day pass by without reading some portion of the Sacred Scriptures, at such convenient hour as offers, and giving some space to meditation. And never cast off the habit of reading in the Holy Scriptures; for nothing feeds the soul and enriches the mind so well as those sacred studies do. (Theonas of Alexandria, *Epistle to Lucianus*, sec. 9, ANF VII, p. 161)

V. 🐦 THE PRACTICE OF SCRIPTURAL COUNSELING

The best pastoral care is that which has become thoroughly infused with the spirit and language of scripture:

We must not deliver anything whatsoever, without the sacred Scriptures, nor let ourselves be misled by mere probability, or by marshalling of arguments. And do not simply credit me, when I tell you these things, unless you get proof from the Holy Scriptures of the things set forth by me. (Cyril of Jerusalem, *Catechetical Lectures*, IV.17, LCC, IV, pp. 108–109)

Here the pastoral guide is warning his hearer not to take him seriously if he does not ground his teaching in scripture. What if one is tempted to distort scripture in the interest of what seems to be the good cause of stretching a bit to make it more relevant to a particular situation of counsel?

Collecting a set of expressions and names scattered here and there [in Scripture], they twist them, as we have already said, from a natural to a non-natural sense. In so doing, they act like those who bring forward any kind of hypothesis they fancy, and then endeavor to support them out of the poems of Homer, so that the ignorant imagine that Homer actually composed the verses bearing upon that hypothesis, which has, in fact, been but newly constructed (Irenaeus, *Against Heresies*, Bk. I, Ch. IX, sec. 4, ANF I, p. 330)

Irenaeus' caution is directed against using scripture for any purpose alien to its intent. At least the minimal level of hermeneutical integrity that one would expect in the study of Homer would also be expected in the study of scripture. By what rule is scripture to be interpreted?

When there is a question about the true and full sense of any Scripture (which is not manifold, but one), it must be searched and known by other places that speak more clearly. The Supreme Judge, by which all controversies of religion are to be determined, and all decrees of councils, opinions of ancient writers, doctrines of men, and private spirits, are to be examined, and in whose sentence we are to rest, can be no other than the Holy Spirit speaking in the Scripture. (Westminster Confession, Ch. IX, *CC*, p. 196)

Unclear passages are to be illumined by clear passages, Luther argued:

Such is the way of the whole of Scripture: it wants to be interpreted by a comparison of passages from everywhere, and understood under its own direction. The safest of all methods for discerning the meaning of Scripture is to work for it by drawing together and scrutinizing passages. (Luther, "Lectures on Deuteronomy 1–34, 1525," LW 9, p. 21; WA 14, p. 556)

The comparison of what is more fully known with what is only partially known is often called the analogy of faith. It prevents individualistic or idiosyncratic interpretation of the Spirit's address through scripture:

It is indeed true that some passages of Scripture are dark; however they contain nothing but precisely that which is found at other places in clear, open passages. But now the heretics come on, understand the dark passages according to their own mind, and contend with them against the clear passages, the foundation of our faith. Then the fathers fought them with the clear passages, threw light with these on the dark passages, and proved that the dark passages taught precisely the same thing as the clear passages. . . . whoever cannot understand the dark passages should stay with the clear ones. (Luther, WA 8, pp. 237ff., in WLS 1, #229, p. 75)

One cannot rightly treat any sentence of scripture merely as separable words without attending to how they relate to each other and to their context of meaning. Tertullian stated this principle of interpretation:

One's aim is carefully to determine the sense of the words consistently with that reason which is the guiding principle in all interpretation. No divine saying is so unconnected and diffuse, that its words only are to be insisted on, and their connection left undetermined. (Tertullian, "On Prescription Against Heretics," Ch. IX, ANF III, p. 247)*

The operative distinction here is between the words themselves and their relationship to each other. Scripture is composed of coherent sentences, not separable individual words. The plain sense of scripture is to be sought, but that may require a figurative interpretation. How, then, shall one know when a scriptural command is to be interpreted figuratively?

If a command seems to order something immoral or criminal, or to forbid what is useful or beneficial, then it is figurative. "Unless," he says, "you eat the flesh, and drink the blood, of the Son of Man, you will not have life in yourselves" [John 6:53]. This seems to order crime or immorality: therefore it is figurative, and enjoins that we should participate in the Passion of the Lord, and store up in our memory, for our joy and our profit, the fact that his flesh was crucified and wounded for us. (Augustine, *On Christian Doctrine*, Bk. III, Ch. 16, sec. 24, LCF, p. 246; cf. NPNF 1, II, p. 563)

This Part of our collection has attempted to bring together texts that place human caring in the context of divine care. God the Spirit is the prototypical Counselor whose wisdom human counsel may to some degree refract. Scripture is the most reliable source of understanding of God's own caring for humanity and the world. The best pastoral care is that formed by the Spirit's active address through Scripture.

4 Seasonable Wisdom: The Timing of Good Counsel

A GOOD MAXIM given at a bad time is full of mischief. Astute timing of pertinent communications is a central feature of pastoral wisdom. The following selections reveal how important this contextual feature of pastoral care has been from the outset of the pastoral tradition, and how frequently it has been explored and interpreted.

I. 🍂 GREGORY NAZIANZEN'S PRINCIPLE OF VARIABLE RESPONSIVENESS

How do temperament and context impact upon a particular moment of pastoral care? The most widely quoted classical answer to this question is an incisive passage from Gregory Nazianzen. Strictly speaking Gregory did not invent this idea—it can be found in Ignatius, Clement of Alexandria, and others, but he gave the principle its classic formulation as a central premise of pastoral care:

How great is the difference between pastoral counsel for the married and the unmarried. Significant differences remain between those who live alone compared to those who live together. And even among celibates who live in a community, there are still important differences in counseling those advanced and those beginning in the art of contemplation. Differences abound between pastoral care for urban and rural folk, between the simple and the crafty, between persons of leisure and persons of affairs, between those who have met with reverses and those who in their prosperity have never experienced misfortune. If you compare the temperaments of these persons you will see that they differ more widely than they differ even in physical features. So to give pertinent guidance to them is no easy task.

The principle is this: just as the same food and medicine is not appropriate to every bodily ailment, so neither is the same treatment and discipline proper for the guidance of souls. Those with

109

wide pastoral experience will best know how to recognize the difference. Some persons are better motivated by words, others by example. Some who are sluggish and dull need to be stirred up to the good, while others are already inordinately fervent and so rushed about that they need to be calmed. Praise will benefit some, while correction will benefit others, provided that *each counsel is administered in a seasonable way*. Out of season counsel may do more harm than good.

Some respond best to confidential correction, while others seem unmovable except by public rebuke. Some pay no attention to a private admonition but are easily corrected if it risks public embarrassment, while others cannot bear a public disgrace and would if publicly rebuked grow morose and impatient, yet they would be happy to accept quiet correctives in response to sympathetic treatment. Some make it necessary to watch them closely even to the minutest details because they prefer to hide their faults and arrogate to themselves the praise of being politic and crafty. Toward others, however, it is better to take no notice as if seeing we do not see and hearing we do not hear. For if we call their faults to their attention, we may bring them to despair so that even with repeated reminders they tend recklessly to lose self-respect and grow in their guilt. In some cases it is necessary that the pastor show anger in the interest of love, or seem to despair of a parishioner as if a hopeless case, even though from another perspective he is far from hopeless.

Each pastoral response hinges strongly on the particular temperament of the person. Some we must treat with meekness in order to encourage them to a better hope. Others seem to require that we combat and conquer them and never yield an inch.

The pastoral principle: variability. All persons are not to be treated in the same way. We do not simply say this is virtue and this is vice uncontextually. For one spiritual remedy may prove dangerous in some cases and wholesome in other cases. The right medicine must be applied for the right occasion as the temper of the patient allows and as the time and circumstance and disposition of the individual indicate. This, of course, is the most difficult aspect of pastoral wisdom, to know how to distinguish which counsel is needed in which situation with a precise judgment so as to administer appropriate remedies for different temperaments. Only actual experience and practice are the basis for skillfully applying this art. (Gregory Nazianzen, Oration II.28–33, NPNF 2, III, pp. 210–211)*

This great text established a cluster of maxims of pastoral care that had previously been intuited, but never so clearly and systematically stated: (1) Temperaments differ widely. (2) Each pastoral response hinges on the specific contours of individual temperament. (3) No two persons need precisely the same pastoral care. (4) Otherwise good counsel, if unseasonable, may harm. (5) Hence the right remedy must be applied to the right occasion.

II. 🐝 INDIVIDUATION OF TREATMENT CONSISTENT WITH DOCTRINAL UNITY

These maxims of Gregory Nazianzen have been confirmed many times by many subsequent teachers of the pastoral tradition. The pastoral care of each individual is different. Soul care is gauged to context. Yet this does not imply that there are no general rules whatever that govern pastoral care.

Two centuries later Gregory the Great reflected practically upon how the pastor's counsel can be adapted to each personal situation, yet still maintain the unity of apostolic teaching. It is only by attending carefully to the context that the apostolic teaching can be meaningfully stated and appropriated:

Discourse. . . . should be adapted to the character of the hearers, so as to be suited to the individual in his respective needs. . . . Hence, too, every teacher, in order to edify all in the one virtue of charity, must touch the hearts of his hearers by using one and the same doctrine, but not by giving to all one and the same exhortation. . . . Wherefore, the words of a preacher should be quickly adapted to the life led by his hearer (Gregory the Great, *Pastoral Care*, Part III, Ch. 2, ACW 11, pp. 90, 93)

Here is the paradox that defies a purely relativistic situationalism: Only if one is grounded in consensual Christian teaching is one well prepared to respond attentively to the uniqueness of ever varying circumstances of need. When such counsel is given should the counselor offer the individual only one correct path, or examine varied alternatives?

A cautious guide points out many paths, so that each one may proceed along that which he wishes and considers suitable for himself, provided he happens on one by which he can reach the camp. (Ambrose, *Letters*, To the Church at Vercelli, FC 26, p. 335)

The acceptable paths to be pointed out may be many, but there are two necessary requirements for pathfinding: The individual must recognize inwardly that the best path feels intuitively right and suitable for himself; and the guide must make sure that the path chosen, even if chosen among many alternatives, will lead in the right direction.

We do not forfeit unity in the bond of love when we affirm the diversity of situational responses:

> Each soul has its own proper nutriment; some growing by knowledge and science, and others feeding on the Hellenic philosophy, the whole of which, like nuts, is not eatable. "And he that planteth and he that watereth," "being ministers" of Him "that gives the increase, are one" in the ministry [1 Cor. 3:7, 8]. (Clement of Alexandria, *The Stromata, or Miscellanies*, Bk. I, Ch. I, ANF II, p. 300)

If it is not proper to offer each soul the same food, how shall one determine what is needed most? Some need philosophical understanding more than scientific information, but if either are eaten exclusively, they will be as indigestible as are nuts if eaten alone. Using the metaphor of diversity of gifts, Clement celebrated as a gift of providence this recurrent situation of variability of need, wherein one may respond rightly at one stage in one way while another way is fitting at a different stage. Only through such a diversity of gifts can the unity of ministry be manifested. The Didache pointed to three types of pastoral responses that differ according to circumstances:

> Some you are to reprove, some to pray for, and some again to love more than your own life. (*Didache*, sec. 3, ECW, p. 228)

The pastoral eye must be trained to recognize who needs which. In all this diversity, should priority be given to bodily over spiritual needs? There are some memorable maxims of the earliest oral and written tradition that help train the eye to situational responsiveness, which were passed along by Ignatius of Antioch. That these maxims have been preserved since the third generation of believers is remarkable:

> Vindicate your office with all care both fleshly and spiritual. Think upon unity, than which nothing is better. Lift up all men, as the Lord lifts you; put up with all in love. . . . Bring the more troublesome into subjection by gentleness. "Not all wounds are healed by the same plaster [salve]." "Relieve convulsions by moist applications." "Be prudent as the serpent" in every matter "and sincere as the dove" (Matt. 10:16). You are both fleshly and spiritual for this reason, that you may deal gently with what appears before your face; but ask that invisible things may be made manifest to you so that you may lack nothing and abound in every gift of grace. The occasion calls upon you to attain to God, just as pilots seek winds and the storm-tossed sailor a harbor. . . . Stand

firm as a hammered anvil. Great athletes are battered, but yet they win. (Ignatius of Antioch, *Letter to Polycarp*, sec. 1:2–3:1, AF, pp. 116–117)

These maxims work off of the tension between inner stability and situational variability. The leading images—anvil, harbor, wind, and athletic struggle—suggest reliability and centeredness which are thereby able to make situational adjustments. The wounds differ but the athletic purpose persists. The storms differ but the pilot's intelligence remains centered. The cohesion of purpose, far from being destroyed, is sustained by the variability of response.

Gregory the Great succinctly illustrated how good counsel for one is harmful counsel for another, acknowledging his debt to Gregory Nazianzen:

Long before us Gregory of Nazianzus of revered memory has taught, one and the same exhortation is not suited to all, because they are not compassed by the same quality of character. Often, for instance, what is profitable to some, harms others. Thus, too, herbs which nourish some animals, kill others; gentle hissing that calms horses, excites young puppies; medicine that alleviates one disease, aggravates another; and bread such as strengthens the life of robust men, destroys that of little children. (Gregory the Great, *Pastoral Care*, Part III, Prologue, ACW 11, p. 89)

Thus there was no naive assumption in classical pastoral care that a single remedy is always the correct one irrespective of circumstances. Rather, exceptional attention was given to situationality, timeliness, and prudent judgment relating norm and context.

III. 🐑 THE UNITY AND COHERENCE OF SITUATIONAL COUNSEL

Given the principle of varied responsiveness, more must be said about the underlying unity of pastoral care that is sustained even through its situational varieties. Otherwise one might gain the mistaken impression that pastoral wisdom is pervaded by moral relativism. Some may prematurely seize this principle of variability without understanding its more fundamental hidden unity. What enables such a situationally-based process to cohere?

The deceitful and treacherous guide . . . leads the luxurious in one direction, and those who are called temperate in another; the ignorant in one direction, the learned in another; the sluggish in one direction, the active in another. . . . But nevertheless all those paths which display an appearance of honors are not different roads, but turnings off and bypaths, which appear indeed to be separated from that common one, and to branch off to the right, but yet return to the same, and all lead at the very end to one issue. . . . But this way—which is that of truth, and wisdom, and virtue, and justice, of all which there is but one fountain, one source of strength, one abode—is both simple, because with like minds, and with the utmost agreement, we follow and worship one God; and it is narrow, because virtue is given to the smaller number; and steep, because goodness, which is very high and lofty, cannot be attained to without the greatest difficulty and labor. (Lactantius, *The Divine Institutes*, Bk. VI, Ch. VII, ANF VII, p. 170)

Counsel, despite its variability, is fundamentally centered and focused in simplicity upon the here and now address of God, and in this sense it is steep and narrow. The principle of variability must not be recklessly separated from its self-authenticating center, so as to be reduced merely to emotive self-indulgence or situational self-actualization. The counsels of license only have the appearance of flexibility, while they actually tend toward unconstrained expression of emotive impulse, an embittering tyrant.

Clement of Alexandria set forth this series of distinctions that must be sorted out contextually:

Ruling, then, over himself and what belongs to him, and possessing a sure grasp of divine science, he makes a genuine approach to the truth. . . . One must learn to see what is conjoined and what is disjoined. One must distinguish between the position each one holds and the power and service each contributes; between what one is and what one has been given either naturally or preternaturally; between activity and passivity; between one's virtues and one's vices; between things good and bad, and those indifferent; and between moral virtues like courage, prudence and self-restraint on the one hand, and on the other hand that righteousness that completes all virtues. (Clement of Alexandria, *The Stromata, or Miscellanies*, Bk. VII, Ch. III, ANF II, p. 527)*

Learning to make such distinctions contextually is the constant task of the wise counselor. The ability to distinguish between activity and passivity must have presented the same challenges for Clement as it did later for Freud. The knower must recognize the difference between a person's social location and his actual power of functioning, as much for Clement as later for K. Marx or M. Weber or C. W. Mills or J. Habermas.

What specific varieties of temperaments and personality types must the care-giver serve? If pastors are to be prepared to meet this variety, they need some sense of its range. An inventory of personal differences was set forth by Gregory the Great in the sixth century. In each case counsel requires precise discernment of these differences:

In giving admonition we must distinguish between:
men and women;
the young and the old;
the poor and the rich;
the joyful and the sad;
subjects and superior;
slaves and masters;
the wise of this world and the dull;
the impudent and the timid;
the insolent and the fainthearted;
the impatient and the patient;
the kindly and the envious;
the sincere and the insincere;
the hale and the sick;
those who fear afflictions and, therefore, live innocently,
and those so hardened in evil as to be impervious to the
correction of affliction;
the taciturn and the loquacious;
the slothful and the hasty;
the meek and the choleric;
the humble and the haughty;
the obstinate and the fickle;
the gluttonous and the abstemious;
those who mercifully give of their own
and those addicted to thieving;
those who do not steal yet do not give of their own, and
those who do not give of their own yet do not desist from
despoiling others;
those living in discord and those living in peace;
those who do not understand correctly the words of the
Holy Law and those who do, but utter them without humility;
those who, though capable of preaching worthily, yet are
afraid to do so from excessive humility, and those whose
unfitness or age debars them from preaching, yet who are
impelled thereto by their hastiness;
those who prosper in their pursuit of temporal things,
and those who desire, indeed, the things of the world
yet are wearied by suffering and adversity;

those who are bound in wedlock and those who are free
from the ties of wedlock;
those who have had carnal intercourse and those who have
had no such experience;
those who grieve for sins of deed and those who grieve for
sins of thought only;
those who grieve for their sins yet do not abandon them,
and those who abandon their sins yet do not grieve
for them;
those who even approve of their misdeeds and those who
confess their sins yet do not shun them;
those who are overcome by sudden concupiscence, and
those who deliberately put on the fetter of sin;
those who commit only small sins but commit them
frequently, and those who guard themselves against small
sins yet sometimes sink into grave ones;
those who do not even begin to do good and those who
begin but do not finish;
those who do evil secretly and good openly, and those who
hide the good they do, yet allow themselves to be thought
ill of because of some things they do in public.
But what is the use of running through all these groups
and cataloguing them, if we do not also explain the several
methods of giving admonitions to each with what brevity
we can? (Gregory the Great, *Pastoral Care*, Part III, Ch. 1,
ACW 11, pp.90–92)*

The entire third book of Gregory's *Pastoral Care*, the heart of the treatise, is effectively summarized by the above paragraph. The argument
following this introduction proceeds to discuss each distinction separately, and how pastoral practice varies with each.
   This variability principle was similarly applied in Protestant pastoral
care:

We must study to build up those who are already truly con-
verted. In this respect our work is various, according to the various states of Christians.
   There are many of our flock that are young and weak, who,
though they are of long standing, are yet of small proficiency
or strength. This, indeed, is the most common condition of
the godly. . . . One word of seasonable, prudent advice, given by
a minister to persons in necessity, may be of more use than
many sermons. . . . The last class whom I shall here notice, as

requiring our attention, are the strong; for they, also, have need of our assistance: partly to preserve the grace they have; partly to help them in making further progress. (Baxter, *RP*, p. 97, 100)

Those who wrongly imagine an ethic of context to be an invention of the twentieth century do well to study this variability principle, which has stably accompanied pastoral care through centuries of change.

IV. 🍂 ANALOGIES OF FLEXIBLE CONTINGENCY MANAGEMENT

Four metaphors have assisted the pastoral writers in setting forth this key principle of variable responsiveness. The pastor deals with emergency variables much like a high seas navigator, a military logistics coordinator, a surgeon, or a wrestler:

(1) The Navigator

Clement of Alexandria summarized the task of the soul guide under the metaphor of a navigator—practiced in contingency management, tough, aware, trim.

The guide is like a navigator directing the ship according to the star; prepared to hold himself in readiness for every suitable action; accustomed to despise all difficulties and dangers when it is necessary to undergo them; never doing anything precipitate or incongruous either to himself or the common weal; taking thought for the future; and not captive to his emotions either in waking hours or in dreams. For, accustomed to spare living and frugality, he is moderate, active, and serious; requiring few necessaries for life; occupying himself with nothing superfluous. (Clement of Alexandria, *The Stromata, or Miscellanies*, Bk. VI, Ch. IX, ANF II, p. 498)*

Guiding the soul through troublesome times is something like guiding a ship through hazardous waters.

(2) The Military Logistics Coordinator

The pastor is no narrow specialist. Versatility is required to work with varied data. John Chrysostom applied a logistics metaphor to the variable requirements of pastoral counsel. The scene is a battlefield. The opposing army is powerful, flexible, and determined:

For our preparation is not against a single kind of attack. This warfare of ours assumes complex forms and is waged by various enemies. They do not all use the same weapons and they have not all trained to attack us in the same manner. Anyone who undertakes to fight them all must know the arts of all. He must be at the same time archer and slinger, cavalry officer and infantry officer, private soldier and general, foot-soldier and hussar, marine and engineer. In military warfare each man is given a particular task and repulses the attacker in that particular way. But in our warfare this is not so. Unless the man who means to win understands every aspect of the art, the devil knows how to introduce his agents at a single neglected spot and so to plunder the flock. But he is baffled when he sees that the shepherd has mastered his whole repertoire and thoroughly understands his tricks. (Chrysostom, *On the Priesthood*, Ch. IV.3, p. 116)

Soul care is something like being a defensive commander of an army deploying forces sparely and astutely. The Enemy is wily, opportunistic, and well-prepared for any combat. So must the pastor be.

(3) The Surgeon

At times an act of soul care is like a moment of surgery:

Sometimes what serves as a medicine for one is poison for another; and sometimes something given to one and the same person at a suitable time serves as a medicine, but at the wrong time it is a poison. I have seen an unskilled physician who, by subjecting to dishonor a sick man who was contrite in spirit, only drove him to despair. And I have seen a skilled physician who operated on an arrogant heart with the knife of dishonor, and drained it of all its evil-smelling pus. (Climacus, *The Ladder of Divine Ascent*, Step 26, sec. 25f., p. 166)

If the pastor must use a spiritual lancet, he must make precisely the right move at precisely the right time.

(4) The Wrestler

So deft must be the timing of the physician of souls that Gregory the Great compared it to the movement of a wrestler, dodging this blow, taking that unexpected action, and working on several ploys at the same time. This becomes particularly difficult when dealing with persons who experience contrary compulsions and ambivalences:

It is, indeed, difficult for a preacher in speaking to a congregation to pay regard to the hidden emotions and motives of individuals, and after the manner of the wrestlers, to turn skillfully from side to side. But the burden of his task is much heavier, when he has to preach to an individual who is a slave to contrary vices. Take the common case of one of a quite too gay temperament becoming extremely depressed, when sadness suddenly comes upon him. Here the preacher must take care to dispel the temporary sadness, without permitting his gay temperament to assert itself too much; at the same time he must so moderate his gay nature as not to aggravate the temporary sadness. Here is a man burdened with the habit of inordinate hastiness, but now and then, when something should be done quickly, he is thwarted by fear, gripping him suddenly. Another man is burdened with the habit of immoderate fear, yet occasionally is impelled by rash precipitancy to fulfill some desire or other. Consequently, in the one the sudden fear must be repressed, but so that his persistent precipitancy does not increase; in the other his sudden hastiness must be checked, but so that his temperamental fear does not revive. Indeed, is it a matter of wonder that the physicians of souls should be on their guard in such cases, seeing that those who heal, not hearts, but bodies, regulate their treatment with such skillful discrimination? Often, for instance, a violent illness assails the weak body, and such illness should really be treated with the antidote of drastic remedies, and yet a weak body cannot endure a strong remedy. The doctor, therefore, makes it his business to draw out the present malady in such a way that the existing weakness of the body is not increased, lest perchance the illness ends with life itself. He, therefore, compounds the remedy with such great refinement, that at the one and the same time he counteracts both the malady and the infirmity. If, then, medicine for the body can be so compounded and administered as to serve separate ends—for it is then truly medicine when it serves as a remedy for an existing disease, while at the same time meeting the needs of the prevailing constitution—why should medicine for the soul, administered by one and the same preaching, fail to be able to combat moral evils of different kinds, seeing that it is a more delicate art, in that it deals with what is unseen? (Gregory the Great, *Pastoral Care*, Part III, Ch. 37, ACW 11, pp. 228, 229)

Under complicated conditions of contrary compulsions, the physician of souls must act, like a wrestler, to set up one defense without becoming vulnerable to another attack. Deftness, strength, agility, and flexibility are marks of the wrestler. Here the principle of variability of treatment becomes highly refined: one must provide a remedy that does not tend toward a new symptom.

V. 🦋 CIRCUMSTANCE

Degree of need is a significant determinant of pastoral response. Baxter anticipated the triage principle:

He that seeth one man sick of a mortal disease, and another only pained with the toothache, will be moved more to compassionate the former, than the latter; and will surely make more haste to help him, though he were a stranger, and the other a brother or a son. (Baxter, *RP*, pp. 94–95)

The performance of pastoral duty must be suited to the occasion. Thomas Aquinas defined the notion of circumstance in a way that illuminates the particularities of any discrete situation to which counsel is addressed.

Circumstance means something standing around the substance of the act and yet somehow touching it. This may happen in three ways: first, as touching the act itself; second, as touching the cause of the act; third, as touching the effect.

Now, it touches the act either through quantity, of time or place; or through the quality of the act, e.g., the way of acting. From the standpoint of the effect, we refer to what a man did. From the side of the cause of the act, in respect to the final cause, the reference is to that *for which*; in respect to the material cause or object, it is that *in which*; in respect to the principal, efficient cause, it is *who acted*; and in respect to their instrumental, efficient cause, it is *by what means*.

The motive force and object of the will is the end. Therefore, the most important circumstance is that which touches the act from its end aspect, namely that for the sake of which; secondarily, it is that touching the very substance of the act, i.e., what one did. (Thomas Aquinas, *Summa Theologica*, Part I–II, Q. 7, Art. 3, 4, AR, p. 344; cf. Vol. II, p. 625, italics added)

A multi-layered cause-effect analysis illumines the context of duty. Analysis of context is illumined by accurately describing: When and where is the act itself occurring? What is causing the act—especially what is its purpose or end (its final cause, in addition to its material and efficient causes)? And what effects does the act have?

Erasmus thought that the ancients had recognized that an extreme or wooden concept of equal justice can become unjust:

However, Plato did not think that everything should be offered equally to young and old, learned and unlearned, stupid and wise, strong and weak, but that distribution should be made to each according to his worth. Otherwise, as he says in the same passage, "to unequal people equal things will be unequal," and just as extreme right turns into extreme wrong, so equality pushed to extremes becomes extreme inequality. (Erasmus, "Adages," I i 2/ LB II 14F, in *Collected Works*, Vol. 31, p. 31)

If ten people are waiting in a line for emergency treatment, and one is extremely weak and vulnerable to immediate death, one does not treat all equally. For in that case it would be unjust to treat all equally.

Ambrose viewed Paul as the model of flexibility of response in good counsel:

Such, then, ought he to be who gives counsel to another, in order that he may offer himself as a pattern in all good works, in teaching, in trueness of character, in seriousness. Thus his words will be wholesome and irreproachable, his counsel useful, his life virtuous, and his opinions seemly.

Such was Paul, who gave counsel. . . . Therefore the man of good counsel says: "I have learnt in whatsoever state I am therewith to be content" [Phil. 4:11]. . . . Sufficient for me, he says, is what I have; whether I have little or much, to me it is much. It seems as though he wanted to state it as clearly as possible. . . . Gloriously, therefore, does he say: "I know how to be abased" [Phil. 4:12], that is to say, where, in what moderation, to what end, in what duty, in which office. The Pharisee knew not how to be abased, therefore he was cast down. The publican knew, and therefore he was justified.

Paul knew, too, how to abound, for he had a rich soul, though he possessed not the treasure of a rich man. He knew how to abound, for he sought no gift in money but looked for fruit in grace. (Ambrose, *Duties of the Clergy*, Bk. II, Ch. XVII, secs. 86, 89–91, NPNF 2, X, p. 57)

Each pastoral response has its own unique time. Hence it requires an astute sense of timing. Knowing when to fulfill a duty is as important as to know formally what one's duty is. Ambrose provided these comic illustrations:

If you restore money to a raving lunatic when he cannot keep it; if you hold up to a madman a sword that had been earlier set aside, by which he may kill himself, is it not an act contrary to duty to complete the transaction? Is it not contrary to duty to take knowingly what has been stolen by a thief, so that he who has lost it is cheated out of it?. . . . [Pastors need to] know the times for the fulfilling of their duty, as also which duty is the greater, which the lesser, and to what occasion each is suited. (Ambrose, *Duties of the Clergy*, Bk. II, Ch. 50, secs. 263, 267, NPNF 2, X, pp. 42–43)*

VI. 🐝 Pastoral Discernment

To discern is to recognize the difference between things that are otherwise quite similar, to see finer threads of distinctions clearly, to see subtle differences or similarities of color, texture, or timing, and to penetrate the layers of confusion or clouds of ambiguity, so as to be able to articulate distinctions accurately.

An important aspect of discernment in the classical pastoral tradition has been the attempt to see how the Spirit through scripture addresses the highly specific situation of a particular person at a given time. Various scripture texts may seem competitively to apply to a given situation:

Let us hearken to Divine Scripture when it says concerning some, "Cut it down, why cumbereth it the ground?" [Luke 8:7] And, "Put away from yourselves that wicked person" [I Cor. 5:13] and, "Pray not for this people" [Jer. 7:16], which was also said concerning Saul [I Kings 14:1]. The shepherd must know for whom, and in what manner, and when all these measures are to be applied. . . . The guide ought not to tell all those who come to him that the way is strait and narrow, nor should he say to each that the yoke is easy and the burden is light. Rather, he should examine the case of each man and prescribe medicines which are suitable. To those who are weighed down by grievous sins and are prone to despair, he should administer the second as an appropriate remedy, but to those who are inclined to haughtiness and conceit, the first. (Climacus, *To the Shepherd*, sec. 29, p. 32, in *The Ladder of Divine Ascent*, p. 236)

Each and every scripture must not be bluntly or indiscriminately applied to a context. An important aspect of pastoral wisdom is the discernment of how the Spirit is addressing a currently developing situation. This is why overly simplified views of absolute equality fail to grasp the complex contextuality of pastoral care. Though every person is equal in dignity, each person's history and emergent situation is unique. Therefore persons are not to be treated the same as if they had no pertinent differences in situation:

It is impossible to treat all his people in one way, any more than it would be right for the doctors to deal with all their patients alike or a helmsman to know only one way of battling with the winds. (John Chrysostom, *On the Priesthood*, Ch. VI.4, p. 142)

Luther provided a clear statement of the reason why no single standard of moderation can be uniformly applied in a strict rule ethic:

St. Peter does not want to prescribe any rule, measure, or limit concerning moderation, as the monastic orders have undertaken to do. They desired to achieve all by rule, and they framed statutes which were to be exactly observed. It is not to be tolerated in Christendom that men should establish by laws a generally applicable standard of moderation. For people are different; one is of a strong, another of a weaker nature, and the condition of no person is in every respect and always the same as that of another. For this reason everybody should keep an eye on himself in order to determine what his condition is, and what he is able to bear. (Luther, "Sermons on the Second Epistle of St. Peter," WLS 1, #1284, p. 432; cf. LW, 30, p. 156; WA 14, p. 20)

If temperaments differ, then the capacity of persons to receive and assimilate counsel differs. The prudent application of good counsel will be attentive precisely to these differences. John Climacus, who stood in the center of the monastic tradition Luther was criticizing, was very close to Luther on this point:

It often happens that a way that is unsuitable for one just fits another; and the intention of both is acceptable to the Lord. (Climacus, *The Ladder of Divine Ascent*, Step 26, sec. 105, p. 177)

A case study of the suitability principle comes from a remarkable incident in the beleaguered career of Menno Simons, founder of the Mennonites. Normally one would expect that pastoral care be provided openly, and not in secret. Yet the political circumstances of persecution under which Menno was working caused him to write the following defense, under circumstances of extreme persecution, of a concealed ministry done by night and by stealth in order to save lives:

He accuses us of preaching at night. . . . We sometimes do have to prosecute the Lord's Word and work at night. This is largely due, I fear, to Gellius and the learned ones. For they have so embittered and still embitter all lords, princes, rulers, and magistrates against us by their hateful, unmerited revilings, slanderings, and defamings that we cannot, alas, move them sufficiently with Scriptures, supplications, tears, misery, sorrow, loss of possessions, blood, or life, and so that we cannot secure a promise of safe conduct to face these evident enemies of the cross of Christ to defend the doctrine of God, the blessed truth. But we must (we preachers, that is) regularly conceal ourselves, in shops and secret places, from the persecutors and the bloodthirsty, if we do not wish, all of us, to be rent into pieces and devoured by the terrible beasts which come up out of the sea.

Dear readers, observe well what I write. . . . About the year 1539, a householder who was a very pious man, named Tjaert Reynerdson, was seized in my stead, because out of compassion and love he had received me in his house secretly. He was a few days later put on the wheel after a free confession of faith, as a valiant knight of Christ, after the example of his Lord, although even his enemies testified that he was a pious man without reproach. Also in 1546, at a place where they boast of the Word, a four-room house was confiscated, because the owner had rented one of the rooms for a short time, unknown to anybody, to my poor sick wife and her little ones. What edicts have been read against some of us in some cities and countries, and what fines stipulated, what imperial mandates and condemnations of the Roman Empire have been resolved against us, and how we are treated everywhere is not unknown to Gellius and to the preachers of his class. That they are the real cause and instigators of these things, I write and testify without hesitation. (Menno Simons, Reply to Gellius Faber, *CWMS*, p. 634)

Under violent circumstances it became evidently proper to engage in a non-canonical act (preach in secret at night) that one would not ordinarily do. Discernment seeks to make just such distinctions with wisdom and prudence.

Whether action or contemplation is more needed is itself a question of discernment:

The wages of self-mastery are detachment; of faith, knowledge. Now detachment begets discernment, while knowledge love for God. The mind that follows well the active life advances in prudence; the contemplative life, in knowledge. To the one it belongs to bring the contender to a discernment of virtue and vice; to the other, to lead the participant to the essences of the incorporeal and corporeal creation. (Maximus the Confessor, *The Four Centuries on Charity*, Ch. 2, sec. 25–26, ACW 21, p. 157)

Action increases moral prudence which learns to discern differences between vice and virtue in a given situation; contemplation increases spiritual knowledge, which learns to discern the difference between finitude and God, nature and self-transcendence, body and spirit.

When the pastoral tradition speaks of the need for discernment of thoughts, passions and virtues, it is not always referring to something completely other than what modern writers might call intuitive insight, self-understanding, or discrete self-awareness. This capacity grows slowly through variable developmental stages which culminate in a fully matured life of love. The wind does not blow the same way every day, as John Climacus remarked:

> Discernment in beginners is true knowledge of themselves; in intermediate souls, it is a spiritual sense that faultlessly distinguishes what is truly good from what is of nature and opposed to it; and in the perfect, it is the knowledge which they have within by Divine illumination, and which can enlighten with its lamp what is dark in others. Or perhaps, generally speaking, discernment is, and is recognized as, the certain understanding of the Divine will on all occasions, in every place and in all matters; and it is only found in those who are pure in heart, and in body and in mouth.... After God, let us have our conscience as our mentor and rule in all things, so that we may know which way the wind is blowing and set our sails accordingly. In all our actions in which we try to please God, the demons dig three pits for us. By the first, they endeavour to prevent any good at all from being done. By the second, after their first defeat, they try to secure that it should not be done according to the will of God. But when these rogues fail in this too, then, standing quietly before our soul, they praise us for living a thoroughly godly life. The first is to be opposed by zeal and fear of death, the second by obedience and humiliation, and the third by unceasing self-condemnation. (Climacus, *The Ladder of Divine Ascent*, Step 26, secs. 1–7, pp. 161–162)

Discernment of oneself, discernment of good and evil, and finally divine illumination are distinguishable stages. The variable demonic temptations must be resisted throughout, yet in different ways for different seasons. At the end of the process, self-condemnation may seem an exaggerated notion, but the ascetics thought that it was the only way to counteract the demonic temptation to pride.

Quality of discernment distinguishes the helpful counselor from the inexperienced and harmful counselor:

> Many inexperienced persons have done damage to many unwise people, for which they will be judged in eternity. Everyone does not have the right to guide others, but only those who have been endowed with divine discernment according to the Apostle, namely, that discerning of spirits which distinguishes good from

evil by the sword of the Word. Every person has his own natural reason and discernment, either practical or scientific, but not all have discerning of spirits. Therefore the wise man of Sirach says: "Be in peace with many: nevertheless have but one counselor in a thousand." It is difficult to find a guide unerring either in deeds, words, or understanding. A person who is without error can be recognized if he has his testimony from the Scriptures both for personal practice and for understanding, and is humbly wise in the sphere of wisdom. For it takes no small amount of labor to know truth clearly and to keep away from what is opposed to grace. For the devil is accustomed to present his illusions in the garb of truth, especially to beginners. (Gregory of Sinai, *Rules for Hesychasts*, MPG 150, WSD, p. 42)

VII. ❦ THE EXQUISITE TIMING OF SEASONABLE COUNSEL

Since changing symptoms require specific treatments, timing is of the essence of counsel. The situation-specificity of good counsel is absolutely critical to its proper functioning. A brilliant word spoken at an inopportune time can be ill-advised counsel. The pastoral tradition has thought profoundly about the mysteries of time in counsel, and the synchronicity of need and word. In the passages that follow, we will explore how this conjunction has been understood.

It is characteristic of compulsive and immature perfectionism to seek too early to do a completed good without adequate growing time and inward preparation. Why, John Climacus speculated, does the Deceiver so desperately want us to desire impossible virtues prematurely, ill-timed to our capacity to actualize them?

The devil suggests to those living in obedience the desire for impossible virtues. Similarly, to those living in stillness he proposes unsuitable ideas. Scan the mind of inexperienced novices and there you will find deluded notions: a desire for stillness, for the strictest fast, for uninterrupted prayer, for absolute freedom from vanity, for unbroken remembrance of death, for continual compunction, for perfect freedom from anger, for deep silence, for surpassing purity. And if, by divine providence, they are without these to start with, they leap in vain from one thing to another, having been deceived. For the enemy urges them to seek these perfections prematurely, so that they may not persevere and attain them in due course. (Climacus, *The Ladder of Divine Ascent*, Step 4, sec. 118, p. 52)

In this way the devil uses against us even our best motivations. If you were trying to think of a way to prevent perseverance, or set obstacles in the way of slow, steady growth toward behavioral excellences, wouldn't you want to hold out the tempting idea that these excellences would be quite easily achieved, and immediately available? So Climacus reasoned about the demonic.

This raises the intriguing issue of whether the hard-won insight of yesterday can be directly applied to problems to be faced tomorrow. Ambrose commented on the Exodus passage in which the miraculous food, manna, is said to have lasted only a single day:

This manna, therefore, was fine and it was gathered each day, not kept for the day following, because what wisdom finds in a moment is more pleasing, nor is that more admirable for being found in leisure time than what is struck at once from the spark of genius. It may be that future mysteries are revealed: the manna kept until sunrise is unfit to be eaten (Ambrose, *Letters*, 77, To Irenaeus. *FC* 26, p. 434)

If the manna of Moses' journey is viewed metaphorically as wisdom, then the conclusion is that it is dangerous to use one day's wisdom for another day. For the faithful pilgrim, each day's wisdom is given as if miraculously on that day alone, and cannot be gained in advance.

There are some times when the possibility of renewal of spirit seems to be quite out of reach, when no manna is given, when truth seems totally eclipsed. A different sort of spiritual discipline is required to sustain one amid such droughts:

Abba Poemen asked [Abba Macarius] weeping: "Give me a word that I may be saved." But the old man replied, "What you are looking for has disappeared now from among monks." (Macarius the Great, in *Sayings of the Desert Fathers*, sec. 25, p. 112)

Hugh of St. Victor warned against focussing inordinately upon the immediate results of a good action. Pursue the good directly and let the long range consequences overrule immediate setbacks:

Let him not trust too much to fortune when she smiles, or lose his confidence when things go badly; and let it be a matter of indifference to him whether the result that he achieves be good or bad. (Hugh of St. Victor, *SSW*, p. 111)

In travelling, the pastor does not leave behind his ministry. Each occasion brings a new opportunity to extend ministry:

The Country Parson, when a just occasion calleth him out of his Parish (which he diligently and strictly weigheth, his parish being all his joy and thought), leaveth not his Ministry behind him, but is himself wherever he is. Therefore those he meets on the way he blesseth audibly; and with those he overtakes, or that overtake him, he begins good discourses, such as may edify; interposing sometimes some short and honest refreshments. (Geo. Herbert, *CP*, Ch. XVII, CWS, p. 78)

In what way does the soul guide offer aid to some by positive, others by negative, reinforcement, some gently and others toughly?

The benign Educator bestows aid on us in different ways, now offering advice, now rebuke; He holds up to us the dishonor reaped by those who have sinned, and reveals the punishment they have merited, both to attract our notice and to warn us. In this way does He devise a gentle means of restraining us from evil, by such a picture of those who have already suffered. He forcibly deters those who are bent on evil by these images, hinders some who are ready to dare similar crimes, strengthens others in their endurance, draws still others from evil, and heals many, converting them to a better life by letting them see such an image. (Clement of Alexandria, *Christ the Educator*, Bk. III, Ch. 8.43, FC 23, p. 234)

Inquirers should be encouraged to take due time before making solemn commitments that may not be fulfilled. This was especially so during periods of persecution. At times a trial period was advised for persons considering the narrow way. In the pre-Nicene novel called The Recognitions of Clement, Peter was portrayed as advising Clement, whose father was considering conversion:

I am afraid that you will urge [him] too soon to take upon himself the yoke of religion while he is not yet prepared for it, and to this he may perhaps consent through his affection for you. But this is not a course to be depended upon. For what is done for the sake of men is not worthy of approbation and soon falls to pieces. Therefore it seems to me that you should permit him to live for a year according to his own judgment, and during that time he may travel with us, and while we are instructing others he may hear with simplicity, and as he hears if he has any right purpose of acknowledging the truth, he will himself request that he may take up the yoke of religion. Or if he does not please to take it up, he may remain a friend. For those who do not take it up heartily, at the point when they begin not to be able to bear it, not only cast off that which they had taken up, but by way of excuse, as it were, for their weakness, they begin to speak evil of the way of religion, and to malign those whom they have not been able to follow or to imitate. (Clementina, *Recognitions of Clement*, Bk. X., Ch. I, ANF VIII, p. 192)*

The yoke of rigorous commitment must be freely chosen, not forced, or rushed, and not excessively influenced by others' expectations. Willingness must grow over time.

A sudden illness reveals the vulnerability of the human frame:

Variable, and therefore miserable condition of man! This minute I was well, and am ill, this minute. I am surprised with a sudden change, and alteration to worse, and can impute it to no cause, nor call it by any name. We study health, and we deliberate upon our meats, and drink, and air, and exercises, and we hew and we polish every stone that goes to that building; and so our health is a long and a regular work: but in a minute a cannon batters all, overthrows all, demolishes all; a sickness unprevented for all our diligence. (John Donne, *Devotions*, p. 7)

VIII. 🦋 Developmental Stages as Variables of Seasonable Counsel

The pastor is daily in conversation with persons at different stages of their growth. On the same day a pastor may witness the birth of a child, assist the parents in early child nurture, see a child struggle with a crisis of adolescence, and bury a parishioner. During a long tenure of ministry a pastor may come very close to all the members of a single family through premarital counsel, marriage, marital conflict, childbirth, vocational crises and death. The pastor will be called upon to deal with persons facing quite different stages of life crises. He must remain responsive to all the different levels and developmental stages of the life cycle. Counsel must be attentive to these developmental differences.

There are times when a good physician will allow a particular illness to continue if the prospect for overall recovery is thereby improved. Similarly, if the human predicament is deep and intricate, then is a slow, but surer rate of recovery at times better than an imagined quick recovery that may elicit a relapse?

For as physicians, who are able to cure a man quickly, when they suspect that a hidden poison exists in the body, do the reverse of healing, making this more certain through their very desire to heal, deeming it better for a considerable time to retain the patient under inflammation and sickness, in order that he may recover his health more surely, than to appear to produce a rapid recovery, and afterwards to cause a relapse, and (thus) that hasty cure last only for a time; in the same way, God also, who knows the secret things of the heart, and foresees future events, in His long-suffering, permits (certain events to occur), and by means of those things which happen from without extracts the secret evil, in order to cleanse . . . so also the great Husbandman of all nature postpones that benefit which might be deemed premature, that it may not prove superficial. (Origen, *De Principiis*, Bk. II, Ch. I, sec. 13–14, ANF IV, pp. 314–315)

The attention of the soul guide, like the astute physician, is directed toward long term recovery rather than the superficial or immediate appearance of improvement. The comfort of God cannot be precisely similar for persons who are different, or who are in widely different stages of development.

More than speculative theological knowledge is required for the pastor to enable growth. Without humility his competencies are easily exaggerated. The spiritual novice is less likely to be prepared for the same counsel that one might give to one who is more mature in faith and action:

I fear that I may do harm to "you who are infants" (1 Cor. 3:1). You must pardon me, lest you be choked by what you cannot swallow. For though I am in bonds and can know heavenly things such as the angelic locations and the archontic [ruling] conjunctions, visible and invisible (cf. Col. 1:16), for all that I am not already a disciple. For many things are lacking to us so that we may not lack God. (Ignatius of Antioch, *Trallians*, 5, AF, p. 93)

As the infant may be choked by too large a bite, so in counsel. To speak of "archontic conjunctions" to novices in the faith is not likely to help them. Even the best of theologians lacks full knowledge of God, but these inadequacies have a deeper meaning, in that through confronting them we may better discover the adequacy of trust in God.

A gentle remedy may be due to the soul deluded by distorted imaginings:

It is not time to use severer remedies, and since we know that it is the way of all minds to clothe themselves ever in false opinions as they throw off the true, and these false ones breed a dark distraction which confuses the true insight, therefore will I try to lessen this darkness for a while with gentle applications of easy remedies, that so the shadows of deceiving passions may be dissipated. (Boethius, *Consolation of Philosophy*, Bk. I, p. 19)

Boethius understood this psychological dynamic: in the search for honesty one must of necessity test out on many false interpretations. When these distortions excite the passions to broad confusion, the treatment required is that of gently settling down the emotive energy, so that deceit can be penetrated.

There are opportune times when some spurt of personal growth may be possible at that time only, which if delayed, will never again be offered:

So, brethren, since we have been granted no small opportunity to repent, let us take the occasion to turn to God who has called us, while we still have one to accept us.... Recognize that "the day" of judgment is already "on its way like a furnace ablaze" (Mal. 4:1).... Fasting is better than prayer, almsgiving better than both; for "love covers a multitude of sins" (Prov. 10:12; 1 Pet. 4:8). (An Epistle, Commonly Called Second Clement, VI.16, AF, p. 68)

IX. 🥁 THE LIMITS OF SITUATIONAL WISDOM

Each time and place offers its unique opportunity to learn something about oneself, and in a larger sense to enable the soul to deepen wisdom and increase good judgment. But time is short and each moment remains finally unrepeatable:

For a second life is not granted to us, so that when we seek wisdom in this life, we cannot delay becoming wise, for each stride we make must be taken within the strict bounds of this life. Let us hope that wisdom may be quickly found, in order that its fruits may soon be borne, lest our lives be cut short and come to an uncertain end. (Lactantius, *The Divine Institutes*, Bk. III, Ch. XVI, ANF VII, p. 85)*

The Shepherd of Hermas employed the chilling metaphor of winter in order to speak of the limits of the self-understanding even of the faithful and wise. If you go into a forest in mid-winter, can you readily tell which trees are alive and which are dead? It is difficult. So also when we look at a forest of persons, it may be very difficult to recognize where life is latent and ready to spring back, as opposed to where it is quite dead. In this winter world, it is not always possible to detect where the soul remains alive, where righteousness dwells, or where sin has eroded.

He showed me many trees which had no leaves, but appeared to me to be as if dried up; for they were all alike. And he said to me, "Do you see," he said, "these trees?" "I see, sir," I said, "that they are alike and dried up." He answered me and said, "These trees which you see are the ones who dwell in this world." "Why, then, sir," I said, "are they as if dry and all alike?" "Because," said he, "neither the righteous nor the sinners are apparent in this world, but are all alike. For this world is winter for the righteous, and they are not apparent even though they are living with sinners. For just as in the winter, the trees, having shed their leaves, are alike, and it is not apparent which are the dried up or which are the living, so also in this world neither the righteous nor the sinners are apparent, but all are alike" (*The Pastor of Hermas*, Similitude III, AF, p. 209)

The metaphor of flowering was used by Hugh of St. Victor to stress the timing of a good act:

As a flower is beautiful in its form and pleasing in its scent, so a good work gives a bright example when it seems laudable to those who witness it and incites them to do the like. And its fragrance is pleasing when the good report of it reaches those who are far off. . . . The tree of wisdom *ripens through patience* and perseverance. Virtue begun is useless if it be not carried through. So anyone who makes a beginning in virtue forms so to speak a sort of fruit of goodness in himself; but, if he gives up the virtue before the end, his fruit falls untimely, being as it were unripe and not fit to eat. (Hugh of St. Victor, *SSW*, p. 118)

Events that once appeared enigmatic have a different appearance once their meaning is illuminated by subsequent events. When particular times seem to be full of enigma and uncertainty, the paucity of our knowing must be viewed in the context of resurrection hope:

Christ is the treasure which was hid in the field, that is, in this world (for "the field is the world", Matt. 13:38); but the treasure hid in the Scriptures is Christ, since He was pointed out by means of types and parables. Hence His human nature could not be understood, prior to the consummation of those things which had been predicted, that is, the advent of Christ. And therefore it was said to Daniel the prophet: "Shut up the words, and seal the book even to the time of consummation, until many learn, and knowledge be completed. For at that time, when the dispersion shall be accomplished, they shall know all these things" [Daniel 12:4,7]. But Jeremiah also says, "In the last days they shall understand these things" [Jer. 23:20]. For every prophecy, before its fulfillment, is to men (full of) enigmas and ambiguities. But when the time has arrived, and the prediction has come to pass, then the prophecies have a clear and certain exposition. (Irenaeus, *Against Heresies*, Bk. IV, Ch. XXVI, sec. 1, ANF I, p. 496)

Pastoral counsel remains keenly attentive to the promise/fulfillment character that pervades human events. Promising events look toward their fulfillment, and promise is understood from the vantage point of fulfillment.

Purely individualistic, experimental trial and error is not the best way to learn to offer counsel. For persons will be hurt by the counselor's errors. Therefore, according to Gregory of Nyssa, a corporate tradition of experienced wisdom has built up, and is available for those who would listen:

> For all that we do in life, it is better for a person entering upon a task to get a knowledge of whatever he is seeking to know from teachers than to attempt to learn by himself. This task of ours is not so easy that one can necessarily judge for himself what is best, and when a person dares to attempt something he is not familiar with, he takes a risk. Just as men, through experience and close scrutiny, have gradually found out the previously unknown art of healing, so that the helpful and the dangerous are recognized through experiments, knowledge is collected for the profession, and instruction as to what is to be observed is handed down by those who have learned before, and thus the novice does not have to decide the effects of medicines, whether a drug is harmful or helpful through his own experiments. He becomes a successful physician by learning what is known from another. In the same manner, it is not necessary to learn the healing art of the soul through trial and error. (I am speaking of the principles through which we learn the cure for all diseases touching the soul.) It is learned through the authority of the learning of one who has developed the ability through long and extensive hours. (Gregory of Nyssa, *On Virginity*, XXIII, WSD, p. 51; cf. NPNF 2, V, p. 368)

X. 🍎 PRUDENCE AS A PRIMARY QUALITY OF GOOD COUNSEL

Good counsel searches for prudent judgments. But what is prudence? How does the excellent habit of prudence help order good judgment? Many pastoral writers have dealt with this question, but none more influentially than Thomas Aquinas. The following selections define prudence and show how it stands as a crucial premise of good counsel. Our principle guide is Thomas' Treatise on the Virtues, in *Summa Theologica*, which set forth a classical definition of prudence:

It belongs to the ruling of prudence to decide in what manner and by what means man shall obtain the mean of reason in his deeds. . . . Prudence is "right reason applied to action" [Aristotle, Ethics, vi. 10]. Hence that which is the chief act of reason in regard to action must needs be the chief act of prudence. Now there are three such acts. The first is "to take counsel," which belongs to discovery, for counsel is an act of inquiry, as stated above (I–II, Q. 14, Art. 1). The second act is "to judge of what one has discovered, and this is an act of the speculative reason. But the practical reason, which is directed to action, goes further, and its third act is "to command," which act consists in applying to action the things counselled and judged. And since this act approaches nearer to the end of the practical reason, it follows that it is the chief act of the practical reason, and consequently of prudence. (Thomas Aquinas, *Summa Theologica*, Part II–II, Q. 47, Art. 8, Vol. II, pp. 1393f.)

Prudent counsel is seeking to find the proper balance of moral virtues applicable to a given situation. It is to decide as a wise person would decide about how reason is applied to activity. "Taking counsel" was, for Thomas, an intrinsic part of prudence, namely, that part of prudence which makes inquiry into the right means to obtain a good end. One is prudent whose estimate of an action is accurate, who understands what is needed, attuned to circumstances:

Since prudence is right reason applied to action, the whole process of prudence must needs have its source in understanding. . . . Prudence is concerned with particular matters of action, and since such matters are of infinite variety, no one man can consider them all sufficiently; nor can this be done quickly, for it requires length of time. Hence in matters of prudence man stands in very great need of being taught by others, especially by old folk who have acquired an understanding of the ends in practical matters. . . . Thus it is written (Prov. 3:5): "Lean not on thy own prudence," and (Ecclus. 6:35): "Stand in the multitude of the ancients" (i.e., the old men), "that are wise, and join thyself from thy heart to their wisdom." Now it is a mark of docility to be ready to be taught; and consequently docility is fittingly reckoned a part of prudence. . . .

Prudence consists in a right estimate about matters of action. Now a right estimate and opinion is acquired in two ways, both in practical and in speculative matters, first by discovering it oneself, secondly by learning it from others. Now just as docility consists in a man being well disposed to acquire a right opinion from another man, so shrewdness is an apt disposition to acquire a right estimate of oneself, yet so that shrewdness be taken for *eustochia*, of which it is a part. For *eustochia* is a happy conjecture about any matter, which shrewdness is "an easy and rapid conjecture in finding the middle term" (Aristotle, *Posteriori*, i.34). . . . "Shrewdness is a habit whereby congruities are discovered rapidly" (Aristotle, ibid.) . . . Shrewdness is concerned with the discovery of the middle term not only in demonstrative, but also in practical syllogisms. . . . *Euboulia*, i.e., good counsel, is not *eustochia*, which is commended for grasping quickly what should be done. Now a man may take good counsel, though he be long and slow in so doing, and yet this does not discount the utility of a happy conjecture in taking good counsel. . . . It is for this reason that shrewdness is fittingly reckoned a part of prudence. (Thomas Aquinas, *Summa Theologica*, Part II–II, Q. 49, Art. 2–6, Vol. II, pp. 1402–1404)

Good counsel makes a shrewd conjecture about a given situation, concerning what is needed. Prudence is slowly trained by the ages of human experience, willing to listen to accumulated wisdom of social experience. Yet in the actual moment of decision, it does not delay but is alert to analyze and discern accurately the subtly competing values and contextual needs. One cannot provide prudent counsel without both listening carefully to the wisdom of others, and rapidly conjecturing the proportionality of a given situation. Shrewdness must survey a situation quickly for analogies, congruities, and for the proper means to good ends. But it must be informed by slow accumulations of human experience.

According to Thomas, a good thing may become unsuitable in a given circumstance. Prudent counsel must discern not only what is good abstractly, but when (under what circumstances) that good may be actualized:

It belongs to prudence chiefly to direct something aright to an end; and this is not done aright unless both the end be good, and the means good and suitable.

Since, however, prudence, as stated above (II–II, Q. 47, Art. 3) is about singular matters of action, which contain many combinations of circumstances, it happens that a thing is good in itself and suitable to the end, and nevertheless becomes evil or unsuitable to the end, by reason of some combination of circumstances. . . . Circumstances are the concern of prudence. . . .

Just as it belongs to foresight to look on that which is by its nature suitable to an end, so it belongs to circumspection to consider whether it be suitable to the end in view of the circumstances. Now each of these presents a difficulty of its own, and therefore each is reckoned a distinct part of prudence.... Prudence needs caution, so that we may have such a grasp of good as to avoid evil. (Thomas Aquinas, *Summa Theologica*, Part II–II, Q. 49, Art. 7, 8, Vol. II, pp. 1405f.)

The process of offering wise and prudent counsel is an extremely complex perceptive-intuitive act. Its principle interest is in circumstances (which constantly change) and especially with the fit application of achievable goods to changing circumstances, by correlating due means with good ends. The effective counselor must have that behavioral excellence that Thomas called "circumspection" (from *circumspectus*, looking around oneself carefully at the circumstances), being attentive to all circumstances that may affect an action or decision. Thomas was not developing these ideas originally, but rather synthesizing a long pastoral tradition that may be seen forming in Gregory of Nazianzus, Augustine, and Gregory the Great, yet with Thomas this is all viewed subsequently through the lens of the Aristotelian view of a four-fold ordering of causality.

XI. 🐭 On Learning Wisdom and Wise Counsel

To say that good counsel is wise counsel (hence informed by wisdom) is a truism. For a clarification of *how* wisdom informs counsel, we turn again to Thomas Aquinas:

It belongs to wisdom to consider the highest cause. By means of that cause we are able to form a most certain judgment about other causes, and according thereto all things should be set in order.... The wisdom which is called a gift of the Holy Ghost, differs from that which is an acquired intellectual virtue, for the latter is attained by human effort, whereas the former is "descending from above" (James 3:15)....
Accordingly wisdom as a gift, is not merely speculative but also practical. The higher a virtue is, the greater the number of things to which it extends, as stated in *De Causis*, prop. x, xvii. Wherefore from the very fact that wisdom as a gift is more excellent than wisdom as an intellectual virtue, since it attains to God more intimately by a kind of union of the soul with Him, it is able to direct us not only in contemplation but also in action. (Thomas Aquinas, *Summa Theologica*, Part II–II, Q. 45, Art. 2–3, Vol. II, pp. 1380–1381)

Wise judgments are distinguished from (though not separable from) prudential judgments in that they are not merely looking for means to ends, but rather for the highest end to which all other ends must finally be accountable. Wise counsel works both within and beyond natural intelligence, i.e., it both emerges out of natural intelligence, and addresses natural intelligence through revelation as known in scripture and tradition. Wise counsel is in part clarified by asking what foolish counsel is:

Stultitia (folly) seems to take its name from stupor; wherefore Isidore says (*Etym.* x, S): "A fool is one who through dullness (*stuporem*) remains unmoved." And folly differs from fatuity, according to the same authority (ibid.), in that folly implies apathy in the heart and dullness in the senses while fatuity denotes entire privation of the spiritual sense. Therefore folly is fittingly opposed to wisdom.

For *sapiens* (wise) as Isidore says (ibid.), "is so named from *sapor* (savor), because just as the taste is quick to distinguish between savors of meats, so is a wise man in discerning things and causes. . . . Unwisdom is contrary to wisdom because it lacks the savor of discretion and sense." (Thomas Aquinas, *Summa Theologica*, Part II–II, Q. 46, Art. 1, Vol. II, p. 1384)

Using the metaphor of tasting, to counsel wisely is to learn to distinguish clearly and immediately between subtly competing values (nuances of taste) in a given situation. A dull palate cannot so distinguish, and thus offers foolish counsel. Thomas then proceeded to show dialectically that there could be an evil wisdom as well as a good folly:

Just as there is an evil wisdom, as stated above (II–II, Q. 45, Art. 1), called worldly wisdom, because it takes for the highest causes and last end some worldly good, so too there is a good folly opposed to this evil wisdom, whereby man despises worldly things. . . . To be unconcerned when one is injured is sometimes due to the fact that one has no taste for worldly things, but only for heavenly things. (Thomas Aquinas, *Summa Theologica*, Part II–II, Q. 46, Art. 1, Vol. I, p. 1384)

Pastoral guidance does not necessarily become wiser as it becomes more complex. In one of the aphorisms of John Climacus, this reasoning appears:

I beg you, do not instruct the simpler sort in the complexities of deceitful thoughts, but rather, if possible, make complex men simple—a marvelous thing indeed! (Climacus, *To the Shepherd*, Aphorism 95, in *The Ladder of Divine Ascent*, p. 246)

The shepherd of souls pays careful attention to how language is used, aware of potential edges of misunderstanding:

The Spirit of Wisdom is described in the Book of Wisdom as subtle and lively, because in her is the spirit of understanding, holy, one, manifold, subtle, lively; and she grinds her words before speaking so that she may not offend in any mode or meaning. (Ambrose, *Letters*, 77, To Laymen, FC 26, p. 434)

That wisdom "grinds her words" means that they must be made digestible within particular circumstances.

Hugh of St. Victor delineated these stages (first storey, pondering the virtues of others; second storey, making their virtue my own; third storey, habituated virtue) through which the wisdom of good counsel proceeds:

If, therefore, I have begun to love to meditate upon the Scriptures, and have always been ready to ponder the virtues of the saints, and the works of God, and whatever else there is that serves to improve my conduct and stimulate my spirit, then I have already begun to be in the first storey of the ark. But if I neglect to imitate the good I know, then I can say that my thought is right, but unprofitable. For it is good that I should think what I do think and know what I know about others, but it profits me nothing if I do not take it to myself as a pattern for living. For another person's virtue is of not profit to me.... But if I have taken pains not only to know, but also to perform good and profitable actions, and if my heart's preoccupation is to see how by self-control and a right way of living I can make my own the virtues which I love and admire in others, *then* I can say that my thought is profitable, *then* I have gone up to the second storey. My heart is now more at one with itself; in consequence, it does not gad about among vain and profitless things.

There remains the third kind of thought, that when I have begun to do the works of the virtues, I should labour to have the virtues themselves—that is to say, that I should possess within myself the virtue which I show in outward works. Otherwise it will not be much good for me to have performed the works, unless I have also the virtues of the works. If, then, I direct the thought of my heart to this end, that I may strive to show inwardly before the eyes of God whatever good appears in me outwardly to human sight, then I have gone up into the third storey, where the essential virtues are to be found. But among all these there is one that is supremely necessary, namely, charity, which unites us to God. (Hugh of St. Victor, *SSW*, pp. 81–82)

The gradual process by which wisdom grows is further delineated in this way by Hugh:

This, therefore, is the tree indeed, the word of the Father, the wisdom of God in the highest, which in the hearts of the saints, as in an unseen paradise, is sown in fear, watered by grace, dies through grief, takes root by faith, buds by devotion, shoots up through compunction, grows by longing, is strengthened by charity, grows green by hope, puts out its leaves and spreads its branches through caution, flowers through discipline, bears fruit through virtue, ripens through patience, is harvested by death, and feeds by contemplation. . . . Our saying that the tree of wisdom *is sown through fear* will then correspond to "Blessed are the poor in spirit: for theirs is the kingdom of heaven." Our saying that it *is watered by grace* will answer to "Blessed are the meek: for they shall inherit the earth." Our saying that it *dies through grief* will answer to "Blessed are they that mourn; for they shall be comforted." Our saying that it *takes root by faith* will answer to "Blessed are they that hunger and thirst after righteousness; for they shall be filled." Our saying that it *germinates through devotion* will answer to "Blessed are the merciful: for they shall obtain mercy." Our saying that it *shoots up through compunction* will answer to "Blessed are the pure in heart: for they shall see God." Our saying that it *grows by longing* will answer to "Blessed are the peacemakers: for they shall be called the children of God." Our saying that it is *strengthened by charity* will answer to "Blessed are they that are persecuted for righteousness' sake: for theirs is the kingdom of heaven." (Hugh of St. Victor, *SSW*, pp. 93, 107; see Matt. 5:2–11)

Benedict set forth these mandates for the spiritual pilgrim:

> To relieve the poor.
> To clothe the naked.
> To visit the sick.
> To bury the dead.
> To help those that are in trouble.
> To comfort the afflicted. . . .
> Not to cover deceit in the heart.
> Not to make a pretended peace.
> Not to forsake charity.
> Not to swear, for fear of being perjured.
> To speak truth from the heart as well as the mouth. . . .
> To keep death every day before our eyes.
> To keep a continual watch over our actions.
> To be convinced that God sees us wherever we are.

To dash evil thoughts as soon as they arise in the heart, against the Rock Christ; and to discover them to our spiritual father. . . .
To be reconciled to those who have quarrelled with us, before the sun go down.
And never to despair of God's mercy. (Benedict of Nursia, Rule, LCC XII, pp. 297–299)

This Part of our collection has sought to show that astute timing of pertinent prudential judgment is a central feature of pastoral wisdom. Beginning with Gregory Nazianzen's principle of variable responsiveness, the texts have showed how the individuation of treatment is not inconsistent with doctrinal cohesion, that context and norm must interface in pastoral counsel, that the essence of counsel is the discernment of truth amid variable contingences and circumstances, hence timing is of the essence of counsel. Classic pastoralia was fully aware of the need to deal with developmental differences of persons in various stages of personal growth. It sought to define and practice the virtue of prudence in the offering of wise situational counsel.

5 The Language, Silence, and Gesture of Counsel

How DOES one read body language, and how do non-verbal gestures work for and against constructive change? How may language become a vehicle either for deceit or truth-telling? The following texts concern soul care as a language event, an occurence that proceeds primarily by conversation. Though dependent upon words, pastoral care reaches out beyond words. We will discuss the therapeutic function of both language and silence.

It may seem at first glance that the thread that holds all these themes together is slender. Why talk of the function of language in pastoral care? And why of silence? Partly because this constellation of issues remains such a recurrent preoccupation of the classic pastoral writers.

The heart of the issue is: How do we communicate with and without language? What are we saying through bodily movement, countenance, gesture, and posture that serves or disserves the care of souls? How does the responsible or irresponsible use of language impinge upon health of soul?

I. ❦ THE FUNCTION OF SILENCE IN COUNSEL

First, what constructive role does silence play in significant moments of human communication? The pastoral writers have known for centuries that it is possible to say nothing, yet communicate profoundly. This is particularly evident in care of the dying, but it may also be seen as a general truth of pastoral communication:

It is better to be silent and be there than to speak and not be there. It is only good to teach if one does what one teaches. Indeed there was one teacher of whom it was said that he "spoke and it happened" (Ps. 33:9). Even what he did in silence (cf. 1 Pet. 2:22,23) was worthy of the Father. He who has truly heard the word of Jesus can also hear his silence, so that he may become perfect and act through what he says and be known also through what he does not say. (Ignatius of Antioch, *Ephesians*, 15, AF, p. 82)*

141

The best teacher of the meaning of silence was Jesus himself, who remained silent before Pilate, and in the presence of adversaries. He taught as much through what he did not say, as by what he said.

Some situations of conflict which particularly tempt us to abuse language are to some degree correctable simply through silence:

It is better to keep silent than to engage in bickering, adding the fault of action to that of boorishness. Surely "Happy the man who has never let slip a careless word, who has never felt the sting of remorse" (Ecclus. 14:1), or at least has repented of the sins committed in speech, or has conversed without inflicting pain on anyone. (Clement of Alexandria, *Christ the Educator*, Bk. II, Ch. 7.53, FC 23, p. 140)*

Words may seem innocent but they can inflict considerable harm or pain. Language is not intrinsically healing, although care of souls cannot do without it altogether. If so, then is it proper that careful and deliberate constraints be placed upon public use of language by persons in ministry?

Scripture has said: "Let not many be teachers among you, my brethren, and be not all of you prophets" [1 Cor. 12:29] . . . For "at one time it is proper to keep silence, and at another time to speak" [Eccl. 3:7]. And again it says: "When a man speaks in season, it is honorable to him" [Prov. 25:11]. And again it says: "Let your speech be seasoned with grace. For it is required of a man to know how to give an answer to every one in season" [Col. 4:6]. For "he that utters whatsoever comes to his mouth, that man produces strife; and he that utters a superfluity of words increases vexation; and he that is hasty with his lips falls into evil" [Prov. 18:6; 13:3]. (Clementina, Two Epistles Concerning Virginity, I, Ch. XI, ANF VIII, p. 59)

Even in these early documents of Christianity there was a felt need to muster scripture to check the unconstrained words of the religious guides.

II. 🐚 LEARNING TO READ THE LANGUAGE OF THE BODY

We have heard much recent talk in popular psychology about the significance of body language, often on the assumption that these insights were utterly fresh and unparalleled in human history. Once again the pastoral tradition anticipated this modern premise with penetrating reflections on how bodily movements and gestures and involuntary responses often provide signals of unconscious attitudes or hidden feelings, and clues to the inner person.

Lactantius, for example, thought that the mind of another could often be discerned by careful attentiveness to the eyes. In love and anger the eyes "tell all":

Since we see at the same moment of time, and for the most part, while engaged on other business, we nevertheless behold all things which are placed opposite to us, it is more true and evident that it is the mind which, through the eyes, sees those things which are placed opposite to it, as though through windows covered with pellucid crystal or transparent stone; and therefore the mind and inclination are often known from the eyes. (Lactantius, *On the Workmanship of God*, Ch. VIII, ANF VII, p. 289)

The eyes speak from the heart:

The Lover and the Beloved met, and the Beloved said to the Lover, "You do not need to speak to me. Simply sign to me with your eyes—for they are words to my heart—that I may give you what you ask from me." (Raymond Lull, *The Book of the Lover and the Beloved*, sec. 29, p. 19)

When we are seeking earnestly to communicate our deep concern and care for another, it may be better to do so without words:

Do not wish to assure everyone in words of your love for them, but rather ask God to show them your love without words. (Climacus, *The Ladder of Divine Ascent*, Step 6, sec. 22, p. 69)

An illumined aura about the face has often been thought to be a nonverbal indication that one has been addressed by God's own holiness so as to reflect that holiness amid the life of the world. Clement of Alexandria reflected intentionally upon what such an aura signifies, and how it may be understood:

And as in the case of Moses, from his righteous conduct, and from his uninterrupted intercourse with God, who spoke to him, a kind of glorified hue settled on his face; so also a divine power of goodness clinging to the righteous soul in contemplation and in prophecy, and in the exercise of the function of governing, impresses on it something, as it were, of intellectual radiance, like the solar ray, as a visible sign of righteousness, uniting the soul with light, through unbroken love, which is God-bearing and God-borne. (Clement of Alexandria, *The Stromata, or Miscellanies*, Bk. VI, Ch. XII, ANF II, p. 504)

When one's soul is united with the source of light, the brightness of that light seems to radiate upon all beholders.

When we use our voice, we communicate who we are, and how we understand ourselves to be oriented toward the horizon of time. Our voices outwardly express what we inwardly feel or think. If so, the tone or modulation or stridency of one's voice may become an indirect indicator of a more deeply-set interpersonal style or orientation toward others. Clement understood how much beyond words was being signalled by voice:

> Loud talking is annoying, yet speaking inaudibly to one close by suggests ineptitude, inability to make oneself heard. The one is a sign of timidity, the other of brashness. Do not let quarrelsomeness with its love of empty victory creep into our midst, for our aim is the elimination of all discord. . . . We should not be long-winded in our conversations, nor wordy, nor engage in idle chatter, nor rattle on rapidly without drawing a breath. Surely, even the voice ought to have its share, so to speak, of moderation, and those who talk out of turn and those who shout should be silenced. . . . "A man full of tongue is terrible in his destruction" (Ecclus. 9:18). The rest of the body of a chatterer is worn away like an old shoe by evil, with only the tongue left to inflict harm. (Clement of Alexandria, *Christ the Educator*, Bk. II, Ch. 7, FC 23, pp. 58–59)

Length of speech is best moderated by awareness of how much the hearer is capable of receiving. Out of simple courtesy and attentiveness, the tone of voice is to be moderated so as to be neither too loud or too soft, too abrupt or too long-winded, too bland or too sharp, since any of these excesses betray an uncaring insensitivity to the neighbor.

III. 🐛 Use and Abuse of Language in Counsel

Counsel occurs primarily through language. It happens in part through non-verbal communication, but seldom completely without words. Good counsel pays careful attention to how language is used, how distinctions are made or left unmade, how to answer another responsibly, how to penetrate deceptions both in one's own and in the other's use of language. The good pastor listens to language with exceptional attentiveness. The exercise is demystifying:

> No more will he dread cunning words who is capable of distinguishing them, or of answering rightly to questions asked. . . . For the cause of all error and false opinion is inability to distinguish in what respect things are common, and in what respects they

differ. For unless, in things that are distinct, one closely watches speech, he will inadvertently confound what is common and what is peculiar. And where this takes place, he must of necessity fall into pathless tracts and error. . . . For it is necessary to understand expressions which signify several things, and several expressions when they signify one thing; the result of which is accurate answering. (Clement of Alexandria, *The Stromata, or Miscellanies*, Bk. VI, Ch. X, ANF II, p. 499)

The cause of most errors of communication is the failure accurately to distinguish between things that are similar and different (things common and things peculiar). When one learns to unravel layers of ambiguity and equivocal language (where a single expression may signify several things), and to distinguish these expressions from those in which several words point to the same reality, then one is on the way to becoming better prepared to counsel, having learned to avoid "pathless tracts" of obfuscations. The care-giver needs a shrewd ability to recognize palaver:

The lover of truth does not give heed to ornamental speeches, but examines the real matter of speech, what it is, and what kind it is. (Theophilus, *To Autolycus*, Bk. I, Ch. I, ANF II, p. 89)

The counselor must learn to penetrate evasions. In his dialogue on *The Teacher*, Augustine sought through Socratic questioning to elicit from his son, Adeodatus, a clear awareness of the purpose of language. In asking to what purpose language functions, he got this spare answer:

Augustine.—What do you suppose is our purpose when we use words? Adeodatus.—The answer that occurs to me at the moment is, we want to let people know something, or we want to learn something. (Augustine, *The Teacher*, I.1, LCC VI, p. 69)

Accordingly, self-disclosure and learning are complementary functions of dialogue, which requires the listening speech of another and the listening speech of oneself. Yet language may serve to conceal thoughts as well as reveal them:

You can easily understand that words not only do not reveal the mind, but even serve to conceal it. . . . We have often experienced in ourselves and others that words do not correctly convey thoughts. (Augustine, *The Teacher*, I.13, LCC VI, p. 98)

If language conceals meaning, then the one who loves truth through language must also learn to use language to penetrate concealment. Origen used the metaphor of "gentle rain" to refer to the patient dialogue of the soul guide:

"Let my speech be expected as rain, and let my words come down as dew, as the gentle rain upon the tender grass, and as the showers upon the herb, for I have called upon the name of the Lord" (Deut. 32:2–3). . . . The one who is able to utter speech "like rain," which works together with those who hear it for the production of the fruits of their souls, and who can give encouraging words "like dew," bringing extremely profitable "gentle rain" in words with the force of edification upon the hearers or most effectual showers—this man can do all this because of the name [of the Lord]. (Origen, *On Prayer*, 3, CWS, p. 130)

A hard, flooding rain may uproot tender plants, but gentle rain lets the smallest seed grow. The speech of good counsel is something like water being made tenderly available to the thirsty. In modest quantities (like the heaviness of dew), it is exceedingly useful and assimilable, but not in floods.

Pastoral counsel does well to make frequent use of metaphor, in Luther's view:

For ordinary people are caught more easily by analogies and illustrations than by difficult and subtle discussions; they would rather look at a well-drawn picture than a well-written book. . . . For teaching it is useful to be able to produce many analogies and illustrations; not only Paul but also the prophets and Christ used them. (Luther, "Lectures on Galatians, Ch. 1.4, 1535," LW 26, p. 359; WA 40 I, p. 548)

In distinguishing the spoken and written word, Clement showed how important non-verbal clues may be in testing of speech for truthfulness:

He who addresses those who are present before him, both tests them by time, and judges by his judgment, and from the others distinguishes him who can hear; watching the words, the manners, the habits, the life, the motions, the attitudes, the look, the voice; the road, the rock, the beaten path, the fruitful land, the wooded region, the fertile and fair and cultivated spot, that is able to multiply the seed. But he that speaks through books, consecrates himself before God, crying in writing thus: Not for gain, not for vainglory, not to be vanquished by partiality, nor enslaved by fear nor elated by pleasure; but only to reap the salvation of those who read, which he does not at present participate in, but awaiting in expectation the recompense which will certainly be rendered by Him who has promised to bestow on the labourers the reward that is meet. (Clement of Alexandria, *The Stromata, or Miscellanies*, Bk. I, Ch. I., ANF II, p. 301)

The written word differs from conversation, for in conversation one is able to pick up immediate signals of response, both verbal and non-verbal. The written word lives out of the promise of potential responses in which it "does not at present participate," yet for which it hopes.

There are strong Old Testament injunctions against deceitful use of language which were often recollected in the Christian pastoral tradition:

Thou shalt not be doubleminded nor doubletongued; for "a man's own lips are a strong snare to him" [Prov. 6:2], and "a talkative person shall not be prospered upon earth" [Ps. 140:11]. Thy words shall not be vain; for "ye shall give an account of every idle word" [Matt. 12:36; Lev. 19:11]. Thou shalt not tell lies (*Constitutions of the Holy Apostles*, Bk. VII, sec. I, ANF VII, p. 466)

Similarly there were appeals to use speech sparely and responsibly, not waste it, to be accountable to God for each word. There is more than an incidental correlation between idleness and a loose tongue:

When persons are idle and do not work, they are inclined to pry into those things which go better unspoken. Then they may be tempted by means of seemingly plausible words, to make merchandise of the name of Christ. . . . As it is written: "Thorns sprout in the hands of the idle" [Prov. 26:9], and, "The ways of the idle are full of thorns" [Prov. 15:19, LXX]. . . . Such are the ways of all those who do not work, but go hunting for tales, and think to themselves that this is profitable and right. (Clementina, Two Epistles Concerning Virginity, I, Ch. 10, ANF VIII, p. 58)

Significant conversation is often recalled with exceeding joy. Note the quality of congruence between word and facial gesture in this medieval text, the intimate union of interiority and exteriority:

Do you not joyfully recall how frequently our hearts also were burning within us thanks to Jesus, when we were speaking about him on the way? For what we said about him, he first said within us. . . . Few are your words but full of insights. You seem to summon every word before a law-court, so true is it that no word escapes you unquestioned. . . . I remember, if I mistake not, that sometimes in the very act of speaking, you checked your discourse, alert and astonished at the light and gladness flaring in your heart. Your voice broke off and was changed into a sigh which became audible. Now though your tongue is evidence enough, still interior astonishment and love and amazement at the light radiating from above attracts and ravishes and completely captures your mind which had been expressing itself in words and as with Moses cloaks your mind in a cloud of the spirit, makes a cloud its mantle, makes darkness its retreat, so that your mind becomes stunned at what is happening within, and dumb to what is happening without. . . . Just as solid and tougher logs offer greater resistance to the power of fire, while tinder that is fine and dry and light is more quickly kindled and consumed in the devouring flame, so spiritual and refined meditations more quickly welcome but do not endure very long the sweet violence of enkindled love. "Your spirit," says Isaiah [33:11], "will consume you like fire." (Gilbert of Hoyland, "On Conversation and Colloquy, the Shadows of Substance," *Treatises, Epistles, and Sermons*, CFS 34, pp. 36–38)

When one is speaking from the depths, the face and body gestures are expressive of those depths. Often when words must be dug out from the greatest depths, it takes more time and energy, just as a huge log takes more time to burn—one becomes wholly wrapped up in the effort to retrieve these deep thoughts, and astonished when they are finally brought into speech.

IV. ❦ DECEPTION AND SELF-DECEPTION

Early pastoral care-givers sought to offer those interpersonal gifts that would invite full personal self-disclosure. Contemporary psychotherapists continue in the tradition of seeking to enable self-disclosure.

Here is a telling description by the historian Eusebius of how fourth century pastors were trying to penetrate the hidden depths of the believer's soul.

They so touched the depths of their souls, caught hold of and pierced the individual conscience, that men no longer hid anything away in concealment, but brought their forbidden things to light, and themselves completed the indictment of themselves. (Eusebius, *The Proof of the Gospel*, Bk. III, Ch. 6, p. 148)

When persons are addressed at close quarters by one who cares deeply for their soul, forbidden things are voluntarily brought to light. Such probing self-disclosure was not forced upon them from without, but emerged freely from within as individuals found themselves in the presence of radical trust and truth-telling. This differs dramatically from those contexts in which one is forced to be constantly self-protective.

Some tell the truth about themselves only when filled with insobriety, unaware of their truth-telling! If candor is so healing, why is lying so prevalent, many-faced, and destructive?

One lies for sheer wantonness, another for amusement; one, to make the bystanders laugh; and another, to trap his brother and do him injury. . . . He who gives way to lying does so under the pretext of prudence, and he often regards what is the destruction of his soul as an act of righteousness. . . . A babe knows nothing of lying. . . . He who has become merry with wine involuntarily speaks the truth on all subjects, and he who is drunk with compunction cannot lie. (Climacus, *The Ladder of Divine Ascent*, Step 112, secs. 9, 11, 13–14, pp. 94, 95)

The newborn child reveals everything and conceals nothing about his own developing feeling process, disclosing accurately to others what is being currently experienced, even if that requires screaming to reveal hunger or anger. But as introjected cultural and parental patterns overlay our experiencing, we learn how to not disclose our feelings, and eventually to deceive not only others, but also ourselves. In time we learn to pretend to be prudent, using the appearance of prudence as a cloak for self-assertion. Those who regard such an interpretation of the lapse of neonate awareness as a strictly modern description do well to read further in the early pastoral writers on the *lapsus* of the will. One filled with the wine of compunction (*compunctiones*, the sting of conscience) dares not lie.

In his essay *On the Priesthood*, John Chrysostom produced an extended list of intertwining enemies of plain truth-telling:

Anger, dejection, envy, strife, slanders, accusations, lying, hypocrisy, intrigue, imprecations against those who have done no harm, delight at disgraceful behaviour in fellow priests, sorrow at their successes, love of praise, greed for preferment (which more than anything else hurls the human soul to destruction), teaching meant to please, slavish wheedling, ignoble flattery, contempt for the poor, fawning on the rich, absurd honours and harmful favours which endanger giver and receiver alike, servile fear fit only for the meanest of slaves, restraint of plain speaking, much pretended and no real humility, failure to scrutinize and rebuke, or, more likely, doing so beyond reason with the humble while no one dares so much as to open his lips against those who wield power. (Chrysostom, *On the Priesthood*, Ch. III.7–9, pp. 77, 78)

The length of such a list indicates how explicitly the ancient Christian writers were thinking about the destructive dynamics of deception. Amid such distortions, we find ways of pretending that the truth has been told:

Sometimes, because of double-mindedness and the unbelief lodged in our hearts, we do what is wrong without knowing it, and "our understanding is darkened" (cf. Eph. 4:17,18; Rom. 1:21) by vain desires. (An Ancient Homily by an Unknown Author [Second Letter of Clement], 19, AF, p. 70)

Deception thereby becomes habituated, "lodged in our hearts." The behaviorist principle of daily replacing of bad with good habits was earlier commended by Erasmus. The struggle with daily, ordinary temptation is a deadly combat fraught with gravity and constantly prone to self-deception. People are prone to see others' vices more clearly than their own, and rationalize their own faults as acceptable. Disastrous social consequences follow upon the heels of widespread hypocrisy:

Treat each battle as if it were the last. . . . I find that not a few mortals miserably deceive themselves. For they deceive themselves when they connive in one vice or another, which each one thinks venial for his own morals, yet they incessantly curse the remaining vices. The better part of those whom the crowd calls unblemished and incorrupt certainly do detest theft, pillage, homicide, adultery, incest. Yet simple fornication and moderate enjoyment of pleasure, as lightly committed, they in no wise eschew. One person, sufficiently incorrupt as far as other vices are concerned, is somewhat of a drunkard or somewhat intemperate in eating. Another has a rather unbridled tongue. Another is somewhat vain and boasting.
What vice will we lack, if each one of us is deluded by his own in this way? The point is not that those who enjoy any vice indeed possess the remaining virtues, but rather [they possess only] certain likenesses of virtues which either nature or education or finally habit has imparted likewise to the minds of pagans. . . . And if perchance you are as yet unable to root out the whole tribe of vices, yet daily we ought to pluck out something of our sins, and always at the same time replace them with good habits. (Erasmus, *Enchiridion*, LCC, XIV, pp. 364–366)

The battle is endless, the enemy irrepressible. Little progress will be made when we imagine our own special vice to be permissible while the vices of others are not, or imagine that our native gifts are virtuous.

V. 🐛 PROBING THE LAYERS OF DECEPTION

The special burden of entrenched duplicity increases greatly the difficulties of giving and receiving counsel, as Gregory the Great observed:

The insincere are to be admonished to realize how burdensome is the business of duplicity which they guiltily bear. For in the fear of discovery they ever try to defend themselves even dishonourably, and are ever agitated with fear and apprehension. Now, nothing is more safely defended than sincerity, nothing easier to speak than the truth. But when a man is forced to defend his deceit his heart is wearied with the toilsome labour of doing so. Wherefore, it is written: The labor of their lips shall overwhelm them. [cf. Ps. 139.10]. . . . For commonly, though they are discovered in their fault, they shrink from being known for what they are, and they screen themselves under a veil of deceit, and the fault which is quite obvious they try to excuse. The result is that often one who aims at reproving them, led astray by the mists of disseminated falsehood, finds that he has all but lost the certain conviction he had been holding concerning them . . . they, poor fools, take delight in what is to their own harm. (Gregory the Great, *Pastoral Care*, Part III, Ch. 11, ACW 11, pp. 117–119)

It takes special labor to lie, because it requires protecting of oneself from detection by others whose affirmation one values. Even when trapped in layers of deceit and actually caught, we may pretend to ourselves that we still remain uncaught. This is why it is so difficult for corrective love to penetrate the masks of deception. Yet deception cannot proceed without our consent:

[One] is deceived not when he sees falsely but when he assents to what is false. (Augustine, *The Soliloquies*, II.iii.3, LCC, VI, p. 43)

There is always some level of assent in deception. Note that unintentional inaccuracy of perception is not necessarily deception. But when one has freely assented to a false perception, there begins the winding trail of deceit. Augustine's teacher, Ambrose, doubted that one who practiced deception at certain times could offer wisdom at other times:

He cannot give what he does not have; nor can one who does not possess the light give light, but he transforms himself into an angel of light to deceive the unbelieving. He transforms himself, moreover, under the pretense of a false light, and not in the splendor of a perpetual brightness. For this reason also the Savior says, "I was watching Satan fall as lightning from heaven" [cf. Luke 10.18]. He is not lightning, but he is as lightning. Think upon some heretic who is devoted to bodily abstinence and the knowledge of heavenly mysteries. He is accounted like one who is everlasting, but he does not possess the recompense of eternal life. (Ambrose, *Exegetical Works*, The Prayer of Job and David, Bk. II, 4.16, FC 65, p. 362)

Each little moment of stumbling into lies is thus made analogous to the awesome and tumultuous fall of the Deceiver from heavenly dwelling. The dynamics are the same: We pretend to have a light and truth that we do not have. We may appear bright, but it is a false, deceptive brightness. So we try to make our folly appear wise:

As that [believing] way of wisdom contains something which resembles folly, as we showed in the preceding book, so this [disbelieving] way, which belongs altogether to folly, contains something which resembles wisdom, and they who perceive the folly of men in general seize upon this; and as it has its vices manifest, so it has something which appears to resemble virtue: as it has its wickedness open, so it has a likeness and appearance of justice. (Lactantius, *The Divine Institutes*, Ch. VII, Bk. VI, ANF VII, p. 170)

If wisdom and folly are not easily distinguishable under conditions of deception, this makes the care of souls more difficult. For health of soul depends upon truth-telling. Amid the syndromes of duplicity, it is not surprising that one's judgment may become sometimes skewed by unnecessary suspicions. Thomas Aquinas defined the hermeneutic of suspicion:

Suspicion denotes evil thinking based on slight indication, and this is due to three causes. First, from a man being evil in himself, and from this very fact, as though conscious of his own wickedness, he is prone to think evil of others, according to Eccl. 10:3, "The fool when he walketh in the way whereas he himself is a fool, esteemeth all men fools." Secondly, this is due to a man being disposed towards another: for when a man hates or despises another, or is angry with one envious of him, he is led by slight indictions to think evil of him, because everyone easily believes what he desires. Thirdly, this is due to long experience: wherefore the Philosopher says (Rhet. ii.13) that old people are very suspicious, for they have often experienced the faults of others. (Thomas Aquinas, *Summa Theologica*, Part II–II, Q. 60, Art. 3, Vol. II, p. 1448)

Yet amid the syndromes of suspicion, which arises in part because of our own projections and defensiveness, and in part because of our realistic awareness of human self-assertiveness, God's own wisdom remains wholly undeceived. God's Spirit continues in our presence to work against petty deceptions:

For even if some desired to deceive me in a merely human way, the Spirit is not deceived, for it is from God. For it "knows whence it comes and whither it goes" (cf. John 8:14, 3:8) and exposes secrets (see 1 Cor. 2:10; 14:24, 25). (Ignatius of Antioch, *Philippians*, 7, AF, p. 106)

God's own Spirit is radically undeceived, aware of each whence, wherefore, and why. Human freedom, on the other hand, is tempted to call unlawful that which it merely dislikes.

Shepherdless, in no other fold but that of their own will, have no other law but what is agreeable and pleasing; they measure the proportion of holiness by their own choice and ideas, and call unlawful what they dislike. (Benedict of Nursia, *Rule*, LCC XII, p. 294)

Orosius provided a comic-pathetic example of how far self-deception can go, even to the sustained illusion of a defeated Roman society that it had remained undefeated:

Thus, in the one thousand one hundred and sixty fourth year after the founding of the City, an attack was made upon the City by Alaric; although the memory of this event is fresh, nevertheless, if anyone sees the multitude of the Roman people themselves and hears their talk, he will think that nothing took place, as even they themselves confess, unless by chance he is informed by the ruins of the fire still remaining. (Paulus Orosius, *The Seven Books of History Against the Pagans*, VII, FC 50, pp. 355–356)

It was amazing to Paulus Orosius how quickly a massive historical event could be assimilated into a pattern of reassuring self-deception. What actually happened in the sack of Rome appeared only years later as if nothing important occurred. So easily do we adjust to rationalization.

VI. 🐚 TELLING THE TRUTH

The pastoral writers viewed lying and truth-telling in the context of an organic metaphor: The Christian community is a living single body with many members. Each part is important for the health of the whole. A blockage or dysfunction in one member causes ill health for the whole organism. If one member lies to another, pain is felt by the whole body. Chrysostom stated the argument clearly in his exegesis of Ephesians:

There is nothing, no, nothing so productive of enmity as deceit and guile. Observe how every lie becomes shameful in relation to this analogy of the body. Let not the eye, Paul says, lie to the foot, nor the foot to the eye. Suppose for example that there is a deep pit ahead. Suppose weak reeds are laid on top of the pit, yet remain concealed under earth. By its appearances it furnishes the eye with an expectation that this is solid ground. But won't the eye use the foot, if suspicious, to discover whether it is firm and resists? Would the foot under those circumstances tell a lie, and not report the truth as it is? Again, if the eye were to spy a snake or a wild beast, would it ever lie to the foot? Would it not at once inform it, and the foot thus informed would refrain from stepping down? Again, suppose that neither the foot nor the eye would know whether to proceed, and everything might depend entirely upon smelling, as, for example, whether a drug had a deadly odor or not—would the nose ever lie to the mouth? Why not? Because it would be destroying itself at the same time. Rather it tells the truth exactly as it appears to itself. Again, would the tongue ever lie to the stomach? Wouldn't it reject what is bitter and permit what is edible? Observe the joint ministry, the complex interchange of services of the body. Here we observe a provident care of the truth that arises spontaneously from the heart. So surely should it be with us also. Let us not lie, since we are "members one of another" [Eph. 4:25]. (Chrysostom, *Homilies on Ephesians*, Hom. XIV, NPNF 1, XIII, p. 117)*

Though we sometimes find that truth is misperceived, when this happens it is as if one part of the body were not reporting accurately, thereby absurdly harming the whole body. The health of the body politic requires that each person tell the truth. The pastor seeks to elicit and increase accurate perception at each of the varied levels of sensory input. The training or education of the soul will always prefer the clearest perception available:

If the interior vision, instead of being trained by learning and diligence so as to acquire the power of discerning good and evil through much experience, gets its eyes misted as it were by ignorance and inexperience, or bleary as from the feebleness induced by some disease, it cannot manage to discern good from evil by any means at all. And so it happens that it does bad things instead of good, and rejects the good in favour of the bad. And if you apply this analogy, which we have treated in regard to the sight of body and soul, to hearing, and taste, and smell, and touch also, and work out the parallel between all the several powers of the bodily senses according to their kind and the corresponding powers of the soul, you will then clearly perceive that training should be undertaken in each case, and what correction ought to be set going. (Origen, *The Song of Songs*, Bk. 1, ACW 26, p. 80)

The training of the soul that every reasonable person should undertake, seeks to improve the accuracy of perception at every level and every sensory interface, so that whatever harms the soul may be accurately perceived. By this process, the entire sensory apparatus becomes awakened and sensitized in the soul's hunger for truth, as Origen pointed out in this amusing erotic metaphor:

> The Bride, [the church], who has associated with herself the many maidens—they are said to be numberless a little further on—relates that she is running towards the fragrance of the Bridegroom's ointments under the compulsion of one single sense, the sense of smell alone. . . . What, do you think, will they do when the Word of God takes possession of their hearing, their sight, their touch, and their taste as well, and offers excellences from Himself that match each single sense according to its nature and capacity. (Origen, *The Song of Songs*, Bk. 1, ACW 26, p. 78)

The church is portrayed as the bride rushing toward the bridegroom, truth incarnate. The entire sensory apparatus is being activated: hearing, sight, touch, and taste, but above all the truth smells terrific. The truth is eliciting from each sense that which is appropriate to its capacity, in order that the truth may become fully known.

The Shepherd of Hermas offered an interpretation of deception. Lying is like refusing to return a deposit due back at a given time. The deposit in this case is the image of God in human creation. Humanity has taken the deposit and misused it, wasted it, and not been able to return it as received:

> Love truth, and let nothing but the truth proceed from your mouth, so that the spirit which God caused to dwell in this flesh will be found truthful by all men (cf. 1 John 2:27), and in that way the Lord who dwells in you will be glorified, because the Lord is truthful in every word and there is nothing false in him. So those who falsify, reject the Lord and become defrauders of the Lord, not returning to him the deposit which they received. For they received from him a spirit free of falseness. If they give this back as a false one, they have defiled the commandment of the Lord, not returning to him the deposit which they received. . . . So when I heard these things I cried a great deal. And when he saw me crying, he said, "Why are you crying?" "Sir," I said, "because I do not know whether I can be saved." "Why?" said he. "Because, sir," I said, "I have never yet in my life spoken a true word, but I have always lived deceitfully with everyone." (Shepherd of Hermas, *The Mandates*, III, sec. 28, 1–3, AF, p. 184)

The Shepherd "cried a great deal" because he knew how much he had lived on lies.

VII. 🐏 DE-CODING DECEPTIONS

The soul guide is well served by what has been called the gift of discernment—that special capacity to penetrate deceptions and grasp the truth of a situation, which is so much a part of good counsel, such as that found in St. Anthony:

Who came troubled with doubts and did not get quietness of mind? For this was the wonderful thing in Anthony's discipline, that, as I said before, having the gift of discerning spirits, he recognized their movements, and was not ignorant whither any one of them turned his energy and made his attack. And not only was he not deceived by them himself, but cheering those who were troubled with doubts, he taught them how to defeat their plans, telling them of the weakness and craft of those who possessed them. Thus each one, as though prepared by him for battle, came down from the mountain braving the designs of the devil and his demons. (Athanasius, *Life of Antony*, sec. 87, 88, NPNF 2, IV, p. 219)

The discernment that Athanasius beheld in Anthony was an ability to distinguish between many possible spirits that seize consciousness, to turn our hearts, to attack our motivations and habit formations. The struggle of the soul was viewed by early Christian soul guides as a contest between friendly and unfriendly superpersonal intelligences, yet not without the collusion of our wills. It can also be viewed by modern interpretations as a struggle against interpersonal and intrapersonal deception. Athanasius pictured the soul guide at work, as if preparing for battle with a crafty, multifaceted enemy, providing the faithful with practical means of resisting temptation.

On what sort of battleground is the soul most likely to be seriously injured, and by what weapons? The much earlier Epistle of Barnabas provided a frightful catalogue of the instruments by which persons would be deceived. Note how many of them hinge on lack of candor and truth telling, and how duplicity is woven throughout demonic temptation:

The Way of the Dark Lord is devious. . . . In it is found all that destroys the souls of men: idol worship, brazen self-assertion, and the arrogance of power; and duplicity; adultery, manslaughter, and robbery; vanity, rascality, sharp practice, spitefulness and contumacy; and black magic; greed, and defiance of God. They persecute the virtuous; they hate truth and love falsehood; they know nothing of the rewards of righteousness, or of devotion to goodness and just judgement. The widow and the orphan are nothing and their sleepless nights are spent, not in fearing God, but in pursuit of vice. Gentleness and patience are altogether alien to them; all they care for is paltry and worthless, all they look for is their own advantage. They have no pity for the poor, not ever trouble their heads about any poor soul in distress. They are always ready with malicious rumours, for knowledge of their Creator is not in them. They make away with infants, destroying the image of God; they turn the needy from their doors, and deal harshly with the afflicted. (*Epistle of Barnabas*, sec. 20, ECW, p. 219)

Wherever one finds deception, idolatry, and arrogance, there one finds the footsteps of the Enemy, the demonic power that vexes human passions. The soul guide sought to discern the varied types of lies. By the medieval period, these types had become formalized in three phases: Vanity lies spontaneously by imagining that one is better than others. Deceit lies by premeditated trickery to draw others into the sphere of lying. The intentional lie destroys human community by maliciously speaking what is known to be false. Those charged with care of souls must know the nature of lies, according to Alan of Lille:

There are three kinds of lies: the lie of vanity, the lie of deceit, and the lie of intention. Of the first it is said: "Everyone speaks vanity to his neighbor." Of the second it is said: "Every man is a liar." Of the third: "You will destroy all who speak lies." The first is wretched, the second blameworthy, the third an abomination. The first is a matter for punishment, the second for blame, the third of malice. The first is spontaneous, the second premeditated, the third elaborated. (Alan of Lille, *The Art of Preaching*, Ch. XXVII, CFS 23, p. 112)

In his comment on the command, "Thou shalt not bear false witness," Luther set forth the types of deceivers, who break the command:

[One] who conceals or suppresses the truth in a court of law. He who lies and deceives to another's hurt. All hurtful flatterers, whisperers and double-dealers. He who speaks evil of his neighbor's possessions, life, words, and works, and defames them. He who gives place to slanderers, helps them on and does not resist them. He who does not use his tongue to defend his neighbor's good name. He who does not rebuke the slanderer. He who does not say all good of every man and keep silent about all evil. He who conceals or does not defend the truth. (Luther, *Brief Explanation*, WML II, p. 363)

In these ways we have spent away our original inheritance of openness, truth-telling, and accurate feeling disclosure. The remedy, however, is not out of reach: plain speech.

Do not equivocate in thought or speech, for a double tongue is a deadly snare; the words you speak should not be false or empty phrases, but fraught with purposeful action. (*Didache*, sec. 2, ECW, p. 228)

Should the truth be told to oppressive state powers who seek to force idolatrous confessions, when life is at risk? Just such a case arose in the ministry of Peter, Bishop of Alexandria after the Diocletian persecution. Having survived the persecution, he drew up rules for the readmission of persons who had lapsed from Christian confession during severe conditions of persecution, torture and roaming death-squads. When under conditions of persecution, certain individuals dissimulated in an idolatrous oath to the Emperor, the refusal of which caused the death of many Christians, should this be regarded as lying, and penance required? Peter thought so.

But upon those who have used dissimulation like David, who feigned himself to be mad to avoid death, being not mad in reality; and those who have not nakedly written down their denial of the faith, but being in much tribulation, as boys endowed with sagacity and prudence amongst foolish children, have mocked the snares of their enemies, either passing by the altars, or giving a writing, or sending heathen to do sacrifice instead of themselves, even though some of them who have confessed have, as I have heard, pardoned individuals of them, since with the greatest caution they have avoided to touch the fire with their own hands, and to offer incense to the impure demons; yet inasmuch as they escaped the notice of their persecutors by doing this, let a penalty of six months' penance be imposed upon them. For thus will they be the rather profited, meditating upon the prophet's words, and saying, "Unto us a child is born, unto us a Son is given; and the government shall be upon His shoulder" [Is. 9:6]. (Peter of Alexandria, *The Canonical Epistle*, Canon V, ANF VI, p. 271)

If six months penitence was required of those who dissembled obedience to idolatrous power under conditions of persecution, what might Peter say of those who dissemble obedience to idolatrous power under conditions where there is no persecution? Gregory the Great thought that the truth should be withheld on some occasions. For while telling a lie is intrinsically culpable, this is to be distinguished from rightly with-holding the truth when the occasion for its disclosure might do harm:

The sincere are to be admonished in one way, the insincere in another. The sincere are to be commended for their intention of never saying anything false, but they should be warned that they should know how to withhold the truth on occasion. For, just as falsehood always harms him who utters it, so the hearing of the truth has sometimes done harm. Wherefore, the Lord, temper-ing speech with silence in presence of His disciples, says: I have yet many things to say to you, but you cannot bear them now [cf. Jn. 16:12]. (Gregory the Great, *Pastoral Care*, Part III, Ch. 11, ACW 11, p. 116)

When the care-giver is tempted to cheat for a good cause, what may be said? If one can offer bread to the poor only by stealing, should one steal? Ambrose answered succinctly:

Everything gained by craft and got together by cheating loses the merit of openness. . . . If it is not possible to help one without injury to another, it is better to help neither than to press hard upon one. Therefore it is not a priest's duty to interfere in money affairs. (Ambrose, *Duties of the Clergy*, Bk. III, Ch. IX, secs. 58, 59, NPNF 2, X, pp. 76, 77)

The pastoral guide does well to set a firm example of truth-telling, else he will be unable to elicit it in others.

This Part of the collection has attempted to show that soul care is essentially a language event, an occurence that proceeds primarily by conversation, yet constantly reaches out beyond words. Non-verbal com-munication is an important dimension of classical pastoralia. Language may become a vehicle either for deceit or truth-telling. There are heal-ing functions embedded in both language and silence. What one says through bodily movement, countenance, gesture, and posture may serve or disserve the care of souls.

6 The Work of the Holy Spirit in Admonition, Discipline, and Comfort

ALTHOUGH CONSPICUOUSLY absent in modern pastoral writings, admonition is a recurrent theme of classical sources on soul guidance. The Latin term *admonitio* translates the Greek *nouthesia*—corrective guidance, a warning to the soul that comes out of love, a reminder of the soul's greatness. It is confrontation, reproof, or counsel on behalf of the good of the soul.

I. 🐾 THE PASTORAL DUTY OF ADMONITION

Anyone who is to grow healthy inwardly and interpersonally needs clear, caring, tough, constructive criticism from others. This correlation was well understood by the pastoral writers.

Although persons need caring admonition in all significant relationships, they have a right to expect it from a physician of souls—one called, mandated, and duly ordained to offer the Word, sacrament, and discipline.

We begin with a passage from the Desert Fathers that reflects the need for a certain caring toughness in interpersonal candor:

Abba Sisoes, the Theban, said to his disciple, "Tell me what you see in me and then I will tell you what I see in you." His disciple said to him, "You are a good man, but a little hard." The old man said to him "You are good, too, but you are not tough enough." (Sisoes, sec. 51, in *Sayings of the Desert Fathers*, p. 185)

Those not tough enough with each other lose the rare benefit of each other's experience, intuitions, hunches, and prudential judgments. Yet in tough-minded feedback there is no way to avoid some discomfort:

Unless the sheaves are bruised and the straw winnowed, the corn within cannot appear and be separated. Let the soul that would advance in virtue first bruise and thresh out its superfluous passions that at the harvest it may have its fruits to show. How many weeds choke the good seed! These first must be

160

rooted out, so that they will not destroy the fruitful crop of the soul. The careful guardian of the soul then sees how he may restrain her in her pleasures, and cut off her desires, to prevent her being overwhelmed with delight in them. The correction of the father who does not spare the rod is useful, that he may render his son's soul obedient to the precepts of salvation.... No one who is chastened and corrected need lose hope, for one who loves his son chastises him. No one should despair of a remedy. (Ambrose, *Letters*, 45, To Horontianus, FC 26, pp. 233–234)

Weeds (inordinate or undisciplined pleasures) choke out seeds (early efforts at excellent habitual behavior patterns). Even after the steady, slow, protected growth of the plant, one cannot harvest the grain until first the fruit is cut, separated from its stem, and split asunder. If you are fortunate enough to have a good soul guide, then if you happen to be chastened (that word does not mean punished, but disciplined out of love), then that chastening stands as the surest evidence that you are being cared for, and that you need not despair of a remedy.

In failing to provide seasonable admonition, the pastor may do an irremediable injustice to one committed to his care. Not speaking is not caring:

To give sleep to the eyes is to cease from care, and thus to neglect altogether the charge of subjects. The eyelids slumber, when our thoughts, weighed down by sloth, connive at what we know should be reproved. To be in deep sleep is neither to know, nor to correct, the actions of those committed to us. To slumber but not to sleep is to be well aware of what should be reprehended, but not to amend it with proper reproof, owing to mental sloth. Yet by slumbering, the eye is induced to sleep profoundly, because commonly the superior who does not eradicate the evil which he observes, comes to that state which his negligence deserves, namely, not even to recognize the sins of his subjects. (Gregory the Great, *Pastoral Care*, Part III, Ch. 4, ACW 11, p. 99)

Some pastors become desensitized to human pain. They may have difficulty even in vaguely recognizing that someone in their care is depressed, anxious, troubled, or hungry, so practiced have they become at not looking. Helping requires admonishing. Admonition is not an end in itself, but a means to reconciliation.

Let us then help each other to restore especially those who are weak in goodness, so that we may all be saved, both converting and admonishing one another. (An Ancient Homily by an Unknown Author [Second Clement], 17, AF, p. 68)

Some parishioners may vaguely want increased happiness or maturity of spirit without any sacrificial effort. Of them Baxter wrote:

The hypocrite's hope is, that though Christ put him upon these promises, he will never put him to the trial for performance, nor ever call him to forsake all indeed: and therefore, if ever he be put to it, he will not perform the promise which he hath made. He is like a patient that promiseth to be wholly ruled by his physician, as hoping that he will put him upon nothing which he cannot bear. But when the bitter potion or the vomit cometh, he saith, "I cannot take it, I had hoped you would have given me gentler physic." (Baxter, Christian Directory, *Works*, Vol. XXX, Part II, p. 391)

Thus if one hopes to live a mature Christian life and at the same time be spared of all inconvenience, the chief duty owed to that person by a spiritual director may be to take away that hope. The false hope must be compassionately guided toward greater realism.

One major deficit of fee-based counseling is that to the degree that the counselor boldly confronts such illusions, the client is less likely to continue paying for it. Admonition is more viable where fees are not contingent.

II. 🐌 FRATERNAL CORRECTION

Thomas Aquinas will serve as a guide in defining fraternal correction, showing why it is needed, how it functions, and its realistic limitations. Thomas began his treatise on fraternal correction by asking to what extent correction is a necessary expression of love (*caritas*), first considering contrary arguments, then answering them:

It would seem that fraternal correction is not an act of charity. For . . . it is an act of charity to bear with a sinner, according to Gal. 4:2: "bear ye one another's burdens, and so you shall fulfill the law of Christ," which is the law of charity. Therefore it seems that the correction of a sinning brother, which is contrary to bearing with him, is not an act of charity.

On the contrary, to correct the wrongdoer is a spiritual almsdeed. But almsdeeds are works of charity, as stated above (Q. 32, A. 1). Therefore fraternal correction is an act of charity.

I answer that, the correction of the wrongdoer is a remedy which should be employed against a man's sin. Now a man's sin may be considered in two ways, first as being harmful to the sinner, secondly as conducing to the harm of others. . . . This is fraternal correction properly so called, which is directed to the amendment of the sinner. Now to do away with anyone's evil is the same as to procure his good; and to procure a person's good is an act of charity. (Thomas Aquinas, *Summa Theologica*, Part II–II, Q. 33, Art. 1, Vol. II, p. 1333)

One does not do another a favor by withholding one's honest, experience-based critique that might contribute to improved functioning. To take the risk of accurately sharing that view is an act of caring love (*caritas*). We express our love for others less well if we perpetually fail to offer any corrective perception of their temptations and egocentricities. To admonish little is to love little:

I should certainly rebuke and reprimand my brother, but I should not be hostile to him. If I say to him out of a brotherly heart: You fool [Luke 12:22], as Christ says to His disciples: O fools, and slow of heart [Luke 24:25], and St. Paul to the Galatians: O foolish Galatians, [Gal. 3:1] this is not sign of anger; it is a sign of friendly love. For if I did not have the welfare of my brother at heart, I would certainly be quiet and let him go. But the fact that I open my mouth and rebuke him is an indication that I love him and seek his welfare. For my failure to instruct and rebuke my brother is actually an evidence of anger. (Luther, "Sermon on Matthew 5:20-26," WLS 3, #3740, p. 1169; WA 37, p. 114)

Often the opposite is assumed, that we rebuke only in anger. Luther grasped with remarkable lucidity the psychological dynamic that if we withhold genuine corrective feedback from our neighbor, we are thereby indirectly expressing our hostility toward him or her, whereas when we openly state negative feedback, we then are showing evidence that we care enough to wish something better for our neighbor. Admonition begins privately, and only upon the failure of this may public admonition be considered:

Our Lord wished the beginning of fraternal correction to be hidden, when one brother corrects another between this one and himself alone.... When the secret admonition has been given once or several times, as long as there is probable hope of his amendment, we must continue to admonish him in private, but as soon as we are able to judge with any probability that the secret admonition is of no avail, we must take further steps. (Thomas Aquinas, *Summa Theologica*, Part II–II, Q. 33, Art. 8, Vol. II, p. 1340)

There is an unsuitable and a suitable time for speaking a word of admonition. It can hardly be construed as an act of caring love to pick an unsuitable time. Corrective love is good, but not good in every situation. The degree to which the partner in dialogue is prone or willing to hear that word of correction is an important component in the equation of determining suitability of timing:

> Fraternal correction is directed to the amendment of the wrongdoer, whom it does not coerce, but merely admonishes. Consequently when it is deemed probable that the sinner will not take the warning, and will become worse, such fraternal correction should be foregone. . . . Whatever is directed to an end, becomes good through being directed to the end. Hence whenever fraternal correction hinders the end, namely the amendment of our brother, it is no longer good, so that when such a correction is omitted, good is not omitted lest evil should befall. (Thomas Aquinas, *Summa Theologica*, Part II–II, Q. 33, Art. 7, Vol. II, p. 1338)

Augustine described the tendency to self-deception in giving ourselves reasons for avoiding or evading admonition when it is called for:

> For often we perversely blind ourselves to the occasions of teaching and admonishing them, sometimes even of reprimanding and chiding them, either because we shrink from the labor or are ashamed to offend them or because we fear to lose good friendships, lest this should stand in the way of our advancement, or injure us in some worldly matter, which either our covetous disposition desires to obtain, or our weakness shrinks from losing. . . .
>
> At times one hesitates to reprove or admonish those who are doing wrong because he seeks a more seasonable opportunity, or because he fears they may be made worse by his rebuke, or that other weak persons may be disheartened from endeavoring to lead a good and pious life, and may be driven from the faith. Under these conditions the omission seems to be occasioned not by covetousness, but by a charitable consideration. But what is reprehensible is, while leading good lives themselves, and finding the conduct of the wicked abhorrent, yet they spare those faults in others which they ought to reprehend and wean them from, because they fear to give offence. . . .
>
> Accordingly this seems to me to be one principal reason why the good are chastised along with the wicked. . . . They are punished together, not because they have spent an equally corrupt life, but because the good as well as the wicked, though not equally with them, love this present life. (Augustine, *City of God*, Bk. I.9, NPNF 1, II, pp. 6–7)*

Jeremy Taylor cautioned against allowing admonition to become individually specific or excessively personalized in sermons:

> In the reproof of sins, be as particular as you please, and spare no man's sin, but meddle with no man's person; neither name any man nor signify him, neither reproach him nor make him to be suspected. He that doth otherwise, makes his sermon to be a libel, and the ministry of repentance an instrument of revenge; and, so doing, he shall exasperate the man, but never amend the sinner.... Press those graces most that do most good, and make the least noise. (Jeremy Taylor, *RAC*, secs. 46–48, in *CS*, pp. 15–16)

These passages show how delicate is the process of admonition, how subtle its timing, how deeply rooted in love it must be to reach its mark.

III. 🐛 To Whom Does Admonition Belong?

There is agreement that admonition belongs to the pastoral office. The classical tradition has debated about the extent to which admonition belongs to the general ministry of the laity.

Should all believers be involved in the responsibility of mutual correction, or is this essentially a function reserved for the pastoral office? The central stream of the tradition has taken the view that admonition, properly conceived, should be a concern of the whole company of believers. But precisely because it is so important to the whole community, the ordained minister must pay special attention to corrective love, which is thought to be intrinsic to the ministry of Word, sacrament, and pastoral care. Thomas thoughtfully distinguished between admonition considered as an act of charity for and by all the laity, and admonition considered as an act of justice to be received from those from whom it is especially due, viz., the ordained clergy:

> It would seem that fraternal correction belongs to prelates alone. For Jerome says: "Let priests endeavor to fulfil this saying of the Gospel: 'If thy brother sin against thee'".... On the contrary, it is written (Dist. xxiv, qu. 2, Can. *Tam Sacerdotes*): Both priests and all the rest of the faithful should be most solicitous for those who perish, so that their reproof may either correct their sinful ways, or, if they be incorrigible, cut them off from the Church.
>
> I answer that, as stated above (Art. 1), correction is twofold. One is an act of charity which seeks in a special way the recovery

of an erring brother by means of a simple warning; such like correction belongs to anyone who has charity, be he subject or prelate.

But there is another correction which is an act of justice purposing the common good which is procured not only by warning one's brother, but also, sometimes, by punishing him, that others may, through fear, desist from sin. Such a correction belongs only to prelates. (Thomas Aquinas, *Summa Theologica*, Part II–II, Q. 33, Art. 3, Vol. II, p. 1335)

Thus without denying the importance of mutual correction in the general ministry of the laity, Thomas reserved to ordained ministry a clear and distinct call to the practice of admonition. When Thomas spoke of punishment, however, he was referring quintessentially to penance, to penitential acts presided over by the pastor, not to any other punitive action.

If mutual correction belongs also the laity, should a lay person correct a minister? Thomas thought that superiors need correction too:

The fraternal correction which is an act of charity is within the competency of everyone in respect of any person towards whom he is bound by charity, provided there be something in that person which requires correction.... When a subject corrects his prelate, he ought to do so in a becoming manner, not with impudence and harshness, but with gentleness and respect.... If the faith were endangered, a subject ought to rebuke his prelate even publicly. Hence Paul, who was Peter's subject, rebuked him in public, on account of the imminent danger of scandal concerning faith, and, as the gloss of Augustine says on Gal. 2:11, "Peter gave an example to superiors, that if at any time they should happen to stray from the straight path, they should not disdain to be reproved by their subjects." (Thomas Aquinas, *Summa Theologica*, Part II–II, Q. 33, Art. 4, Vol. II, p. 1336)

Francis de Sales used the same biblical text to show that pastors and spiritual guides too need correction:

The sisters ought not to be surprised that the Superior commits imperfections, since St. Peter, Chief Pastor as he was of Holy Church, and universal Superior of all Christians, fell into a fault, and that so grave a one that he deserved correction for it, as says St. Paul. Neither must the Superior show any astonishment if her faults are noticed; but she should observe the humility and gentleness with which St. Peter received the correction of St. Paul, whose Superior, nevertheless, he was. It is hard to say which is the most to be admired, the strength of St. Paul's courage in reproving St. Peter, or the humility with which St. Peter submitted to the correction given to him. (Francis de Sales, Conference XVI, *SC*, p. 310)

Being monitor of another's sins is itself a spiritual risk, as Baxter recognized:

I know myself to be unworthy to be your monitor; but a monitor you must have; and it is better for us to hear of our sin and duty from anybody than from nobody. Receive the admonition, and you will see no cause in the monitor's unworthiness to repent of it. (Baxter, *RP*, p. 132)

Those who admonish others need themselves all the more admonition:

Do those who reproach the faults of others strip themselves thoroughly of the contamination of every sin? Indeed, by a dispensation of great kindness, God often allows those through whom He arranges to correct the errors of others to fall unpleasantly, so that from their own fault they may learn how merciful they ought to be in the reproach of others. (Richard of St. Victor, *The Twelve Patriarchs*, Ch. 45, p. 102)

When the monitor falls into the need for admonition, providence is offering a gracious reminder of the need for mercy amid the imperfections that so widely characterize human life.

IV. 🦌 GENTLENESS IN ADMONITION

If the spirit of admonition is grounded in love, then it will necessarily be gentle, not harsh or mean-tempered. For that would defeat its purpose, betraying a spirit of aggression instead of love. Good parents warn and remind children because they care, not because they want them to feel repressed or pained.

I desire, according to my humble talents, to teach a Gospel that builds up, and not one that breaks down; one that gives off a pleasant odor, and not a stench. (Menno Simons, Instruction on Discipline to the Church at Emden, *CWMS*, p. 1051)

When we are necessarily and accountably placed in a corrective role in relation to another, there is understandably a potential confusion between our own tendency to be angry toward another, and our duty to admonish or correct. How is that inward conflict to be understood and dealt with? Macarius distinguished between venting our feelings and gentle admonition:

The same Abba Macarius said, "If you reprove someone, you yourself get carried away by anger and you are satisfying your own passion; do not lose yourself, therefore in order to save another." (Macarius the Great, sec. 17, in *Sayings of the Desert Fathers*, p. 110)

The proportional balance between gentleness and discipline is always subject to tendencies to excess, which may need correctives that may at times seem excessive:

Certainly both the gentleness which we desire to maintain, and the discipline which we shall endeavour without passion to administer, may be hindered, if God in His hidden counsels order it otherwise, and either appoint that this so great wickedness be punished with a more severe chastisement or in yet greater displeasure leave the sin without punishment in this world, its guilty authors being neither reproved nor reformed. (Augustine, *Letters*, XCI, To Nectarius, sec. 6, NPNF 2, I, p. 378)

This selection assumes a dialectical balance between gentleness and discipline. These depend upon each other in proper proportion. Yet both gentleness and discipline may at times be set aside by God's own counsel in order to pursue a more dramatic teaching function, either by a more severe chastisement that hopefully would sooner bring the behavioral deficit to correction, or at worst, by a benign neglect that would postpone the needed chastisement and allow sinners to live out the consequences of their sin. A similar interpretation was set forth by Jeremy Taylor:

Be not hasty in pronouncing damnation against any man or party in a matter of disputation. It is enough that you reprove an error; but what shall be the sentence against it at the day of judgment, thou knowest not; and therefore pray for the erring person, and reprove him, but leave the sentence to his Judge. (Jeremy Taylor, *RAC*, IV, sec. 52, in *CS*, p. 17)

To admonish or warn is not the same as to judge, as if one had the right to stand in judgment of another from some transcendent perspective. It is difficult to do, but we can gently admonish while leaving judgment to another more wise and just than we. Is it on the whole better, therefore, that the pastor be lenient or tough?

You must leave no room for the suspicion that you wish to judge so sternly that you would reject sinners entirely, or refuse to offer them exhortations that might lead them to a better path.

God spoke through Isaiah in a way that speaks to church leaders today: "Comfort ye, comfort ye my people, ye priests: speak comfortably to Jerusalem" [Is. 40:1]. It therefore behooves you, upon hearing those words of his, to encourage those who have offended, and lead them to repentance, and afford them hope. . . . For if a person were walking by the side of a river and almost ready to stumble, and you should nudge him and make him go on into the river, instead of offering him your hand for his assistance, wouldn't you be guilty of the murder of your brother? Rather you owe it to him to lend him a helping hand just as he is about to fall, lest he perish without remedy. . . . It is your duty, O bishop, neither to overlook the sins of the people, nor to reject those who are penitent. (*Constitutions of the Holy Apostles*, Bk. II, sec. III, ANF VII, p. 402)*

Luther employed a surgical metaphor in showing that admonition, though painful, remains necessary:

For you have to inflict the wound in such a way that you also know how to alleviate and heal it. You have to be severe in such a way as not to forget kindness. Thus God, too, puts lightning into the rain and breaks up gloomy clouds and a dark sky into fruitful showers. (Luther, "Lectures on Galatians, 1519," LW 27, p. 305; cf. WA 2, p. 546)

Baxter commented on the question of whether the pastor should be severe or mild in discipline:

There must be a prudent mixture of severity and mildness both in our preaching and discipline; each must be predominant, according to the quality or character of the person, or matter, that we have in hand. If there be *no* severity, our reproofs will be despised. If *all* severity, we shall be taken as usurpers of dominion, rather than persuaders of the minds of men to the truth. (Baxter, *RP*, p. 117)

Be candid, but not judgmentally absolute:

I would, however, advise you to be very cautious how you pass too hasty or absolute censures on any you have to do with; because, it is not so easy a matter to discern a man to be certainly graceless, as many imagine it to be; and you may do the work in hand as well without such an absolute conclusion as with it. . . . Truly, my friends, I have no mind, the Lord knows, to make your condition worse than it is, nor to occasion you any causeless fear or trouble; but, I suppose, you would account me a treacherous enemy, and not a faithful minister, if I should flatter you, and not tell you the truth. If you seek a physician in your sickness, you would have him tell you the truth, though it were the worst. . . . Set these things home with a peculiar earnestness; for if you get not to the heart, you do little or nothing; and that which affecteth not is soon forgotten. (Baxter, *RP*, pp. 248–50)

The failure of the pastor to address the correction at an emotive depth may allow it to be soon forgotten. Hence the correction must be driven home. Flattery is of no help, only truth. Yet it is equally unwise to take on the presumption of absolute censure. Benedict stressed the timing of admonition as a key determinant of whether it should be firm or lenient:

Observe this rule of the apostle: "Reprove, beseech, correct" [2 Tim. 4:2]: which consists in a judicious timing: to mix gentleness with sternness: at one time to show the severity of a master, at another the tenderness of a father: to use rigour with the irregular and the turbulent, but win to better things the obedient, mild, and patient. I warn him to reprove and chastise the careless or contemptuous. Nor is he to dissemble the faults of those that go amiss. (Benedict of Nursia, *Rule,* LCC XII, p. 295)

Tenderness belongs to those situations where severity would wound too deeply. Severity belongs to those situations where tenderness would reinforce dependency.

V. ☙ On Avoiding Fault-Finding

Corrective love is entirely different from the spirit of fault-finding, which Luther described so vividly:

Everyone enjoys hearing and telling the worst about his neighbor and it tickles him to see a fault in someone else. If a woman were as beautiful as the sun but had one little spot or blemish on her body, you would be expected to look only for that spot and to talk about it. (Luther, "Lectures on Galatians, 1519," LW 27, p. 308)

Admonition does not spring out of despair of genuine change, but out of hope for constructive, realistic, meaningful behavioral change:

No one should immediately rebuke as if he despaired of the restoration of the sinner; he should do so with a definite indication that he is hoping for the best. (Luther, "Lectures on Galatians, 1519," WLS 3, #3745, p. 1170; cf. LW 27, p. 326; WA 2, p. 560)

If compulsive anger parades under the banner of loving others, it needs deliberate resistance. One must learn to say "Stop this!" to a "malicious reckoner of accounts":

I have heard people slandering, and I have rebuked them. And these doers of evil replied in self-defence that they were doing so out of love and care for the person whom they were slandering. I said to them: "Stop that kind of love." . . . Do not regard the feelings of a person who speaks to you about his neighbour disparagingly, but rather say to him: "Stop, brother! I fall into graver sins every day, so how can I criticize him?" In this way you will achieve two things: you will heal yourself and your neighbour with one plaster. . . . Listen to me, listen, all you malicious reckoners of other men's accounts! If it is true (as it really is true) that "with what judgment ye judge, ye shall be judged" [Matt. 7:2], then whatever sins we blame our neighbour for, whether bodily or spiritual, we shall fall into them ourselves. That is certain. Hasty and severe judges of the sins of their neighbour fall into this passion because they have not yet attained to a thorough and constant remembrance and concern for their own sins. For if anyone could see his own vices accurately without the veil of self-love, he would worry about no one else in this life, considering that he would not have time enough for mourning for himself, even though he were to live a hundred years, and even though he were to see a whole River Jordan of tears streaming from his eyes. . . . A good grape-picker, who eats the ripe grapes, will not start gathering unripe ones. A charitable and sensible mind takes careful note of whatever virtues it sees in anyone, but a fool looks for faults and defects. And of such it is said: "They have searched after iniquity, and in searching they are grown weary of searching" [Ps. 63:7]. (Climacus, *The Ladder of Divine Ascent*, Step 10, secs. 4, 7, 9–10, 16, pp. 89–91)

The hasty judge has forgotten his own sins. To deliberately look for defects in the character of others is not to admonish rightly. Athanasius described how the Arian party became so fixated upon the expression of anger that it became a self-accelerating syndrome:

They also gave permission to the females of their party to insult whom they chose; and although the holy and faithful women withdrew on one side, and gave them the way, yet they gathered round them like Bacchanals and Furies, and esteemed it a misfortune if they found no means to injure them, and spent that day sorrowfully on which they were unable to do them some mischief. (Athanasius, *History of the Arians*, sec. 59, NPNF 2, IV, p. 292)

The dynamics of overzealous admonition, "the vice of curious inquiry," were astutely analyzed by Hugh of St. Victor:

Because a person once puffed up has learnt to think thus highly of himself, he disdains to bring his own actions before the bar of reason, and the less he thinks there is within himself that merits blame, the readier he is to hunt down someone else. Yet this pride cloaks itself at first under the semblance of good zeal, and it persuades the deluded heart that he who acquiesces in another's fault is no perfect lover of righteousness, and that he undoubtedly so acquiesces, who neglects to rebuke an offender while he can.

Deluded by this error, therefore, the sorely imperceptive soul gives itself over wholly to the vice of curious inquiry. And by degrees, as the disease increases, while at the outset it makes a habit of chasing after other people's faults without restraint, it ultimately reaches a condition in which, with everything it sees, it tries either to misrepresent it openly, or to interpret it unfavourably.

Thus, for instance, if such persons see that some people are a trifle anxious about common needs, they call them covetous. Those whom they see provident they call misers. Those again who are friendly and cheerful towards everyone are, so they say, given to the vice of flattery; and at the same time they believe that those who generally go about with a sad face are eaten up with jealousy. (Hugh of St. Victor, *SSW*, pp. 109–110)

VI. 🐝 THE PRACTICE OF ADMONITION

Whatever theories may prevail about admonition, the pastor must finally test them out in practice. What follows are some selections that deal with practical approaches of the pastor to the sensitive situation of offering corrective love to those in his charge.

Admonition is reserved primarily for situations in which persons are *overtaken* in faults. It is for upbuilding, not judging. John Chrysostom thought that the manner of offering admonition was as important as the content of the communication itself:

Under the pretense of offering admonition, they were merely gratifying their private feelings. While professing to correct faults that had been committed, these were merely advancing their own ambition. Hence Paul wrote: "Brothers, if someone is caught in a sin." He did not say if a man commit but if he be "caught" in a sin, that is, if he be overtaken, carried away. "You who are spiritual should restore him gently" [Gal. 6:1, NIV]. He said not "chastise" nor "judge," but "restore." Nor does he stop here, but in order to show that it behooved them to be very gentle towards those who had lost their footing, adds, "in a spirit of meekness." He says not, "in meekness," but, "in a spirit of meekness," signifying thereby that this is acceptable to the Spirit, and that to be able to administer correction with mildness is a spiritual gift. Then, to prevent the one being unduly exalted by having to correct the other, Paul puts both under the same fear, saying, "But watch yourself, or you also may be tempted." It is like the rich who give contributions to the indigent in the awareness that they themselves might have been trapped in poverty and would have wished to receive the same generosity. So should we proceed with admonition. (Chrysostom, *Commentary on Galatians*, Ch. VI, NPNF 1, XIII, p. 43, NIV)*

As the rich do well to give to the poor keenly aware that they have no enduring claim upon wealth, so the pastor does well to admonish those overtaken in fault by keen awareness of his own faults.

Very early in the pastoral tradition, deliberate constraints were placed upon admonition: Curb resentment and arrogance; do not speak equivocally or prematurely; avoid unnecessary dissension; do not correct another without confessing your own faults. The Epistle of Barnabas provided these practical guidelines for the giving and receiving of admonition:

Do not exaggerate your own importance, but be modest at all points, and never claim credit for yourself. Cherish no ill-natured designs upon your neighbour. Forbid yourself any appearance of presumption . . . If you have to rebuke anyone for a fault, do it without fear or favour. Keep calm and mild; reverence the words you have heard, and bear no resentment towards a brother. Never be in two minds as to whether something is or is not to be. . . . Never equivocate, either in thought or speech. . . . Never be in a hurry to speak, for the tongue is a fatal snare. For your soul's sake, be as pure as you can. . . . Do nothing to encourage dissensions. Bring the disputants together and compose their quarrel. And make confession of your own faults; you are not to come to prayer with a bad conscience. That is the Way of Light. (*The Epistle of Barnabas*, sec. 19, ECW, pp. 217–219)

Paul served as model for the duly balanced application of negative and positive reinforcement:

[Paul] first praised them for those things in which they displayed courage, and afterwards, with prudent admonition, strengthened them in that matter wherein they were weak. . . . True teacher that he was, he conducted matters so that they were first to recall something for which they were praised, and afterwards follow his admonition. The words of praise were to fortify their minds against feeling disturbed over the admonition. (Gregory the Great, *Pastoral Care*, Part III, Ch. 8, ACW 11, p. 106)

Fourteen centuries after Gregory this same principle was rediscovered by behavior therapists and child psychologists: the criticism of behavioral deficits is best achieved in the context of a trusting relationship in which the good things one is doing are recognized and affirmed.

Admonition is closely connected with the fitting reception of the Lord's Supper:

About the time of the Sacrament, every Minister that knows any one of his Parish guilty of eminent Sins, ought to go and Admonish him to change his Course of Life, and not to profane the Table of the Lord; and if private Admonitions have no Effect; then if his Sins are Publick and Scandalous, he ought to deny him the Sacrament. . . . Both Private and Publick Admonitions might be more used than they are. There is a flatness in all these things among us. Some are willing to do nothing, because they cannot do all that they ought to do; whereas the right way for procuring an enlargement of our Authority, is to use that which we have well; not as an Engine to gratifie our own and other Peoples' Passions, not to vex People, not look after Fees, more than the Correction of Manners, or the Edification of the People. . . . For the truth is, Mankind is so strongly compounded, that it is very hard to restrain Ecclesiastical Tyranny on the one hand, without running to a Lawless Licentiousness on the other. . . . Fit times are to be chosen for this; it may be often the best way to do it by a Letter; For there may be ways fallen upon, of reproving the worst Men, in so soft a manner, that if they are not reclaimed, yet they shall not be irritated or made worse by it. (Burnet, *Of the Pastoral Care*, Ch. 8, pp. 91–93)

If the pastor is lax in admonition, pastoral authority generally will be weakened. The practice of admonition tests the metal of clergy because it is so difficult to accomplish without falling into either overbearing legalism or neglectful license.

Gregory thought one should approach the admonition of a haughty person with exceptional caution. He employed two shrewd metaphors—the gentle training of horses, and the gradual palatability of medicines:

> Thus, too, in the case of unbroken horses we first stroke them gently with the hand, so that afterwards we may tame them completely even by using the whip; and to the bitter draughts of drugs a portion of sweet honey is added, so that what will benefit the health may not be crude and bitter to the taste, and while the taste is beguiled by the sweetness, the deadly humours are expelled by what is bitter. So, in the very beginning reproof of the haughty must include a proportionate amount of praise, so that while they accept the approbations which they like, they may also accept the reproofs which they dislike. Again, generally, we are better able to persuade the haughty to their profit, if we say that their progress is more likely to benefit us than themselves, and if we beg their amendment as a favour to us rather than to themselves. For the haughty are more easily led to good, if they believe that in turning to good they will profit others also. (Gregory the Great, *Pastoral Care*, Part III, Ch. 17, ACW 11, p. 143)

One had best be realistic in dealing with self-assertive egocentrism. It may be necessary first to encourage such persons by temporarily attributing more to them than they are due in order to provide a platform on which they may later be brought to a more humble self-recognition.

Ambrose described the way in which corrective love seeks practical amendment in a relationship between friends, by avoiding harshness, bitterness, flattery and arrogance, expressing sympathy from the heart:

> When one knows of any fault in a friend, one ought to rebuke him secretly—if he does not listen, one must do it openly. For rebukes are good, and often better than a silent friendship. Even if a friend thinks himself hurt, still rebuke him; and if the bitterness of the correction wounds his mind, still rebuke him and fear not. "The wounds of a friend are better than the kisses of flatterers" [Prov. 27:6]. . . . Open thy breast to a friend that he may be faithful to thee, and that thou mayest receive from him the delight of thy life. "For a faithful friend is the medicine of life and the grace of immortality" [Ecclus. 6:16] . . . Do not desert a friend in time of need, not forsake him nor fail him, for friendship is the support of life. . . . Let us aid by giving counsel, let us offer our best endeavours, let us sympathize with them with all our heart. . . . Let not thy warning be harsh, nor thy rebuke bit-

ter, for as friendship ought to avoid flattery, so, too, ought it to be free from arrogance. For what is a friend but a partner in love, to whom thou unitest and attachest thy soul, and with whom thou blendest so as to desire from being two to become one; to whom thou entrustest thyself as to a second self, from whom thou fearest nothing, and from whom thou demandest nothing dishonourable for the sake of thine own advantage. Friendship is not meant as a source of revenue, but is full of seemliness, full of grace. Friendship is a virtue, not a way of making money. It is produced, not by money, but by esteem; not by the offer of rewards, but by a mutual rivalry in doing kindnesses. (Ambrose, *Duties of the Clergy*, Bk. III, Ch. XXII, sec. 127–128, 134, NPNF 2, X, pp. 88–89)

The true friend is an alter ego to whom one entrusts oneself with complete openness, from whom no advantage is sought. If faults are ignored in such a relationship, they take root.

VII. 🐝 Admonition Private and Public

Baxter urged public forms of discipline, on behalf of the health of the community, only after private forms had been extensively pursued:

We must reprove and admonish those who live offensively or impenitently. . . . In most cases it will be necessary to speak with the greatest plainness and power, to shake their careless hearts. . . . The last part of our oversight, which I shall note, consists in the exercise of Church discipline. This consists, after the aforesaid private reproofs, in more public reproof, combined with exhortation to repentance, in prayer for the offender, in restoring the penitent, and in excluding and avoiding the impenitent. . . . The principal use of this public discipline is not for the offender himself, but for the Church. It tends exceedingly to deter others from similar offenses, and so to keep the congregation and their worship pure. Seneca could say, "He who excuses present evils transmits them to posterity." And elsewhere, "He who spares the guilty harms the good." (Baxter, *RP*, pp. 104–106)*

It is dangerous to the health of the community when gentle reproof is lacking. Discipline serves both toward the restoration of the penitent and the integrity of the *communio sanctorum*. Private sympathy toward an offender cannot override caring for the good of the commonweal.

Persistent lack of reproof only increases the momentum of evil. The pastor cannot collude with those who would systematically circumvent the moral law:

If he absolutely shut up men's mouths, and forbid all disclosing of faults, many an evil may not only be, but also spread in his Parish, without any remedy, (which cannot be applied without notice), to the dishonor of God, and the infection of his flock, and the discomfort, discredit and hindrance of the Pastor. . . . all are honest, till the contrary be proved. Besides, it concerns the Commonwealth that Rogues should be known; and Charity to the public hath the precedence of private charity. So that it is so far from being a fault to discover such offenders, that it is a duty rather; which may do much good, and save much harm. (Geo. Herbert, *CP*, Ch. XXXVII, CWS, pp. 112, 113)

Under what circumstances, then, is it fitting that one correct another? Ignatius Loyola set forth clear criteria for making this judgment:

When the sin is public, as in the case of a . . . known error which is corrupting the souls of those with whom we are conversing.
[Or] When the hidden sin is made known to someone to help him rise from his own sin. There must, however, be some grounds or probable reasons for expecting that this will help him. (Ignatius Loyola, *Spiritual Exercises*, p. 52)

Baxter set forth these key biblical imperatives guiding pastoral admonition:

God who calleth all men to repentance, hath commanded us to "exhort one another daily, while it is called To-day, lest any be hardened through the deceitfulness of sin," (Hebrews 3:13) and that we do not hate our brother in our heart, but in any wise rebuke our neighbour, and not suffer sin upon him, (Leviticus 19:17) and that if our brother offend us, we should tell him his fault between us and him; and if he hear us not, we should take two or three more with us; and if he hear not them, we should tell the church; and if he hear not the church, he must be to us as a heathen man and a publican; (Matthew 18:15–17) and those that sin, we must rebuke before all, that others may fear, (I Timothy 5:20) and rebuke with all authority, (Titus 2:15), yea, were it an apostle of Christ that should sin openly, he must be reproved openly, as Paul did Peter, (Galatians 2:11, 14), and if they repent not, we must avoid them, and with such not so much as eat, (2

Thessalonians 3:6, 11, 12, 14; I Corinthians 5:11–13). (Baxter, *RP*, pp. 106, 107)

Private admonition is best written into the daily walk of Christians. Only when it fails is there public recourse, and that only with witnesses. The breaking off of communication can come only after a lengthy and serious process of attempted reconciliation.

VIII. ❦ Dynamics of Internal Resistance

Good pastoral admonition will listen intently to the resistance received. For it will provide the most important clues on how to proceed further. Resistance shows where there is tenderness, soreness, and inflammation. It was particularly in the monastic tradition that resistance to admonition was thought to be indicative of serious concern and a hazard to the soul's growth:

He who will not accept a reproof, just or unjust, renounces his own salvation. But he who accepts it with an effort, or even without an effort, will soon receive the remission of his sins. . . . He whose will and desire in conversation is to establish his own opinion, even though what he says is true, should recognize that he is sick with the devil's disease. (Climacus, *The Ladder of Divine Ascent*, Step 4, secs. 44, 48, p. 38)

The inordinate desire to establish one's own opinion, even if it is a true opinion, was thought to be a flawed habit, according to the monastic tradition.

Richard Baxter thought that the pastoral counselor had best be realistic about the diverse and subtle forms of resistance likely to be met:

How many weighty and yet intricate cases of conscience have we almost daily to resolve! And can so much work, and such work as this, be done by raw, unqualified men? O what strongholds have we to batter, and how many of them! What subtle and obstinate resistance must we expect from every heart we deal with! (Baxter, *RP*, p. 69)

Correction is preferably to be received as a valuable gift, and not resisted. For how may love be expressed if there are no means of correcting itself? How could happiness grow without corrective love? Parenting does not occur without chastisement:

O my friends, do let us accept correction; it is something nobody ought to resent. Mutual admonition is wholly good and beneficial, for it leads us into conformity with the will of God. The sacred word says, "The Lord chastised me severely, yet without delivering me to death" [Ps. 118:18]. "Those whom the Lord loves, he chastises; everyone whom he acknowledges as a son, he scourges" [Heb. 12:6; Prov. 3:12].... Again it says, "Happy is the man whom the Lord reproves. Reject not the admonitions of the Almighty, for though he inflicts pain, yet afterwards he makes whole again; he wounds, but his hands bring healing. He will bring you out of six troubles, and in the seventh no ill will touch you" [Job 5:17–19]. (Clement of Rome, *To the Corinthians*, sec. 56, ECW, p. 52)

There was a firm conviction in early Christian counseling (even as early as the late first century) that admonition had a beneficial purpose, and that one simply could not grow in faith and grace without it. Modern views mistake the purpose of admonition as tending toward neuroticism or masochism. One would be far worse off if no one cared enough to say in a friendly way: Do not go so near that cliff! Do not permit that bad habit to take root! Do not hurt yourself that way! The overly defensive are prone to regard corrective criticism as a threat to them or a rejection of them.

It is as if one were to call the words of a physician "threats," when he tells his patients, "I will have to use the knife, and apply cauteries, if you do not obey my prescriptions and regulate your diet and mode of life in such a way as I direct you." (Origen, *Against Celsus*, Ch. LXXII, ANF IV, p. 529)

How can a physician of souls cure the sicknesses of the soul if one begins by saying: "You can treat me in any way you see fit, as long as there is no discomfort of any sort"? At times a needful admonition will involve the direct censure of an ill-advised behavior pattern. Lactantius considered how such a censure might be given and received:

They are deceived by no slight error who defame all censure, whether human or divine, with the name of bitterness and malice, thinking that he ought to be called injurious who visits the injurious with punishment. But if this is so, it follows that we have injurious laws, which enact punishment for offenders, and injurious judges who inflict capital punishments on those convicted of crime. But if the law is just which awards to the transgressor his due, and if the judge is called upright and good when he punishes crimes,—for he guards the safety of good men who punishes the evil—it follows that God, when He opposes the evil, is not injurious; but he himself is injurious who either injures an innocent man, or spares an injurious person that he may injure many. (Lactantius, *A Treatise on the Anger of God*, Ch. XVII, ANF VII, p. 273)

The judge who cares about the safety of the innocent does injury to the innocent by not opposing vigorously threats to their safety. John Climacus thought that the counselee should be far less worried when he is getting active resistance from his counselor, than when his counselor gives him nothing or treats him innocuously:

If your director constantly rebukes you, and you thereby obtain great faith and love for him, then know that the Holy Spirit has invisibly made His abode in your soul, and the power of the Most High has overshadowed you. But do not boast or rejoice when you bear insults and indignities courageously, but rather mourn that you have done something meriting rebuke and incensed the soul of your director against you. Do not be surprised at what I am going to say (for I have Moses to support me). It is better to sin against God than against our father; for when we anger God, our director can reconcile us; but when he is incensed against us, we no longer have anyone to make propitiation for us. But it seems to me that both cases amount to the same thing. (Climacus, *The Ladder of Divine Ascent*, Step 4, sec. 121, p. 53)

This is a remarkable passage coming from the heart of the monastic tradition of spiritual direction that reveals how important it is to receive the caring resistance of the counselor. For the advisor who cares enough about you to give firm and constant resistance to your misconceptions and misdeeds is far more valuable to you than the one who may be content to let you deteriorate.

IX ❦ CANDOR AS A PASTORAL VIRTUE

The pastoral writers spoke often of the "duty to disturb false peace." However important may be the values of peace and tranquility, they are not absolute, and at times the pastor must deliberately penetrate the facade of false peace in order to speak the truth in love.

The peaceful are to be admonished not to fear disturbing their temporal peace, by breaking out into words of reproof. Further, they are admonished to keep inwardly with undiminished love the same peace which outwardly they disturb by their reproving voice. David declares that he had prudently observed both of these, when he says: "With them that hated peace I was peaceable" (Ps. 119:7). . . . So, too, Paul says: "If it be possible, as much as is in you have peace with all men" (Rom. 12:18). When he was about to exhort his disciples to have peace with all, he said first, "if it be possible," and added, "as much as is in you." For if they reproved evil deeds, it would have been difficult for them to have peace with all men. But when temporal peace is disturbed in the hearts of evil men by our reproof, peace must be kept inviolable in our own hearts. (Gregory the Great, *Pastoral Care*, Part III, Ch. 22, ACW 11, p. 167)*

It is for this reason that fearless candor is a crucial virtue of the pastor:

He should not be silent or mumble but should testify without being frightened or bashful. He should speak out candidly without regarding or sparing anyone, let it strike whomever or whatever it will. It is a great hindrance to a preacher if he looks around and worries about what people like or do not like to hear, or what might make him unpopular or bring harm or danger upon him. (Luther, "The Sermon on the Mount," LW 21, p. 9)

Luther's dissatisfaction with Erasmus focussed precisely on this point. For he thought Erasmus, despite his great qualifications as a scholar, had equivocated, and chosen to hide beneath intentional ambiguities:

Erasmus is a veritable Momus. He ridicules and derides everything, all religion and Christ. And in order to be able the better to do so, he by day and night thinks up equivocal and ambiguous words so that his books may be read also by a Turk. And when he is thought to have said many things, he has said nothing at all. All his writings may be construed in any way [that anyone desires]. (Luther, Table-Talk, WLS 1, #936, p. 317–318; WA-T 1, No. 811)

Admonition must be given straightforwardly, and not withheld as if contingent upon what another's response to it might be. If Moses had withheld the divine word from the Pharaoh because he was unsure he could get a positive response, how long would he have waited? God called Moses to preach even when there was no ready listener:

The question is why God bids Moses to preach although He Himself says: Pharaoh will not listen to you. Is it not foolish for someone to say to another: Friend, preach to Pharaoh, but be advised that he will not listen to you. . . . Only the Word of God is entrusted to Moses, not the responsibility of making Pharaoh soft or hard by preaching. . . . [Says God]: Go on, Moses, preach! If you are despised because of it, commit that to Me. (Luther, "Sermon on Exodus 7:3–5, Dec. 11, 1524," WLS 3, #3568, p. 1117; WA 16, p. 116f.)

Pastoral candor can be at times either soft or firm, but in either case it must be clear and straightforward:

> Let a faithful minister of the Word consider that he has been set by God as a watchman and lookout of the church, so that, when he notices that some of his sheep have gone aside from the way of the righteous and have turned aside into the way of sinners, he be neither a sleeping and blind watchman nor a dumb dog (Is. 56:10). Nor ought he provide soft pillows for the impious (Ezek. 13:18). But let him cry out against sins with a loud voice (Is. 58:1). And let him be instant in prayer and exhortations, threats and rebukes in all patience and teaching, both in season and in a spirit of gentleness and also out of season with severe rebukes (Ezek. 3:17; 33:7; 2 Tim. 4:2; Titus 2:15; 1 Cor. 4:21). For through these means God recalls the erring and raises the fallen. (Martin Chemnitz, *Ministry, Word and Sacrament*, Part 2, sec. 52, p. 47)

Open reproof is better than silent resentment:

> In company with the other brethren do not adulterate a brother's customary due of praise because of the grief against him still hidden in your heart, by imperceptibly mixing censure in your conversation. . . . Do not say: I do not hate my brother in putting him out of mind. Listen to Moses who said: "Thou shalt not hate thy brother in thy heart, but reprove him openly, and thou wilt not incur sin through him" (Lev. 19:17). . . . Do not goad a brother by speaking in riddles, lest you receive the like from him in turn and you drive from both of you the disposition for charity. But go and reprove him in the freedom of charity that you may remove the causes of grief and free the both of you from trouble and grief. . . . In the time of peace do not recall what a brother said in the time of grief, even though the offensive things were said to your face, even though they were said to another about you and you heard them afterwards, lest in suffering grudging thoughts you turn again to destructive hate of a brother. (Maximus the Confessor, *The Four Centuries of Charity*, Ch. 4, sec. 28–29, 32, 34, ACW 21, pp. 196–197)

In admonishing, do not speak in riddles, but openly.

X. 🥀 ADMONITION AS A PRESERVATIVE OF COMMUNITY

Modern views of pastoral counseling tend to assume a highly individualistic view of counsel. They presuppose that pastoral counseling has as its major purpose the service of individuals, of individual self-actualization, of the mental and emotional health of individual persons. Classical pastoral care was not so individualistic. It was concerned as well with the health of the community before God. The reason why admonition was so important hinged on the fact that it helped to preserve the stability, tranquillity, good name, and proximate goodness of the community. Without admonition, the community of faith would slowly but surely become like an unweeded garden.

The pastoral writers thought that the church could be profoundly harmed by only a few of its members. If the body is a single organism, then the defect of any part of the body passes its malfunction to the whole body:

If any one be convicted as having done a wicked action, such a one not only hurts himself, but occasions the whole body of the Church and its doctrine to be blasphemed; as that we declare to be good and honest, and we ourselves shall be reproached by the Lord, that "they say and do not" [Matt. 23:3]. (*Constitutions of the Holy Apostles*, Bk. II, sec. III.8, ANF VII, p. 399)

This is why discipline was considered so important for the entire community. The pastoral writers thought that the responsibility-taking of a single member was closely correlated with the responsibility-taking of the whole community. For if the community is accountable for each member, then when one falters all come to grief.

While we are alive and healthy all parts of our body fulfil their functions. If one part is in pain anywhere, all the other parts suffer with it. But because the part is in the body it can suffer, but it cannot die. To die is to "expire," which means to "lose the spirit." If a part of the body is cut off . . . it retains the form of a finger, hand, arm, ear; but it has no life. Such is the state of a man separated from the Church. (Augustine, *Sermons*, 268.2, LCF, p. 237)

Some Protestants may assume that the doctrine of the keys, of excommunication, and absolution are primarily Catholic doctrines, but as the following passage from the standard Reformed confession, the Westminster Confession, shows, these themes were all continued in a revised form in Protestant pastoral care:

The Lord Jesus, as king and head of his Church, hath therein appointed a government in the hand of Church officers, distinct from the civil magistrate. To these officers the keys of the kingdom of heaven are committed, by virtue whereof they have power respectively to retain and remit sins, to shut that kingdom against the impenitent, both by the Word and censures; and to open it unto penitent sinners, by the ministry of the gospel, and by absolution from censures, as occasion shall require. Church censures are necessary for the reclaiming and gaining of offending brethren; for deterring of others from the like offenses; for purging out of that leaven which might infect the whole lump; for vindicating the honor of Christ, and the holy profession of the gospel; and for preventing the wrath of God, which might justly fall upon the Church, if they should suffer his covenant, and the seals thereof, to be profaned by notorious and obstinate offenders. For better attaining of these ends, the officers of the Church are to proceed by admonition, suspension from the Sacrament of the Lord's Supper for a season, and by excommunication from the Church, according to the nature of the crime and demerit of the person. (Westminster Confession, Ch. XXX, *CC*, p. 227)

Richard Baxter recognized the irony in the fact that communicants were on the whole less resistant to serious pastoral admonition than pastors were to giving it:

The common cry is, "Our people are not ready for it; they will not bear it." But is not the fact rather, that you will not bear the trouble and hatred which it will occasion? If indeed you proclaim our churches incapable of the order and government of Christ, what do you but give up the cause to them that withdraw from us, and encourage men to look out for better societies, where that discipline may be had? (Baxter, *RP*, p. 47)

Baxter was pleading that pastors not give up on the difficult task of discipline, since that function inheres in the pastoral office. People who intuitively know they need discipline will look for it outside the church if they cannot find it within.

According to Catherine of Siena, the best counselors of the church tradition are those who have paid constant and serious attention to admonition. They have better preserved and formed the community than those who pretended unremitting good will without constructive criticism. Catherine mentioned particularly Peter, Gregory, Sylvester, Augustine, Thomas, and Jerome as great pastors who have properly exercised this corrective function:

If you turn to Augustine, and to the glorious Thomas and Jerome, and others, you will see how much light they have extended over this subject, extirpating error, like lamps placed upon the candelabra, with true and utter humility. . . . They have followed the Lord's footsteps. They did not hesitate to correct. They did not let their members become rotten for want of correcting. They charitably corrected them with the unction of benignity, and with the sharpness of fire, cauterizing the wound of sin with reproof and penance, little or much, according to the graveness of the fault. And in order to correct it and to speak the truth, they did not even fear death. They were true gardeners who, with care and holy tears, took away the thorns of mortal sins, and cultivated plants that rendered the fragrance of virtue. . . .

One who remains uncorrected, and who does not correct others, becomes like a limb which putrefies, and corrupts the whole body. It is like an inept physician who, when a limb had already begun to be corrupted, placed ointment immediately upon it, without having first burnt the wound. So it is with the pastor or any other person having received the duty of care of souls, on seeing someone putrefying from the corruption of mortal sin. If one applies to him the ointment of soft words of encouragement alone, without reproof, one would never cure him. The putrefaction would rather spread to the other members, who, with him, form one body under the same pastor. But if he were a good physician who cares about those souls, as were those glorious pastors of old, he would not give comforting ointment without the fire of reproof. . . . Many do not act in this way today, but rather when they see evil, they pretend not to see. (Catherine of Siena, *A Treatise of Prayer*, pp. 244–247)*

Catherine spoke plainly: If pastors refuse even to recognize or acknowledge undesirable and misled behaviors, they default on the pastoral task. The great pastors of the tradition have offered admonition precisely because they cared about the health of the community.

In this Part of the collection, the classic texts have pointed to the work of the Holy Spirit in admonition, discipline, and comfort. Admonition belongs intrinsically to the pastoral office, and to some extent to the general ministry of the laity. It best emerges out of love, not a judgmental spirit of fault-finding. Admonition does not spring out of despair of genuine change, but out of hope for constructive, realistic, meaningful behavioral change. Classic pastoralia sought to identify practical means of offering corrective love. Admonition is reserved primarily for situations in which persons are *overtaken* in faults. It is dangerous to the health of the community when gentle reproof is lacking. Discipline serves both toward the restoration of the penitent and the integrity of the *communio sanctorum*. Resistance to admonition is a hazard to the soul's growth. The pastor must deliberately penetrate the facade of false peace in order to speak the truth in love.

7 Moral Counseling and the Nurture of Responsible Freedom

THIS PART OF OUR JOURNEY draws together a crucial series of classic pastoral passages on the moral dimensions of pastoral counseling. The internal witness of conscience remains a central premise of soul care. Conscience is consistently viewed in the pastoral tradition as a universal human capacity.

Pastors have from time immemorial been involved in dealing with anguished cases of conscience, where the clarification of the dynamics of guilt in a particular situation is of utmost concern. Pastoral counseling cannot avoid being also moral counseling. It is this dimension that we now address.

Where moral requirements are neglected in the ministry of forgiveness, pastoral care has tended to turn into antinomian license. Self-controlled freedom is nurtured through attentiveness to discipline under the guidance of law and moral order. The passions must be understood and rightly ordered. In this connection, various ascetic strategies have been employed in the pastoral tradition to enable growth in grace, and to come to terms with the mortification of life under the power of sin.

I. ❦ THE INTERNAL WITNESS OF CONSCIENCE AS A PREMISE OF SOUL CARE

The care-giver does not begin to guide the soul on the pretentious assumption that the care-giver possesses all the relevant moral knowledge. Rather the assumption is that God has already been providentially present in the soul from the outset, and has made known the divine requirement. Especially through conscience, God is already present in every rational being. No one can arbitrarily turn off that capacity for moral self-awareness. It is the capacity within oneself to judge oneself, to ask whether one's behavior is acceptable or unacceptable. Luther defined conscience in this way:

For conscience is not the power to do works, but to judge them. The proper work of conscience (as Paul says in Romans 2:15), is to accuse or excuse, to make guilty or guiltless, uncertain or certain. Its purpose is not to do, but to pass judgment on what has been done and what should be done, and this judgment makes us stand accused or saved in God's sight. (Luther, "Judgment of Martin Luther on Monastic Vows, 1521," LW 44, p. 298; WA 8, 606)

The seventeenth century Anglican pastor, Joseph Hall, wrote of the power of conscience:

It is a true word of the Apostle, "God is greater than our conscience," [1 John 3:20], and surely none but He. Under that great God, the supreme power on earth is the conscience. Every man is a little world within himself; and, in this little world, there is a court of judicature erected, wherein, next under God, the conscience sits as the supreme judge from whom there is no appeal; that passeth sentence upon us, upon all our actions, upon all our intentions; for our persons, absolving one, condemning another; for our actions, allowing one, forbidding another. If that condemn us, in vain shall all the world beside acquit us; and, if that clear us, the doom which the world passeth upon us is frivolous and ineffectual. I grant this judge is sometimes corrupted with the bribes of hope, with the weak fears of loss, with an undue respect of persons, with powerful importunities, with false witnesses, with forged evidences, to pass a wrong sentence upon the person or cause, for which he shall be answerable to Him that is higher than the highest; but yet this doom, though reversible by the tribunal of Heaven, is still obligatory on earth. So as it is my fault, that my conscience is misled; but it is not my fault to follow my conscience. How much need have I therefore, O my God, to pray that Thou wouldst guide my conscience aright, and keep this great judge in my bosom from corruption and error! (Joseph Hall, Soliloquies, *Works*, Vol. VIII, p. 274; *Angl.*, p. 645)

Although conscience can admittedly be corrupted, it remains obligatory. If I allow my conscience to be misled, I am responsible. Conscience remains the judge of both my actions and intentions, without which reasonable self-assessment could not continue. Isaac Barrow contrasted the reliability of the person who is attentive to conscience to one who is relatively inattentive:

It is a fair ornament of a man, and a great convenience both to himself and to others with whom he converses or deals, to act regularly, uniformly, and consistently; freeing a man's self from distraction and irresolution in his mind, from change and confusion in his proceedings; securing others from delusion and disappointment in their transactions with him. Even a bad rule constantly observed is therefore better than none. Order and perseverance in any way seem more convenient than roving and tossing about in uncertainties. But if one rules out a regard to the precepts of religion, there can hardly be any sure or settled rule which firmly can engage a man to, or effectually restrain a man from, any thing.

There is scarce in nature anything so wild, so untractable, so unintelligible, as a man who has no bridle of conscience to guide or check him. A profane man is like a ship, without anchor to stay him, or rudder to steer him, or compass to guide him; so that he is tossed with any wind, and driven with any wave, who knows where,—whither bodily temper might sway him, or passion might hurry him, or interest might pull him, or example lead him, or company inveigle and drag him, or humour transport him; whither any such variable and unaccountable causes determine him, or several of them together distract him; whence he so rambles and hovers that he can seldom himself tell what in any case he should do, nor can another guess it; so that you cannot at any time know where to find him or how to deal with him; you cannot with reason ever rely upon him, so *unstable he is all his ways*. He is in effect a mere child, all humour and giddiness, somewhat worse than a beast, which, following the instinct of its nature, is constant and regular, and thence tractable, or at least so untractable that no one will be deceived in meddling with him. Nothing therefore can be more unmanly than such a person, nothing can be more unpleasant than to have to do with him.

But a pious man, being steadily governed by conscience and a regard to certain principles, both understands himself and is intelligible to others. He presently detects what in any case he is to do, and can render an account of his acting. You may know him clearly, and assuredly tell what he will do, and may therefore fully confide in him. (Isaac Barrow, "The Profitableness of Godliness," Sermon III, *Works*, 1845 ed., Vol. 1, pp. 20, 21)*

When we are awakened to the voice of conscience, we tend to become more reliable, more consistent, lacking delusions, so that others can confide in us. We understand why we are doing what we do, and can explain it to others. Without this inner attentiveness, we are inconsistent, impossible to deal with, rudderless, and beastly.

Even when unexamined, conscience remains, according to John Donne, in the background of consciousness:

Thou hast imprinted a pulse in our soul, but we do not examine it; a voice in our conscience, but we do not hearken unto it. We talk it out, we jest it out, we drink it out, we sleep it out. (John Donne, *Devotions*, p. 10)

Conscience is as constant in human consciousness as a pulsebeat, even when unattended.

II. ❦ CONSCIENCE AS A UNIVERSAL HUMAN CAPACITY

The extent to which conscience is considered a universally reliable guide for human decision-making everywhere has been a perplexing issue for classical pastoral writers. Most have tended to regard conscience as a universal human capacity, not limited to a particular history of special revelation, yet capable of being sensitized and further taught by revelation and reason.

Conscience is commonly viewed as an inescapable, ever-impinging resource for self-examination and self-understanding. If so, then are the great world religions, like Hinduism and Islam, also aware of profound moral and spiritual claims, and capable of admirable behaviours? The Pauline way of stating the question was whether the Gentiles had the law "written on their hearts." Some early Christian writers had a surprisingly high opinion of the moral vitality and possibilities of non-Christian moral conscience.

There are likewise amongst the Bactrians, in the Indian countries, immense multitudes of Brahmans, who also themselves, from the tradition of their ancestors, and peaceful customs and laws, neither commit murder nor adultery, nor worship idols, nor have the practice of eating animal food, are never drunk, never do anything maliciously, but always fear God. (Clementina, *Recognitions of Clement*, Bk. IX, Ch. XX, ANF VIII, p. 187)

Quite apart from Jews and Christians, or from the Mosaic law and the law of Christ, the Christian pastoral tradition has recognized that the fear of God, moral virtue and just laws can be found wherever conscience is listened to. An actively attended moral awareness is possible in non-Jewish and non-Christian cultures, but its possibility in principle does not mean that it is always actualized and attended to in fact.

The early pastoral writers were probably more aware of cultural pluralism than we often suppose. The sociological observation of radical cultural differences is hardly an invention of modernity, as we see in this passage from Minucius Felix:

I see that you at one time expose your begotten children to wild beasts and to birds; at another, that you crush them when strangled with a miserable kind of death. There are some women who, by drinking medical preparations, extinguish the source of the future man in their very bowels, and thus commit a parricide before they bring forth. . . . Among the Tauri of Pontus, and to the Egyptian Busiris, it was a sacred rite to immolate their guests, and for the Galli to slaughter to Mercury human, or rather inhuman, sacrifices. The Roman sacrificers buried living a Greek man and a Greek woman, a Gallic man and a Gallic woman; and to this day, Jupiter Latiaris is worshipped by them with murder. . . . Among the Persians, a promiscuous association between sons and mothers is allowed. . . . You worship incestuous gods, who have intercourse with mothers, with daughters, with sisters. With reason, therefore, is incest frequently detected among you, and is continually permitted. (Minucius Felix, *The Octavius*, Ch. XXX–XXXI, ANF IV, p. 192)

This passage shows evidence that a third century Latin pastoral writer was quite aware of radical cultural differences among peoples. The amazing variety of cultural traditions, far from nullifying conscience, was thought to validate it. For it points to the fact that conscience can be well or poorly attended, shaped this way and that, yet even when corrupted or ignored it is finally irrepressible.

In defending the notion that conscience is being transmuted by Christ, Minucius Felix argued that Christian conscience had internalized a high moral life that is found only in the best examples of its cultural counterparts. He was answering, with evidence to the contrary, the charge against Christianity that it was morally inferior:

You forbid, and yet commit, adulteries, while we are committed only to our own wives. You punish crimes as they are committed, while with us, even to think of crimes is to sin. You fear those who might become aware of what you are doing, while we are even afraid of our own conscience alone, without which we cannot exist. Finally, from your numbers the prison boils over, yet no Christian is in prison unless put there on account of his religion. (Minucius Felix, *The Octavius*, Ch. XXXV, ANF IV, p. 195)*

Far from inferior morally, Christians during the period of persecution lived exemplary lives. Tertullian pointed to the excellence of Christian conscience, compared to the secular Roman environment:

For our religion commands us to love even our enemies, and to pray for those who persecute us, aiming at a perfection all its own, and seeking in its disciples something of a higher type than the commonplace goodness of the world. For all love those who love them; it is peculiar to Christians alone to love those that hate them. (Tertullian, "To Scapula," Ch. I, ANF III, p. 105)

Conscience does not mean conformity to culture. Amid persecution it became necessary for Christian pastors to ask: Under what circumstance may one consider civil disobedience? Lactantius, who was deprived of his teaching post upon his conversion to Christianity (c. 300 A.D.), and who later became the tutor to the son of Constantine, forthrightly answered:

When men command us to act in opposition to the law of God, and in opposition to justice, we should be deterred by no threats or punishments from preferring the command of God to the command of man. Likewise it is a virtue to despise death; not that we seek it, and of our own accord inflict it upon ourselves, as many and distinguished philosophers have often done, which is a wicked and impious thing; but that when compelled to desert God, and to betray our faith, we should prefer to undergo death, and should defend our liberty against the foolish and senseless violence of those who cannot govern themselves, and with fortitude of spirit we should challenge all the threats and terrors of the world. (Lactantius, *The Divine Institutes*, Bk. VI, Ch. XVIII, ANF VII, p. 183)

Although no one may justly seek his own death, the willingness to die in following the divine requirement is preferable to life in a state which unequivocally requires disobedience to God. The gift of being unintimidated by death and by those who hold the power of death gave Christianity a remarkable courage under extremely hazardous circumstances of persecution during its first three centuries.

Ambrose argued that the utility of an act should not be preferred above conscience, but that an act that follows conscience will in the long run prove useful:

What a virtuous action that was when David wished to spare the king his enemy, though he could have injured him! How useful, too, it was, for it helped him when he succeeded to the throne. . . . Thus what is virtuous was preferred to what was useful, and then usefulness followed on what was virtuous. (Ambrose, *Duties of the Clergy*, Bk. III, Ch. IX, sec. 60, NPNF 2, X, p. 79)

III. 🐚 CARE OF THE DISTRAUGHT AND ANGUISHED CONSCIENCE

The pastor will be called upon, ready or not, to respond to those undergoing intense struggles of conscience. Often from the outside such a struggle may seem small, but from within it may take on desperately large proportions.

Learning wisely to do no harm while one is seeking positively to do some modest good amid conditions of moral stress is no easy matter, and has been the subject of much interest among the pastoral writers. Luther testified to the damage that a rotten conscience could do:

A bad conscience is hell. This is created by the rod of the oppressor, the Law. When this oppressor bears down on a man, when it severely drubs and drives with club and cudgel, then no soundness remains in the flesh and in the bones. The soul or the conscience is tortured as if it were in hell. (Luther, "Sermon on Isaiah 9:1–7, 1543," WLS 1, #994, p. 336; WA 40 III, 630)

The tender, inordinately sensitive conscience falls prey to demonic intensification:

[The Deceiver] can magnify a little sin for the purpose of causing one to worry, torture, and kill oneself with it. That is why a Christian should learn not to let anyone easily create an evil conscience in him. . . . Rather let him say: Let this error and this failing pass away with my other imperfections and sins, which I must include in the article of faith: I believe in the forgiveness of sins, and the Fifth Petition of the Lord's Prayer: Forgive us our trespasses. (Luther, "Sermon on John 18:28," WLS 1, #983, pp. 333, 334; WA 28, 296f.)

Each one is responsible for not letting oneself be manipulated into false guilt. While affirming the importance of "knowing oneself," the pastoral writers did not think that listening to one's feelings was enough when it comes to dealing with the dynamics of guilt. The objective word of forgiveness in scripture is more reliable than the proneness of feelings to exaggerate guilt. Luther stated the point powerfully:

If conscience accuses you of sin . . . you must not assent but must judge against your conscience and feelings that God is not angry and that you are not damned. For scripture says that the kingdom of Christ lies beyond (*extra*) the domain of feeling. Therefore we must judge against our feeling. (Luther, "Sermon on Isaiah 65:17–19, 1532," #1535, WLS 1, p. 512; WA 25, 387f.)

When someone is disturbed by bizarre and evil thoughts, the caregiver must ascertain the extent of the complicity of the will with incipient temptation. According to Gregory, it may relieve the conscience of the person prone to evil imaginings to realize that the degree of personal consent, after all, is minimal:

Sin is committed in three stages namely, the suggestion of it, the pleasure experienced, and the consent. The first is the act of the Enemy, the second that of the flesh, the third that of the spirit. . . . Those, therefore, who grieve for the evil of thoughts only, are to be admonished to consider carefully the degree of sin into which they have fallen, to the end that they may raise themselves to a degree of sorrow in proportion to the known degree of their fall. (Gregory the Great, *Pastoral Care*, Part II, Ch. 29, ACW 11, p. 202)

Note that the individual is not responsible for the first stage of sin (temptation), but is clearly responsible for the third stage (consent). The middle stage is mixed. In any event, it is hardly healthy psychologically for the individual to have an elevated degree of grief or guilt disproportional to the actual degree of consent. A careful examination of this may relieve the excessively scrupulous conscience. Classical pastoral writers were actively interested in sorting out the subtle dynamics of the scrupulous conscience:

I call that a scruple when a man is reasonably well persuaded of the lawfulness of a thing, yet remains fearful and doubtful nonetheless that perhaps it might be after all unlawful. Such scruples are most incident to men of melancholy dispositions, or of timorous spirits, especially if they be tender conscienced. They are much increased by the false suggestions of Satan, by reading the books, or hearing the sermons, or frequenting the company of men more strict, precise, and austere in sundry points than they need or ought to be, and by sundry other means which I now mention not. Of such scruples it behooves everyone first to be wary that he does not admit them to dwell within if he can choose. Or, if he cannot wholly avoid them, that, secondly, he should endeavour, as far as may be, to eject them speedily out of his thoughts as Satan's snares and things that may breed him worse inconveniences. Or, if he cannot so rid himself of them, then thirdly, he should resolve to go on according to the more probable persuasion of his mind and despise those scruples. And this he may do with a good conscience, not only in things commanded him by lawful authority, but even in things indifferent and arbitrary, and where he is left to his own liberty. (Robert Sanderson, Sermons, *Works*, Vol. II, p. 139; Angl. p. 658)*

A scruple is an intensified awareness of a guilty disposition. They should be resisted speedily. Exceeding religious austerity may deepen the syndrome.

Jeremy Taylor reflected upon the ways one struggles inwardly with conscience, and the process by which the conscience may be gradually changed from doubtful to probable:

When the conscience is doubtful, neither part can be chosen till the doubt be laid down. But to choose the safer part is an extrinsical means instrumental to the deposition of the doubt and changing the conscience from doubtful to probable. . . . For in matters of conscience, it is as hard to find a case so equally probable that a man shall find nothing without or within to determine him as it is to find that which the philosophers call *temperamentum ad pondus,* "a constitution so equal that no part shall excel the other." For if there were nothing in the things to distinguish them, yet in the man there is a natural propensity which will make him love one sort of arguments more than another. (Jeremy Taylor, *Ductor Dubitantium,* Bk. I, Ch. V, *Works,* Vol. XII, p. 127; *Angl.* #309, p. 659)

Ignatius Loyola set forth this well-defined "Method of Making the General Examination of Conscience":

1. The first point is to render thanks to God for the favors we have received.
2. The second point is to ask the grace to know my sins and to free myself from them.
3. The third point is to demand an account of my soul from the moment of rising until the present examination; either hour by hour or from one period to another. I shall first make an examination of my thoughts, then my words, and then my actions in the same order as that given in the Particular Examination of Conscience.
4. The fourth point is to ask pardon of God our Lord for my failings.
5. The fifth point is to resolve to amend my life with the help of God's grace. Close with the "Our Father." (Ignatius Loyola, *Spiritual Exercises,* p. 53)

Luther thought it was as hard to comfort a depressed conscience as it was to challenge a hardened conscience:

No one believes what an effort is required again to comfort and raise up a despondent, fearful conscience, and, on the other hand, what an effort is required to terrify and frighten a stubborn, hardened conscience. Both seem impossible, and God himself must perform the task. (Luther, "Sermon on Zechariah 6:8," #985, WLS 1, p. 334; WA 23, p. 583)

Only by forgiveness is the troubled conscience made untroubled.

IV. ❦ GUILT AS MORAL INDEBTEDNESS

The experienced pastor is often able to observe at close quarters the dynamics of accelerating guilt. Guilt can create extreme havoc in the soul. Its power cannot prudently be ignored. However experienced the pastor may be in applying tested remedies, they cannot be simplistically applied. The pastor must come to understand how guilt is functioning in a particular situation. The task, in Luther's view, is no easy one:

One cannot say or believe how difficult it is to buoy up and revive a heart in despair and a conscience overwhelmed by sadness. Those who are not being tried are easily gladdened, but it requires toil and labor to bring a man who lies oppressed by spiritual grief and sorrow back to a knowledge of and faith in the goodness and mercy of God. (Luther, "Lectures on Genesis Chapters 45 to 50," LW 8, p. 26; WA 44, p. 598)

The economic analogy of unremitting indebtedness has been powerfully used to describe the predicament of guilt. This analogy is curiously mixed by Origen with the metaphor of the debt an actor owes to his audience:

If we are in a theater of the world both of angels and of men, we must know that, just as the [actor] in a theater is a debtor to say or to do certain things in the view of the spectators and if he fails to do them is punished or having insulted the whole theater, so also we are debtors to the whole world, both to all the angels and to the human race, for those things that we shall learn from Wisdom if we are willing. Apart from these more general responsibilities, a widow cared for by the Church has a debt, a deacon another, a presbyter another, and a bishop an extremely heavy debt for which payment is demanded by the Savior of the whole Church and punishment exacted if he does not pay it (cf. 1 Tim. 5:3, 16, 17). And the Apostle names a debt common to man and wife when he says, "Let the husband pay his debt to his wife, and likewise the wife to her husband." And he adds, "Do not refuse one another" (1 Cor. 7:3). (Origen, *On Prayer*, XXVIII.3–4, CWS, p. 148)

An actor who gives a bad performance has not paid his debt to his audience. So in the care of souls, the care-giver does who not guide well remains indebted. Debt is a diffuse symbol of generally-shared guilt. The indebtedness metaphor was further elaborated by Origen. Not all are equally in debt. The debts emerge out of concrete relationships and covenants in which one exists:

There is not a single hour of night or day in life when we are
not in debt. Now when he is in debt someone either pays or refuses payment. And it is possible in our lifetime to pay, but it is
also possible to refuse payment. And some people are in debt to
no one for anything (cf. Rom. 13:8). Some pay most debts and
are in debt for a few things, while others pay a few and are in
debt for the greater part. And perhaps there is someone who
pays nothing, but is in debt for everything. . . . If we are in debt
to so many people, it is inevitable that there are people in debt to
us. Some are in our debt since we are men, others since we are
citizens, others since we are fathers or sons. And in addition
wives are in debt to us if we are husbands, and friends if we are
friends. Therefore, whenever any of our numerous debtors are
somewhat lax about paying what they owe us, we should act
kindly toward them and not hold a grudge, remembering our
own debts and how often we have put them off. (Origen, *On
Prayer*, XXVIII.4–5, CWS, p. 148–149)

This passage contains a primitive interpretation of human community
as social contract, and a consequent injunction. The interpretation
hinges on the burdened awareness that we owe something to each other.
Children owe their lives to parents. Friends owe loyalty to friends. A
spouse owes fidelity and care to a spouse. Merely being human places
us in a web of relationships that imply various vectors of indebtedness.
The injunction is: Do not be too hard on those who owe you, because
you yourself are so profoundly in debt at so many levels. Ambrose understood how heavily the burden of sin may be felt:

There is no greater sorrow than to have a man wound his conscience with the sword of sin; there is no heavier burden than the
load of sin and the weight of transgression. It bows down the
soul, it bends it to the ground, so that it cannot raise itself. Heavy,
my son, exceedingly heavy are the burdens of sin. (Ambrose, *Letters*, 45, To Horontianus, FC 26, p. 233)

Loyola set forth an interpretation of the way in which demonic temptation always attacks the weakest vulnerability of the over-scrupulous
conscience:

The enemy observes very carefully whether one has a delicate
or lax conscience. If the conscience is delicate he strives to make it
excessively so in order to disturb and ruin it more easily. For example, if the enemy sees that a soul consents to no sin, mortal or
venial, or even to the appearance of deliberate sin, since he cannot make the soul fall into what has the appearance of sin, he
strives to make it judge that there is sin where there is none, as in

some insignificant word or thought. If the conscience is lax, the enemy strives to make it still more lax. (Ignatius Loyola, *Spiritual Exercises*, pp. 137–38)

Whether lax or stringent, demonic temptation addresses the greater vulnerability. Since there is no end to freedom, there is no end to temptation, in this life.

V. 🦌 MORAL COUNSEL: WARDING OFF ANTINOMIAN DISTORTIONS

The gospel of God's free mercy leads to the temptation to treat divine grace lightly and licentiously, as if one could "sin that grace may abound" (Rom. 6:1). From the earliest decades of Christian pastoral care, the pastor has been placed in the paradoxical situation of having to admonish believers to take the law seriously, even while unmerited forgiveness is being proclaimed. For there can be no liberty without law, as Augustine argued:

There is no true liberty except the liberty of the happy who cleave to the eternal law. (Augustine, *On Free Will*, Bk. XV.32, LCC VI, p. 132)

But if God is truly merciful and forgiving, does not that tend to encourage sin, given our human inclination to take every advantage? Tertullian answered with a metaphor of the aftermath of shipwreck:

Let no one be worse because God is better, sinning just as often as he is forgiven. Otherwise, while there will be no end to his sin, there will be, of a certainty, an end to his immunity. We have escaped once. Let us not place ourselves in danger again, even though it seems that we shall again escape. Most men who are saved from shipwreck divorce both ship and sea from that time on, and they show their appreciation of the gift of God, that is, their salvation, by remembering their peril. I praise their fear and I appreciate their timidity. They are unwilling, a second time, to burden the mercy of God. (Tertullian, "On Penitence," ACW 28, p. 28)

Survivors of a disaster, grateful to be alive, are not likely to return to take the same risk again. Tertullian thought that a second repentance could not be relied upon if the first repentance does not lead to enduring behavioral change. Forgiveness is freely offered, but it is not given in order to invite us to take immoral advantage of it.

Hatred of moral requirement, along with hatred of creation, is a distinguishing mark of heterodox teaching, according to Clement:

We may divide all the heresies into two groups in making answer to them. Either they teach that one ought to live on the principle that it is a matter of indifference whether one does right or wrong, or they set a too ascetic tone and proclaim the necessity of continence on the ground of opinions which are godless and arise from hatred of what God has created. (Clement of Alexandria, *On Marriage*, Ch. V. sec. 40, LCC II, p. 58)

Thus for Clement the opposite extremes—licentious antinomianism and masochistic asceticism—are the two perennial errors spawned by neglect of the whole counsel of God.

The more accurately one listens to conscience, the more one is actively loving and caring for oneself:

So, should you feel more ashamed of what God made well, than of what you have done evilly? Certainly God made even those parts of the body that we call shameful.... And so in a marvelous way, when convicted from its own conscience and deservedly cast down by disorder, the mind of each person simultaneously delivers a judgment against itself. It exacts satisfaction from itself. In this judgment, the person who judges and the person judged are one and the same. He who condemns is precisely he who is condemned. He who punishes is none other than he who is punished.... In this judgment, the more ardently each person loves himself, the more bitterly he rages against himself. The more eagerly he desires to spare himself, the less he spares himself. If he should fear or avoid his own disorder, the result is that his disorder troubles everyone else more severely. (Richard of St. Victor, *The Twelve Patriarchs*, Ch. 47–48, pp. 104–105)*

In conscience, the judgment comes not from without, externally, but from the deepest inward source. Shame is not to be avoided, but faced and learned from.

May guilt, therefore, be a necessary stage of a healthily developing self-awareness?

Let those entering a hospital for the first time indicate their pains, and let those entering upon obedience show their humility. For the former, the first sign of their health is the relief of their pains, and for the latter a growing self-condemnation; and there is no other sign so unerring. Let your conscience be the mirror of your obedience, and it is enough. (Climacus, *The Ladder of Divine Ascent*, Step 4, sec. 74, p. 43)

Modern psychologically-trained readers may tend to ignore this point: the first sign of reversal of the sin-sick human condition and of embryonic movement toward health is the accurate identification of symptoms. Upon entering a hospital, the first thing to be done is to describe explicitly one's symptoms. Similarly, in Christian counsel, the beginning point is attending to conscience as it mirrors the truth.

VI. 🐝 LAW AND GOSPEL—A RECURRENT PASTORAL DIALECTIC

These paired concepts suggest perennial tensions in the practice of pastoral care:

guilt	forgiveness
grace	effort
discipline	freedom
law	gospel

We will show, in examining these tensions, that the artificial separation of psychology, ethics, and theology (such as prevails in the modern university) was never thinkable for classical Christian pastoral care.

The balance between the sternness of the law and the mercy of the gospel remains a continuing perplexity for situational pastoral judgment. Luther thought there was no teaching more important to good conscience than the relation of law and gospel:

The knowledge of this topic, the distinction between the Law and the Gospel, is necessary to the highest degree; for it contains a summary of all Christian doctrine. Therefore let everyone learn diligently how to distinguish the Law from the Gospel, not only in words but in feeling and in experience; that is, let him distinguish well between these two in his heart and in his conscience. For so far as the words are concerned, the distinction is easy. But when it comes to experience, you will find the Gospel a rare guest but the Law a constant guest in your conscience, which is habituated to the Law and the sense of sin; reason, too, supports this sense. (Luther, "Lectures on Galatians, Chapters One to Four, 1535," LW 26, p. 117; WA 40 I, p. 207)

One can count on conscience, but situational awareness of mercy in Christ requires a different kind of attentiveness. In his treatise on Christian Liberty, Luther stated the essential difference between commands and promises:

All the Scriptures of God are divided into two parts— commands and promises. The commands indeed teach things that are good, but the things taught are not done as soon as taught; for the commands show us what we ought to do, but do not give us the power to do it; they are intended to teach a man to know himself, that through them he may recognize his inability to do good and may despair of his powers. . . . Here the second part of the Scriptures stands ready—the promises of God, which declare the glory of God and say, "If you wish to fulfill the law, and not to covet, as the law demands, come, believe in Christ, in Whom grace, righteousness, peace, liberty and all things are promised you." (Luther, *Treatise on Christian Liberty*, WML II, pp. 316, 317)

It is hardly enough for pastors to help people understand what they ought to do. Rather the pastoral task is that of nurturing persons toward active responsiveness to what God has done for them in Christ:

No one doubts that the Ten Commandments must be taught and, what is much more, must be kept. But they are not kept; this is our complaint. Therefore something more than merely preaching the Law is required, that a man may also know how he may be enabled to keep it. Otherwise what good does it do to preach that Moses and the Law merely say: This thou shalt do; this God requires of thee. Yes, my dear Moses, I hear what you say; and it is no doubt right and true. But do tell me where am I to get the ability to do what I have unfortunately not done and cannot do. It is not easy to count money from an empty purse or to drink from an empty tankard. (Luther, "Sermon on 2 Cor. 3:4–11," WLS 2, p. 738; WA 22, pp. 220, 221)

Soul care that focuses upon simple "oughts" continues to try to extract money from an empty purse, another drop from an empty cup. Evangelical soul care celebrates God's own filling of cup and purse. The Westminster Confession set forth the distinguishable yet inseparable ministries of law and gospel in this dispensational way, where the one covenant appears is two forms:

This covenant was differently administered in the time of the law and in the time of the gospel: under the law it was administered by promises, prophecies, sacrifices, circumcision, the paschal lamb, and other types and ordinances delivered to the people of the Jews, all foresignifying Christ to come, which were for that time sufficient and efficacious, through the operation of the Spirit, to instruct and build up the elect in faith in the promised Messiah, by whom they had full remission of sins and eternal salvation; and is called the Old Testament.

Under the gospel, when Christ the substance was exhibited, the ordinances in which this covenant is dispensed are the preaching of the word and the administration of the sacraments of Baptism and the Lord's Supper; which, though fewer in number, and administered with more simplicity and less outward glory, yet in them it is held forth in more fullness, evidence, and spiritual efficacy, to all nations, both Jews and Gentiles; and is called the New Testament. There are not, therefore, two covenants of grace differing in substance, but one and the same under various dispensations. (Westminster Confession, Ch. VI, sec. v–vi, *CC* pp. 202–203)

Early Christian pastoral writers remembered the "golden rule" not only as summarizing Jesus' teaching of the law, but also Jewish teaching:

There is one law of God, simple, true, living, which is this: "Do not do that to another which thou hatest another should do to thee" (Tobit 4:15). (*Constitutions of the Holy Apostles*, Bk. I, sec. 1, ANF VII, p. 391)

From the earliest times of Christian preaching and ministry, the law was diligently studied and viewed in the light of Christ:

Let [the bishop] be patient and gentle in admonitions, being himself well instructed, diligently studying and meditating upon the Lord's books, and reading them frequently, so that he may be able carefully to interpret the Scriptures, expound the Gospel in correspondence with the prophets and with the law; and let the exposition from the law and prophets correspond to the Gospel. For the Lord Jesus says: "Search the Scriptures; for they are those which testify of me" [John 5:39]. And again: "For Moses wrote of me" [John 5:46]. But, above all, let him carefully distinguish between the original law and the additional precepts and show which are the legitimate commands for believers, and which the bonds for unbelievers, lest any should fall under those bonds. Be careful, therefore, O bishop, to study the word, that you may be able to explain everything exactly, and that you may abundantly nourish your people with much doctrine, and enlighten them with the light of the law. (*Constitutions of the Holy Apostles*, Bk. II, sec. II, ANF VII, p. 397)*

The teaching office required the *episkopoi* to work constantly to help their flock understand what God requires, and how that is intrinsically related to God's mercy.

VII. 🐑 Pastoral Uses of the Law

Does the law have a constructive function leading to faith active in love? Why does it continue to be so necessary for the soul guide to speak of what God requires, of the divine claim, of God's command, *if* radical divine forgiveness is offered and available? We can find no one in the pastoral tradition more intent than Luther to drive home the ethical meaning of divine forgiveness. This makes it all the more impressive that Luther repeatedly emphasized the importance of preaching, teaching and counseling the law:

Since we are still living in flesh and blood, it is necessary to preach the letter as well, so that people are first killed by the law and all their arrogance is destroyed. Thus they may know themselves and become hungry for the Spirit and thirsty for grace. So (the letter) prepares the people for the preaching of the Spirit, as it is written about St. John (the Baptist), that he made the people ready for Christ through the preaching of repentance (Matt. 3:1–12). This was the office of the letter. After that he led them to Christ, saying, "Behold, the Lamb of God, who takes away all the sins of the world" (John 1:29). This was the office of the Spirit. These then are the two works of God, praised many times in Scripture: he kills and gives life, he wounds and heals, he destroys and helps, he condemns and saves, he humbles and elevates, he disgraces and honors, as is written in Deuteronomy 32:39, I Kings 2, I Sam. 2:6–8, Psalm 12:7–8, and in many other places. He does these works through these two offices, the first through the letter, the second through the Spirit. The letter does not allow anyone to stand before his wrath. The Spirit does not allow anyone to perish before his grace. (Luther, "Answer to the Hyperchristian, Hyperspiritual, and Hyperlearned Book by Goat Emser in Leipzig, 1521," LW 39, p. 188; WA 7, pp. 658, 659)

There is no way to go beyond the harsh claims of the law without first becoming thirsty for forgiveness. The law helps prepare the heart for grace. The Reformed pastoral tradition spoke more broadly of pastoral uses of the law not only as preparatory to faith, but for the faithful:

Although true believers be not under the law as a covenant of works, to be thereby justified or condemned; yet is it of great use to them, as well as to others; in that, as a rule of life, informing them of the will of God and their duty, it directs and binds them to walk accordingly; discovering also the sinful pollutions of their nature, hearts, and lives; so as, examining themselves thereby, they may come to further conviction of, humiliation for, and hatred against sin; together with a clearer sight of the need they have of Christ, and the perfection of his obedience. It is likewise of use to the regenerate, to restrain their corruptions, in that it forbids sin; and the threatenings of it serve to show what even their sins deserve. . . . Neither are the forementioned uses of the law contrary to the grace of the gospel, but do sweetly comply with it. (Westminster Confession, Ch. XIX, sec. VI, *CC*, pp. 214–215)

The classic pastoral exegetes did not assume that ascetic self-control was in every case most urgently needed. The Pastor of Hermas early in the second century distinguished between the need for discipline and the call to freedom:

[The Shepherd said:] "Self-control is also twofold. For in some things it is necessary to exercise self-control, in others it is not." "Let me know, sir," I said, "in what it is necessary to exercise self-control, and in what it is not." "Listen," he said, "Exercise self-control over what is evil, and do not do it; but do not be self-controlled in what is good, but do it." (The Pastor of Hermas, *The Mandates*, VIII, sec. 38.1, 2, AF, p. 193)

While doing good, the watchword is not restraint. The soul guide only wishes to elicit the unimpeded freedom to do good. It is the avoidance of evil that requires intentional, disciplined self-constraint. The Pastor of Hermas offered a long list of examples of situations in which one need not focus primarily upon self–control, but rather upon implementing freedom:

"Listen," [the Shepherd] said, "to the works that are good, which are necessary for you to do and not be restrained. First of all is faith, fear of the Lord (cf. Ps.111:10; Prov. 1:7), love, harmony, words of righteousness, truth, patience; there is nothing in the life of humanity better than these. For if anyone keeps these virtues and does not hold back from them, he will be blessed in this life. Then hear what follows these things: serving the widows, looking after orphans and those who are needy, delivering the servants of God from distress, being hospitable (for doing good is found in hospitality), resisting no one, being quiet, being more needy than all others, revering the aged, practicing righteousness, protecting brotherhood, enduring insults, being patient, not bearing a grudge, encouraging those who are tired of life, not casting aside those who have stumbled from the faith, but converting and encouraging them, admonishing those who sin, not oppressing those who are in debt and in need, and whatever is like these things. Does it seem to you," he said, "that these

things are good?" "What sir," I said, "is better than these things?"
"Then live by them," he said, "and do not be restrained in relation to them." (The Pastor of Hermas, *The Mandates*, VIII, sec.
38, AF, pp. 194–195)*

In all these ways, wisdom lets freedom flow untrammelled. To approach these simply as matters of constraint would be to restrain good
works.

What the law requires is found to be more extensive the more one
meditates upon it. Not simply avoiding sin, but doing good, is required:

Suppose then [the case of] an husbandman. He does no damage to our property, he lays no plots against us, and he is not a
thief, he only ties his hands behind him, and sits at home, neither
sowing, nor cutting a single furrow, nor harnessing oxen to the
yoke, nor looking after a vine, nor in fact discharging any one of
those other labors required in husbandry. . . . He does wrong in
that he does not contribute his own share to the common stock of
good. (Chrysostom, *Homilies on Ephesians*, Hom. XVI, NPNF 1,
XIII, p. 126)

VIII. 🐾 ON ELICITING DISCIPLINED SELF-CONTROL

The education of the soul by the narrow way proceeds through an
extended series of stages. Maturity is not acquired by a simple insight
from which perfect love immediately follows without the disciplining of
the will to habitual excellence. John Climacus, the seventh century monastic teacher, provided a proposed trajectory of stages of maturation, a
kind of map of the narrow way which leads to life:

The lessening of evil breeds abstinence from evil;
abstinence from evil is the beginning of repentance;
the beginning of repentance is the beginning of salvation;
the beginning of salvation is a good resolve;
and a good resolve is the mother of labours.
And from the beginning of labours comes the virtues;
the beginning of the virtues is a flowering;
the flowering of the virtue is the beginning of activity.
And the offspring of virtue is perseverance;
the fruit and offspring of persevering practice is habit,
and the child of habit is character.
Good character is the mother of fear;
fear gives birth to the keeping of commandments,
   both Heavenly and earthly.

> The keeping of the commandments is a sign of love;
> the beginning of love is an abundance of humility;
> an abundance of humility is the daughter of dispassion;
> the acquisition of the latter is the fullness of love—
> the perfect indwelling of God in those
> who through dispassion are pure in heart,
> for they shall see God. (Climacus, *The Ladder of Divine Ascent*, Step 26, sec. 65, pp. 196-197)*

One does not even set one's foot on this path unless one first seeks to reduce ill will, repents, resolves the good, and then moves along the path, working daily toward excellent habitual behaviors, persevering through drought, and developing character, which enables faithful obedience, love and humility. All these in time enable the channeling of emotive energies toward the fullness of love.

Hugh of St. Victor employed a gardener's analogy: A tree is challenged to grow broad and strong by being weighed down. So it is in the training of the soul through discipline amid its fears, anxieties, necessities, and attractions:

> Then at last will that tree of wisdom, which had begun by growing badly as a bare stem, like a bending reed, be strengthened by continual exercise of the virtues and clad with the foliage of a universal caution. It will lift up its head to the heights once more, all the better now for being stronger, sturdier, more experienced, and the more fair with caution, so that even its very truncation seems to have turned out to its advantage.
>
> But since it is through caution that this same wisdom spreads abroad its branches, let us lay down some common circumstances in which caution comes into play. There are four of these—fear, anxiety, necessity, attraction.
>
> Fear is worry lest we fall into danger.
>
> Anxiety is concern to avoid the unpleasant and to obtain the pleasant.
>
> Necessity is the duty to give, or the need to receive.
>
> Attraction is the desire to enjoy things.
>
> Fear is a burden, anxiety a weight, necessity a restriction, attraction a wound. Thus when farmers want their trees to spread out, they are wont either to put weights on top of them to press them down, or else to tie weights under them to pull them down. Or else they drive in stakes and tie the branches to those, so that they cannot rise, but spread out sideways. Or else again they insert grafts in the bare stem, that these, when they have taken, may cover the tree. Fear then, is like a weight put on top, anxiety is like a weight hung underneath, necessity is like a stake that teth-

ers, attraction is as it were a graft that on its insertion makes a wound.

Those four are born of the four kinds of evils to which man is subject in this world—namely, the wrath of God, the vanity of the world, the weakness of our human state, and the malice of the devil.

The wrath of God is when we are chastened with afflictions.

The vanity of the world is when, by going beyond the measure of our real need, we fall into self-indulgence.

The weakness of our human state is that we are easily upset when things go badly, and recover only with difficulty our power to act well.

The malice of the devil is when at his instigation we are stimulated to vice.

So the wrath of God weighs us down, the vanity of the world by filling us with needless cares drags us down, the weakness of our human state ties us down with ruthless restrictions, the malice of the devil wounds us by inciting us to unlawful desires.

In all these things, however, God's servant is practiced to his profit, and even these evils do him abject service. (Hugh of St. Victor, *SSW*, pp. 112-113)

God is the gardener. God permits fear to burden, anxiety to be a weight, necessity a restriction, and distraction by the world a wound. In all of these ways, freedom is being strengthened, as a plant becomes strengthened by being challenged by the storm, by bearing a weight, by being tied in a certain angle, or by being ingrafted. By this analogy we see that a handicapping condition may become the basis for very special forms of growth and strength.

The soul guide is not without risk in the process. For if the guidance is skewed, the guide is responsible:

Now I think the advice I have given about self-control is not unimportant, since one who follows it will not regret doing it but will save both himself and me his counselor (cf. Ezek. 14:1, Tim. 4:16). For the reward is not small if we turn back to salvation a soul wandering and perishing (cf. James 5:20). (An Ancient Homily by an Unknown Author [Second Letter of Clement], sec. 15, AF, p. 67)

IX. ❦ THE INCREMENTAL GROWTH OF FREEDOM THROUGH DISCIPLINE

It is only through discipline that freedom emerges. The perennial question can be framed psychoanalytically: Shall soul care encourage and allow the id free play to release it from superego constraints, so that the self learns to treat all things as lawful?

He who indulges his pleasures gratifies his body; but he who is controlled liberates from its passions his soul which is master of the body. And if they tell us that we are called to freedom, only let us not use our freedom as an opportunity for the flesh, as the Apostle says. [Cf. Gal. 5:13]. If lust is to be gratified and a life of sin regarded as morally neutral, as they say, either we ought to indulge our desires in every direction and, if this is our desire, do the most lascivious and immoral acts, in that we are following our instincts in every way; or we may suppress certain desires and live no longer a life which recognizes no distinction of right and wrong. . . . Desire is nourished and invigorated if it is encouraged in indulgence, just as, on the other hand, it loses strength if it is kept in check. . . . But how is it possible to become like the Lord and have knowledge of God if one is subject to physical pleasures? Every pleasure is the consequence of an appetite, and an appetite is a certain pain and anxiety, caused by need, which requires some object. In my opinion those who choose this kind of life are simply "suffering pain to their shame," as the well-known verse puts it [Hesiod], choosing evil which they bring upon themselves, now and hereafter. If then, all things were lawful and one need have no fear that because of one's wicked deeds one's hope of salvation would be lost, perhaps they might have some excuse for living this wicked and wretched life. But through the commandments a life of blessedness is shown to us. . . . We must not live as if there were no difference between right and wrong, but, to the best of our power, must purify ourselves from indulgence and lust and take care for our soul which must continually be devoted to the Deity alone. For when it is pure and set free from all evil the mind is somehow capable of receiving the power of God and the divine image is set up in it. (Clement of Alexandria, *On Marriage*, Ch. V, secs. 41-42, LCC II, pp. 58–59)

The caring pastor is seeking to nurture genuine freedom. Such freedom is distinguished from being bound to the tyrannies of emotive impulse. The logic of freedom leads in one of two fundamental directions: either we satisfy all desires and let the passions be loosed or in a sense "freed" to reign over the soul, or we carefully train the desires so that the soul freely reigns over the passions. Those who give wide range to the first alternative soon find that the garden of freedom is full of the weeds of emotive impulse. The blessed and happy life wishes rather to tend carefully the garden of freedom. Good counsel is a part of that tending process, which occurs through caring speech. Each person is primarily responsible for what one allows to be put into one's own mind. Anselm's parable of the mill made the point powerfully:

Our heart is like a mill, ever grinding, which a certain lord gave in charge to his servant, enjoining that he should only grind in it his master's grain, whether wheat, barley, or oats, and telling him that he must subsist on the produce. But that servant has an enemy who is always playing tricks on the mill. If any moment he finds it unwatched, he throws in gravel to keep the stones from acting, or pitch to clog them, or dirt and chaff to mix with the meal. If the servant is careful in tending his mill, there flows forth a beautiful flour, which is at once a service to his master and a subsistence to himself; but if he plays the truant, and allows his enemy to tamper with the machinery, the bad outcome tells the tale, his lord is angry, and he himself is starved. This mill ever grinding is the heart ever thinking. God has given one to each man to guard and tend, and bids him grind in it only those thoughts which He Himself supplies.... These thoughts God would have us keep continually revolving in our minds; but the devil is man's adversary, and, if at any moment he finds the heart empty of good thoughts, he instantly throws in some bad ones. Some of these bad thoughts—such as wrath and envy—dissipate the mind; others—such as sensuality and luxury—clog its action; and others—such as vain imagination—fill up the place of better thoughts. (Anselm of Canterbury, "Similitudes," OCC I, pp. 34–35)

In this way, the blessed life is not impossible, but requires constant attention to the smallest daily matters in the nurture of the soul. Yet even though the pastoral writers paid great attention to small goods habitually done, they nonetheless assert that one well-timed good action may overcome many evils:

As one spark has frequently set fire to much wood, so it has been found that one good deed can wipe out a multiple of great sins. (Climacus, *The Ladder of Divine Ascent*, Step 26, sec. 35, p. 194)

Not external changes but inward serenity and humble patience is the only answer to some intractable human difficulties:

What can't be cured, must be endured. Aulus Gellius writes that certain sayings of Publius the moralist, which were couched in everyday language, were often bandied about in common speech. This is one of them, more wholesome than any dictum of the philosophers: "What can't be cured must be endured." These words warn us that destined evils, when they cannot by any means be avoided nor warded off, can at least be alleviated by resignation. (Erasmus, "Adages," I iii 14/LB II 17E, *Collected Works*, Vol. 31, p. 246)

X. ❦ MORAL PROGRESS AND REGRESS IN THE ORDERING OF THE PASSIONS

Modern evolutionary optimism has tended to assume that humanity is essentially good and, despite setbacks, historical progress is gaining steadily and human beings are fundamentally getting better and better. This very idea was, in its elementary form, thoughtfully examined and rejected by the pastoral tradition. For under the aegis of this notion, which eliminates the premise of the last judgment, there would be no way to sustain morality or virtue:

For if it is true that souls . . . are ever advancing with all generations, what danger is there in giving themselves up to the pleasures of sense—despising and neglecting the virtues by regard to which life is more stinted in its pleasures, and becomes less attractive—and in letting loose their boundless lust to range eagerly and unchecked through all kinds of debauchery? (Arnobious, "Against the Heathen," sec. 30, ANF VI, p. 445)

This is the heart of Christian objections to the notion of progress: Nothing is left for strenuous moral effort to undertake, if one should assume that moral improvement spontaneously occurs merely by allowing nature to take its course over a long sequence of progressive historical developments. On the contrary, Christian criticism focussed on the damage that uncorrected behaviors of individuals wreak intergenerationally on human families and communities:

An offender, when he sees any other doing as bad as himself, will be encouraged to do the very same things. . . . Sin which passes without correction grows worse and worse, and spreads to others; since "a little leaven infects the whole lump," [Gal. 5:9.] and one thief spreads the abomination over a whole nation, and "dead flies spoil the whole pot of sweet ointment" [Eccles. 10:7]; and "when a king hearkens to unrighteous counsel, all the servants under him are wicked" [Prov. 29:12]. So one scabbed sheep, if not separated from those that are whole, infects the rest with the same distemper; and a man infected with the plague is to be avoided by all men; and a mad dog is dangerous to every one that he touches. (*Constitutions of the Holy Apostles*, Bk. II, Ch. 17, sec. III, ANF VII, p. 403)

This revulsive series of contagion metaphors has a single aim: to reveal the problems the community must face if it neglects the early admonition and correction of offenders. Thus it becomes an act of prizing, conserving, and caring for the community to provide loving correction to the offending individual. The analogy anticipates the dilemma emerging from such modern phenomena as computer viruses, the cocaine epidemic, and AIDS.

Is the person responsible for erotic feelings, or are they exhaustively determined by heredity and environment? The seeming archaism of this answer by Maximus should not hamper our ability to hear its substance:

> Some say the demons touch the private parts of the body in sleep and rouse the passion of fornication; the roused passion then suggests to the mind, by the memory, female forms. Others say the demons appear to the mind in the guise of a woman and then touching the body rouse desire, and thus imaginings arise. Still others say that the passion dominant in the approaching demon rouses the passion and thus the soul is prepared for thoughts and recalls the forms by memory. For other impassioned images it is the same; some say it happens so, some say in some other way. However, in none of these ways are the demons able to rouse any passion whatsoever in a soul whether awake or asleep, when charity and self-mastery are present. (Maximus the Confessor, *The Four Centuries of Charity*, Ch. 2, sec. 85, ACW 21, p. 170)

Three primitive dream and psychological theories are here presented and rejected, all denying that freedom is accountable for the origin of its own fantasies. All three assume that there is an external demonic origin to sexual fantasy that transcends human self-control. Maximus was arguing for accountable self-determination in the life of erotic fantasy. We are responsible for how we use our eyes—for what we choose to look at:

> Hence, we can fully understand how chaste the Saviour wished us to be, who forbids us licentiousness of the eyes. Knowing that our eyes are, to an extent, the windows of our minds and that all evil desires enter the heart by using the eyes as natural underground passageways, God wished to destroy these evil desires while they were still outside, lest they gain strength within the mind and their deadly fibres grow if they once were germinated in our eyesight. (Salvian, *The Governance of God*, Bk. III, sec. 8, FC 3, p. 81)

If the eyes are windows through which either vice or virtue may grow, and each one controls what one is looking at in a given moment, then each one is finally responsible for those acts which draw near to those temptations which would by the eyes lead the whole body astray. In Salvian we have an early anticipation of the reinforcement metaphor that would later shape behavior therapy.

X. 🦌 GRACE AND EFFORT

If grace ranks so importantly in spiritual formation, some may conclude prematurely that human effort is thereby made less important or altogether unimportant. This misunderstanding had to be corrected and vigorously combatted. Most pastoral writers dealt with it in some form. For example, Abba Sisoes, the desert father, answered this question: Having fallen, how many times shall one get up again?

A brother asked Abba Sisoes, "What shall I do, abba, for I have fallen?" The old man said to him, "Get up again." The brother said, "I have got up again, but I have fallen again." So then the brother said, "How many times?" The old man said, "Until you are taken up either in virtue or in sin. For a man presents himself to judgement in the state in which he is found." (Sisoes, in *Sayings of the Desert Fathers*, sec. 38, p. 184)

It matters less how many times one has fallen, than that one has continued to get up again that same number of times, however many it is. If one takes the teaching about eternal judgment with radical seriousness, as did the desert fathers, then that final judgment was thought to be possible at any moment. One does not come to judgment as one appeared ten years ago, but at the very time that judgment occurs, which could be anytime. If now, then the time is up, and one has no more time to seek a better way, or prepare further for some subsequent judgment. Yet if the gospel comes to us through God's free mercy, why is any effort at all required of us? Luther pounced on the question:

The holy Gospel is a powerful Word. Therefore it cannot do its work without trials, and only he who tastes it is aware that it has

such power. Where suffering and the cross are found, there the Gospel can show and exercise its power. It is a Word of life. Therefore it must exercise all its power in death. In the absence of dying and death it can do nothing, and no one can become aware that it has such power and is stronger than sin and death. (Luther, "Sermon on the First Epistle of St. Peter, 1522," LW 30, p. 126, WA 12, p. 381)

Even though God's accepting love comes only through God's grace, not through our effort, it nonetheless calls for our active effort in response to it. If one believes the gospel but never has to face any opposition, then one has no way of discovering its power to overcome opposition. Divine providence and human will both work to elicit health:

> Now, then, many things in life take their rise in some exercise of human reason, having received the kindling spark from God. For instance, health by medicine, and soundness of body through gymnastics, and wealth by trade, have their origin and existence in consequence of Divine Providence indeed, but in consequence, too, of human co-operation. (Clement of Alexandria, *The Stromata, or Miscellanies*, Bk. VI, Ch. XVII, ANF II, p. 517)

Neither medicine, athletics, nor economic production take place merely by the action of providence, without any human effort or cooperative reasoning and activity.

May some periods of intensive effort be required to make up for an accumulated previous neglect? May an intensive self-examination abruptly turn around a life of long-seated bad habituation?

> Lop off superfluous occupations and anxieties, lest a noxious growth choke the good seed of the word. For it may be that a short and earnest diligence may repair a long time's neglect; for the time of every one's life is uncertain. (Clementina, *Recognitions of Clement*, Bk. VI, Ch. II, ANF VIII, p. 153)

There are moments of a process of personal or social development when a specially courageous or intelligent or caring act may make more difference than hundreds of other acts. There is not built into history an absolute equality of the value of all actions. So the caring person is attentive to those opportunities of especially energetic action that have the possibility of making the most difference for the good. Must everyone make a reasonable effort for themselves?

> A brother said to Abba Anthony, "Pray for me." The old man said to him, "I will have no mercy upon you, nor will God have any, if you yourself do not make an effort and if you do not pray to God." (Anthony the Great, in *Sayings of the Desert Fathers*, sec. 16, p. 3)

Two sides of the dynamics of behavior change are presented in paradoxical tension: effort and prayer. Cooperative grace seeks to elicit the cooperation of human wills. But is salvation offered and received irresistibly, totally apart from all human willing?

> We believe and we know from experience that this abundant grace acts in man and has a powerful influence; but in our opinion this influence is not such as to be overpowering, to the extent that whatever transpires in men's salvation is achieved by God's

will alone; . . . But man's will is also associated with grace as a secondary factor. For it is roused by the above-mentioned aids in order that it may co-operate with God's work which is being accomplished in man, and that it may begin to practice and gain merit from that for which the divine seed inspires the effective desire. Thus its eventual failure is due to its own fickleness; but its success is due to the help of grace.

This help is given in countless ways, some of which are hidden, and others are easily discernible. If many refuse this help, it is only their malice that is the cause. If many accept it, then this is due to both divine grace and their human will. We may examine the beginning of faith in the faithful or their progress or final perseverance in it, nowhere shall we discover any sort or kind of virtue which is not the fact of both the gift of grace and the consent of our wills. For grace, in all the variety of remedy or help which it provides, first operates to prepare the will of the recipient of its call to accept and follow up its gifts. Virtue is non-existent with men who do not wish to be virtuous, and you cannot say that men could have faith or hope or charity, if they refuse their free consent to these virtues. (Prosper of Aquitaine, *The Call of All Nations*, Bk. II, Ch. 26, ACW 14, pp. 134–135)

Grace preveniently operates to elicit in the broken will the possibility of cooperation, then operates to elicit cooperation. That faith which becomes habitually active in love is enabled by grace to increase in the strength of its activity. Acts of charity thus work retrospectively to blot out fleeting temporal memories of rancor and bitterness, and prospectively to strength courage to receive more grace. In all this, charity is a little like wine:

The tree of wisdom is strengthened by charity. Charity is like wine. For wine makes those whom it inebriates sprightly, bold, brave, forgetful, and in a certain way insensible. So charity, by cleansing the conscience, puts new spirit into the heart; and then, as through purity of conscience it gains confidence, emboldens it. Hence it grows strong because, as Scripture testifies, he who trusts in the Lord is as strong as a lion. For a pure conscience cannot be overcome by any adverse circumstances. So long as it is inwardly confident that it will always have God's help, it readily despises and conquers whatever outward contradiction it endures. It also induces forgetfulness, because while it draws the whole attention of the souls towards desire for eternal things, it drives from it entirely the memory of all those [things] that pass.

It makes the soul insensible, filling the heart to overflowing with inward sweetness; so that it despises whatever outward bitterness it suffers, as though it did not feel it. (Hugh of St. Victor, *SSW*, pp. 106–107)

XI. 🐝 Ascesis and Spiritual Athleticism

In the previous sections the pastoral writers have been strongly commending the value of cooperative effort in response to grace, and of discipline as the road to freedom. This requires the training of the body in much the same way that an athlete might train. This Christian "training" seeks to channel the body's energies to the service of the soul's growth, nurture and enlightenment. *Ascesis*, from which our word ascetic comes, simply means discipline or exercise (from *askein*, to exercise). A monk on nun or ascetic (*asketes*) was one who devoted intensive attention to this sort of exercise for the soul's growth, seeking to make the soul as strong as possible, much like the athlete in preparation for a final contest.

This contest was placed in a cosmic-historical context in which not only the end time was expected, but also in which the struggle with demonic powers was being enacted within the inner depths of every person. It is admittedly difficult, yet possible, for modern persons to empathize with, understand, and perhaps demythologize the traditional language of demonic temptation and ascetic exorcisms of demons. It was in this charged context that the ascetic discipline worked to put demonic powers to flight, willing to suffer for the good. However much modern consciousness may peremptorily reject it, we owe it to ourselves to at least try to understand these dynamics in terms of modern sensibilities and symbol systems.

One of the most graphic explanatory descriptions of demon-possession is found in the Clementina:

The reasons why the demons delight in entering into men's bodies is this. Being spirits, and having desires after meats and drinks, and sexual pleasures, but not being able to partake of these by reason of their being spirits, and wanting organs fitted for their enjoyment, they enter into the bodies of men, in order that, getting organs to minister to them, they may obtain the things that they wish, whether it be meat, by means of men's teeth, or sexual pleasure, by means of men's members. Hence, in order to the putting of demons to flight, the most useful help is abstinence and fasting, and suffering of affliction. For if they enter into men's bodies for the sake of sharing pleasures, it is manifest that they are put to flight by suffering. . . . The demons themselves, knowing the amount of faith of those of whom they take possession, measure their stay proportionately. Wherefore they stay permanently with the unbelieving, tarry for a while with the weak in faith; but with those who thoroughly believe, and who do good, they cannot remain even for a moment. For the soul being turned by faith, as it were, into the nature of water, quenches the demon as a spark of fire. The labour, therefore, of every one is to be solicitous about the putting to flight of his own demon. (Clementina, *Homilies*, Hom. VIII, Chs. X–XI, ANF VIII, p. 271)

However alien this reasoning feels within the premises of modernity, one must feel its power if one is to enter empathically into the arena in which *askesis* was undertaken. If the incorporeal demonic powers desire the fleshly experience of human bodies and passions, and if they are able to deceive, enter, and use the human body as surrogate for their own pleasure, then the most direct way to hinder this possession would be to refuse them the pleasurable result, hence withhold food and sex. One does not need to grant those premises in order to understand the power of the conclusion. Admittedly, such talk may lead toward an ex-aggerated disavowal of responsibility for oneself or toward a masochistic self-negation or even to outright self-harm. But the reasoning, cast in cosmic context of embattlement, provided an explanation to the ascetic of his struggle with hunger, sexual desire, and anger.

It was in response to such reasoning that the question had to be raised, whether, if we harm our bodies, does that in any way glorify God?

Surely, when they boast that a bodily mutilation is evidence of their inclusion among the elect, as though it gave them some special claim on God's love, what does this deserve but to be laughed out of court? (Epistle to Diognetus, sec. 4, ECW, p. 176)

As early as Diognetus, the Christian community was resisting bodily mutilation as a degrading of the created good of the body.

If discipline is to be rigorous, there is indeed some danger that the body may be too harshly treated, just as the athlete may overtrain, as Abba Poemen wryly noted:

Abba Isaac came to see Abba Poemen and found him washing his feet. As he enjoyed freedom of speech with him he said, "How is it that others practice austerity and treat their bodies hardly?" Abba Poemen said to him, "We have not been taught to kill our bodies, but to kill our passions." . . . He also said, "There are three things which I am not able to do without: food, clothing and sleep; but I can restrict them to some extent." (Poemen, in *Sayings of the Desert Fathers*, sec. 184, p. 162)

The pastoral tradition unambiguously condemned and proscribed the unconscionable masochistic practices of self-harm (suicide, self-dismemberment, and castration were all strongly condemned), on the grounds that the body as created is God's gift.

Let not him who has disabled himself be made a clergyman; for he is a self-murderer, and an enemy to the creation of God. If any one who is of the clergy disables himself, let him be deprived, for he is a murderer of himself. (*Constitutions of the Holy Apostles*, Ecclesiastical Canons, 22–23, ANF VII, p. 501)

Ignatius Loyola, standing in the Augustinian tradition, distinguish all creaturely goods from the end toward which all creaturely goods are ordered. One had best nurture a fitting sense of indifference toward creaturely goods that do not help one attain one's true end. If it should be the case that poverty is more likely to lead to salvation than wealth, what reasonable person would choose wealth?

Man is created to praise, reverence, and serve God our Lord, and by this means to save his soul. All other things on the face of the earth are created for man to help him fulfill the end for which he is created. From this it follows that man is to use these things to the extent that they will help him to attain his end. Likewise, he must rid himself of them in so far as they prevent him from attaining it. Therefore we must make ourselves indifferent to all created things, in so far as it is left to the choice of our free will and is not forbidden. Acting accordingly, for our part, we should not prefer health to sickness, riches to poverty, honor to dishonor, a long life to a short one, and so in all things we should desire and choose only those things which will best help us attain the end for which we are created. (Ignatius Loyola, *Spiritual Exercises*, pp. 48–49)

Loyola offered the following meditations on attachment and detachment. Each phase is a separate extended meditation. The series focuses upon whether one should or should not desire to retain worldly goods:

I will behold myself standing in the presence of God our Lord and all His saints, that I may desire and know what is most pleasing to His Divine Goodness . . . [and] ask for what I desire. Here it will be to beg for the grace to choose what is for the greatest glory of His Divine Majesty and the salvation of my soul.
The first class. They would like to free themselves of the attachment they have for the money they acquired, in order to find peace in God our Lord and to be able to save their souls, but up to the hour of death they do not take the means.

The second class. They want to free themselves of the attachment, but they wish to do so in such a way as to retain what they have acquired. They thus want God to come to what they desire, and they do not resolve to give up the money in order to go to God, even though this would be the better state for them.

The third class. They wish to free themselves of the attachment, but in such a way that their inclination will be neither to retain the thing acquired nor not to retain it, desiring to act only as God our Lord shall inspire them and as it shall seem better to them for the service and praise of His Divine Majesty. Meanwhile they wish to consider that they have in their hearts broken all the attachments, striving not to desire that thing nor anything else, unless it be only the service of God our Lord that prompts their action. (Ignatius Loyola, *Spiritual Exercises,* p. 78)

Rather than desperately seeking to be free from attachment or to retain what one has acquired, the supplicant prays neither to retain or not to retain, but to desire God's will in whichever alternative is of higher service.

XII. 🐝 THE GOVERNANCE OF HUNGER

The spiritual athlete will be expected to take great care about what foods shall enter the body. Yet early in the tradition it was recognized that a spare diet like anything good can be overdone. A moderating view was stated by John Climacus:

Gluttony is hypocrisy of the stomach; for when it is glutted, it complains of scarcity; and when it is loaded and bursting, it cries out that it is hungry . . . [Evagrius] says: "When our soul desires different foods, then confine it to bread and water." To prescribe this is like saying to a child: "Go up the whole ladder in one stride." And so, rejecting his rule, let us say: When our soul desires different foods, it is demanding what is proper to its nature. Therefore, let us also use cunning against our most wily foe. And unless a very severe conflict is on us, or penance for falls, let us for a while only deny ourselves fattening foods, then heating foods, and only then what makes our food pleasant. If possible, give your stomach satisfying and digestible food, so as to satisfy its insatiable hunger by sufficiency, and so that we may be delivered from excessive desire, as from a scourge, by quick assimilation . . . Master your stomach before it masters you. . . . By stinting the stomach, the heart is humbled. (Climacus, *The Ladder of Divine Ascent,* Step 14, secs. 2, 12, 17, 22, pp. 98–100)

How current the advice—a three-stage sequence of omitting foods to strengthen the body: first high lipids, then high carbohydrates (heating foods), and finally salts and sugars (which make food pleasant). No dietary changes were to occur abruptly, but only in a due sequence. A low caloric diet was commended to strengthen vitality. The spare diet was at times argued essentially on grounds of physical health, rather than primarily as a spiritual regimen:

Be sober in diet. Nature is contented with little. Where sobriety is absent, nothing is enough. The body must have sufficiency, lest it faint in the midst of necessary duties. But beware of gluttony and drunkenness. Christ said, "Take ye heed, overload not your hearts with these burthens of excess" [cf. Luke 11:46]. . . . Such excess is an enemy both to wealth and health. It has shortened the lives of those who stay near the kitchen. It has brought many to extreme beggary. And even as many great diseases are cured by abstinence, likewise the full stomach has been the cause of many strange and unusual sicknesses. Aurelian the emperor did not ever send for a physician in time of his sickness, but cured himself only by thin diet. And as much as immoderate feeding hurts the body, it is even more noisome to the mind. For as the ground, if it receives too much rain, is not watered but drowned and turns into mire, which is neither fit for tillage nor for yielding of fruit, so our flesh, over-watered with wine, is not fit to admit the spiritual plough, or to bring forth the celestial fruits of righteousness. The herbs that grow about it will be loathsome and stinking weeds, as brawling, chiding, blasphemy, slander, perjury, hatred, manslaughter, and such bad works of drunkenness and darkness. Are not these unsavoury fruits enough to make us abhor the tree? (George Sandys, Sermon, "The Evil of All Things Is at Hand," OCC I, pp. 86, 87)

The heart must not be overloaded with excess food. Penitential fasting has deep symbolic significance, far beyond its physical utility:

Now fastings signify abstinence from all evils whatsoever, both in action and in word, and in thought itself. As appears, then, righteousness is quadrangular; on all sides equal and like in word, in deed, in abstinence from evils, in beneficence. (Clement of Alexandria, *The Stromata, or Miscellanies*, Bk. VI, Ch. XII, ANF II, p. 503)

Fasting may serve good purposes, according to Luther, but never as a means of supposed religious merit:

Of fasting I say this: It is right to fast frequently in order to subdue and control the body. For when the stomach is full, the body does not serve for preaching, for praying, for studying, or for doing anything else that is good. Under such circumstances God's Word cannot remain. But one should not fast with a view to meriting something by it as by a good work. (Luther, "Sermon on Matthew 4:1," WLS 1, p. 506; WA 15, p. 450)

Does the scripture suggest that a single pattern of fasting should be commended for all, whatever the circumstances?

St. Peter . . . does not prescribe any definite length of time for fasting, . . . but he leaves it to everyone's discretion to fast in such a way that he always remains sober and does not burden the body with gluttony. He must remain reasonable and sensible, and he must see to what extent it is necessary for him to mortify the body. It does no good at all to impose a command about this on a whole crowd or community, since we are so different from one another. One has a strong body, another has a body that is weak. Therefore one person must deny it much, and another person must deny it little, in such a way that when this is done, the body remains healthy and able to do good. (Luther, "Sermons on the First Epistle of St. Peter, 1523," LW 30, pp. 27–28; WA 1, p. 507)

Fasting is contextual and highly individuated, and does not lend itself easily to highly abstract or general legalistic rules. Does fasting cleanse the body of dangerous obstructions?

Now fasting days contain a treble obligation; first, of eating less that day than on other days; secondly, of eating no pleasing or over-nourishing things, as the Israelites did eat sour herbs; thirdly, of eating no flesh, which is but the determination of the second rule, by Authority, to this particular. The two former obligations are much more essential to a true fast, than the third and last; . . . One thing is evident; that an English body, and a Student's body, are two great obstructed vessels; and there is nothing that is food, and not physic, which doth less obstruct, than flesh moderately taken; as, being immoderately taken, it is exceeding obstructive. And obstructions are the cause of most diseases. (Geo. Herbert, *CP*, Ch. X, CWS, pp. 70, 71)

Gregory the Great recognized the danger inherent in an inordinately rigid, tight, ascetic discipline:

Were it not that impatience commonly shakes the abstinent out of the bosom of tranquillity, Peter would by no means, when saying, "Supply in your faith virtue, and in your virtue knowledge, and in your knowledge abstinence" (2 Pet. 1:5), have straightway vigilantly added, "And in your abstinence patience." For He foresaw that the patience which he admonished them to have would tend to be lacking among the abstinent. . . . When the flesh is worn by abstinence more than is necessary, humility is displayed outwardly, but inwardly there is grievous pride on account of that very humility. . . . The abstemious are to be admonished to be always carefully on their guard that in fleeing from the vice of gluttony, worse vices are not generated. . . . Hence it is rightly said through the prophet, . . . "Ye fast for debates and strifes, and ye smite with the fists" [Is. 58:4]. . . . In vain, then, is the body worn by abstinence, if the mind, abandoned to disorderly emotions, is dissipated by vices. . . . In this matter we must consider how little the virtue of abstinence is accounted, unless it deserves commendation by reason of other virtues. So, Joel says: "Sanctify a fast" [Joel 2:15]. To sanctify a fast is to show abstinence of the flesh to be worthy of God by other good things being added to it. (Gregory the Great, *BPR*, Part III, Ch. XIX, NPNF 2, XII, pp. 43, 44; cf. ACW 11, pp. 148–150)*

Abstinence is not to be commended to all in an undiscriminating way. The gluttonous are to be counseled in a very different way than the abstemious. Gregory viewed these as polar types:

Those who are addicted to gluttony are to be admonished in one way, those who are abstemious in another. Loquacity, levity in conduct, and impurity, accompany the former; impatience and the sin of pride often accompany the latter. . . . Let the former hear the words: Meat for the belly, and the belly for the meats, but God shall destroy both it and them [cf. 1 Cor. 6.13]. . . . Let the latter be told that all things are clean to the clean, but to them that are defiled, and to unbeliever, nothing is clean. . . . Use a little wine for thy stomach's sake and thy frequent infirmities. (Gregory the Great, *Pastoral Care,* Part III, Ch. 19, ACW 11, pp. 147–151)

Every good is subject to abuse, and every virtue to becoming a vice. No genuine good in creation can be received without taking contextually into account its due proporation:

What goodness can there be in the world without moderation, whether in the use of God's creatures or in our own disposition and carriage? Without this, justice is no other than cruel rigour; mercy, unjust remissness; pleasure, brutish sensuality; love, frenzy; anger, fury; sorrow, desperate mopishness; joy, distempered wildness; knowledge, saucy curiosity; piety, superstition;

care, wracking distraction; courage, mad rashness. (Joseph Hall, Christian Moderation, Introduction to Book I, *Works*, Vol. VI, pp. 367f.; *Angl.*, #348, p. 763)

Any good may be pressed immoderately or insensitively to become an excess.

XIII. 🍎 THE INCREASE OF HUMILITY: DYING TO ONE'S OLD SELF

The caring pastor seeks to elicit in others a realistic self-assessment. Since persons are prone to pride, on the one hand, and self-deprecation on the other, the balance is never easily struck. One person may even retain both dysfunctional tendencies simultaneously. Early in the Christian pastoral tradition there developed a fund of resourceful wisdom concerning how pastors might deal differently with persons who are inordinately humble on the one hand, and inordinately self-elevated on the other.

The humble are to be admonished in one way, the haughty in another. The former should be told how genuine is that excellence which they have by hoping for it; the haughty, how worthless is the temporal glory which is not retained even when in their grasp. Let the humble be told of the eternal nature of the things which they strive after, and of the transitoriness of the things which they despise. Let the haughty be told how transitory the things are which they set themselves to acquire, how eternal the things which they forfeit. (Gregory the Great, *Pastoral Care*, Part III, Ch. 17, ACW 11, p. 141)

Common self-deceptions accompany false humility and self-congratulatory pride, which the astute pastor will learn quickly to recognize:

Some deceive themselves by a semblance of humility, while others are beguiled by ignorance of their own haughtiness. For commonly some who think themselves humble are given to an unmanly fear, while an assertion of free speech commonly goes with the haughty. When correction of certain faults is required, the former are silent out of fear, yet imagine themselves as being silent out of humility. The latter speak in the impatience of haughtiness, yet imagine themselves to be speaking in the freedom of uprightness. The former (the fearful) are prevented from admonishing wrongs by a faulty timidity under the guise of humility. The haughty are moved by the unbridled impetuosity of pride, under the image of freedom, to rebuke what should not be rebuked, or to rebuke them more than they ought. (Gregory the Great, *BPR*, Part III, Ch. 17, NPNF 2, XII, p. 41; cf. ACW 11, p. 142)*

The desert fathers used humor and dramatic exercise to teach humility—the first step, the primary learning, for any serious spiritual pilgrim:

A brother came to see Abba Macarius the Egyptian, and said to him, "Abba, give me a word, that I may be saved." So the old man said, "Go to the cemetery and abuse the dead." The brother went there, abused them and threw stones at them; then he returned and told the old man about it. The latter said to him, "Didn't they say anything to you?" He replied, "No." The old man said, "Go back tomorrow and praise them." So the brother went away and praised them, calling them, "Apostles, saints and righteous men." He returned to the old man and said to him, "I have complimented them." And the old man said to him, "Did they not answer you?" The brother said no. The old man said to him, "You know how you insulted them and they did not reply, and how you praised them and they did not speak; so you too if you wish to be saved must do the same and become a dead man. Like the dead, take no account of either the scorn of men or their praises, and you can be saved." (Marcarius the Great, in *Sayings of the Desert Fathers*, sec. 23, pp. 111–112)

A situation that at first appears to be humiliating may turn out to be a powerful context for learning. Deliberately designing such learning experiences must have been a vital concern of spiritual directors in the desert tradition. It was only by such means, they thought, that the demons could be "outwitted." Take, for example, the remarkable case of Isidore:

A certain man called Isidore, of magisterial rank, from the city of Alexandria, had recently renounced the world in the above-mentioned monastery, and I found him still there. That most holy shepherd, after accepting him, found that he was full of mischief, very cruel, sly, fierce and arrogant. But with human ingenuity, that most wise man contrived to outwit the cunning of the devils, and said to Isidore: "If you have decided to take upon yourself the yoke of Christ, then I want you first of all to learn obedience." Isidore replied: "As iron to the smith, so I surrender myself in submission to you, holy father." The great father, making use of this comparison, at once gave exercise to the iron Isidore, and said: "I truly want you, brother, to stand at the gate of

the monastery, and to make a prostration to everyone coming in
or going out, and to say: 'Pray for me, father; I am an epileptic.' "
And he obeyed as an angel obeys the Lord. When he had spent
seven years there, he attained to deep humility and compunction.
Then the glorious father, after the lawful seven years and the
man's incomparable patience, judged him fully worthy to be numbered among the brethren, and wanted to have him ordained.
But Isidore, through others and through my feeble intervention,
implored the shepherd many times to let him finish his course as
he was living before, vaguely hinting that his end and call were
drawing near. And that was actually the case. For when his director had allowed him to remain as he was, ten days later in this
state has passed gloriously to the Lord. And on the seventh day
after his own falling asleep, the porter of the monastery was also
taken. For the blessed man had said to him: "If I have found
favour in the sight of the Lord, in a short time you also will be
inseparably joined to me there." And that is what happened, in
witness of his unashamed obedience and divine humility.

When he was still living, I asked this great Isidore what occupation his mind had found during his time at the gate. And the
renowned ascetic, wishing to help me, did not hide this from me.
"In the beginning," he said, "I judged that I had been sold into
slavery for my sins; and so it was with bitterness, with a great
effort, and as it were with blood that I made the prostration. But
after a year had passed, my heart no longer felt sorrow, and I
expected a reward for my patience from God Himself. But when
another year had gone by, I began to be deeply conscious of my
unworthiness even to live in the monastery, and see and meet the
Father, and partake of the Divine Mysteries. And I did not dare
to look anyone in the face, but bending low with my eyes, and
still lower with my thought, I sincerely asked for the prayers of
those coming in and going out." (Climacus, *The Ladder of Divine
Ascent*, Step 4, sec. 23, pp. 28–29)

Even though this recollection is likely to be taken as horribly demeaning by those who cannot see beyond the counter-egalitarian issues, this
remains a moving ascetic pericope. It seeks to teach that demonic power
is not broken easily, and then only through rigorous discipline. Taking
the lowly way voluntarily, as in voluntary poverty, may bring one to an
exceptionally powerful awareness of joy and freedom. The meaning of
"dying to one's neighbor" is the subject of one of Black Moses' most
moving aphorisms:

The old man said, "If we are on the watch to see our own
faults, we shall not see those of our neighbour. It is folly for a

man who has a dead person in his house to leave him there and go to weep over his neighbor's dead. To die to one's neighbour is this: To bear your own faults and not to pay attention to anyone, do not think anything bad in your heart towards anyone, do not scorn the man who does evil, do not put confidence in him who does wrong to his neighbour, do not rejoice with him who injures his neighbour. This is what dying to one's neighbour means. Do not rail against anyone, but rather say, 'God knows each one'." (Black Moses, Instructions to Abba Poemen, in *Sayings of the Desert Fathers*, sec. 7, p. 120)

Black Moses, the third century desert monastic, assumed in this word-picture that each of us has a dead person in our own house (our own history of sin) who is enough to weep over, without having to rail at other's offenses. Each person has enough to deal with in conscience before God that it is not necessary to also pretend to serve as conscience for the neighbor. Augustine argued that pride and humility have precisely opposite, and therefore ironically very similar, psychological dynamics:

There is, therefore, something in humility which, strangely enough, exalts the heart, and something in pride which debases it. This seems, indeed, to be contradictory, that loftiness should debase and lowliness exalt. But pious humility enables us to submit to what is above us; and nothing is more exalted above us than God; and therefore humility, by making us subject to God, exalts us. . . . By craving to be more, man becomes less; and by aspiring to be self-sufficing, he fell away from him who truly suffices him. (Augustine, *The City of God*, B. XIV.13, NPNF 1, II, p. 273)

He demeans himself who seeks to push himself above others. He who permits himself to value what is lowly in life and share in its lowliness, is paradoxically more deeply prized by God who Himself took the lowly way in the incarnation. What follows? What paradoxical psychological dynamics are at work in the lowly way? A powerful series of aphorisms of lowliness were associated with the memory of Abba Pambo:

There was a monk named Pambo and they said of him that he spent three years saying to God, "Do not glorify me on earth." But God glorified him so that one could not gaze steadfastly at him because of the glory of his countenance. . . . Abba Pambo said, "By the grace of God, since I left the world, I have not said one word of which I repented afterwards." He also said, "The monk should wear a garment of such a kind that he could throw it out of his cell and no-one would steal it from him for three days." . . . They said of Abba Pambo that he was dying, at the very hour of his death, he said to the holy men who were standing near him, "Since I came to this place of the desert and built my cell and dwelt here, I do not remember having eaten bread which was not the fruit of my hands, and I have not repented of a word I have said up to the present time, and yet I am going to God as one who has not yet begun to serve him." He was greater than many others in that if he was asked to interpret part of the Scriptures or a spiritual saying, he would not reply immediately, but he would say he did not know that saying. (Pambo, in *Sayings of the Desert Fathers*, pp. 164–166).

I know of no place in the Christian tradition where humor is more at play in spiritual formation than among these desert ascetics. The idea of wearing a piece of clothing so beaten up that even if one tosses it out of one's room for three days, no one else would even be tempted to pick it up! This is an outrageous confluence of comedy and pathos, yet with just such ridiculous word-pictures the truth is driven home. What paradoxical learnings emerge from enduring such scorn and absorbing the hostility of others?

It is not when we courageously endure the derision of our [spiritual] father that we are judged patient, but when we endure it from all manner of men. For we bear with our father both out of respect and as a duty to him. Eagerly drink scorn and insult as the water of life from everyone who wants to give you this drink that cleanses from lust. Then a deep purity will dawn in your soul and the light of God will not grow dim in your heart. (Climacus, *The Ladder of Divine Ascent*, Step 4, secs. 84–85, p. 44)

"Drinking scorn" is hardly a modern virtue. Admittedly it can be twisted in the direction of demeaning self-bereavement. But apparently it did not move in that direction for the desert fathers. Instead it became a means of illumination, tranquility, and purification.

This Part of our discussion has drawn together classic passages on the moral dimensions of pastoral counseling. Pastors have from time immemorial been involved in dealing with anguished cases of conscience, where the clarification of the dynamics of guilt in a particular situation is of utmost importance. Pastoral counseling cannot avoid being also moral counseling. Where moral requirements are forgotten in the ministry of forgiveness, pastoral care has tended to turn into antinomian license. Self-controlled freedom is nurtured through attentiveness to discipline under the guidance of law and moral order. The aim is the right ordering of the life of the passions.

8 Anticipations of Psychotherapy

THE CLASSICAL PASTORAL tradition has anticipated many of the strategies for behavior change that now prevail in various contemporary psychotherapies. The same dynamics of self-deception, guilt, anxiety, repression and sublimation that we find in contemporary psychological analyses were also studied by pastoral writers, in some cases with extraordinary balance and insight. The same necessary and sufficient conditions for constructive psychological change (accurate empathy, congruence, and unconditional positive regard) are abundantly attested in the ancient Christian tradition.

This chapter brings together more coherently the particular ways in which three major schools of contemporary psychotherapy have been to some degree anticipated by the classical pastoral tradition. A convenient way of dividing up major schools of psychotherapy is to distinguish between (1) behavior therapy, (2) psychoanalysis, and (3) the so-called "Third Force" or humanistic psychology that presents itself as an alternative to the first two families of therapeutic approaches.

In what follows we will first show textual evidence that many of the specific strategies of behavior therapy (the daily descriptive recording of behavior observations, the scheduling of targeted objectives, positive and negative reinforcement, immediacy of reinforcement) have been well understood and diligently applied by early pastoral writers. Secondly, many key elements of psychoanalysis have been grasped in a rudimentary form: the dynamics of repression, the therapeutic value of freedom from super-ego dominance, the mediation between libidinal and superego conflicts by the analytical ego, religion as a projection of needs, creative sublimation, and other Freudian themes. Finally, the "Third Force" or humanistic psychologies stand even closer to classical pastoral care in their personalization of therapeutic care, their emphasis on the primacy of the therapeutic relationship (as opposed to the instrumentalization of chemical or psychopharmacological views of therapy), and in their stress on empathic understanding.

Classical Christianity remains ironically "ahead" of modernity in its balance of complementary values and virtues so prone to imbalance in modern discussions. To gain a broader vantage point, we begin with a more general question:

226

I. ❦ To What Extent Can Pastoral Care Employ Secular Psychologies and Therapies Without Losing Its Identity?

The work of Christian soul care has proceeded through many centuries in companionship with alternative views of human nature, varied psychologies, and therapeutic approaches. Thus it has become a recurrent point of needful debate to ask how deeply Christian soul care can legitimately borrow from its humanistic partners in dialogue among secular psychologies (such as Platonic, Neo-platonist, Gnostic, Epicurean, Stoic, etc.), and still remain rigorously faithful to the Christian understanding of persons.

In addressing the question of whether Christian soul-guides should have a general humanistic education (including the study of psychology), and substantial knowledge of the truth as perceived by these non-Christian thinkers on the soul and its care, Clement of Alexandria, took an open and tolerant view:

> To the Christian teacher, knowing whatever is knowable is his principal concern. Consequently, he applies himself to the subjects that constitute a training for knowledge. He takes from each branch of study its contribution to the truth. He inquires into the proportion of harmonies in music. He notes the increasing and decreasing of numbers in mathematics, and their relations to one another, and how most things fall under some proportion of numbers. . . . He further avails himself of dialectics, fixing on the distinction of genera into species, and seeks to master the distinction of existences, till he comes to what are primary and simple. . . . How could he serve as a money changer if he is not able quickly to test and distinguish spurious from true coinage? (Clement of Alexandria, *The Stromata, or Miscellanies*, Bk. VI, Ch. X, ANF II, p. 498)*

The money-changer metaphor is telling: The soul guide must be able quickly to recognize the differences between truthful and counterfeit claims to the truth about human personality. This discernment cannot be achieved without serious study of varied comparative psychologies and philosophies. This is why Clement commended these studies as preparatory for undertaking pastoral care:

> Anyone who has hands finds it natural to grasp. Anyone with good eyes can naturally see the light. So it is the natural prerogative of him who has received faith to apprehend knowledge, if he desires, on "the foundation" which has already been laid, to work and build up "gold, silver, precious stones" [cf. I Cor. 3:12]. . . . Who would not admit that to be is far better than not to be. Each

person, according to their capabilities, naturally strives to advance toward that which is better. So there is no absurdity in philosophy [including psychology] having been given by Divine Providence as a preparatory discipline for the maturity which has appeared in Christ (unless philosophy itself is absurdly ashamed of learning from distant forms of knowledge how to advance to truth). But if "the very hairs are numbered" [Matt. 10:30], and the most insignificant motions, how shall philosophy not be taken into account? For to Samson power was given in his hair, in order that he might perceive that the worthless arts that refer to the things in this life, which lie and remain on the ground after the departure of the soul, were not given without divine authorization. . . . The philosophers, therefore, who, trained to their own peculiar power of perception by the spirit of perception, when they investigate, not a part of philosophy, but philosophy absolutely, testify to the truth hidden in truth—hence they love a humble spirit. (Clement of Alexandria, *The Stromata, or Miscellanies*, Bk. VI, Ch. XIII, ANF II, p. 516)*

The study of psychology was included in what Clement called philosophy—for it included the study of motivation, perception, passion, habit, and behavior modification. Clement thought that secular learning could be viewed historically and psychodevelopmentally as a stage on the way to fuller manifestation of the truth in Christ. Everything learnable was, insofar as possible, commended to be learned. Yet, as in the case of Samson, each learning testifies of its own vulnerability and inadequacy.

Even before Clement, another early pre-Nicene writer, Justin Martyr, would similarly pursue the question of how far soul guides may freely make use of secular disciplines:

I do not say that the teachings of Plato are wholly different from those of Christ, nor are they in all respects similar, as neither are those of the other philosophers, Stoics, poets, and historians. For each of these spoke well in proportion to the share he had of the spermatic [generative divine] word, grasping as they could behold what was related to it. But those thinkers who contradict themselves on the more essential points appear not adequately to have grasped the heavenly wisdom, against which no one can knowledgeably speak.

Whatever truth has been fittingly spoken in human history is also therefore the property of Christians. For next to God, we worship and love the Word who is from the unbegotten and ineffable God, since He even became a human being for our sakes so that, by sharing in our sufferings, He might also bring us healing. Indeed, all these writers were enabled to glimpse dimly the truth through the sowing of the implanted word that was in them. For the seed of something and its imitation, imparted in proportion to one's capacity, is one thing, while the thing itself which is shared and imitated according to grace which is from God, is something else. (Justin Martyr, *Second Apology*, Ch. XIII, ANF I, pp. 192–193; cf. FC 6, pp. 133, 134)*

Whatever Christian inquiry finds to be truthful in secular psychological reflection or experiment belongs to Christians as well as non-Christians. If the best secular writers see the truth, yet through a glass darkly, then that truth may be claimed, embraced and transmuted in Christ. Origen used an aesthetic metaphor of fragrance to clarify how God's personal self-giving love complements humanistic psychology and philosophy:

The fragrance of His ointments is above all spices. We shall make use of a like interpretation whenever we transfer these words to every individual soul that is fixed in the love of the Word of God and in desire for Him; a soul that will have traversed in order all the sorts of instruction in which she was exercised and taught before she attained to the knowledge of the Word of God, whether those teachings be based on ethics or on natural philosophy. For all those things were so many spices for that soul, in that by their means an agreeable disposition and improvement of behaviour are acquired, and because in them the vanity of the world is discovered and the deceitful marvels of perishable things are rejected. All these things were, then, as spices and perfumes, cosmetics as it were of the soul. But when she has come to knowledge of the mysteries and the divine judgements, when she has reached the gates of wisdom itself, of the wisdom that is not of this world, neither of the world who came to nought, but is the very wisdom of God which is discoursed upon among the perfect, and when the mystery that was not made known to former generations has been revealed to the sons of men—when, I say, the soul ascends to recognition of this so great secret, she has cause to say: "The fragrance of Thine ointments"—that is, the spiritual and mystical meaning—"is above all spices" of moral and natural philosophy [Song of Songs 4:10]. (Origen, *The Song of Songs*, Bk. 1, sec. 3, ACW 26, pp. 73, 74)

There are two levels of knowing in this intriguing metaphor: objective-empirical and intuitive-mystical. Psychological insights and empirical researches are like spices for the soul, or perfumes or cosmetics: They improve human behavior and make human life more agreeable. Yet there is another level of knowing, a transcendent and mystical sense of the mystery of God, which the soul guide is entrusted to share, which is "above all spices of moral and natural" knowledge. One might say that the right pinch of good psychology spices up a savory dish of pastoral care.

II. ❦ HABIT MODIFICATION

The previous section has established that Christian soul guides should have a general humanistic education (including the study of psychology), and substantial knowledge of the truth as perceived by the best non-Christian thinkers on the soul and its care, and that classical Christian wisdom from its beginnings has remained in dialogue with natural and secular ways of understanding human behavior.

We now proceed with classic antecedents of behavior modification, the first of three major modern schools of psychotherapy anticipated by classical pastoralia.

Behavior modification techniques are often assumed by modern advocates to be original discoveries by psychologists of the last century, from Pavlov and Skinner through the traditions following Wolpe and Lazarus. However, the essential ideas of behavior modification—accurate observation and recording of behavior, sequencing of targeted behavior changes, positive and negative reinforcement, immediacy of reinforcement, etc.—are found abundantly in the classical western religious tradition.

We will first ask whether early Christian writers had a clear notion of the importance of keeping careful records of behavioral changes in correcting chronic dysfunctions. We will let Kierkegaard's favorite monastic writer, Johannes Climacus, be first to answer:

As one who has suffered a prolonged illness can scarcely obtain health in an instant, so it is impossible suddenly to overcome the passions, or even one passion. Keep track of the extent of every passion and of every virtue, and you will know what progress you are making. (Climacus, *The Ladder Of Divine Ascent*, Step 26, sec. 55–56, p. 196)

The management and redirection of emotive distortions is not easily accomplished. The first step is accurate observation. But it is also widely recommended that one regularly write down misdeeds and skewed behaviors that one wishes to change, in order to monitor the pace and progress of change. The greatest of the desert fathers, Anthony, made this point quite sharply, as related by his biographer, Athanasius:

That this state may be preserved in us it is good to hear the apostle and keep his words, for he says, "Try your own selves and prove your own selves" [2 Cor. 13:5]. Daily, therefore, let each one take from himself the tale of his actions both by day and night. . . . let the following be observed. Let us each one note and write down our actions and the impulses of our soul as though we were going to relate them to each other. . . . If we record our thoughts as though about to tell them to one another, we shall the more easily keep ourselves free from vile thought through shame lest they should be known. (Athanasius, *Life of Antony,* sec. 55, NPNF 2, IV, p. 211)

Anthony's recommended procedure: (1) Habit modification is a daily exercise; (2) it requires careful self-assessment both day and night, presumably inclusive of dreams; (3) the writing down the "tale of one's actions," and the "impulses of one's soul" concretizes the observation for later comparison; and (4) it must be done as if one were speaking to another, openly revealing oneself to another, in confidence. But why is this last point considered necessary? What behavior change function is served by the imagination that we are revealing our misdeeds openly to another caring person?

Just as we would not practice fornication if we were observing each other directly, so also we will doubtless keep ourselves from impure thoughts, ashamed to have them known, if we record our thoughts as if reporting them to each other. Let this record replace the eyes of our fellow ascetics. (Athanasius, *The Life of St. Anthony,* ACW 10, p. 73)

In this way the caring community becomes the supportive context in which this exercise of self-observation and behavioral monitoring takes place. The thought of reporting to another (even in fantasy) about one's misdeeds surely functions as a curb or negative reinforcement to undesired behaviors. But why is such a daily monitoring of behavior considered so necessary for the good of the soul?

After a few days he [Anthony] returned once more to the mountain, and thereafter many visited him, and some who suffered were bold enough to approach him. For all the monks who came to him he unfailing had the same message: to have faith in the Lord and love him; to guard themselves from lewd thoughts and pleasures of the flesh, and as it is written in Proverbs, not to be deceived by the feeding of the belly; to flee vanity, and to pray constantly; to sing holy songs before sleep and after, and to take to heart the precepts in the Scriptures; to keep in mind the deeds of the saints, so that the soul, ever mindful of the commandments, might be educated by their ardor. But he especially urged them to practice constantly the word of the Apostle: Do not let the sun go down on your anger, and to consider that this had been spoken with every commandment in mind—so that the sun should set neither on anger nor on any other sin of ours. He continued: "For it is good, even urgent, that the sun should not condemn us for an evil of the day, nor the moon for a sin, or even for an inclination, of the night.... For frequently we are unaware of the things we do, but even though we do not recognize them, the Lord comprehends all things." (Athanasius, *Life of St. Anthony*, sec. 55, ACW 10, p. 72)

The purpose of Anthony's daily behavioral monitoring was to increase accurate observation and awareness of the things we do, of known and observed behaviors. Meanwhile this human awareness was framed in the context of the incomparably accurate awareness of God who fails to note nothing.

It is hardly wise for the spiritual director to try to undertake responsibility for correcting numerous vexing problems of the troubled neighbor at the same time. Climacus and most monastic spiritual directors thought it better to focus on a single, manageable behavioral change objective than many:

It is better for us not to diversify ourselves and divide up our poor soul in doing battle with thousands of thousands and ten thousands of ten thousands of enemies; for it is not in our power to comprehend or even to discover all their hosts. (Climacus, *The Ladder of Divine Ascent*, Step 26, sec. 32, p. 167)

There is a sobering realism in the pastoral literature about the difficulty of changing entrenched behavioral habits. Both positive and negative reinforcement, patiently applied over a sufficient time span, are required to effect long-lasting and substantive change. But in the case of the fainthearted or anxious person, is not positive reinforcement more effective? Gregory's principle of variability applies—that different types of reinforcement are required for persons with different symptoms:

The insolent are to be admonished in one way, the fainthearted in another. The former, greatly relying on themselves, scorn reproofs from all others, but the latter, too conscious of their weakness, commonly fall into despondency. The former esteem everything they do to be singularly excellent, the fainthearted think what they do is extremely despicable, and, therefore, their spirit is broken in dejection.... Now, we best reprove the insolent, when we show them that what they believe they have done well has been ill-done, so that a wholesome confusion may ensue from what they believe won glory for them.... But the opposite course holds for the fainthearted. We are more apt to bring them back to the path of well-doing, if by way of indirect approach we refer to some of their good points. Thus, by reproving and correcting some things, and approving and praising others, their sensitiveness is palliated by the praise they hear, though it is chastised by the rebuking of their fault. Generally we make more profitable progress with these people, if we also speak of their good deeds. (Gregory the Great, *Pastoral Care,* Part III, Ch. 8, ACW 11, pp. 104–105)

The fainthearted who are prone to anxiety (as distinguished from the insolent who are prone to pride), are better helped by positive reinforcements, with correction mixed sparely with undergirding affirmation and praise.
Persons at different stages of behavioral transformation must be pastorally dealt with in terms of the differences of those stages:

Milk must go before strong meat; the foundation must be laid before we attempt to raise the superstructure. Children must not be dealt with as men of full stature. Men must be brought into a state of grace, before we can expect from them the works of grace. . . . We must not ordinarily go beyond the capacities of our people, nor teach them the perfection, that have not learned the first principles of religion: for, as Gregory of Nyssa saith; "We teach not infants the deep precepts of science, but first letters, and then syllables, &c." (Baxter, *RP,* pp. 112–113)

The early Christian writers viewed habit formation in the light of an assumed cosmology in which angelic and demonic powers struggled proximately for the destiny of the soul (though never denying freedom, for the struggle is precisely about freedom). This is the context in which the following interpretation is offered of how bad habits are formed:

In seeking good things, the human will is of its own strength unable to accomplish any good, for it is only by divine aid that freedom is brought to maturity in any matter. Similarly in our involvement with evil, we inconspicuously receive from the beginning, as it were, the seeds of sin, as we are employing temporal things according to our nature. But we often indulge in these created goods in ways far beyond their intrinsic value. Thus we do not sufficiently resist the first impulses to intemperance. Then at that point the enemy, seizing the occasion of our first transgression, incites our passions and presses us hard at every point, seeking to extend our sins over an ever-wider field. By this means persons are forever being furnished with occasions and beginnings of sin. . . . Thus, when someone at first experiences a small desire for money, covetousness begins to grow. The passion increases. Finally the fall into avarice takes place. . . . It is recorded in certain histories that some have fallen into madness from a state of love, others from a state of anger, not a few from a state of sorrow, and even from excessive joy! This is the result of the fact that these inimical, demonic powers have already gained lodging in originally free minds, which have quietly become vulnerable to intemperance, only to find themselves suddenly taken over completely in their passions, especially when they have no experience of the feeling of the glory of virtue that might have aroused in them resistance to these powers. (Origin, *De Principiis*, Bk. III, Ch. II, sec. 2, ANF IV, p. 330)*

Bad habits are formed out of the inordinate pursuit of good things. Through excesses of love, candor, or desire, (or even joy!), bad habits gain firm lodging in our minds. Incrementally the unsavory habits grow when any proportional creaturely good is indulged in a disproportional way. Finally they take possession of an ever widening range of the emotive life. Although this insight admittedly was conceived in a context of superpersonal intelligences influencing behavior, the basic psychological process is able to be described in empirical terms, without use of demonic imagery.

III. 🐑 Reinforcement Techniques

We continue with classic antecedents of behavior therapy. The prudent balancing of what modern writers call positive and negative reinforcements was a central theme of ancient pastoral reflection. Astute pastors were attentive to the etiology of accumulated habit formations and to the viability of incremental behavioral change. The means of accomplishing such change must be studied carefully and critically. Such studied attention by care-givers has continued over many centuries.

In accord with the pivotal metaphor of shepherding, the pastor worked by both positive and negative reinforcements. This involved both a constant feeding and curbing, both nurturing and limiting, and constant monitoring in the interest of the growth and protection of the flock. In pastoral descriptions like the following, we have a glimpse of the complexity of this patient behavior-guidance task. Note the balance:

As to a good shepherd, let the lay person honour him, love him, reverence him as his lord, as his master, as the high priest of God, as a teacher of piety. . . . In like manner let the bishop love the laity as his children, fostering and cherishing them with affectionate diligence; . . . chiding them in order to their reformation and better course of life; watching the strong, that is, keeping him firm in the faith who is already strong; feeding the people peaceably; strengthening the weak, that is, confirming with exhortation that which is tempted; healing that which is sick, that is, curing by instruction that which is weak in the faith through doubtfulness of mind; binding up that which is broken, that is, binding up by comfortable admonitions that which is gone astray, or wounded, bruised, or broken by their sins, and put out of the way (*Constitutions of the Holy Apostles*, Bk. II, sec. II.2, ANF VI, p. 404)

Pastoral work proceeded typically by both negative reinforcement (chiding, watching, firming) and positive reinforcement (feeding, strengthening, confirming, healing, instructing). If negative reinforcements or constraints were to be used, they had to be carefully timed and gauged to the proportion of the undesired behavior.

How is it equitable or wise, that any one should be punished on account of a slight offence, and should be unpunished on account of a very great one? (Lactantius, *A Treatise on the Anger of God,* Ch. XVIII, ANF VII, p. 275)

Clement of Alexandria argued for the therapeutic benefit of timely pain viewed as a corrective function:

Accordingly, pain is found beneficial in the healing art, and in discipline, and in punishment; and by it men's manners are corrected to their advantage. (Clement of Alexandria, *The Stromata, or Miscellanies,* Bk. VI, Ch. III, ANF II, p. 527)

But it is ineffective to offer corrections without building first a foundation of understanding love. The pastoral writers viewed the corrective process essentially as an act of love.

[The Apostle Paul] first praised them for those things in which they displayed courage, and afterwards, with prudent admonition, strengthened them in that matter wherein they were weak. . . . True teacher that he was, he conducted matters so that they were first to recall something for which they were praised, and afterwards followed his admonition. The words of praise were to fortify their minds against feeling disturbed over the admonition. (Gregory the Great, *Pastoral Care,* Part III, Ch. 8, ACW 11, p. 106)

Prior to gentle admonition, one does well to look for an occasion to praise. In habit modification, the guide must work incrementally at small behaviors in order eventually to effect larger patterns of behavior change. This is why Gregory thought it important to ask: How, then, shall the pastor counsel those who transgress only in small matters, but very frequently? He beautifully applied the raindrop metaphor, which remains consonant with modern views of incremental habit reinforcement:

> Indeed, it is small raindrops, but countless ones, that make up the towering torrents of streams; and bilge water rising imperceptibly produces the same effect on a ship as a hurricane raging after the main. Small, too, are the sores which erupt on the bodily members in pimples, but when a countless number of these invade the body, they destroy life as effectually as a single serious wound inflicted on the breast. (Gregory the Great, *Pastoral Care*, Part III, Ch. 33, ACW 11, p. 215)

John Chrysostom also argued for the primary importance of the smallest quantum of behavior modification. This goes contrary to caricatures of Christian conversion and behavioral change that imagine that total transformations should occur in an instant (which later became a special problem of Protestant revivalism):

> A want of zeal in small matters is the cause of all our calamities; and because slight errors escape fitting correction, greater ones creep in. As in the body, a neglect of wounds generates fever, mortification, and death; so in the soul, slight evils overlooked open the door to grave ones.... Thus a thousand and similar errors are daily introduced into the Church, and we are become a laughing stock to Jews and Greeks, seeing that the Church is divided into a thousand parties. But if a proper rebuke had at first been given to those who attempted slight perversions, and a deflection from the divine oracles, such a pestilence would not have been generated, nor such a storm have seized upon the Churches.... Hence our affairs are now in confusion and trouble, hence have our learners being filled with pride, reversed the order of things throwing every thing into confusion, and their discipline having been neglected by us their governors, they spurn our reproof however gentle. (Chrysostom, *Commentary on Galatians*, Ch. 1, NPNF 1, XIII, p. 8)

Great troubles of the Christian community grow gradually out of the want of discipline in small matters. Christian pastors learned early this important behavioral maxim: repeatedly reinforced undesirable habits continued over a long period of time are far more difficult to change. This calls attention again to the crucial importance of early parental education, and of the formation of desirable habitual behavior from the beginning.

Ignatius Loyola developed a daily pattern of reinforcement for amending behavioral addictions:

As soon as he arises in the morning the exercitant should resolve to guard himself carefully against the particular sin or defect which he wishes to correct or amend. The second time: After the noon meal he should ask God our Lord for what he desires, namely, the grace to remember how many times he has fallen into the particular sin or defect, and to correct himself in the future. Following this he should make the first examination demanding an account of his soul regarding that particular matter which he proposed for himself and which he desires to correct and amend. He should review each hour of the time elapsed from the moment of rising to the moment of this examination, and he should make note on the first line of the following diagram, a mark for each time that he has fallen into the particular sin or defect. (Ignatius Loyola, *Spiritual Exercises,* p. 48)

The effectiveness of the Ignatian system of behavior change is partly due to this regularity of accurate (hourly!) observation of defects, and its precise recording, which was to be shared and talked through with the spiritual guide.

Richard Baxter used the metaphor of addiction to speak of powerfully reinforced behavioral excesses. One who cares about the addict will resist his or her addiction:

Some are specially addicted to pride, and others to worldly-mindedness; some to sensual desires, and others to frowardness or other evil passions. Now it is our duty to give assistance to all these; and partly by dissuasions, and clear discoveries of the odiousness of the sin, and partly by suitable directions about the remedy, to help them to a more complete conquest of their corruptions. . . . how much more we love their persons, by so much the more must we manifest it, by making opposition to their sins. (Baxter, RP, p. 98–99)

George Herbert thought that reinforcers that otherwise might be considered unworthy (such as profit and fame) could be legitimately made use of in encouraging behavior change:

The country parson, who is a diligent observer and tracker of God's ways, sets up as many encouragements to goodness as he can, both in honor and profit and fame; that he may, if not the best way, yet any way make his Parish good. (Geo. Herbert, *CP,* Ch. XI, CWS, p. 72)

Targeted behaviors to be changed must be specific. Otherwise effort is diffused. John Cassian used a striking metaphor of an archer shooting at a target out of sight as an analogy to the problems of attempting behavioral change without specific goals:

When expert archers want to display their prowess before a king, they try to shoot their arrows into little targets which have the prizes painted on them: they know they can only win the prize which is their real goal by shooting straight into the mark which is their immediate goal. But suppose that the target were carried out of sight. They would then have no means of knowing how unskillfully and crookedly they were shooting, but would be shooting their arrows at random into the air without any guide to accurate or inaccurate aim and without the possibility of estimating what correction was needed. . . . If we do not keep this mark continually before the eyes, all our travail will be futile waste that wins nothing, and will stir up in us a chaos of ideas instead of singlemindedness. Unless the mind has some fixed point to which it can keep coming back and to which it tries to fasten itself, it will flutter hither and thither according to the whim of the passing moment and follow whatever immediate and external impression is presented to it. (Cassian, *Conferences*, First Conference of Abba Moses, sec. 5, LCC XII, pp. 197–98)

Thomas Aquinas set forth this influential opinion on how habits are formed:

The philosopher in *Metaphysics* V, 25 states that by habits we are directed well or ill with regard to the passions. For whenever anything is appropriate to a thing's nature, it is recognized as a good; but when inappropriate, it seems evil. . . . Sense powers can be considered in two ways. First, insofar as they act from natural impulse, and second, insofar as they act under reason's rule. Insofar as they act by natural impulse they are ordered, just as nature is, to one thing. So that just as habits are not present in natural powers, so habits are not present in sense powers, insofar as they act from natural impulse. Insofar as they act under reason's rule, they can be ordered to various things. In this way sense powers can have habits by which they are well or badly disposed toward something. . . . In *Ethics I* the philosopher says that just as one swallow does not make spring, so neither does one day nor a brief time make a man blessed or happy. But happiness comes from action according to a perfect, virtuous disposition, as stated in *Ethics I*. Hence, one act does not cause a virtuous habit nor, for the same reason, any other habit. . . . In respect to the inferior knowing powers, the same acts must be many times repeated to imprint something firmly upon the memory. . . . The same thing does not cause contrary things. But as stated in *Ethics II* some acts lessen the disposition from which they come, namely, if they are carelessly done. Hence not every act increases disposition. (Thomas Aquinas, *Summa Theologica*, Part I-II, Q. 49, Art. 2, Q. 50, Art. 3, Q. 51, Art. 3, Q. 52, Art. 3, AR, pp. 351–353)

Habit formation occurs in the arena of tension between reason and natural impulse. Some acts strengthen, others lessen a particular disposition. The repetition of good behavior is required to make it habitual. Happiness comes from action according to a virtuous disposition. Conversely, undesirable behaviors acquire momentum through repetition:

One degree prepareth the heart for another, and one sin inclineth the mind to more. If one thief be in the house, he will let in the rest; because they have the same disposition and design. A spark is the beginning of a flame; and a small disease may cause a greater. (Baxter, *RP*, p. 73)

Amid temptation, one may substitute the thought of a real good for the thought of an imaginary good. This replacement process is very much like the behavior therapy proposed by Spinoza in *Ethics*, and later by the "positive thinking" tradition following William James:

Canny generals are accustomed, even in times of peace, to set guards. In like manner you too ought always to have a mind vigilant and circumspect to the future assaults of the enemy. "For he ever goes about, seeking whom he may devour" [1 Pet. 5:8]. . . . But the tempter is best repelled by these means: if you either vehemently put out of mind and immediately as it were spit upon the suggester, or earnestly pray, or wholeheartedly betake yourself to some holy task, or answer the tempter with words chosen from Holy Scripture, just as we have admonished above. (Erasmus, *Enchiridion*, Rules 9-10, LCC XIV, p. 363)

By a contemptuous act of spitting (symbolically) on the suggester, (thereby demeaning the tempter's power), temptation may be averted. A worse notion is resisted and a better notion is lodged in the mind.

Maximus reduced the prime motivations to improve behavior to these five:

Fear of men, fear of judgment, future reward, love of God, or promptings of conscience. (Maximus the Confessor, *The Four Centuries of Charity*, Ch. 2, sec. 81, ACW 21, p. 169)*

Where unresisted, vice which is unnatural, takes on the appearance of being the natural condition of humanity:

But no vice is natural to man, whereas virtue is. None the less the force of habit deriving from a corrupt will or a deep-seated carelessness tends to make a host of vices become as if natural to the conscience which has been neglected. As medical men say, habit is second nature. . . . However, vice although it is considered to be nothing other than the privation of virtue can assume such enormous proportions as to be felt crushing and overwhelming. Its vileness can be such that it defiles and infects. It can cling with so pertinacious a force of habit that nature is scarcely able to shake it off. . . . In this way every kind of vice derives its origin from some disorder of the will or from the force of bad habit. The more attractive to the mind it is and the more firmly rooted, the more tenaciously it clings and the more vigorous are the remedies it calls for and the more painstaking the care it needs.

For diseases of this sort, vices, pursue the solitary into the furthest recesses of his solitude. And just as solid virtue that is firmly established in the spirit does not abandon the man who possesses it however many people there may be around him, so the vice of bad habit leaves the man over whom it has asserted its mastery no freedom in any solitude. For unless the habit be rooted out by persevering effort and prudent toil, it may be attenuated but it can hardly be overcome. However carefully the spirit may set itself in order, the habit clings; in whatever degree of solitude it dwells, the habit precludes solitude or silence in the heart.

The stronger the bent of the habit, and of the will, the more powerfully is felt the rebellion of what may be termed not so much spiritual malice as a swarm of pests of all sorts or a heavy tumor weighing down the body that must be cast out as it were with manual force. (William of St. Thierry, *The Golden Epistle*, II.7, *Works*, Vol. 4, #219, 222, 224–226, pp. 84–85)

IV. 🐭 BEHAVIORAL CHANGE STRATEGIES

What psychologists today call behavior change strategies or behavioral modification, the classical tradition was more likely to call the struggle for virtue (meaning behavioral excellences), and the struggle against specific vices (behavioral excesses and deficits). Every pastor is necessarily involved in this struggle to curb behavioral excesses to make behavior more humane, desirable, and ordered more effectively toward higher ends. In this sense it was intrinsic to the pastoral office to be a mentor of behavioral change.

It is not easy to foster virtues, however, without eliciting corresponding vices. For if a vice is a virtue taken to excess, then assessing the due proportionality of behaviors had to become an important aspect of pastoral counsel, but one which ran endless hazards. Note the subtlety of the struggle for behavioral equilibrium in this famous passage from Gregory:

These are things that a director of soul should observe in the various phases of his preaching, so that he may carefully propose the remedies indicated by the wound in each given case. But whereas in exhorting individuals great exertion is required to be of service to each individual's particular needs, whereas it is very laborious to instruct each one in what applies to him in particular by urging appropriate considerations, the task is a far more laborious one when on one and the same occasion one has to deal with a numerous audience subject to different passions. In this case the address must be formulated with such skill that, notwithstanding the diversity of failings in the audience as a whole, it carries a proper message to each individual, without involving itself in self-contradictions. Thus, in one direct stroke it should pass straight through the passions. Yet, this should be as with a double-edged sword, so as to lance the tumours of carnal thoughts on both sides: humility is to be preached to the proud in a way not to increase fear in the timorous, and confidence infused into the timorous, as not to encourage the unbridled impetuosity in the proud. The idle and the remiss are to be exhorted to zeal for good deeds, but in a way not to increase the unrestraint of intemperate action in the impetuous. Moderation is to be imposed on the impetuous without producing a sense of listless security in the idle. Anger is to be banished from the impatient, but so as not to add to the carelessness of the remiss and easy-going. The remiss should be fired with zeal in such a manner as not to set the wrathful ablaze. Bountiful almsgiving should be urged on the niggardly without slackening the rein on prodigality. Frugality is to be indoctrinated in the prodigal, but not so as to intensify in the niggardly their tenacity of things doomed to perish. Wedlock is to be preached to the incontinent, but not so as to recall to lust those who have become continent. Physical virginity is to be commended to the continent, yet so as not to make the married despise the fecundity of the body. Good things are so to be preached as not to give incidental help to what is bad. The highest good is to be so praised, that the good in little things is not discarded. Attention should be called to the little things, but not in such a way that they are deemed sufficient and there is no striving for the highest. (Gregory the Great, *Pastoral Care*, Part III, Ch. 36, ACW 11, pp. 226–227)

This passage from the leading treatise of the Christian pastoral tradition, is worthy of detailed meditative study. For each virtue is to be encouraged in such a way that its corresponding vice not be unintentionally elicited. This raises an ancillary question: If one could deprive another of the possibility of vices, would one also be deprived of the possibility of virtue?

When they take away vices from man, they also take away virtue, for which alone they are making a place. For if it is virtue in the midst of the impetuosity of anger to restrain and check oneself, which they cannot deny, then he who is without anger is also without virtue. If it is virtue to control the lust of the body, he must be free from virtue who has no lust which he may regulate. If it is virtue to curb the desire from coveting that which belongs to another, he certainly can have no virtue who is without that, to the restraining of which the exercise of virtue is applied. Where, therefore, there are no vices, there is no place even for virtue, as there is no place for victory where there is no adversary. And so it comes to pass that there can be no good in this life without evil. (Lactantius, *The Divine Institutes*, Bk. VI, Ch. XV, ANF VII, p. 180)

Human existence is precisely characterized by the finite freedom that is able to stand but liable to fall. If God had created humanity without the capacity or permission to fall, but determined humanity only to virtue, that by definition would undermine virtue, and be a denial of the possibility of virtue, which itself is only possible in the arena of freedom. So Lactantius early formulated the simple equation that some still find difficult to accept, that there can be no virtue without the possibility of vice. Now we return to the central pastoral issue of how virtues are prone to become vices:

Who cannot distinguish a liberal man from one who is prodigal (as they do), or a frugal man from one who is mean, or a quiet man from one who is slothful, or a cautious man from one who is timid? Because these things which are good have their limits, and if they shall exceed these limits, fall into vices; so that constancy, unless it is undertaken for the truth, becomes shamelessness. In like manner, bravery, if it shall undergo certain danger, without the compulsion of any necessity, or not for an honourable cause, is changed into rashness. Freedom of speech also, if it attack others rather than oppose those who attack it, is obstinacy. Severity also, unless it restrains itself in meting out fit punishment to those who are harmful, becomes harsh cruelty. (Lactantius, *The Divine Institutes,* Bk. VI, Ch. XIV, ANF VII, p. 179)*

The soul must master the passions, or be mastered by them. As the charioteer struggles to control wayward or well-trained horses, so human freedom seeks reasonable control in the struggle between passion and virtue:

If the soul is a chariot, she has horses that are either good or bad. The good horses are the virtues of the soul, the bad horses the passions of the body. So the good master restrains the bad horses and draws them back but urges on the good. The good horses are four: prudence, temperance, fortitude, justice; the bad horses: wrath, concupiscence, fear, injustice. Sometimes these horses are in dissension with one another, either wrath or fear strains forward, and they hinder one another and slow their progress. But the good horses fly up, ascend from earth to the higher regions, and light burden of Him who says, "Take my yoke upon you" [Matt. 10:29]. (Ambrose, *Isaac, or The Soul,* FC 65, p. 53)

If courage is to be developed, fear must be restrained. If temperance is to be nurtured, then desire must be checked. While the emotive life is everywhere described by the pastoral writers as powerful, it is seldom seen as absolutely or unilaterally powerful, without consent or without any possibility of control or sublimation. In fact the nurture of ascetic discipline was precisely concerned with the constraint of libidinal energies through understanding them. Clement anticipated a dialectic that would later occupy Spinoza in much more detail:

The understanding in the soul has much power for cutting off all its desires, specially when it has acquired the knowledge of heavenly things, by means of which, having received the light of truth, it will turn away from all darkness of evil actions. For as the sun obscures and conceals all the stars by the brightness of his shining, so also the mind, by the light of knowledge, renders all the lusts of the soul ineffective and inactive, sending out upon them the thought of the judgment to come as its rays, so that they can no longer appear in the soul. (Clementina, *Recognitions of Clement,* Bk. IX, Ch. XIV, ANF VIII, p. 186)

There was considerable confidence among pastoral writers in the capacity of the grace-enabled mind to penetrate and illuminate the dark side of affective states. Lust was not thought to be sheer unmanageable impulsive energy destined always to have its way. Rather it could be understood and shaped to a significant degree by reason, sublimation, and habituation. If we have these analytical and rational competencies, which are being enhanced and nurtured by prevenient grace, why then must virtue wrestle so mightily with desire? To what purpose is the acquisition of virtue necessarily thought to be a rigorous struggle?

And eagerness, or desire of action, if this is the right meaning to put upon the Greek *horme* [impulse] is also reckoned among the primary advantages of nature; and yet is it not this which produces those pitiable movements of the insane, and those actions which we shudder to see, when sense is deceived and reason deranged? In fine, virtue itself, which is not among the primary objects of nature, but succeeds to them as the result of learning, though it holds the highest place among human good things, what is its occupation save to wage perpetual war with vice—not those that are outside of us, but within; not other men's, but our own—a war which is waged especially by that virtue which the Greeks call *sophrosune,* and we temperance, and which bridles carnal lusts, and prevents them from winning the consent of the spirit to wicked deeds? For we must not fancy that there is no vice in us, when, as the apostle says, "The flesh lusteth against the spirit" [cf. Gal. 5:17]; for to this vice there is a contrary virtue, when, as the same writer says, "The spirit lusteth against the flesh." "For these two," he says, "are contrary one to the other, so that you cannot do the things which you would." (Augustine, *City of God,* Bk. XIV.4, NPNF 1, II, p. 402)

Accordingly, virtue cannot appear without struggling inwardly with desire. That does not mean that desire is *ipso facto* evil or demeaning, but that it is not in itself the source of happiness. No one becomes happy merely by desiring it. One who struggles mightily for the good is likely to value it more than if it were cheaply given:

Things are not esteemed so highly which come spontaneously, as those which are reached by much anxious care. . . . Moreover, the faculty of seeing would not appear to be so desirable, unless we had known what a loss it were to be devoid of sight; and health, too, is rendered all the more estimable by an acquaintance with disease; light, also, by contrasting it with darkness; and life with death. (Irenaeus, *Against Heresies,* Bk. IV, Ch. XXXVII, ANF I, p. 520)

As light is undefinable without darkness, so one would not even be able to recognize a good activity if one had nothing with which to compare it (that which is less good). The acquisition of a moral good cannot come merely by fiat, apart from the human will:

God does not wish that the good should belong to anyone by necessity but willingly. (Origen, *On Prayer*, XXIX, CWS, p. 160)

Maximus astutely described the stages by which a vice becomes gradually reinforced, both through imagination and action, through dreaming and choosing:

As the hungry man's mind forms phantoms of bread and the thirsty man's of water, so the glutton imagines a variety of food, the voluptuary forms of women, the vain man attentions from men, the avaricious gain, the vengeful man vengeance on the offender, the envious man evil for the object of his envy—and similarly for the other passions. For the mind beset by passions receives impassioned thoughts, whether the body be waking or sleeping.

When concupiscence is grown strong, the mind dreams of the objects that give pleasure; when anger is strong, the mind looks on the things that cause fear. . . . When the concupiscible part of the soul is frequently roused, there is induced in the soul a fixed habit of pleasure. The temper continually stirred makes the mind cowardly and unmanly. They are healed, the first by a continual exercise of fasting, vigils, and prayer; the other by kindness, benevolence, charity, and mercy. . . .

The mind receives impassioned thoughts from three sources— from the senses, from the body's condition and temperament, from the memory. From the senses, when they, receiving impressions from the objects of the passions, move the mind to impassioned thinking; through the body's condition and temperament, that is, when this condition, altered by undisciplined living, by the activity of demons, or some disease, moves the mind to impassioned thinking, or against Providence; through memory, namely, when the memory recalls the thoughts of things that have stirred our passion, it likewise moves the mind to impassioned thinking. (Maximus the Confessor, *The Four Centuries of Charity*, Ch. 2, secs. 68–70, 74, ACW 21, pp. 166–167)

Particular bits of sensory input, the particular mood or condition of the psychosomatic interface, and recurring memory (all acts of freedom) work together in the reinforced habituation of concupiscence. Failure to exercise a virtue leads to atrophy:

Some virtuous dispositions are decreased or destroyed by lack of exercise. . . . Failure to act over a lengthy period may diminish or totally destroy such dispositions, as can be seen in respect to both science and virtue. It is clear that a disposition of moral virtue inclines a man to choose promptly the means in his moral activity and the use of his passions. But when anyone fails to use a virtuous disposition to temper his passions or actions, many acts and passions escape virtue's control because of the impulses of the sensitive tendencies and external causes. (Thomas Aquinas, *Summa Theologica,* Part I-II, Q. 53, Art. 3, AR, p. 354)

The objection follows: Did not God make quite a mess of it by creating humanity with such fundamental flaws and proneness to disaster? If God had the power to create us all perfect, why didn't God care enough about us to do so? These questions were posed by the detractors of Christian soul care very early in its history. Here is Clement's thoughtful response—in defense of human freedom:

How are we to solve the question pressed by false teachers as to whether Adam was created perfect or imperfect? If imperfect, who is to say that the work of a perfect God is imperfect, especially in the crucial case of the creation of humanity? If made perfect, how did it come about that human beings transgressed the commandments? Our answer is that humanity was from the outset adapted to the reception of virtue, yet not completed from the outset. For it is of great importance in regard to virtue to be made fit for its potential attainment. And it was intended that we not be saved without some cooperative effort by ourselves. This, then, is the nature of the soul, to move of itself. This is why we, being rational, and philosophy being rational, have some affinity for philosophy. Now an aptitude is a movement towards virtue, not virtue itself. All, then, as I said, are naturally constituted for the acquisition of virtue. But one person applies himself less, another more, to learning and training. Furthermore, some have even been able to come to a complete expression of virtue, while others have attained only to some measure of it. And some, on the other hand, through negligence have turned away from virtue, even though in other respects they may have begun with a good disposition. (Clement of Alexandria, *The Stromata, or Miscellanies,* Bk. XII, Ch. VI, ANF II, p. 502)*

The pastor at times must learn to state this argument plausibly and contextually: It was to our benefit that we were not created perfect from the beginning, but rather given the possibility of fitting responses to unfolding divine grace. For if God had made us perfect, we would have been made without finite freedom, and without any capacity for fallible self-determination. The idea that we are saved only by some cooperative effort does not imply that we could save ourselves without God's saving help, but rather that we will not be saved without some responsive effort of our own that answers freely to the unmerited mercy of God.

Since virtue shares in the good, and the good is eternal, virtue was thought to endure beyond temporal achievements and failures. On this premise was based the conclusion that virtue could not be rewarded in this life, but only in a life that endures:

Virtue is perpetual, without any intermission. . . . It has not been grasped, if it deserts its post. . . . The uninterrupted duration of virtue itself shows that the soul of man, if it has received virtue, remains permanent. . . . Because vices are temporary, and of short duration; virtue is perpetual and constant, and always consistent with itself. . . . Because the advantage of vices is immediate, therefore that of virtue is future. Thus it happens that in this life there is no reward of virtue, because virtue itself still exists. For as, when vices are completed in their performance, pleasure and their reward follow; so, when virtue has been ended, its reward follows. (Lactantius, *The Divine Institutes*, Bk. VI, Ch. X, ANF VII, p. 207)

Lactantius sought to make a point here that was crucial for classical pastoralia, but which is difficult for modern readers, saturated with moral relativism, to accept: virtue puts us in touch with that which transcends fleeting, temporal existence:

Suppose it possible that one by natural and innate goodness should gain true virtues. It is said that Cimon of Athens was such a man—he gave alms to the needy, entertained the poor, and clothed the naked. Yet suppose that the one thing which of greatest importance were wanting—the knowledge of God—then all those good things are rendered superfluous and empty, so that he labored in vain in performing them.

Such efforts at justice resemble a human body which has no head. Although all the limbs would be there in their proper position, and have beauty and proportion, yet the chief thing would remain absent. Since that is lacking which is the principle of all, such virtue would remain destitute of life and hence of all sensation, so that what looked like limbs would have only the shape of limbs, but admit of no use. It would be as if one had a head without a body. Similar to this case is one who has knowledge of God yet lives unjustly. He has that which is of greatest importance, but to no purpose. He is destitute of virtues, of limbs. Therefore, that the body may be alive, and capable of sensation, both head and body are necessary—both the knowledge of God and the virtues. (Lactantius, *The Divine Institutes*, Bk. VI, Ch. 9, ANF VII, p. 171)*

The theological virtues (faith, hope, and love) and cardinal virtues (justice, prudence, fortitude, and temperance) of the divine Lover (Christ) are offered to the believer in the moment of true contrition, according to Lull:

"Tell us, Fool! When did Love first come to you?" He replied, "At that time when my heart was enriched and filled with thoughts and desires, sighs and griefs, and my eyes abounded with weeping and tears." "And what did Love bring you?" "The wonderful virtues of my Beloved, his honours, and his exceedingly great worth." "How did these things come to be?" "Through memory and understanding." "With what did you receive them?" "With charity and hope." "With what do you guard them?" "With justice, prudence, fortitude, and temperance." (Raymond Lull, *The Book of the Lover and Beloved*, sec. 79, p. 32–33)

Thomas Aquinas saw an intrinsic aesthetic connection between joy and virtue. The delight taken in an action perfects that action:

The end of rational nature, through which it is ordered to its proper end, is perfect action proper to its nature. But an action's perfection is threefold: specifically in reference to object, disposition, and delight. For insofar as the object is higher, so the action tending toward it is more beautiful and more perfect; whence in respect to the object an action is not perfect except from a habit [or disposition]. Hence insofar as the disposition is the more perfect, the action will be more perfect; and the most perfect action will be from the noblest habit. Likewise, as the philosopher says in *Ethics* X, 6, "delight perfects action as beauty does youth; for delight itself is a certain grace of action." (Thomas Aquinas, *Commentary on the Sentences*, II.38.1, AR, p. 272)

The will to do a task clearly affects one's strength to do it:

Therefore, we must never grieve over the affliction of bodily sickness which, we understand, is the mother of strength. . . . No matter how light the task, it is heavy to him who performs it unwillingly. No matter how heavy, it seems light to him who executes it willingly. (Salvian, *The Governance of God*, Bk. I, sec. 2, FC 3, pp. 30–31)

The most difficult task becomes easy for one who does it willingly.

V. 🐝 ANTICIPATIONS OF PSYCHOANALYSIS

Freud was well aware that the analysis of the *psyche* (or psychoanalysis) had been a perennial preoccupation of the western intellectual tradition. Post-Freudian psychological traditions, lacking historical awareness, have largely tended to think of psychoanalysis as the single-handed invention of Freud.

The classical texts that follow will show that the Christian pastoral tradition anticipated many key aspects of Freudian and post-Freudian analysis and therapy. They will make clear that Christian soul care is not in every sense antithetical to but some ways consonant with many goals and procedures of psychoanalysis. An entire monograph could be devoted to this one theme. I will briefly set forth textual evidence of classical Christian anticipations of familiar Freudian themes such as repression, free association, sublimation, and projection.

First, concerning *repression*: When anger remains secretly repressed, what dynamics occur? John Chrysostom anticipated Freud's notion of hidden, repressed anger:

> There are some, like those dogs that bite secretly, which do not bark at all at those that come near them, nor are angry, but which fawn, and display a gentle aspect; but when they catch us off our guard, will fix their teeth in us. These are more dangerous than those that take up open enmity. . . . Dost thou not know that those conflagrations are the most destructive of all which are fed within, and appear not to those that are without? And that those wounds are the deadliest which never break out to the surface; and those fevers the worst which burn up the vitals? . . . Nothing good, nothing healthful, can ever come from a bitter soul; nothing but misfortunes, nothing but tears. (Chrysostom, *Homilies on Ephesians*, Hom. XV, NPNF 1, XIII, p. 125)

When the repression of anger festers, it looks for some other way to find expression. Psychosomatic illness may be caused by emotive conflicts that lie beneath the surface of awareness. Feelings that are closed off from awareness cause parataxic distortions and psychological disorders. This is hardly a new or modern discovery. Long before Freud or Sullivan or Binswanger we find clear indications that the dynamics of repression were being studied, astutely analyzed, and dealt with therapeutically. We take for example Gregory's sixth century discussion of the dynamics of severely repressed speech:

> They often bridle the tongue beyond moderation, and as a result suffer in the heart a more grievous loquacity; and so, their thought seethes the more in the mind, in proportion as they restrain themselves by a violent and indiscreet silence. . . . And

when the mouth of its body is closed, it does not recognize how much it exposes itself by pride to vices. The man represses the tongue, but lifts up his mind, and without any regard to his bad qualities, he accuses others within his own heart, the more freely, as he does the more secretly. . . . Often when the taciturn suffer injustice, they come to feel keener grief from not speaking about what they are suffering. For if the tongue were to speak calmly of the annoyances inflicted, grief would fade from consciousness. Wounds that are closed are the more painful. When, however, the suppuration [from *suppurare*, to gather pus underneath, as with a boil or abscess] that burns inwardly is driven out, the pain is opened out for healing. People, therefore, who are more silent than is expedient, should realize that they but aggravate the vehemence of their grief in withholding speech during their annoyance. For as they are to be admonished that if they love their neighbors as themselves, they should most certainly not fail to speak up when they have reason to reprehend them. Thus, by the medication of speech, both parties concur in promoting mutual health, seeing that the one who administers it checks the evil act of the other, and the vehement pain of him who submits to it is relieved by opening the wound.

Indeed, those who observe evil in their neighbor and yet hold their tongue, withhold the use of salves, as it were, from wounds which they see, and thereby become the cause of death, inasmuch as they were unwilling to cure the poison when they could. The tongue, then, must be prudently curbed, but not completely tied up. For it is written: "A wise man will hold his peace till he sees an opportunity" (Ecclus. 20:7), that is to say, when he sees it opportune to speak what is fitting, he sets aside the censorship of silence, and makes it his effort to be of assistance. Again it is written: "There is a time to keep silence, and a time to speak" (Eccles. 3:7). In other words, the various occasions are to be prudently judged: when the tongue ought to be restrained, it should not be unprofitably loosened in speech, or when it could speak with profit, it should not indolently withhold speech. The Prophet considers this matter well when he says: "Set a watch, O Lord, before my mouth, and a door round my lips" (Ps. 140:3). He does not ask that a wall be set before his mouth, but a door, which, you see, can be opened and closed. Wherefore, we must take care to learn when speech should open the mouth discreetly and at the proper time, and when, on the contrary, silence should becomingly keep it closed. (Gregory the Great, *Pastoral Care*, Part III, Ch. 14, ACW 11, pp. 130–132)

These dynamics of repression are hypothesized: (1) When thoughts are repressed, they seethe or burn quietly seeking to be expressed; (2) repression intensifies anger and hubris; (3) this has social and political consequences, and implies that the poor do better to speak out about their suffering; (4) the therapeutic alternative to repression is a community of self-disclosure and corrective love in which caring admonition prevents misdeeds in others and relieves the pressure of wounds by gently opening them; yet (5) good judgment must be exercised in such disclosures, to know when to open the mouth and when to close it. Suppuration was the ancient pastoral metaphor for repression.

A predisposition to *free association* (not unlike that found in early psychoanalysis) was also found in some of the pastoral writers. The pseudonymous Clementine literature, for example, used the persona of Peter to speak of "stating whatever comes to one's mind," so as to elicit fantasies and libidinal energies:

> When Peter spoke in this way, Niceta answered: "I beseech you that you would permit me to *state whatever occurs to my mind.*" Then Peter, being delighted with the eagerness of his disciples, said: "Speak what you will." Then said Niceta . . . is it not marvelous to fly through the air, to be so mixed with fire as to become one body with it, to make statues walk, brazen dogs bark, and other such like things. (Clementina, *Recognitions of Clement*, Bk. III, Ch. LVI–LVII, ANF VII, p. 129, ital. added)*

Thus in the third century Clementine literature we find a pseudonymous portrayal of Peter apparently providing counsel by means of a procedure very much like free association.

The psychoanalytic tradition has taken the couch to be the normative therapeutic context where the truth may become spoken through free association and analysis of the unconscious. Psychoanalytically-oriented readers may be amused to find in Ambrose a specific reference to the symbolic idea of a couch as a paradigm and context of therapeutic work:

> For Christ is the couch of the saints, on whom the hearts of all, weary with the battles of the world, find rest. On this couch Isaac rested, and he blessed his younger son, saying, "The elder shall serve the younger" [Gen. 25:23]. Reclining on this couch, Jacob blessed the twelve patriarchs; reclining on this couch, the daughter of the ruler of the synagogue rose from death; lying on this couch, the dead son of the widow [of Nain] broke the bonds of death when he was called by the voice of Christ. (Ambrose, *Isaac, or the Soul*, sec. 5.45, FC 65, p. 36)

The allegorical imagination viewed the couch as a place where radical changes and reversals of personal history were taking place: illuminations, blessings, resurrections, and renewals. We also find in the pastoral tradition some anticipation of the notion of *sublimation*, as in Ambrose's account of David's use of reason to resist concupiscence:

[David] suffered a kind of irrational longing and wanted that water which was walled in and surrounded by the enemy, so that it could not have been readily brought without great risk. Thus he said, "Who will get me a drink from the cistern that is in Bethlehem by the gate?" [2 Kings 23:15]. And when three men were found to break down the enemy camp and bring the water which he had desired with a very great desire, he knew that he had obtained that water at the cost of danger to others. He poured it out to the Lord, so that he might not seem to be drinking the blood of those who had brought it.

This incident is evidence that concupiscence indeed comes before reason but that reason resists concupiscence. David suffered what is human—an irrational longing—but it is praiseworthy that he cheated the irrational concupiscence in a rational manner with the remedy that was at hand. I praise the men who were ashamed at the desire of their king and preferred to bring his shameful action to an end even with danger to their own well-being. I praise the more him who was ashamed at the danger to others in his own desire, and who compared to blood the water sought at the price of hazardous chance. At once, like a conqueror who had checked his desire, David poured out the water to the Lord, to show that he quenched his concupiscence by the consolation found in His Word.

Therefore the prudent mind can restrain and keep in check the assaults of the passions, even the severe passions, and cooling all the heat of the most burning concupiscence, channel the emotions elsewhere. (Ambrose, *Jacob and the Happy Life*, Bk. I, 1.3–4, FC 65, pp. 120–121)

The rechannelling of dysfunctional emotive energies remains the concern of psychoanalysis, so as to increase ego-strength in the shaping of libidinal energies. Like Freud and Spinoza before him, Ambrose sought to use the capacities of reasoning to analyze, understand, and modestly reorient the directions of the libidinal energies.

VI. 🐛 REPARENTING AND TRANSFERENCE

The struggle of child with parent was a recurring concern of the ancient Christian writers. Christian faith seeks a profound mode of reparenting, analogous to the psychoanalytic concern for utilizing transference to help the individual gain freedom from superego tyrannies. This struggle with parental dictates and their being overcome is seen in the life of St. Francis, as reported by Bonaventure:

When his father learned that the servant of God was staying with this priest, he was greatly disturbed and ran to the place. But Francis, upon hearing about the threats of those who were pursuing him and having a premonition they were approaching, wished to *give place to wrath* (Rom. 12:19), and hid himself—being still untrained as an athlete of Christ—in a secret pit. There he remained in hiding for some days imploring the Lord incessantly with a flood of tears to *deliver him from the hands of those who were persecuting his soul* (Ps. 30:16; 108:31; 141:7) and in his kindness to bring to realization the pious desires he had inspired. He was then filled with excessive joy and began to accuse himself of cowardice. He cast aside his fear, left the pit and took the road to the town of Assisi. When the townspeople saw his unkempt face and his changed mentality, they thought that he had gone out of his senses. They threw filth from the streets and stones at him, shouting insults at him, as if he were insane and out of his mind. But the Lord's servant passed through it as if he were deaf to it all, unbroken and unchanged by any of these insults. When his father heard the shouting, he ran to him at once, not to save him but to destroy him. Casting aside all compassion, he dragged him home, tormenting him first with words, then with blows and chains.... After a little while when his father went out of the country, his mother, who did not approve what her husband had done and had no hope of being able to soften her son's inflexible constancy, released him from his chains and permitted him to go away. He gave thanks to Almighty God and went back to the place where he had been before. Returning and not finding him at home, his father violently reproached his wife and in rage ran to that place. If he could not bring Francis back home, he would at least drive him out of the district. But strengthened by God, Francis went out on his own accord to meet his furious father, calling out in a clear voice that he cared nothing for his chains and blows. Besides, he stated that he would gladly undergo any evil for the name of Christ. When his father, therefore, saw that he could not bring him around, he turned his attention to getting his money back.... He wanted to have Francis renounce into his hands his family possessions and return everything he had. A true lover of poverty, Francis showed himself eager to comply; he went before the bishop without delaying or hesitating.

He did not wait for any words nor did he speak any, but immediately took off his clothes and gave them back to his father. Then it was discovered that the man of God had a hairshirt next to his skin under his fine clothes. Moreover, drunk with remarkable fervor, he even took off his underwear, stripping himself completely naked before all. He said to his father: "Until now I have called you father here on earth, but now I can say without reservation, *Our Father who art in heaven* (Matt. 6:9), since I have placed all my treasure and all my hope in him." (Bonaventure, *The Life of St. Francis*, CWS, pp. 191–194)

Francis dramatically gave back to his father the very clothes on his back. In standing naked in the presence of his earthly father, he thereby chose to take utter responsibility for his own life. His choice was voluntary poverty instead of parental dependence. Something like this responsibility-taking is sought, however inadequately, in the modern psychoanalytic therapy. Yet is it seldom easy to leave one's parents behind and chose one's own life. Salvian reflected upon how parental vices are passed on to children:

Almost all children succeed as much to the vices as to the patrimony of their parents. They take on not only the possessions but also the depravities of their parents, and thus, ever taking up their morals, they begin to be wanton before they possess their inheritance. Children take possession of their parent's goods only when the parents are dead, but, while the parents are living and still in good health, the children assume their morals. Thus, before they begin to have their father's possessions within their own power, they have the image of their fathers in their souls. Before they possess those things which are falsely called goods, they possess those things which are truly proved to be evil. (Salvian, *The Four Books of Peter to the Church*, Bk. I, sec. 3, FC 3, p. 274)

Many layers of experience may need to be penetrated to discover why behavior has become skewed in a certain direction. Suggested, though not developed, in an intriguing passage from the Clementina, is the idea that present relationships recapitulate past relationships:

In all things, the end for the most part looks back upon the beginning and the issue of things is similar to their commencement. (Clementina, *Recognitions of Clement*, Bk. X, Ch. V, ANF VIII, p. 193)

The archeology of layers of emotive life has long been the concern of the soul guide.

VII. 🍎 RATIONAL ANALYSIS OF THE PASSIONS

Crucial to psychoanalytic therapy is the attempt through dialogue to make sense of emotive energies that have been repressed beneath the surface of consciousness. It is difficult to show how this is materially different from the classical attempts of care of souls to provide a rational analysis of the passions, especially those that lie at a low level of awareness.

The texts that follow will show that the adept pastor, as conceived in the classic tradition, helped troubled individuals to search deeply within, through seeming inconsistencies and ambivalences of motive, to discover plausible reasons for their behavior, especially when the behavior appears to be absurd. Gregory Thaumaturgus observed:

> Things which have the appearance of being paradoxical and most incredible, and which have been rejected as false on their own showing, and held up undeservedly to ridicule, have afterwards, on careful investigation and examination, been discovered to be the truest of all things, and wholly incontestable, though for a time spurned and reckoned false. We are taught not simply, then, by dealing with things patent and prominent which are sometimes delusive and sophistical, but also by searching into things within us and to put them all individually to the test, lest any of them should give back a hollow sound. . . . In this way, that capacity of our mind which deals critically with words and reasonings, was educated in a rational manner. (Gregory Thaumaturgus, "Oration and Panegyric Addressed to Origen," VII, ANF VI, p. 30)*

Psychoanalysis seeks to interpret the meaning of dreams. Did early Christian pastoral care view the capacity to reason as active while one sleeps? Reason was thought by the Alexandrines to be constitutive of human existence and therefore inalienable even during sleep. It was not as if reason held sway only during consciousness, and then was dismissed during sleep. Rather a hidden but inexorable intelligibility presides over dreams, thought Clement:

> There is a common saying that we should relax over our cups and postpone serious business until dawn. But it seems to me that it is especially at that time that we should invite reason to be our companion at a feast and the controlling guide of our drinking, lest our feasting turn gradually into rioting. For, just as no one in his right mind would think of going about with his eyes shut until he was trying to sleep, so, too, no one has the right deliberately to dismiss reason from his table, or lull it to sleep on

set purpose before some action. On her part, reason will never be able to separate herself from those who belong to her, even when they sleep; in fact, reason must be summoned to our beds. Wisdom, in its perfection, is the understanding of things human and divine, and includes all things; therefore, it is the art of living in that it presides over the human race. In that way, it is everywhere present wherever we live, ever accomplishing its work, which is living well. (Clement of Alexandria, *Christ the Educator*, Bk. II, Ch. 2.25, FC 23, pp. 115–116)

Reason does not sleep when we sleep. It continues its work of examination. The early pastoral writers delighted in beholding the constant interpenetration of faith, the passions, the understanding, and the emotive life. Long before Augustine, Clement sought to define the relation between investigation (research), experimentation, science, understanding, and faith:

Then, by cultivating the acquaintance not of Greeks alone, but also of barbarians, from the exercise common to their proper intelligence, they are conducted to faith. And when they have embraced the foundation of truth, they receive in addition the power of advancing further to investigation. And thence they love to be learners, and aspiring after knowledge, hasten toward salvation. Thus Scripture says, that "the spirit of perception" [Exod. 28:3, KJV: wisdom] was given to the artificers from God. And this is nothing other than Understanding, a faculty of the soul, capable of studying existences, of distinguishing and comparing what is similar and different, of requiring and forbidding, and of conjecturing the future. This spirit of perception extends not only into the artistic sphere, but also to philosophy itself.

Even the serpent was called wise [Matt. 10:16]. Why? Because even amid its wiles there is found the capacity for causal connection, and distinction, and combination, and conjecturing of the future. So it is by the wiles of reason that even our crimes may become concealed, for the wicked seek to arrange for themselves the means to escape punishment.

Wisdom being manifold, pervading the whole world and all human affairs, is called by various names in each case. When wisdom applies itself to first causes, it is called understanding (*noesis*). When, however, it confirms this by demonstrative reasoning, it is often termed knowledge, or wisdom or science. When wisdom is occupied in what pertains to piety, and receives without speculation the primal Word in order to act in response to this Word, it is called faith. In the empirical sphere of things of sense, establishing that which appears as being truest, it is right opinion. In operations performed by skill of hand, it is called art. But when, on the other hand, without the study of primary causes, yet by the observation of similarities, and by transposition, it seeks to devise a new attempt or combination, it is called experiment. But belonging to wisdom throughout its operations, and supremely essential to it, is the Holy Spirit. One who following divine guidance believes the Spirit will come to a strong faith. (Clement of Alexandria, *The Stromata, or Miscellanies*, Bk. VI, Ch. XVII, ANF II, pp. 516–517)*

Note what wisdom as understanding does: Like psychoanalysis (which stands in the tradition of Spinoza), it makes connections, ferrets out hidden correlations, reveals what had been concealed, and looks for a wider grasp of motivation. This is based on investigation, research, careful observation, and utilizing sense experience. It uses both logical reasoning and intuitive grasping, neither of which is thought to be inconsistent with faith, which listens intently to God's own address. All these elements belong to the "spirit of perception." These operations are precisely the resources that are applied today in psychoanalytic therapy. Modern observers may assume that the study of the relation of knowledge to impulse, and impulse to learning, and learning to action, is a relatively recent subject of investigation. But we find the Alexandrines fascinated with just these questions: Can impulse be understood? Is impulse already a form of knowing? Which comes first, knowledge or impulse? Here is Clement's response:

For both are powers of the soul, both knowledge and impulse. And impulse is found to be a movement after an assent. For he who has an impulse towards an action, first receives the knowledge of the action, and secondly the impulse. Let us further devote our attention to this. For since learning is older than action; (for naturally, he who does what he wishes to do learns it first; and knowledge comes from learning, and impulse follows knowledge; after which comes action); knowledge turns out the beginning and author of all rational action. So that rightly the peculiar nature of the rational soul is characterized by this alone; for in reality impulse, like knowledge, is excited by existing objects. And knowledge (*gnosis*) is essentially a contemplation of existences on the part of the soul, either of a certain thing or of certain things, and when perfected of all together. (Clement of Alexandria, *The Stromata, or Miscellanies*, Bk. VI, Ch. IX, ANF II, p. 496)

The knowledge that informs assent may be in error, and the assent that leads to impulse may be distorted, but no impulse or activity pro-

ceeds, in Clement's platonizing Christian view, without some recognition
of some perceived good. The prudent soul seeks first to understand
things essentially, i.e., how a particular being is to be properly seen in
relation to other beings and to being itself. The knowing process ma-
tures only when all things are seen together. Knowing the soul and believing God were thought by the Alexandrines to have a similar root, as
seen in Clement's etymology of *episteme*:

> If, then, we are to give the etymology of *episteme*, knowledge, its
> signification is to be derived from *stasis*, placing; for our soul,
> which was formerly borne, now in one way, now in another, it
> settles in objects. Similarly faith is to be explained etymologically,
> as the settling (*stasis*) of our soul respecting that which is. (Clem-
> ent of Alexandria, *The Stromata, or Miscellanies*, Bk. IV, Ch. XII,
> ANF II, p. 435)

When the soul knows herself clearly, she provides herself with placement, identity, self-definition.

Some pastoral writers focussed more intently upon the inexorable
limits of reason. Luther thought that reason had a significant and legitimate arena of inquiry and mastery, yet when reason vainly pretends to
extend itself beyond these empirical limits to speak of revelation, its inadequacies were evident:

> You can calculate and figure out that a cow is bigger than a
> calf, that three ells [elbows] are longer than one ell, that a gulden
> is worth more than a groschen, that a hundred guldens are more
> than ten guldens, and that it is better to place a roof over the
> house than under it. Stay with that. You can easily figure out how
> to bridle a horse, for reason teaches you that. Prove yourself a
> master in that field. God has endowed you with reason to show
> you how to milk a cow, to tame a horse, and to realize that a
> hundred guldens are more than ten guldens. There you should
> demonstrate your smartness; there be a master and an apt fellow,
> and utilize your skill. But in heavenly matters and in matters of
> faith, when a question of salvation is involved, bid reason observe
> silence and hold still. Do not apply the yardstick of reason, but
> give ear and say: Here I cannot do it; these matters do not agree
> with reason as do the things mentioned above. There you must
> hold your reason in check and say: I do not know; I will not try to
> figure it out or measure it with my understanding, but I will
> keep still and listen; for this is immeasurable and incomprehensi-
> ble to reason. (Luther, "Sermon on the Gospel of St. John Chap-
> ter Six, 1530–31," LW 23, p. 84; WA 33, 127)

Luther sharply distinguished between two spheres, the one empirical, natural, economic, political, domestic, and technical sphere in which

reason is quite competent, and the other sphere of divine revelation in which reason must learn to listen, behold and praise. Luther frequently warned of the tendency of reason to overestimate its range of competencies:

In temporal things and human relations man is rational enough; there he needs no other light than reason. So God does not teach us in Scripture how to build houses, make clothing, marry, wage wars, sail on the seas, and the like; for there our natural light is sufficient. But in divine things, that is, in those which pertain to God and which must be so performed as to be acceptable to Him and obtain salvation for us, our nature is so stark- and stone-blind, so utterly blind, as to be unable to recognize them at all. Reason is presumptuous enough to plunge into these matters like a blind horse. But all its decisions and conclusions are as certainly false and erroneous as God lives. Here human nature acts like a man who builds on sand. Here it takes cobwebs and wants to make a coat of them, as Isaiah says (Is. 59:6). Here it takes sand instead of flour and wants to bake bread. Here it sows the wind and reaps the whirlwind, as Hosea says (Hos. 8:7). Here it measures the air by spoonfuls, carries light into the cellar in a tray, weighs flames in scales. (Luther, "Sermon on Is. 60:1–6," #3705, WLS 3, p. 1158; WA 10 I, p. 1)

There is the pastoral tradition a guarded affirmation of reason, coupled with an awareness that reason like all human competencies is prone to become corrupted by sin and go awry.

VIII. 🐛 RELIGION AS PROJECTION

The notion that religion often functions as a means to project our own desires toward God, is not an invention of Feuerbach or Freud, but was well-understood by classical pastoral writers:

Men are possessed with so great a fondness for representations, that those things which are true are now esteemed of less value: they are delighted, in fact, with gold, and jewels, and ivory. The beauty and brilliancy of these things dazzle their eyes, and they think that there is no religion where these do not shine. And thus, under pretence of worshipping the gods, avarice and desire are worshipped. For they believe that the gods love whatever they themselves desire. (Lactantius, *The Divine Institutes*, Bk. II, Ch. VII, ANF VII, p. 50)

Thus one may pretend that what one inwardly worships and desires, the gods love, projecting human needs upon a supernal scale. Luther went straight to the heart of the problem of idolatry in his oft-quoted definition of what it means to "have a god."

What does it mean to have a god, or, what is God? I answer: a god is that from which we are to expect everything good and to which we are to take refuge in all times of need. Therefore to have a god is simply to trust and believe in him. It is, as I have often said, only the heart's confidence and faith that make both God and an idol. If your faith and confidence are right, your God will be right too. On the other hand, if your confidence is false and wrong, you do not have the true God; for these two, faith and God, are correlative concepts. Therefore I say that your god in reality is that around which you entwine your heart and on which you place your confidence. (Luther, "Large Catechism, 1529," WLS 2, #1637, p. 541; WA 30 I, pp. 132f.)

The human capacity for fantasizing has an inner connection with the problem of idolatry, as Athenagoras recognized:

These irrational powers and fantasies of the soul produce visions marked by a passion for idols. A tender and susceptible soul which is ignorant of sound teaching and has no experience in it, having neither contemplated the truth nor reflected upon the Father and Maker of the universe, is easily impressed with false notions of itself. . . . That the gods were originally men the most learned of the Egyptians indicate. (Athenagoras, *A Plea in Defense of the Faith*, sec. 27–28, LCC I, pp. 330–331)

The naive soul is susceptible to fantasies that intensify idolatries. The fall into idolatry was portrayed on a cosmic scale as involving the fall of angels into deceit and sorcery:

Now therefore, since you do not yet understand how great darkness of ignorance surrounds you, meantime I wish to explain to you whence the worship of idols began in this world. And by idols, I mean those lifeless images which you worship, whether made of wood, or earthenware, or stone, or brass, or any other metals: of these the beginning was in this wise. Certain angels, having left the course of their proper order, began to favour the vices of men, and in some measure to lend unworthy aid to their lust, in order that by these means they might indulge their own pleasures the more; and then, that they might not seem to be inclined of their own accord to unworthy services, taught men that demons could, by certain arts—that is, by magical invocations—be made to obey men. (Clementina, *Recognitions of Clement*, Bk. IV, Ch. XXVI, ANF VIII, p. 140)

Accordingly, the human tendency to idolatry and the demonic arts was nurtured and encouraged by prototypes of fallen superpersonal intelligence.

IX. 🐝 CARE OF THE EMOTIONALLY ILL

In pre-modern times the pastor was as likely as the physician to be called upon to deal with schizoid or paranoic or psychoneurotic patterns in persons. This led to some surprisingly lucid reflections by the pastoral writers on the etiology of hallucination:

> For those who are beginning to be ... disturbed in their minds, begin in this way. They are first carried away by fancies to some pleasant and delightful things, then they are poured out in vain and fond motions towards things which have no existence. Now this happens from a certain disease of mind, by reason of which they see not the things which are, but long to bring to their sight those which are not. But thus it happens also to those who are suffering phrenzy, and seem to themselves to see many images, because their soul, being torn and withdrawn from its place by excess of cold or of heat, suffers a failure of its natural service. But those also who are in distress through thirst, when they fall asleep, seem to themselves to see rivers and fountains, and to drink; but this befalls them through being distressed by the dryness of the unmoistened body. Wherefore it is certain that this occurs through some ailment either of the soul or body. (Clementina, *Recognitions of Clement*, Bk. II, Ch. LXIV, ANF VIII, p. 115)

The trajectory of hallucination begins with an intensified imagination, which yearns for what is not. The psychosomatic equilibrium becomes distorted through some body/soul imbalance, for the compositum is forever prone to disequilibrium. The most ready-to-hand explanation was excessive cold or heat or moisture or dryness that could upset the natural balance of the body. When excessive or extended, the soul may be wrenchingly drawn out of its normal embodiment, its place in the body, and, due to the failure of the body's service, it moves through "out-of-body" experiences, or hallucinations, seeing things such as rivers if extremely thirsty. Thus, hallucination was not thought to be an absurd or meaningless occurrence, even by very early pastoral writers.

There was some recognition that prevailing social assumptions significantly affect what we call sanity. The question of whether society is

sane, later to be discussed by modern writers such as Erich Fromm,
J. H. van den Berg, Roland Laing, and Thomas Szasz, was keenly debated in earlier periods. Is insanity a socially shaped concept? Should
tranquility of emotions always be the goal of soul care? In the following
passage, Lactantius was objecting to those therapeutic strategies (especially Stoic) that would commend *apatheia* and the quietude of the spirit
as solutions to every human dilemma:

Therefore I can call them by no other name than mad, who
deprive man, a mild and sociable animal, of his name; who, having uprooted the affections, in which humanity altogether consists, wish to bring him to an immoveable insensibility of mind,
while they desire to free the soul from perturbations, and, as they
themselves say, to render it calm and tranquil; which is not only
impossible, because its force and nature consist in motion, but it
ought not even to be so. For as water which is always still and
motionless is unwholesome and more muddy, so the soul which is
unmoved and torpid is useless even to itself nor will it be able to
maintain life itself; for it will neither do nor think anything,
since thought itself is nothing less than agitation of the mind; in
fine, they who assert this immovableness of the soul wish to deprive the soul of life; for life is full of activity, but death is quiet.
(Lactantius, *The Divine Institutes*, Bk. VI, Ch. XVII, ANF VII,
p. 182)

Lactantius thus rejects any view of soul care that would seek inordinately to tranquilize, or to immobilize the soul's intrinsically active
movement. One might also infer from this that he would be wary of
those views of treatment of mental illness that focus upon tranquilizing
medications, so that it is considered a "solution" when the soul becomes
torpid and inactive, drugged and insensate. Since humanity is essentially social, the aim should not be to reduce the soul to an immobilized
vegetative state, but rather to affirm the conflicts (perturbations) as potentially creative, and return the soul to vital, social activity.

Are the mentally ill always fully responsible for their own action?
Athanasius related this sobering story:

Another, a person of rank, came to [Antony], possessed by a
demon; and the demon was so terrible that the man possessed
did not know that he was coming to Antony. But he even ate the
excreta from his body. So those who brought him besought Antony to pray for him. And Antony pitying the young man prayed
and kept watch with him all the night. And about dawn the
young man suddenly attacked Antony and gave him a push. But
when those who came with him were angry, Antony said, "Be not
angry with the young man, for it is not he, but the demon which

is in him. And being rebuked and commanded to go into dry places, the demon became raging mad, and he has done this. Wherefore give thanks to the Lord, for his attack on me thus is a sign of the departure of the evil spirit." When Antony had said this, straightway the young man had become whole, and having come at last to his right mind, knew where he was, and saluted the old man and gave thanks to God. (Athanasius, *Life of Antony*, sec. 64, NPNF 2, IV, p. 213)

What is most important in this account is not merely the cure, but the fact that even in bizarre and violent behavior (eating feces and hostile pushing), it does little good to direct one's anger toward the person suffering gross distortions in judgment. Rather one must try to grasp the etiology of the behavior distortion. Antony's hypothesis of demonic influence may be unpersuasive to modern observers, but given his worldview, it was the most plausible explanation he had available for wildly bizarre and destructive behaviors.

Placing emotive illness within the context of a larger salvation-history struggle that includes superpersonal intelligences (demonic and angelic powers), Origen tried to address the difficult question of why "mental illness" or "lunacy" is so difficult to cure, and whether it has a cure at all:

First let us inquire how he who has been cast into darkness and repressed by an impure and deaf and dumb spirit is said to be a "lunatic," and for what reason the expression to be a "lunatic" derives its name from the great light in heaven which is next to the sun, which God appointed "to rule over the night." Let physicians then, discuss the physiology of the matter, inasmuch as they think that there is no impure spirit in the case, but a bodily disorder, and inquiring into the nature of things let them say, that the moist humours which are in the head are moved by a certain sympathy which they have with the light of the moon, which has a moist nature. . . . It is evident that this disorder it very difficult to cure, so that those who have the power to cure demoniacs sometimes fail in respect of this, and sometimes with fastings and supplications and more toils, succeed. . . . "If ye have faith as a grain of mustard seed, ye shall say unto this mountain" [Matt. 17:20], etc.; but nevertheless also we shall speak in this place the things that appear to us fitted to increase perspicuity. The mountains here spoken of, in my opinion, are the hostile powers that have their being in a flood of great wickedness, such as are settled down, so to speak, in some souls of men. Whenever, then, any one . . . has faith such as that of Abraham, who believed in God to such a degree that his faith was counted for righteousness, he has all faith as a grain of mustard seed; then will such a one say to this mountain—I mean, the dumb and deaf spirit in him who is called lunatic,—"Remove hence," clearly, from the man who is suffering, perhaps to the abyss, and it shall remove. (Origen, *Commentary on Matthew*, Bk. XIII, sec. 6–7, ANF X, pp. 478–479)

In the treatment of delusion, Origen urged that one first look for physiological causes, since the psychosomatic equilibrium is so sensitive and prone to imbalance. Dietary changes or increasing or decreasing of body fluids may make a difference. Fasting and hard work may be correctives when nothing else seems to work. But the central problem of the crisis of the emotive life is that the soul has come to the point of having to deal with a mountain of trouble. No matter how massive the mountain of hostility and despair, Origen declared that it could be removed, as promised, by faith which grasps the divine promise in the same way that a grain of mustard seed looks toward a later, slowly emergent fulfillment.

By what depth of empathy shall the pastor reach out to the depressed or schizoid individual?

Seek for that which is lost. Do not permit one who is despondent of salvation, on account of the enormity of guilt, utterly to perish. Search out those who have grown sleepy, drowsy, and sluggish, those who have lost touch with the value of their own lives. Look for those in a stupor, who dwell at greatest distance from others in the flock. These are most in danger of falling among the wolves, and being devoured by them. Bring these souls back by admonition. Exhort them to be watchful. Engender hope. Do not give in to the conclusion that "Our offenses and sins weigh us down, and we are wasting away because of them. How then can we live?" [Ezek. 33:10]. As far as possible, therefore, let the church leader make the offence his own, and say to the abandoned one: Return, sinner, and I will undertake to suffer death for you, as our Lord suffered death for me, and for all humanity. For "The good shepherd lays down his life for the sheep. The hired hand is not the shepherd who owns the sheep. So when he sees the wolf coming, he abandons the sheep and runs away. Then the wolf attacks the flock and scatters it" [John 10:11,12]. (*Constitutions of the Holy Apostles*, Bk. II, sec. iii, ANF VII, pp. 404–405, NIV)*

Here the pastor is pictured as searching out that very person in his care that is most in trouble, most vulnerable to the wolves, most immobilized by despair. Then by various remedies and approaches—admonition, encouragement, and by taking direct responsibility for him even to the point of suffering for him—he seeks to bring the troubled soul back into health and social discourse.

This Part of the collection has sought to show how the same dynamics of self-deception, guilt, anxiety, repression and sublimation that we find in contemporary psychological analyses were also studied and analyzed by classic pastoral writers. The pastoral tradition anticipated many of the strategies for behavior change that now prevail in various psychotherapies. We have shown textual evidence that many of the specific strategies of behavior therapy (the daily descriptive recording of behavior observations, the scheduling of targeted objectives, positive and negative reinforcement, immediacy of reinforcement) were astutely understood and diligently applied by early pastoral writers. Many key elements of psychoanalysis were grasped in rudimentary form: the malaise of repression, the therapeutic value of freedom from super-ego dominance, the mediation between libidinal and super-ego conflicts by the analytical ego, religion as a projection of needs, and the dynamics of sublimation.

9 The Psychological Dynamics of the Will

In the analysis of the will, its passions, its bondage to passions, and its layers of causality, the early pastoral writers worked energetically and profoundly as psychologists. This Part gathers together some of the fragments of their continuing effort to understand the dynamics of human willing.

I. 🦋 Freedom and the Layers of Necessity

We are familiar with modern voices that restrict psychology to strict empirical evidence, that reject any talk of the soul, that view the person as a mechanism, that reduce every motivation to material causation. We may think of these modern partners in dialogue as only a recent aberration of modern empirical science. But an examination of the pastoral tradition reveals the fact that they have been present in one form or another as partners in dialogue with the tradition from its beginnings.

What of Aristoxenus, who denied that there is any soul at all even while it lives in the body? But as on the lyre harmonious sound, and the strain which musicians call harmony, is produced by the tightening of the strings, so he thought that the power of perception existed in bodies from the joining together of the vitals, and from the vigour of the limbs; than which nothing can be said more senseless. Truly, though his eyes were unimpaired, his heart was blind, with which he did not see that he himself lived, and had the mind by which he had conceived that very thought. But this has happened to many philosophers, that they did not believe in the existence of any object which is not apparent to the eyes; whereas the sight of the mind ought to be much clearer than that of the body, for perceiving those things the force and nature of which are rather felt than seen. (Lactantius, *The Divine Institutes*, Bk. VII, Ch. xiii, ANF VII, pp. 210f.)*

Lactantius was making what we today would call an appeal to intuitive reasoning, as opposed to limiting reasoning strictly to empirically observed phenomena. For not only the body has eyes, but the mind also has eyes. That which the mind sees cannot be constricted to sensory data. More pointedly, the pastoral writers were asking whether free will can finally be reduced to causal determinants of nature or chance. Nemesius argued the case brilliantly in the fourth century:

Let us first assert that we have free-will, and then prove it from facts which even our opponents will concede. For they say that the cause of anything that happens is either God, or necessity, or fate, or Nature, or fortune, or accident. . . . It would be rank blasphemy to ascribe any man's shameful and wicked deeds to God. We cannot ascribe man's deeds to necessity, since they do not follow an invariable pattern. We cannot ascribe them to fate, because fate admits no range of possibilities, but only permits of one inevitable destiny; nor to Nature, artificer of plants and animals; nor to fortune, since the deeds of men are not all singular or unexpected; nor to accident, for accident is the sort of thing that befalls inanimate and irrational things. Surely, there only remains the possibility that man himself, who both does things and makes things, is the initiator of his own works, and possessor of free-will. A further consideration is this; if a man is the initiator of none of his deeds, it is in vain that he deliberates. For what use is taking counsel, if one is master of no single deed? Moreover, it would be a most monstrous thing that the fairest and most honourable attribute of man should turn out to be of no avail. (Nemesius, *Of the Nature of Man*, Ch. XXXIX, LCC IV, pp. 410–411)

Nemesius went through a deliberate process of eliminating six types of causal reductionism: God, necessity, fate, Nature, fortune and accident. Nothing remains but the hypothesis that human freedom is actively self-determining. It is the only hypothesis that makes sense out of the fact that we deliberate on the consequences of our own deeds and feel responsible for them. But couldn't it still be the case the persons are like puppets being moved about by external causes which, if exhaustively known, would show freedom to be a fraud?

Such being the case, to say that we are moved from without, and to put away the blame from ourselves, by declaring that we are like two pieces of wood and stones, which are dragged about by those causes that act upon them from without, is neither true nor in conformity with reason, but is the statement of him who wishes to destroy the conception of free-will. For if we were to ask such an one what was free-will, he would say that it consisted in this, when purposing to do something, no external cause came inciting to the reverse. (Origen, *De Principiis*, Bk. III, Ch. I, sec. 5, ANF IV, p. 304)

To Origen it lacked plausibility to argue that free will is an illusion that finally amounts to the absence of a cause. If we suppose that freedom is to be as strongly affirmed as the pastoral writers insist, then how is it to be related to necessity?

Every motion is divided into two parts, so that a certain part is moved by necessity, and another by will; and those things which are moved by necessity are always in motion, those which are moved by will, not always. For example, the sun's motion is performed by necessity to complete its appointed circuit, and every state and service of heaven depends upon necessary motions. But man directs the voluntary motions of his own actions. And thus there are some things which have been created for this end, that in their services they should be subject to necessity, and should be unable to do aught else than what has been assigned to them. . . . but there are other things, in which there is a power of will, and which have a free choice of doing what they will. These, as I have said, do not remain always in that order in which they were created. (Clementina, *Recognitions of Clement*, Bk. III, Ch. XXIV, ANF VIII, p. 120)

The pastoral writers sought to affirm freedom without denying the web of causality in and through which freedom operates and expresses itself. Some antagonists to the Christian view have been inclined to assign blame for the fallenness of freedom to causes external to freedom. To them Augustine replied using these striking metaphors:

You will not blame gold and silver because there are avaricious people, or food because there are gluttons, or wine because there are drunkards, or female beauty because there are fornicators and adulterers, and so on. . . . And it is manifest that when anyone uses anything badly it is not the thing but the man who uses it badly that is to be blamed. (Augustine, *On Free Will*, Bk. XV, Ch. 33, LCC VI, p. 133)

In any account of human freedom it is well to recall, as did Ambrose, its radical limits:

How pitiable are the conditions of kings, how changeable the status of their power, how short the span of this life, in how great bondage even sovereigns must live, since they live at the will of others and not their own. (Ambrose, *Letters*, 79, To Laymen, FC 26, p. 445)

The Westminster Confession produced one of the most concise and carefully drawn statements of the classical Protestant tradition in its five points concerning free will that reveals the complexity of the problem, which must be seen in stages of development in the divine-human dialogue:

I. God hath endued the will of man with that natural liberty, that is neither forced nor by any absolute necessity of nature determined to good or evil.

II. Man, in his state of innocency, had freedom and power to will and to do that which is good and well-pleasing to God, but yet mutably, so that he might fall from it.

III. Man, by his fall into a state of sin, hath wholly lost, all ability of will to any spiritual good accompanying salvation; so as a natural man, being altogether averse from that good, and dead in sin, is not able, by his own strength, to convert himself, or to prepare himself thereunto.

IV. When God converts a sinner, and translates him into the state of grace, he freeth him from his natural bondage under sin, and by his grace alone enables him freely to will and to do that which is spiritually good; yet so as that, by reason of his remaining corruption, he doth not perfectly, nor only, will that which is good, but doth also will that which is evil.

V. The will of man is made perfectly and immutably free to good alone, in the state of glory only. (Westminster Confession, Ch. IX, sec. I–V, *CC*, pp. 205f.)

This Confession reveals how crucially the Reformed view of freedom depended upon telling a story, the history of salvation, in order to clarify the ground, the predicament and the promise of human freedom.

II. ❦ FREEDOM OF WILL AS A PREMISE OF SOUL CARE

The pastoral writers repeatedly sought to make careful distinctions between freedom and desire, so as to hold fast to the premise that persons are free and therefore responsible, yet at the same time are swept by the emotive power of varied levels of desire. In this section we will seek to set forth some classical thinking on the definition of freedom of will, as distinguished from deliberating, planning, judging, and desiring.

To want is not the same as to choose. To deliberate on something is quite short of choosing it. How then are we to define choice in such a way as to distinguish it from desire? The great Christian psychologist of the fourth century, even greater than Augustine in my view, Nemesius of Emesa, sought to answer this question:

Can it really be, then, that choosing is the same thing as desiring? Once more we answer in the negative. For we can distinguish three kinds of desiring—lust, anger, and simply wanting a thing. But it is clear that neither anger nor lust is an act of choice, as may be seen from the fact that while men share with irrational animals lust and anger, they do not share with them their faculty of choice. . . . Once more, wanting something is not the same as choosing it. This is clear from the fact that not all the things that one may want are properly objects of choice. . . . Wanting is a right word to use even when what we want is impossible of attainment; choice is the right word only when the thing lies within our power to attain it. . . . While we call an opinion true or false, we do not apply the adjectives true or false to an act of choice. Again, while opinion may be with regard to universals, choice has only to do with particulars. For choice is of things to be done, and such things are specific.

Neither is deliberation synonymous with an act of choice, as though it were an actual plan. For deliberation is an enquiry as to things that one might do. But when choice has been made of a course, it has been decided upon by process of deliberation. It is plain, then, that deliberation is about things that are still the subject of enquiry, but choice follows only when decision has been reached. So now that we have stated what an act of choice is not, let us go on to say what it is. It is, then, something that mingles plan, judgment, and desire. It is neither pure desire, nor judgement, nor even plan in isolation, but is a combination of all three. For just as we say that a living creature is composed of soul and body together, so likewise so we define an act of choice; that is to say, it is a kind of plan, followed by deliberation, which ends in a decision. (Nemesius, *Of the Nature of Man*, Ch. XXXIII, LCC IV, pp. 392–393)

While we can want something impossible, strictly speaking we cannot choose something impossible. We can deliberate on a plan without choosing it. But to choose something involves all three elements: we must desire it, we must through deliberation inquire into Plan A as distinguished from Plan B or C, and finally we must make a judgment preferring one to another. Without all three elements, one has not yet made a choice. If this is what it means to choose, what does it mean to will? Are we talking about the same thing, or something quite different? Origen wrote:

Of things that move, some have the cause of their motion within themselves; others, again, are moved only from without . . . such as pieces of wood, and stones. . . . The rational animal, however, has, in addition to its phantasial nature, also reason, which judges the phantasies, and disapproves of some and accepts others. . . . Therefore, since there are in the nature of reason aids towards the contemplation of virtue and vice, by following which, after beholding good and evil, we select the one and avoid the other, we are deserving of praise when we give ourselves to the practice of virtue, and censurable when we do the reverse. We must not, however, be ignorant that the greater part of the nature assigned to all things is a varying quantity among animals, both in a greater and a less degree: so that the instinct in hunting-dogs and in war-horses approaches somehow, so to speak, to the faculty of reason. Now, to fall under some one of those external causes which stir up within us this phantasy or that, is confessedly not one of those things that are dependent upon ourselves; but to determine that we shall use the occurrence in this way or differently, is the prerogative of nothing else than of the reason within us, which, as occasion offers, arouses us towards becoming, or turns us aside to what is the reverse. . . . For, to take an instance, a woman who has appeared before a man that has determined to be chaste, and to refrain from carnal intercourse, and who has incited him to act contrary to his purpose, is not a perfect cause of annulling his determination. For, being altogether pleased with the luxury and allurement of the pleasure, and not wishing to resist it, or to keep his purpose, he commits an act of licentiousness. Another man, again (when the same things have happened to him who has received more instruction, and has disciplined himself), encounters, indeed, allurements and enticements; but his reason, as being strengthened to a higher point, and carefully trained, and confirmed in its views towards a virtuous course, or being near to confirmation, repels the incitement, and extinguishes the desire. (Origen, *De Principiis*, Bk. III, Ch. I, sec. 1–5, ANF IV, pp. 302–304)

Origen's illustration of seduction is intended to show that the same temptation can confront two individuals, yet due to their different levels of understanding and discipline, they will respond in opposite ways. That proves, in Origen's view, that human willing is not reducible to external determinants. It always has within it elements of self-determination, though still functioning within the sphere of many causal influences and determinations. That is precisely what distinguishes human beings (rational creatures) from irrational or brute animals: free self-determination that transcends, though expresses itself within, causal chains. Only human beings are deserving of praise for behavioral excellences and censurable for behavioral deficits, because human freedom is and knows itself to be accountable. This is why human freedom differs dramatically from the consciousness of hunting dogs or war horses, however competent they may be in other ways.

We cannot discuss the dynamics of will, however, without encountering another dilemma of speculation—the perennially perplexing question as to whether everything that God wills must necessarily occur. If this be the case, how could there exist any personal self-determination at all? In the following case the question is being framed by an anonymous third century writer of an imaginary dialogue with the Apostle Peter:

> Then said Peter: "I shall speak, not as under compulsion from you, but at the request of the hearers. The power of choice is the sense of the soul, possessing a quality by which it can be inclined towards those acts it wills." Then Simon said: . . . "What I wish to learn, then, is this: Is it the case that what God wishes to occur does *occur*, and what God does not wish to occur does *not occur*? Answer me this." Then Peter: "Do you not know that you are asking an absurd and incompetent question?. . . . If I were to answer that what God wishes is, and what God wishes not is not, you would say that then God wishes the evil things to be which are done in the world, since everything that God wishes is, and everything that God wishes not is not. But if I had answered that it is not so that what God wishes is, and what God wishes not is not, then you would retort that God must then be powerless, if He cannot do what He wills. (Clementina, *Recognitions of Clement*, Bk. III, Ch. XXIII, ANF VIII, pp. 120–121)*

In the discussion of pastoral theodicy (in *Crisis Ministries*), we deal with the dilemma of the confluence of God's insurmountable power and goodness with the wrenching facts of suffering and distortion. Here we merely note that the Clementine author wisely rejected two false alternatives: attributing either evil to God or powerlessness to God. If the Creator wills to create co-creators or co-choosers, as seems to be the case, so that these co-choosers can will acts that are not strictly necessitated in every respect (although always moving within the relative constraints of multiple levels of necessity), this does not deny that God is absolutely powerful and good, but requires that the assertion of God's power and goodness make room for the free play of human freedom. Pastoral wisdom indeed does argue that God is incomparably powerful and good, but not usually on the basis of a denial of human self-determination, a key biblical premise.

III. 🍇 REASON AND WILL

It might seem that the fall of freedom is basically a problem of inadequate knowing, but Clement of Alexandria proposed, and most of the tradition followed him, that the fall of freedom is willed. Sin, to be sin, must be within our power, and not coerced.

Sinning arises from being unable to determine what ought to be done, or being unable to do it; as doubtless one falls into a ditch either through not knowing, or through inability to leap across through feebleness of body. . . . Again, the Lord clearly shows sins and transgressions to be in our own power, by prescribing modes of cure corresponding to the maladies; showing His wish that we should be corrected by the shepherds, in Ezekiel; blaming, I am of opinion, some of them for not keeping the commandments, "That which was enfeebled ye have not strengthened," and so forth, down to, "and there was none to search out or turn away" [Ezek. 34:4–6]. (Clement of Alexandria, *The Stromata, or Miscellanies*, Bk. II, Ch. XVI, ANF II, pp. 362–366)

Accountability presupposes choice. Choice, according to Origen, depends upon the recognition of the difference between good and evil:

Moses [said]: "I have placed before thy face the way of life, and the way of death: choose what is good, and walk in it" [Deut. 30:15]. Isaiah too: "If you are willing, and hear me, ye shall eat the good of the land; but if ye be unwilling, and will not hear me, the sword will consume you: for the mouth of the Lord hath spoken it" [Is. 1:19, 20]. . . . And let us observe how Paul also converses with us as having freedom of will, and as being ourselves the cause of ruin or salvation. (Origen, *De Principiis*, Bk. III, Ch. I, sec. 6, ANF IV, pp. 305–306)

What is choice?

Since whatever can possibly not be does not necessarily exist, man chooses without necessity. A twofold power of man accounts for his being able to choose or not to choose. Man can will or not will, act or not act; he can will this or that and do this or that. The very power of reason accounts for this. The will can tend toward anything apprehended by reason as good. But the reason can consider to be good not only willing and acting, but not willing and not acting as well. Moreover, the mind can see in every particular good its goodness as well as its lack of goodness, suggesting the notion of evil. Hence the mind can apprehend any one of these goods as worth or not worth choosing. Only the perfect good or happiness cannot in any way be perceived as evil or defective. Thus of necessity man wills happiness and it is impossible for him to will not to be happy, or to be unhappy. But since choice does not deal with the end but with the means to the end, as previously discussed (*Summa of Theology*, I–II, 13, 3) it does not deal with the perfect good or happiness but with other particular goods. Consequently man does not choose necessarily but freely. (Thomas Aquinas, *Summa Theologica*, Part I–II, Q. 13, Art. 6, AR, p. 293)

Personal freedom is not fated, but rather tempted, to corruption:

There is in every soul a potential force and a freedom of the will, by means of which it has the power to do all things good. But this inborn good had been beguiled by the Fall, and perverted to sloth or wickedness. (Origen, *The Song of Songs*, Commentary on the Prologue, CWS, pp. 243–244)

Every soul, therefore, exists in the tension between its originally created possibility and its actual liability to fallenness. This is why a constant struggle for behavioral excellence is required of the soul, and not automatically given. If virtues were but cheaply bestowed quite apart from any effort of freedom, would freedom be harmed? Can one take pleasure in good if cheaply given it apart from any struggle of the will?

Some maintain that all things are drawn by necessity or compulsion to what is good, that there is one mind and one usage in all things which works mechanically in one groove (*inflexibiles et sine judicio*), so that creatures are incapable of being anything else except just what they had been created. But upon this supposition, neither would what is good be grateful to them, nor communion with God be precious, nor would the good be very much to be sought after, which would present itself without their own proper endeavor, care, or study, but would be implanted of its own accord and without their concern. Thus it would come to pass, that their being good would be of no consequence, because they were so by nature rather than by will, and are possessors of good spontaneously, not by choice; and for this reason they would not understand this fact, that good is a comely thing, nor would they take pleasure in it. For how can those who are ignorant of good enjoy it? (Irenaeus, *Against Heresies*, Bk. IV, Ch. XXXVII, ANF I, p. 520)*

Irenaeus argued that it is not conceivable that the mind could even recognize a good, or in fact know any good, without some rational faculty to distinguish perceived goods from perceived evils.

God granted to humans such greatness of mind that they would know both the good of obedience and the evil of disobedience. This was given in order that the eye of the mind, receiving experience of both, might with good judgment make choice of the better things; and that persons might never become indolent or neglectful of God's command; and that they might learn by experience that it is an evil thing which deprives them of life. . . . For if man had no knowledge of the difference between good and evil, how could he have even been instructed as to what is good? (Irenaeus, *Against Heresies*, Bk. IV, Ch. XXXIX.1, ANF I, p. 522)*

Bonaventure argued that the very process of deliberation assumed a highest good in terms of which other goods are judged good:

Deliberation consists in inquiring which is better, this or that. But *better* has meaning only in terms of its proximity to *best*; and this proximity is in terms of greater resemblance. No one, therefore, knows whether this is better than that unless he knows that it bears greater resemblance to the best. . . . Therefore, the notion of the highest good is necessarily imprinted in everyone who deliberates. (Bonaventure, *The Soul's Journey into God*, CWS, p. 83)

Reason implies and requires personal freedom. It is difficult to imagine any rational or self-determining capacity that has no element of freedom. Hence there can be no human *psuche* without positing freedom, even if that freedom becomes trapped in self-chosen bondage. Nemesius formulated the argument on the intrinsic relation of reason and will:

Of the rational faculty, part is devoted to contemplation and part to action. Contemplation is perceiving things, and how they consist. Reason on the active side is deliberative, and determines the right way to do things. The contemplative exercise of the faculty is commonly referred to as mind, while the active exercise is called reasoning; or the first is called wisdom and the second prudence. Everyone who deliberates does so on the supposition that the choice of things to be done lies with him, and that he will choose the preferable course as the result of his taking of counsel; further, that when he has so chosen, he will act upon his choice. There is every necessity therefore, for one who has the capacity for deliberation also to be master of his own actions, for, if it were otherwise, it would be to no profit that he possessed the faculty of deliberation. And if things stand so, then free-will is bound to accompany the faculty of reason. For either a creature will not be endowed with reason, or, if it is endowed with reason, then it will also be master of what it does. And if a creature is master of what is does, without doubt it must possess free-will. (Nemesius, *Of the Nature of Man*, Ch. XLI, LCC IV, p. 418)

The mind contemplates, the reason acts. To take counsel is to act according to the preference of reason, according to due deliberation. If the self deliberates toward action with reason, then any self-determined action implies freedom.

Does animal psychology differ from human psychology? Aelred drew this distinction:

Aelred: Notice how much we have said about that life by which trees live and how much about the life by which beasts live and feel, and all that we have said has been preceded by thought and a certain interior reasoning and judgement. What is it in us that thought out, judged and decided how all this should be said? It is something great, something sublime, something that far transcends the qualities which we have said exist in trees and animals. For they can neither think nor judge, nor can they understand the difference between what is good and bad nor between what is useful and what is not.

John: Do beasts and birds not protect their lives, as far as they are able, by taking to flight and hiding under cover? Do they not take care for their health by procuring food and drink? They have, besides, so great a power of memory that they appear in great measure to come very close to knowledge and reason.

Aelred: None of this is prompted by reason or knowledge. What causes these actions in them is the power not of judgement but of sense. For, as Augustine perceived, many beasts surpass us in the power of sense, and by making sharp use of it in pursuit of the things they want for food or pleasure they acquire such ingrained habits as make them appear to imitate reason in small measure. (Aelred of Rievaulx, *Dialogue on the Soul*, CFS 22, pp. 45–46

IV. 🐝 The Self-alienation of Freedom

The pastor is not dealing with persons whose freedom has remain absolutely undefiled and persists without distortions. The freedom toward which soul care is directed is always already a fallen freedom, freedom abused, freedom that has to some degree plummeted from its original condition (the human condition as originally created, without sin).

A horse with a capacity for self-movement is judged a higher creation than a stone which can only be moved. This is so even if the horse is stubborn. Similarly a human being with capacity for rational self-determination is a higher creation than a horse which lacks reason, and this remains so even if the man is a sinner:

An errant horse is better than a stone that cannot err because it have neither motion nor feeling of its own. So a creature which sins by its own free will is more excellent than one which cannot sin because it has no free will. I would praise wine that was good of its kind, and would censure the man who drank it to excess. And yet I would hold the man whom I had censured, even while he was drunk, to be superior to the wine which made him drunk, even though I had praised it. (Augustine, *On Free Will*, Bk. III, Ch. 15, LCC VI, p. 180)

The pastoral writers thought deeply about the divine purpose in creating persons with vulnerable wills prone to fall into sin. It is not easy to account simply for the divine goodness under these circumstances. The power of willing is a power that God shares with human creation in a way that reveals the hidden affinity between humanity and God. God's primary motive in human creation, according to Clement's exegesis, has been the making of this extraordinary being who is in some ways so like God himself. God loves this human creation and these human souls because they are valuable in themselves, not on the basis that human souls are useful for some other purpose in creation. Through soul care the pastor must somehow try to communicate this extraordinary relationship of love that exists from God toward the human soul:

Now a being which God Himself has fashioned, and in such a way that it resembles Himself closely, must have been created either because it is desirable to God in itself, or because it is useful for some other creature. If man has been created as desirable in himself, then God loves him as good, since He Himself is good, and there is a certain lovableness in man, which is the very quality breathed into him by God [cf. Gen. 2:7]. But, if God made man only because He considered him useful for some other creature, even then He had no other reason for actually creating him than that with him He could become a good Creator, and man could come to a knowledge of God (remember, in this case, unless man had been created, God would not have made the other creature for whose sake man was being created). So, the power which God already possessed, hidden deep within Himself, the power of willing, He was actualizing by this display of the external power of creating, drawing from man a motive for creating him....

Therefore, man, the creation of God, is desirable in himself. But being desirable in oneself means being connatural to the person to whom one is desirable, . . . Man is, then, an object of love; yes, man is loved by God. (Clement of Alexandria, *Christ the Educator*, Bk. I, Ch. 3, FC 23, pp. 9–10)

Could God have made the human will perfect, failsafe, and never even slightly distortable?

Simon [asked]: "Was not He able to make us all such that we should be good, and that we should not have it in our power to be otherwise?" Peter answered: "This also is an absurd question. For if He had made us of an unchangeable nature and incapable of being moved away from good, we should not be really good, because we could not be aught else; and it would not be of our purpose that we were good and what we did would not be ours, but of the necessity of our nature. (Clementina, *Recognitions of Clement*, Bk. III, Ch. XXVI, ANF VIII, p. 121)

If God foresaw that the will would so disastrously fall, wouldn't a wiser and better God have stopped it? Under those circumstances would God's only remedy have been to withhold creation?

Was the Creator ignorant that those whom He created would fall away into evil? He ought therefore not to have created those who He foresaw would deviate from the path of righteousness. Now we tell those who ask such question, that the purpose of assertions of the sort made by us is to show why the wickedness yet to be of those who as yet were not, did not prevail over the goodness of the Creator. For if, wishing to fill up the number and measure of His creation, He had been afraid of the wickedness of those who were to be, and like one who could find no other way of remedy and cure, except that He should refrain from His purpose of creating lest the wickedness of those who were to be should be ascribed to Him, what else would this show but unworthy suffering and unseemly feebleness on the part of the Creator, who should so fear the actions of those who as yet were not, that He refrained from His purposed creation? . . . Therefore He foresaw that there would be faults in His creature. The method of His justice demanded that punishment should follow faults, for the sake of their amendment . . . Moreover, those who have undertaken the contest for eternal reward cannot be left without some enemy to conquer. Thus, therefore, those things thought to be evil are never in God's economy destitute of utility. (Clementina, *Recognitions of Clement*, Bk. IV, Ch. XXIV-XXV, ANF VIII, p. 140)*

God foresaw that the self-determining creature would fall, but this did not deter God in creating. The option of avoiding creating something that might go awry never seems to be viewed by the Christian pastoral tradition as a plausible alternative that could have been consistent with the goodness of God.

> You say, God ought to have made us at first so that we should not have thought at all of such things. You who say this do not know what is free-will, and how it is possible to be really good. One who is good by his own choice is really good, but one who is made good by another under necessity is not really good, because he is not what he is by his own choice. (Clementina, *Homilies*, Hom. XI, Ch. VIII, ANF VIII, p. 286)*

Irenaeus addressed the dilemma of why freedom was made unperfected by the goodness and wisdom of God:

> God thus determining all things beforehand for the bringing of man to perfection, for his edification, and for the revelation of His dispensations, that goodness may both be made apparent, and righteousness perfected, and that the Church may be fashioned after the image of His Son, and that man may finally be brought to maturity at some future time, becoming ripe through such privileges to see and comprehend God. If, however, any one say, ''What then? Could not God have exhibited man as perfect from the beginning?" let him know that, inasmuch as God is indeed always the same and unbegotten as respects Himself, all things are possible to Him. But created things must be inferior to Him who created them ... as it certainly is in the power of a mother to give strong food to her infant, [but she does not do so], as the child is not yet able to receive more substantial nourishment; so also it was possible for God Himself to have made man perfect from the first, but man could not receive this [perfection], being as yet an infant. (Irenaeus, *Against Heresies*, Bk. IV, Ch. XXXVII-XXXVIII, ANF I, pp. 520f.)

As no mother would shove beefsteak down the throat of an infant, before the infant can chew, so God did not elect to give perfection to humanity from the outset, but rather only by gradually preparing the will for perfect responsiveness through the cooperation of grace and freedom.

All these closely reasoned texts on the relation of divine and human freedom, power, and justice may seem tedious to the pastor who is only ready to deal with so-called practical issues of pastoral care. But without good foundation in the reasoning of the pastoral writers on this most fundamental issue of the grandeur and misery of freedom, no pastor is ready to proceed to pastoral practice. These issues, surprisingly, will arise again and again in daily pastoral practice, even though clothed in the rhetoric of modernity.

V. 🐦 Astrology and Magic as Anathema

Early pastoral documents strongly rejected the adaptation of pagan divinizations to diagnosis and treatment of soul sickness:

[Avoid] observations of omens, soothsayings, purgations, divinations, observations of birds; their necromancies and invocations. For it is written: "There is no divination in Jacob, nor soothsaying in Israel" [Num. 23:23]. And again: "Divination is iniquity" [1 Sam. 15:23 LXX]. And elsewhere; "Ye shall not be soothsayers, and follow observers of omens, nor diviners, nor dealers with familiar spirits." [cf. Lev. 19:26; Deut. 18:10] (*Constitutions of the Holy Apostles*, Bk. II, sec. VII, ANF VII, p. 424)

The strong resistance to magical divinization was formulated early in consensual Christianity and sustained consistently:

They who are of the priesthood, or of the clergy, shall not be magicians, enchanters, mathematicians, or astrologers; nor shall they make what are called amulets, which are chains for their own souls. (Synod of Laodicea, Canon XXXVI, The Seven Ecumenical Councils, NPNF 2, XIV, p. 151)

The pastoral writers frequently abhorred horology as a denial of freedom:

They make the stars themselves wicked, as now procuring adulteries, and now inciting murders. Or, rather than the stars, it is God their Creator that bears the blame in their place, seeing that he made them such as would pass on to us an impetus to evil deeds which we cannot resist. (Nemesius, *Of the Nature of Man*, Ch. XXXV, LCC IV, p. 398)

Astrology was indeed a major challenge to early Christian soul care, particularly concerning sexual ethics. Could the placement of stars realistically affect the masculinity of women and the femininity of men?

Then said the old man ... Venus with the Moon, in the borders and houses of Saturn, if she was with Saturn, and Mars looking on, produces women that are viragos [vixens], ready for agriculture, building, and every manly work, to commit adultery with whom they please, and not to be convicted by their husbands, to use no delicacy, no ointments, nor feminine robes and shoes, but to live after the fashion of men. But the unpropitious Venus makes men to be as women. . . . And when the old man had pursued this subject at great length, and had enumerated every kind of mathematical figure, and also the position of the heavenly bodies, wishing thereby to show that fear is not sufficient to restrain lusts I answered again; "Truly, my father, you have argued most learnedly and skillfully; and reason herself invites me to say something in answer to your discourse, since indeed I am acquainted with the science of mathematics. . . . There are in every country or kingdom laws imposed by men, enduring either by writing or simply through custom, which no one easily transgresses. In short, the first Seres [farthest east] who dwell at the beginning of the world, have a law not to know murder, nor adultery, nor whoredom and not to commit theft, and not to worship idols; and in all that country, which is very large, there is neither temple, nor image, nor harlot, nor adulteress, nor is any thief brought to trial. But neither is any man ever slain there; and no man's liberty of will is compelled, according to your doctrine, by the fiery star of Mars, to use the sword for the murder of man; nor does Venus in conjunction with Mars compel to adultery, although of course with them Mars occupies the middle circle of heaven every day. (Clementina, *Recognitions of Clement*, Bk. IX, Ch. XVI-XIX, ANF VIII, p. 187)

The Clementine writer is answering the fiction that sexual patterns are shaped by the stars, especially when pretentious arguments appear to be buttressed by complex mathematical schemes. He thought he possessed solid evidence against the argument that adultery is compelled by stellar placement.

Do not be always looking for omens, my son, for this leads to idolatry. Likewise have nothing to do with witchcraft, astrology, or magic; do not even consent to be a witness of such practices, for they too can all breed idolatry. (*Didache*, sec. 3, ECW, p. 228)

Since magical therapies were so prevalent in the early Christian environment, it became necessary for the classical pastoral writers to go to great lengths to distinguish Christian care of souls from magic, as we see in this selection from Eusebius:

Who has ever so far found the whole body of Christians from His teaching given to sorcery or enchantment? . . . The disciples, who were with Him from the beginning, with those who inherited their mode of life afterwards, are to such an incalculable ex-

tent removed from base and evil suspicion (of sorcery), that they
will not allow their sick even to do what is exceedingly common
with non-Christians, to make use of charms written on leaves or
amulets, or to pay attention to those promising to soothe them
with songs of enchantment, or to procure ease for their pains by
burning incense made of roots and herbs, or anything else of the
kind. . . . All these things at any rate are forbidden by Christian
teaching, neither is it ever possible to see a Christian using an
amulet, or incantations, or charms written on curious leaves, or
other things which the crowd consider quite permissible. (Eusebius, *The Proof of the Gospel*, Bk. III, Ch. VI, sec. 127, p. 146–147)

Similarly, the Apostolic Constitutions rigorously opposed any form of
conjuring pretending to be soul care:

Thou shalt not use magic. Thou shalt not use witchcraft; . . .
Be not a diviner, for that leads to idolatry. . . . Thou shalt not use
enchantments or purgations for thy child. Thou shall not be a
soothsayer nor a diviner by great or little birds. (*Constitutions of the
Holy Apostles*, Bk. VII, Ch. I, sec. 3–6, ANF VII, p. 466–467)

The Athanasian Canons excluded practitioners of divinization and
magic from the sacrament:

Let no presbyter join himself in the sacrament unto wizards or
conjurers or soothsayers [masters of hours]; rather when any enter without reverence, let him set him apart with the catechu-
mens. (Athanasian Canons, p. 30)

The pastor must actively oppose superstition. At one point, for example, St. Patrick of Ireland resisted the imaginings of vampires and
witches:

A Christian who believes that there is such a thing as a vam-
pire, that is to say, a witch, is to be anathematized — anyone who
puts a living soul under such a reputation; and he must not be
received again into the Church before he has undone by his own
word the crime that he has committed, and so does penance with
all diligence. (Patrick of Ireland, "Canons," *Works*, 16, p. 52)

Clement of Alexandria thought that the whole ethos of idolatry tended
to elicit a kind of wildness in its proponents, so that even the demeanor
of the superstitious often itself serves to discredit the spurious divinities
they idolize:

By sad experience, even a child knows how superstition destroys and piety saves. Let any of you look at those who minister

before the idols, their hair matted, their persons disgraced with filthy and tattered clothes; who never come near a bath, and let their nails grow to an extraordinary length, like wild beasts, many of them castrated, who show the idol's temples to be in reality graves or prisons. These appear to me to bewail the gods, not to worship them, and their sufferings to be worthy of pity rather than piety. (Clement of Alexandria, *Exhortation to the Heathen*, Bk. II, Ch. X, ANF V, p. 197)

When allegedly paranormal events occurred, it was thought responsible not to pay excessive attention to them as if they superceded revelation. Anthony felt that paranormal visions, which he experienced, did not make for him a privileged place in relation to the church's apostolic teaching ministry:

And these visions he [Anthony] was unwilling to tell, but as he spent much time in prayer, and was amazed, when those who were with him pressed him with questions and forced him, he was compelled to speak, as a father who cannot withhold ought from his children. And he thought that as his conscience was clear, the account would be beneficial for them, that they might learn that discipline bore good fruit, and that visions were oftentimes the solace of their labours.

Added to this he was tolerant in disposition and humble in spirit. For though he was such a man, he observed the rule of the Church most rigidly, and was willing that all the clergy should be honoured above himself. For he was not ashamed to bow his head to bishops and presbyters, and if ever a deacon came to him for help he discoursed with him on what was profitable, but gave place to him in prayer, not being ashamed to learn himself. (Athanasius, *Life of Anthony*, 66, 67, NPNF 2, IV, p. 214)

Anthony became mentor to a whole generation of spiritual guides in the Egyptian desert. Yet he himself remained tractable, obedient, and teachable. His visions did not, in his view, become normative for teaching or place him in tension with the apostolic tradition.

VI. ❦ THE SOCIAL CONSEQUENCES OF TAKING FREEDOM SERIOUSLY

The pastoral writers recognized serious risks to social continuity and political justice in a society that abused or misconceived responsible freedom. Social disaster follows from the premise that we are radically determined either by heredity or environment, and hence not finally accountable for our own actions:

If men have it not in their own power to do anything? If this opinion be held, all things are torn up by the roots; vain will be the desire of following after goodness, yea, even in vain do the judges of the world administer laws and punish those who do amiss, for they had it not in their power not to sin; vain also will be the laws of nations which assign penalties to evil deeds. Miserable also will those be who laboriously keep righteousness; but blessed those who, living in pleasure, exercise tyranny, living in luxury and wickedness. According to this, therefore, there can be neither righteousness, nor goodness, nor any virtue, nor, as you would have it, any God. (Clementina, *Recognitions of Clement*, Bk. III, Ch. XXII, ANF VIII, p. 120)

The social fabric is preserved only when free responsibility is personally owned and unavoided:

Licentiousness should be regarded as the evil of no other one than of him who is guilty of licentiousness; and temperance on the other hand, as the good of him who is able to practice it. (Clement of Alexandria, *The Stromata, or Miscellanies*, Bk. IV, Ch. XIX, ANF II, p. 432)

Christian pastoral reasoning has been slow to accept any argument that God is directly the cause of any particular sin. Do not blame God for what Judas did, wrote Chrysostom:

Why did he put into the soul of Judas the resolve to bring about my death? Do not tell me now that God had so ordained it; for the fulfillment of God's plan does not belong to the devil, but to God's own wisdom. (Chrysostom, *Homilies on John*, LXVII, on John 12:31, LCF, p. 172; cf. FC 41, p. 232; NPNF 1, VII, p. 288)

Shall we conclude, then, that individuals are very largely the cause of their own imperfection?

The skill of God, therefore, is not defective, for He has power of the stones to raise up children to Abraham [cf. Matt. 3:9]; but the man who does not obtain it, is the cause to himself of his own imperfection. Nor, [in like manner], does the light fail because of those who have blinded themselves; but while it remains the same as ever, those who are [thus] blinded are involved in darkness through their own fault. The light does never enslave any one by necessity; nor, again, does God exercise compulsion upon any one unwilling to accept the exercise of His skill. Those persons, therefore, who have apostatized from the light given by the Father, and transgressed the law of liberty, have done so through their own fault, since they have been created free agents, and possessed of power over themselves. (Irenaeus, *Against Heresies*, Bk. IV, Ch. XXXIX, sec. 3–4, ANF I, p. 523)

Fault cannot be shifted to God for human misdeeds and imperfections. Each moment is a prized gift in which to exercise responsible freedom, in Donne's view:

We are all prodigal sons, and not disinherited; we have received our portion, and misspent it, not been denied it. We are God's tenants here, and yet here, he, our landlord, pays us rents; not yearly, nor quarterly, but hourly, and quarterly; every minute he renews his mercy. (John Donne, *Devotions*, p. 10)

Strong resistance is found everywhere in the pastoral tradition to the assertion that God is determined by some necessity external to God:

He further imposed upon universal Nature, and on particular kinds, the limits they must observe. If any like to call those limits the domain of fate, because such things happen inevitably, altogether and in every respect according to that rule (for example, that everything that, in its turn, comes into being, inevitably also perishes), we have nothing to say against it. For our dispute with them is not about terms. What we say is that God not only stands outside the power of all necessity; he is its Lord and maker. For in that he is authority, and the very source whence authority flows, he himself does nothing through any necessity of nature, or at the bidding of any inviolable law. On the contrary, all things are possible to him, including those we call impossible. . . . The Stoics, on the other hand, assert that when the planets have wheeled about until they reach, once more, the same sign of the Zodiac, and the same height and position in it, which each of them had at the beginning, when the world was first made, at the stated periods of time, a burning up and destruction of all things is brought about. Then the world is reconstituted exactly as it was before, and the stars likewise go through their motions all over again. Each single thing, they say, happens in the same undeviating order as in the previous world-cycle, and takes its course without a single change. (Nemesius, *Of the Nature of Man*, Ch. XXXVIII, LCC IV, pp. 408–409)

The Stoic view of cosmic necessity is contrasted with the Christian view of responsible, grace-enabled freedom under divine sovereignty. Christian teaching does not quarrel with every detail of every doctrine that parades under the topic of fate, but rather with the notion that God is bound to some absolute necessity that transcends God. Instead, fate itself must be viewed as subject to providence:

Whether, therefore, Fate works by the aid of the divine spirits which serve Providence, or whether it works by the aid of the soul, or of all nature, or the motions of the stars in heaven, or the powers of angels, or the manifold skill of other spirits, whether the course of Fate is bound together by any or all of these, one thing is certain, namely that Providence is the one unchangeable direct power which gives form to all things which are to come to pass, while Fate is the changing bond, the temporal order of those things which are arranged to come to pass by the direct disposition of God. Wherefore everything which is subject to Fate is also subject to Providence, to which Fate is itself subject. (Boethius, *Consolation of Philosophy*, Bk. IV, p. 100)

VII. 🐝 GRACE AND FREEDOM

Repeatedly the pastor will be asked: If God ordains everything, is not freedom negated? It may seem, without more serious examination, that the classical tradition is self-contradictory in asserting both divine sovereignty and free will. We will set forth classic arguments that show how both affirmations were held together in strictest tension, as in the Westminster Confession:

God from all eternity did, by the most wise and holy counsel of his own will, freely and unchangeably ordain whatsoever comes to pass; yet so as thereby neither is God the author of sin, nor is violence offered to the will of the creatures, nor is the liberty or contingency of second causes taken away, but rather established. (Westminster Confession, Ch. III, sec. 1, *CC*, p. 198)

It should not be assumed that early pastoral writers had not taken into account serious objections to their views. Note, for example, how fairly Augustine recapitulated and understood the objections to the orthodox Christian teaching that God could foreknow without eliminating human freedom of will:

What is it, then, that Cicero feared in the prescience of future things? Doubtless it was this — that if all future things have been foreknown, they will happen in the order in which they have been foreknown. . . . But if this be so, then is there nothing in our own power, and there is no such thing as freedom of will; and if we grant that, says he, the whole economy of human life is subverted. In vain are laws enacted. In vain are reproaches, praises, chidings, exhortations had recourse to. . . . Cicero chooses to reject the foreknowledge of future things, and shuts up the religious mind to this alternative, to make choice between two things, either that something is in our own power, or that there is foreknowledge—both of which cannot be true. . . . But the religious mind chooses both, confesses both, and maintains both by the faith of piety. But how so? . . . We assert both that God knows all things before they come to pass, and that we do by our free will whatsoever we know and feel to be done by us only because we will it. . . . It does not follow that, though there is for God a certain order of all causes, there must therefore be nothing depending on the free exercise of our own wills, for our wills themselves are included in that order of causes which is certain to God, and is embraced by His foreknowledge, for human wills are also causes of human actions. (Augustine, *The City of God*, Bk. V.9, NPNF 1, II, pp. 90–91)

How, then, may we formulate more positively how grace works through our willing?

Such is the power of Divine Grace, stronger than nature itself, that it can even make subject to itself the faculty of free will which is generally said to be master of itself. (Tertullian, *On the Soul*, Ch. 21, sec. 6, FC 10, p. 229)

Without ceasing to work, we become God's workmanship:

You are not the maker of God. God is the Maker of you. If, then, you are God's workmanship, await the hand of your Maker who creates everything in due time—for it is your own creation that is in due time being carried out. Offer to Him your heart in a soft and tractable state, therefore, and preserve the original form in which the Creator has fashioned you, having moisture in thyself, lest, by becoming hardened, you lose the impressions of His fingers. (Irenaeus, *Against Heresies*, Bk. IV, Ch. XXXIX, sec. 2, ANF I, p. 523)*

If human freedom is to be offered up to the divine Artificer, after the analogy of clay being formed by the potter, then the best that freedom can do is make itself intentionally tractable, to not allow itself to dry up and become unmouldable, but to yield itself to being shaped. That is not a diminishing, but an intensification, of freedom.

The life lived wholly committed to grace is not impossible. In recalling the counsel of the great Egyptian founders of monasticism, John Cassian reflected upon the seeming impossibility of their counsel:

It is evidently my duty that I should, however rashly, set down
on paper something about the way of life and the teaching of
those great Egyptian saints before it is forgotten. . . . I am not
inventing this teaching but simply passing on what I learnt. . . .
But if the reader wants to judge them rightly, and would test
whether what they did is possible, let him without further delay
resolve to adopt their purpose and their earnestness as his own.
Then he will find that what once seemed beyond human capacity
is not only possible but most pleasant. (Cassian, *Conferences*, Pref-
ace, LCC XII, pp. 194–195)

Does one choose one's thoughts?

Thoughts inevitably besiege the mind. But any earnest person
has the power to accept or reject them. Their origin is in some
ways outside ourselves, but whether to choose them or not lies
within us. . . . This movement of the heart may suitably be compared to a mill wheel spinning round under power from a water-
fall. The wheel must revolve so long as the water flows. But the
mill owner can decide whether to grind wheat or barley or dar-
nel, and the wheel will crush whatever he chooses.

So the mind cannot but move hither and thither under the
impetus of external circumstances and the thoughts which pour
in upon it like a torrent. But which thoughts to reject or accept,
an earnest and careful mind will determine. (Cassian, *Conferences*, First Conference of Abba Moses, sec. 17, 18, LCC XII, pp.
207–208)

VIII. 🦚 On Involuntary Acts and Degrees of Consent

This line of reasoning does not imply that no actions are involuntary. If
care of souls is to place primary responsibility upon each soul for its
own improvement, and if voluntary actions are to shape the destiny of
the soul, then it becomes important to distinguish voluntary actions
from those over which one has no control. For it is not reasonable that
one be held responsible for something over which one has had no
choice. The arguments of Nemesius on this issue may be considered typ-
ical of patristic reasoning:

Acts bring in their train praise or blame. Also the doing of
some of them brings pleasure, and of others grief. Some again
the doer chooses and others he shuns. Further, of those he
chooses, some he would choose at any time, but others only on
their proper occasions. Things to be shunned divide in the same
way. Again, some acts excite pity and are held excusable, while

others are loathed and punished. So, then, the norms for judging an act to be voluntary are: that it inevitably brings upon the doer either praise or blame, that it is done with pleasure, and that it is something that some people choose to do either at any time, or at that particular time. And the norms for judging an act involuntary are: that it is held reluctantly and not by choice. With these definitions to guide us, we will treat first of involuntary acts.

Involuntary acts are either those done under constraint or those done unknowingly. In the case of the former, the origination of the deed lies outside the doer. For the cause that constrains us to do such a deed is something alien to us, and is not ourselves. Therefore, what defines a constrained involuntary act, originating outside the doer, is that the person constrained contributed no impulse of his own towards it. The source of the impulse is therefore said to be the effective cause of the act. The question, then, is whether involuntary acts are such things as the jettisoning of cargo by sailors who run into a storm, or someone consenting to suffer some outrage, or even to do some shameful deed, for the sake of saving his friends or his country. We should reply that such things are voluntary rather than involuntary. For it is essential to the definition of an involuntary act that the person constrained to it contributed no impulse of his own towards it. For in acts such as those mentioned above the actors willingly set their own members in motion, and that is how they cast the cargo to the sea. And in the same way those do so voluntarily who suffer outrage, or endure some terrible fate, for the sake of a greater good; like Zeno, who bit out his tongue and spat it at the tyrant Dionysius, rather than divulge secret mysteries to him, or like the philosopher Anaxarchus, who chose to be pounded to death at the hands of the tyrant Nicocreon rather than betray his friends. In general, then, a man does not suffer or do anything involuntarily when he either embraces a lesser evil out of fear of greater ills, or accepts it in the hope of a greater good which he cannot otherwise successfully attain. For what he does he does by his own preference and choice. And when such deeds are done they are deliberate, although not in themselves such as a man would choose to do. Thus, in these acts, the involuntary and voluntary are mingled. They are involuntary, as regards the deed in itself, but voluntary when the circumstances are taken into account. For apart from those circumstances no one would choose to do those deeds. Nevertheless the praise or blame attending such acts demonstrates that they are voluntary. For there will be no word of praise or blame when things are done involuntarily. . . .

Let no one suppose that because lascivious desire or anger
have an inciting source outside the subject, these transgressions
are involuntary. For sure, it may be said that the charms of the
courtesan were what made the man that looked upon her crazy
for indulgence, and that it was the man who gave the provocation
that excited someone's anger. But even though these motions had
a first cause external to the subject, the subjects nevertheless did
their deeds themselves with their own proper members. These
cases do not fall within the definition of involuntary acts, because
the subjects provided themselves with a cause for giving way, in
that poor discipline made them easy captives of their passions. To
be sure, those who so act are blamed, as submitting to an evil
willingly. So it is evident that it is a voluntary act. For the subjects
find pleasure in what they do. And we have shown that an involuntary act is grievous to the doer. (Nemesius, *Of the Nature of
Man*, Ch. XXIX-XXX, LCC IV, pp. 383–386)

Three levels of volitional participation may be seen here. An inciting
source may be outside the individual, yet the misdeed still be voluntary.
A constrained involuntary act occurs only when the individual contributes no impulse of his own toward it, but can do no other than follow
the determination of others. There are in addition mixed actions, voluntary at one level yet involuntary at another, that we would not ordinarily choose to do but under specific circumstances do, in which case
the deed is not preferred, but is nonetheless chosen under certain compelling circumstances. Now we are prepared to ask, to what degree
blame attaches to involuntary acts?

Our next step is to consider these acts whose results are wholly
undesired. For the mere unintended lies nearer to the voluntary,
as having an element of voluntary in it, mingled with the other;
since it begins as unintended, but ends as voluntary. For what began as involuntary was turned, by the result, into voluntary. That
is why the involuntary is defined as follows: an involuntary act is
one which besides being unintentional, is grieved over, and a
cause of regret. . . . Blame attaches only to voluntary acts. . . .
Someone gives a person medicine to make him well, and the patient dies, because the medicine proves to be poison to that particular man. While not even a lunatic could be ignorant of all
these critical circumstances, anyone could be ignorant of most of
them, or of the more important, and act in ignorance. . . . We
have seen that there are two sorts of involuntary act; those done
through ignorance, and those done under constraint. Voluntary
acts are the exact opposite to each of these two groups. A voluntary act is done neither under constraint nor through ignorance.

That, forsooth, is not constrained which originates within ourselves. And that is not done through ignorance, where there is no particular circumstance that directly or indirectly affects the act, of which we did not know. Taking these two qualifications together, we define a voluntary act as one which originates within the doer, who, for his part, is aware of every circumstance attending upon his act. (Nemesius, *Of the Nature of Man*, Ch. XXXI-XXXII, LCC IV, pp. 387–389)

The pastoral care-giver is constantly trying to sort out the degrees of complicity, culpability, and consent in particular acts. For only when that subtle measure is reasonably grasped does one have some notion of where forgiveness is needed, and how acts of restitution may be applied. This is why the clarification of the differences between voluntary and involuntary actions is so important in soul care. For blame attaches only to voluntary acts, which originate in ourselves and which are not done under constraint or in ignorance.

We conclude with a political example. Does not guilt become distributed to a whole community in an act of mass political cowardice? We may use Augustine's account of a riot in which a priest was killed. Augustine's relentless question—was anyone guilty besides the rioters?

Listen to a brief account of what was done, and let the distinction between innocent and guilty be drawn by yourself. In defiance of the most recent laws, certain impious rites were celebrated on the Pagan feast-day, the calends of June, no one interfering to forbid them, and with such unbounded effrontery that a most insolent multitude passed along the street in which the church is situated, and went on dancing in front of the building,—an outrage which was never committed even in the time of Julian. When the clergy endeavored to stop this most illegal and insulting procedure, the church was assailed with stones. About eight days after that, when the bishop had called the attention of the authorities to the well-known laws on the subject, and they were preparing to carry out that which the law prescribed, the church was a second time assailed with stones. When, on the following day, our people wished to make such complaint as they deemed necessary in open court, in order to make these villains afraid, their rights as citizens were denied them. On the same day there was a storm of hailstones, that they might be made afraid, if not by men, at least by the divine power, thus requiting them for their showers of stones against the church; but as soon as this was over they renewed the attack for the third time with stones, and at last endeavoured to destroy both the buildings and the men in them by fire: one servant of God who lost his way and

met them they killed on the spot, all the rest escaping or conceal-
ing themselves as they best could; while the bishop hid himself in
some crevice into which he forced himself with difficulty, and in
which he lay folded double while he heard the voices of the ruf-
fians seeking him to kill him, and expressing their mortification
that through his escaping them their principal design in the
grievous outrage had been frustrated. These things went on from
about the tenth hour until the night was far advanced. No attempt at resistance or rescue was made by those whose authority
might have had influence on the mob. The only one who inter-
fered was a stranger, through whose exertions a number of the
servants of God were delivered from the hands of those who were
trying to kill them, and a great deal of property was recovered
from the plunderers by force: whereby it was shown how easily
these riotous proceedings might have been either prevented
wholly or arrested, if the citizens, and especially the leading men,
had forbidden them, either from the first or after they had begun. Accordingly you cannot in that community draw a distinction between innocent and guilty persons, for all are guilty; but
perhaps you may distinguish degrees of guilt. Those are in a
comparatively small fault, who, being kept back by fear, especially
by fear of offending those whom they knew to have leading influence in the community and to be hostile to the Church, did
not dare to render assistance to the Christians, but all are guilty
who consented to these outrages, though they neither perpetrated
them nor instigated others to the crime: more guilty are those
who instigated them to it. (Augustine, *Letters*, XCI, To Nectarius,
sec. 8, 9, NPNF 1, pp. 378-379)

If Augustine is our guide, everyone who consents to a crime is in
some degree culpable for it, and those who were not present but ab-
sently not preventing it, yet charged with its prevention, and especially
the civil authorities, bear a greater degree of guilt.

It is along these lines that the classical texts have analyzed the dynamics of the will, its passions, its bondage to passions, and its layers of
causality and accountability. Freedom of will remains a steady premise
of Christian soul care. That human freedom is actively self-determining
is the only hypothesis that makes sense out of the fact that we deliberate
on the consequences of our own deeds and feel responsible for them.
Yet the freedom toward which soul care is directed is always already a
fallen freedom, freedom abused, freedom that has to some degree
plummeted from its condition as originally created, without sin. Sin, to
be sin, must be within our power, and not coerced. It is not reasonable
that one be held responsible for something over which one has had no
choice. Every soul exists in the tension between its originally created

possibility and its actual liability to fallenness. This is why a constant struggle for behavioral excellence is required of the soul, and not automatically given. The care-giver is constantly trying to understand the degrees of complicity, culpability, and consent in particular acts.

The pastoral writers sought to affirm freedom without denying the web of causality in and through which freedom operates and expresses itself. To affirm freedom of the will does not imply that freedom is in every sense above all conceivable modes of causality, but rather that it lives within divinely engendered orders of causes known by God, and yet enmeshed in causality it determines itself freely as self-consciously willed by human beings. Only human beings are deserving of praise for behavioral excellences and censurable for behavioral deficits, because human freedom is and knows itself to be accountable.

ABBREVIATIONS

ACW   Ancient Christian Writers. Edited by J. Quasten, J. C. Plumpe, and W. Burghardt. 44 Vols. New York: Paulist Press, 1946–1985

AF   The Apostolic Fathers. Edited by J. N. Sparks. New York: Thomas Nelson, 1978.

AF-Ltft   The Apostolic Fathers. Edited by J. B. Lightfoot, revised by J. R. Harmer, London, New York: Macmillan, 1907.

ANF   Ante-Nicene Fathers. Edited by A. Roberts and J. Donaldson. 10 vols. 1866–1896. Reprint ed., Grand Rapids: Eerdmans, 1979.

Angl.   Anglicanism, The Thought and Practice of the Church of England, Illustrated from the Religious Literature of the Seventeenth Century. Edited by P. E. More and F. L. Cross. London: S.P.C.K., 1935.

AR   An Aquinas Reader. Mary T. Clark, editor. New York: Doubleday, 1972.

BCP   Book of Common Prayer (1662 unless otherwise noted). Royal Breviar's edition. London: S.P.C.K., n.d.

BPR   Book of Pastoral Rule. Gregory the Great, NPNF 2nd X, 1–94.

CC   Creeds of the Churches. Edited by John Leith. Richmond: John Knox Press, 1979.

CFS   Cistercian Fathers Series. 44 vols. Kalamazoo, MI: Cistercian Publications, 1968ff.

COCL   Classics of the Contemplative Life. Edited by J. M. Hussey, 8 vols. London: Faber and Faber, 1960ff.

CS   The Curate of Souls. Edited by John R. H. Moorman, London: SPCK, 1958

CSS   Cistercian Studies Series. 68 vols. Kalamazoo, MI: Cistercian Publications, 1968ff.

CWMS   Complete Writings of Menno Simons (c. 1496–1561). Edited by John C. Wenger, Scottdale, PA: Herald Press, 1956.

CWS   Classics of Western Spirituality. 37 vols. to date. Edited by Richard J. Payne et. al. New York: Paulist Press, 1978ff.

ECF Early Christian Fathers. Edited by H. Bettenson. London: Oxford University Press.

ECW Early Christian Writers: The Apostolic Fathers. Translated by Maxwell Staniforth. London: Penguin Books, 1968.

FC Fathers of the Church. Edited by R. J. Deferrari. 73 vols. Washington, DC: Catholic University Press, 1947ff.

FER The Fathers for English Readers. 15 vols. London: SPCK, 1878–1890.

Inst. Institutes of the Christian Religion, by John Calvin. LCC, vols. 21–22. Philadelphia: Westminster Press, 1960.

KJV King James Version, 1611 (also called the Authorized Version)

LACT Library of Anglo-Catholic Theology. 99 vols. Oxford University Press, 1841–63.

LCC Library of Christian Classics. 26 vols. Edited by J. Baillie, J. T. McNiell, and H. P. Van Dusen. Philadelphia: Westminster Press, 1953–61.

LCF Later Christian Fathers. Edited by H. Bettenson. London: Oxford University Press, 1970.

LF A Library of Fathers of the Holy Catholic Church. Edited by E. B. Pusey, J. Kebel, J. H. Newman, and C. Marriott. 50 vols. Oxford: J. H. Parker, 1838–88.

Loeb Loeb Classical Library. Edited by Page, Capps, Rouse. Cambridge, Mass: Harvard University Press, 1912ff.

LPT Library of Protestant Thought. Edited by John Dillenberger. 13 vols. New York: Oxford University Press. 1964–72.

LW Luther's Works. Edited by J. Pelikan and H. T. Lehmann, 54 vols. St. Louis: Concordia, 1953ff.

MPG J. B. Migne, ed., Patrologia Graeca. 162 vols. Paris: Migne, 1857–76.

MPL J. B. Migne, ed., Patrologia Latina. 221 vols. Paris: Migne, 1841–1865. General Index, Paris, 1912.

MPLS J. B. Migne, ed., Patrologia Latina: Supplementum. 4 vols., Edited by A. Hamman, Turnhout, Belgium: Editions Brepols.

MSW Ministry of Word and Sacrament: An Enchiridion, by Martin Chemnitz (1595). St. Louis: Concordia, 1981.

NE A New Eusebius: Documents Illustrative of the History of the Church to A.D. 337. Edited by J. Stevenson, (based on B. J. Kidd). London: S.P.C.K., 1957.

NEB New English Bible

NIV New International Version

NPNF A Select Library of the Nicene and Post-Nicene Fathers of the Christian Church. 1st Series, 14 vols; 2nd series, 14 vols. Edited by H. Wace and P. Schaff. New York: Christian, 1887–1900.

OCC Our Christian Classics, ed. James Hamilton. London: Nisbet, 1858.

PW   Practical Works, Richard Baxter. 23 vols. London: James Duncan, 1830.

RAC   Rules and Advices to the Clergy of the Dicocese of Nown and Connor, 1661, Jeremy Taylor, Works, ed. R. Heber, 1839, vol. xiv.

RD   Reformed Dogmatics. Edited by J. W. Beardslee. Grand Rapids: Baker, 1965.

RSV   Revised Standard Version

SC   Spiritual Conferences, (1628), St. Francis de Sales. Westminster, Md: Newman, 1943.

SCG   Summa contra Gentiles, On the Truth of the Catholic Faith, Thomas Aquinas. 4 vols. New York: Doubleday, 1955–57.

SED   Standard English Divines. 19 volume series. Oxford: Parker, 1855ff.

SSW   Selected Sacred Writings, Hugh of St. Victor. London: Faber and Faber, 1962.

ST   Summa Theologica, Thomas Aquinas. Edited by English Dominican Fathers. 3 vols. New York: Benziger, 1947–48.

SW   John Calvin, Selections from His Writings. Edited by John Dillenberger. Missoula, Mont.: Scholars' Press, 1975.

TCL   Translations of Christian Literature. Edited by Sparrow Simpson and Lowther Clarke. London: SPCK, 1917ff.

TPW   Taylor's Practical Works, by Jeremy Taylor. 2 vols. London: H. G. Bohn, 1854.

WA   Weimarer Ausgabe, D. Martin Luthers Werke. Kritische Gesamtausgabe, Weimar, 1883ff.

W-Br.   Weimarer Ausgabe, D. Martin Luther, Briefwechsel, Kritische Gesamtausgabe, Weimar, 1930ff., Letters.

WLS   What Luther Says. Edited by E. Plass. 3 vols. St. Louis: Concordia, 1959.

WML   Works of Martin Luther. Philadelphia Edition. 6 vols. Philadelphia: Muhlenberg Press, 1943.

WA-T   Weimarer Ausgabe. D. Martin Luther, Tischreden, Kritische Gesamtausgabe, Table Talk, 1912ff.

WSD   Writings on Spiritual Direction, ed. J. M. Neufelder, and Mary C. Coelho. New York: Seabury Press, 1982.